Melissa's Gift

Melissa's Gift

Olin Dodson

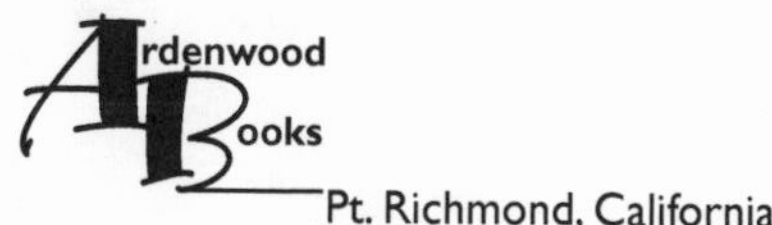

Pt. Richmond, California

Interior design by mltrees

Library of Congress Control Number: 2011961961

Grateful acknowledgement is made for use of the following:

House of The Spirits, Copyright 1982, Isabel Allende. Used with permission.

Selections from Dr. Martin Luther King's sermon, "Interruptions," are reprinted by arrangement with The Heirs to the Estate of Martin Luther King Jr., c/o Writers House as agent for the proprietor, New York, NY. Copyright 1963 Dr. Martin Luther King, Jr.; copyright renewed 1991 Coretta Scott King.

"Wonder " Written by Natalie Merchant, Copyright 1995(ASCAP); All Rights Reserved. Used with permission.

"Stranger in a Strange Land" Words and Music by Leon Russell and Don J. Preston. Copyright © 1971 IRVING MUSIC, INC. Copyright renewed. All Rights Reserved. Used with Permission. Reprinted by Permission of Hal Leonard Corporation.

"Happy Birthday" Words and Music by Stevie Wonder ©1980 JOBETE MUSIC CO. INC. AND BLACK BULL MUSIC c/o EMI APRIL MUSIC INC. All rights reserved. International Copyright Secured Used by Permission. Reprinted with permission of Hal Leonard Corporation.

Shutter Island by Dennis Lehane, Copyright 2003. HarperCollins Publishers. Used with permission.

Their Eyes were Watching God, by Zora Neale Hurston, Copyright 1937, 1965. HarperCollins Publishers. Used with permission.

Selected Poems of Rainer Maria Rilke, A Translation from the German and Commentary by Robert Bly, Copyright, 1981. HarperCollins Publishers. Used with permission.

Antonio Machado's poem "Last Night, As I Was Sleeping" was translated by Olin Dodson.

I have recounted this story as accurately as I could. Some names have been changed to preserve the privacy of various individuals who appear in this account.

Contents

Prelude

Papa,

I was recently reading the story that you wrote me about your life, how you and mommy met. At the end you said that you wanted me to tell mine.

I will try to write about what I feel like and what I remember.

When I was really little, my mom told me that I had a dad who was a North American…I sometimes thought about you, that I would get to meet you one day, or that you could have died. I had so many questions, but nobody had any answers….

Melissa
April, 1996

April, 2004

They said: Buck up, Get over it.

They said: Let go and let God.

They said: Time heals all wounds.

Nothing worked. I'd been beaten to my knees and, after all this time, I couldn't tell if I'd ever gotten off them. I didn't know how badly I was doing, if I was coping well or healing at my own pace or simply reacting to the loss the way anyone would. I had hung on to my job. I functioned. But for seven years, I'd been a creature of shadows and night.

The season of darkness ended on a lush plateau above the Pacific Ocean, 700 miles north of the equator, in the little town of Esparza, Costa Rica.

The bus from the Nicaraguan border braked at a familiar junction of two highways and I raced down the aisle into the afternoon sun. A pleasant breeze tugged at my clothes as I surveyed my surroundings. Up the hill was Esparza, the home of most of Melissa's relatives. My connection with them was rock solid, even though we'd met on only five or six occasions.

Due west, the view of land and ocean touching fingers, north and south as far as the eye could see, transfixed me. A deep breath filled my nostrils with the perfume of flowering hillsides. I tasted the moist salty air which had been of so little benefit to my daughter. Merely catching a breath was, all too often, her only concern.

The lure of more Melissa stories brought me back to Esparza, where the unexpected had been commonplace. It was a hot, humid morning when her uncle Ascension and I strolled around town, working our way down a list of errands. The town was not foreign to me, but its narrow streets and gumdrop-colored houses were like fragments of a distant dream. We rounded a corner into the town plaza with its lofty trees and pillared gazebo, newly painted in aqua and lemon. A cry burst from my mouth and I grabbed Ascension's arm. There, on the plaza's far side, stood the white stucco wall where Melissa and I first laid eyes upon each other and stepped into a new world.

I pulled Ascension to the low wall and brushed my hand across the cool stucco. A vision of Melissa filled my mind, Melissa with her flowing brown locks and mischievous eyes. In her navy and white school uniform, she bid her classmates good-bye and wandered into the plaza. Stopping at the wall, her mind rested on the remarkable confluence of circumstances which brought us together. She smiled as she reflected on how we wrestled, smiled over our deadly serious contest with its calculated moves and counter-moves.

I wondered if, as she stood there, she had agonized over what a daughter was supposed to do or say to her father, a virtual stranger? Did she half-expect me to give up on her? Did she pray that her mother and I might learn to love each other so that everything she ever wanted—a loving family, good health and a long, happy life—could finally be hers?

I believe she did.

There came a memory of a Laurel and Hardy movie, the one in which they play piano movers trying to push a piano up a long outdoor stairway. The duo are pinched, crushed, chased, run over, abandoned and frustrated by the piano, which, like Melissa, seemed to have a mind all its own. Laurel and Hardy never laughed in that movie, although every person in the audience surely did. As for me, I barely chuckled in the years with Melissa, but I smiled then, revisiting the place where we first emerged from innocence and separation into life.

Something had carried me through the darkness to this day, had taught me about love and made me into a person. That something was Melissa's gift.

Part One
1978-1990

1. The Phone Call—August, 1990

Costa Rica no longer entered my mind. Like someone clicked the cosmic channel changer, replacing breath-taking beaches, sunsets and rain forests with classrooms and libraries. My strange new country, three years after returning to the States, was a demanding graduate program in clinical psychology. Three days a week in class, two in supervised counseling, weekends for study, sleep and more sleep. Psyches and marriages of fellow students fell by the wayside with each passing quarter.

Now, with school well behind me, the 90's held promise. No more sleep-deprived slogs through dense textbooks. No more solitary Saturday nights. In charming Petaluma on the border of California wine country, my counseling practice had grown sizeable, the product of seven years of effort. I'd upgraded my ride to a used, cow-pie brown Honda hatchback. An office schedule of late afternoon and evening appointments allowed me to enjoy Sonoma County and its proximity to friends, the Pacific Ocean and San Francisco. Even with major credit card and student loan debt, there was little reason for gloom of any kind.

Yet here I was, feeling an inner gnawing reminiscent of my malaise twelve years earlier—the one which propelled me to the Latin American walk-about. The lesson from that adventure about living for my heart had led me into the field of psychology, a long-time fascination. All my life seemed to lack was the fulfillment of an intimate relationship. A few years of psychotherapy, required by my graduate program, had helped me straighten out a few bent places, but there remained a persistent attraction to restless women with troubled pasts. Some had real jobs; none fit with a recent, surprising interest in having a child of my own.

Many of my friends were married and busy raising children. One was a precocious boy named Henry, son of Jeff and Marnie, friends from the 70's. They brought Henry to Petaluma when he was 8 years of age. Early one morning while his parents slept, he and I left my house for a stroll to the local bakery. We were toodling through a park, engaged in Henry-talk, when he reached up and slipped his hand into mine. His grasp startled me but I received it with thanks. Then I remembered little Yaneth from my 1978 journey to Central America and felt a longing for a love which had escaped me.

I investigated single-parent adoption but eventually pulled back, still hoping for a relationship and a biological child. I volunteered as a Big Brother. My little brother, as an infant, had been abandoned in the bushes of a city park and was more psychologically damaged than his assessment had revealed. His emotional needs were as insatiable as his behavior was problematic. The Big Brothers director finally told me the boy never should have been accepted into the program and requested that I bring the relationship, such as it was, to an end.

I flailed for a lifeline for my impoverished spirit, day-dreamed of pulling up stakes, moving to another city, even changing professions. There was no option too radical to consider if it would jump-start the passion I had discovered in Central America and, later, in my training as a therapist. After the Berlin Wall fell, I impulsively booked a flight to Eastern Europe, lured by the vision of masses of people like me, facing an overwhelming array of life choices. My love of travel to exotic places was fulfilled by overnight train passages through East Germany, Poland and Hungary. I met wonderful people, heard fascinating stories, and returned home with no new direction.

*****

A phone message awaited me after work one August night. A stranger named Laura had called from Chicago, said she'd been trying to find me and would I please call her, collect even? Laura sounded young, possibly calling to give me the "real" scoop about one of my clients who was her ex-husband or boyfriend. It was late in the evening, even later in Chicago, and I was too tired to be intrigued. I phoned her the next morning.

Laura answered, sounding perky as she had on my phone machine. I identified myself in a world-weary tone, like Bogart playing Philip Marlowe. "Who are you?" Laura got to the point. She was a Duke graduate, at home on break from volunteer teaching in Costa Rica, and she had a message from a friend.

"You've been there, right? Do you remember someone named Gloria Maria? Well, she's been trying to find you. She's fine, she just wants to get your address and write to you. About what? I'm sure she'll tell you when she writes you."

"So if everything is fine, why is she trying to contact me? "

"She just wants to talk to you."

"About what?" Laura's coyness annoyed me.

There was a pause. "Are you sure you want me to tell you or would you rather wait and find out from her?"

"Please, Laura. Tell me."

I felt zings of fear and excitement when she said, "Ok….."

"Gloria had a child with you, a girl, and the girl wants to have contact with you."

Laura's words hit my brain with such force it went blank for a moment and my legs buckled. I stumbled to the nearest chair, as if an ocean wave had pounded my chest and ripped my breath away. I tried to stand but my legs gave way, sending me to the floor, back first. I gripped the phone, tied up in the cord and a jumble of feelings.

Laura must have heard the thud and grunt on my end. "Are you okay?"

"I'm great." My words sounded raspy. "What's her name?"

"Melissa."

"Melissa," I whispered. "Oh, my God."

Tears fell from my eyes and the questions tumbled out. Who is this child? What is she like? What does she look like? Who are you? How did you find me? Where do they live? What is their life like? Why did they wait so long to contact me?

"Her full name is Wendy Melissa Reyes Reyes. She's 11. She has wavy brown hair, brown eyes and kind of big ears. I just love her." Laura gushed. "She's one of my favorite students: bright, pretty and kinda shy. Her voice is so tiny you can't hear her across the room. And she's thin, much thinner that the other children her age. She has some kind of pancreatic disorder. She has trouble in P.E. because the physical activity makes her start coughing and she has to stop and sit down. She and her mom live with a retired school teacher. Gloria is his housekeeper."

I scrambled for a pen and paper and asked Laura how she found me. "I'll give you the entire story. Gloria invited me to her house one afternoon after school. Sitting in the backyard, she told me the story of Melissa's missing father and asked if I could help locate him. I promised to do whatever I could after I returned to the States, but my parents, Bob and Anne, who live in Chicago, were the ones who got really interested in helping Melissa and took up the cause."

"I guess you had given Gloria your business card. My parents made several phone calls to the vocational rehabilitation center in Richmond. It had been, you know, twelve years, but they located one man who still worked there and remembered you, a man named Bill. He told my parents that the last he'd heard, you had moved to Ft. Bragg. But they couldn't find you there and even though my dad used all of his business contacts and friends to track you down, after several weeks of no results, he and mom were close to giving up. But they decided to re-contact Bill, just in case, and it was their best move. The man, Bill, phoned someone named Betty, an acquaintance of his who was one of your former co-workers?"

"Yeah, she was my supervisor." My ear hurt from the pressure of the phone.

"Well, Betty had kept in touch with another of your co-workers named Shirley. Betty told Bill that she and Shirley had just been talking about you. Shirley had bumped into you at the Sonoma County Fair three years ago and remembered that you lived in Petaluma. Bill called my parents with the news, and that's how they found you."

With a simple call to long-distance information, Bob and Anne's search was over. I fought to take it all in. My long gone work-mates. A chance encounter at my only visit to the county fair. Total strangers working to find me. I couldn't speak.

Laura told me that she was returning to Costa Rica in a few days and had some questions for me, information she wanted to take back to Gloria and Melissa. When she asked me for a third time if I was married, I erupted. "No! Why do you keep asking me that question?"

She hesitated. "My biggest fear was that I would disrupt a marriage or family. Maybe you would hang up or refuse to become involved."

I laughed. Laura never anticipated my ecstasy.

My heart reached forward, trembling, like one of those jerky, time-lapse films of vines following sunlight. There was a desperation around the edges. If Gloria had deceived Laura, the devastation would rip me apart. And certainly worse for Melissa to believe she'd found her dad, only to find there had been a mistake. Laura said the question of paternity had occurred to her as well and confessed that she could not vouch for Gloria's truthfulness. We dissected the topic for several minutes and formulated a plan. First, Laura would airmail me photos of Melissa which she had brought home. Perhaps there would be an unmistakable resemblance.

Laura, upon her return to Esparza, would casually inquire about Melissa's birth date. I would search my travel journal from 1978, locate the date of the single night Gloria and I had spent together and track forward nine months, give or take a few weeks. Not exactly a scientific method, but what was I supposed to do, ask for a blood test? Hardly. Not then. It would send a message to Melissa that I was reluctant, needing persuasion, when I was just the opposite. Laura and I hoped that the photos and birthday would seal the case.

Laura couldn't answer all my questions but talking to her thrilled me. I treasured her every word about Melissa. Laura was the one who found me, who knew my child and helped track me down. I loved her like a wounded soldier loves his nurse.

We spoke for maybe an hour and agreed to talk again after the photos arrived. We said good-bye and I burst into tears.

* * * * *

Waiting for the photos, there was little to do but avoid walking into walls.

I gave the news to a few of my closest friends, but otherwise kept things to myself until the paternity issue could be resolved. This protective secrecy helped me to maintain a degree of focus on daily tasks. Yet no matter what I did, the phone call would inevitably divert my attention and sweep me away, like a delirious stone skipping across a lake. At times I fidgeted about the photos. Would all of this become nothing but a cruel hoax?

The first night I dreamed of a man, known only as an "ideal father."

> *He and I were in a warehouse. He had stained every hand-carved wood item sitting there in front of us: desks, tables, bookcases. The room glowed.*

Two nights later, surrounded by friends at a dinner party, I hoped for a distraction which never appeared. All the while my body sang its secret happy agony. I returned home sometime after 10:30. The big brown envelope in my mailbox took me by surprise, having arrived from Chicago in only three days. I carried it into the house like an altar boy.

With a deep breath, I ran my finger under the seal. Three photographs rested inside and I removed them touching only their edges. Laura had stuck a yellow post-it with an arrow and the word "Melissa" pointing to a girl in each photo. Two photos showed the entire class, maybe thirty children, outside in the sun. From a distance Melissa's features were indistinct. The third photo showed nine smiling children in white and blue uniforms sitting around a school-room table. I removed the post-it and there she was, seated at the corner closest to the camera. She wore a pleased smile and her eyes were full of life and mischief. It was a look straight out of my third grade school photo.

I looked away and spoke aloud. "Be sure."

I looked again. I was sure.

I ran to the phone and exulted to my good friend, Jeff, a photo journalist. "I got the photos! I have a daughter!"

He congratulated me and I babbled about the photos and the night and the stars before he stopped me. In a dry voice, he said. "O, I have to tell you. I already knew."

"What? You knew? What do you mean, you knew?"

"I knew. I had a dream last night. You were with me at my editing table and I was peering at the photo through my photographer's loupe. I saw Melissa and she had your face, your bald head, everything. I turned to you and said, "Yep, she's yours all right!!!!!"

We howled in laughter.

When we hung up the phone, tears poured down my cheeks. I took more deep breaths, filled with an urge to announce to someone, anyone, everyone, that I was the father of a beautiful child. It was near midnight. I considered driving downtown and crying out to strangers on the street. Maybe I'd go to a bar and buy a round for everyone. Then I remembered that Ralph and Florence, my dinner hosts, were probably awake, cleaning up after the dinner. I phoned and asked if I could return and share some amazing news. Petaluma's old streets always looked quaint but on this night they led through an ethereal darkness, pocked with glowing golden streetlights, and I flowed through them as if I were the driver of a magic carriage.

* * * * *

Those first days left me in a state of shock, like I'd given birth without knowing I'd been pregnant. The miracle of fatherhood struck me, grabbed me, shook me. My insides were an aggregation of every soul-stirring event of my life. Looking down into the fumarole of Mt. St. Helens. Holding on to the open door of an empty freight car, racing across the Wyoming plains at sunset. Descending the stairs into the tomb of Pakal in Palenque. Gazing at the night heavens from the crater of Volcan de Agua in Guatemala.

But the experience was so much more than merely witnessing or feeling. It was more like this: In 1976, I took my girlfriend, Julie, to a Stevie Wonder concert at the Cow Palace in San Francisco. Amidst thousands of rabid fans, we sat awe-struck for nearly four hours, listening to his entire repertoire of hits, played non-stop. Stevie Wonder with a tight, driving group of sidemen and sexy back-up singers.

Imagine being in the middle of that stage with "Signed, Sealed and Delivered," "Living for the City," "Isn't She Lovely," "Sir Duke," etc., pounding your ears to mush. Then imagine being that music. Being the rhythmic drum beats, the thumping bass, the rippling synthesizers and the horn riffs. Being the movement of the dancers, the bodies and muscle and intelligence and breath which went into it all. Imagine that: my delirium over Melissa.

I spent quiet hours in the mist of a dream. I stared at the photos and dreamed of the moment when Melissa and I would meet. At every opportunity I talked and rattled on and raved. I laughed, I cried, I soared, I sighed. Whenever possible, I held off telling friends until I could share the news face-to-face. The reactions always delighted me. Suddenly moist glorious eyes, dropped jaws, and omigod or a similar utterance. By phone Jeff paraphrased my thoughts when he said, "Oh, boy, this little girl is in for an amazing ride. She has no idea what she's getting into!" So much joy awaited Melissa, without a father for all of her life, then wrapped in his loving arms.

Laura called to say goodbye as she prepared for her return to San Jose. I had spoken with her or her parents daily, sometimes twice a day. We agreed on the time I would call her, after she had learned Melissa's birthday. We hoped Laura would also be able to tell me the English name of

Melissa's health problem. Now there were 48 hours to fill until I phoned her in Esparza. On a map of Costa Rica I found Esparza, a little burp in the lowlands near the Pacific Ocean.

I rifled through my record collection for music to match my feelings. Nothing I owned could quite match my euphoria but I spent hours dancing and singing to Marvin Gaye and Tammi Terrell, Aretha Franklin and Bob Marley. Again and again I joined Otis Redding, full volume and open-throated, on his version of "My Girl."

My body felt as if it had been traded in for a new model. My chest would tingle with wonderfully peculiar sensations.

And my brain? It wandered off into other realms. I did everyday tasks on auto pilot, while my attention was attached to the only reality which meant anything. One afternoon I walked down the hall to my office, just as I had several hundred times before. My key went into the lock above the doorknob but it did not turn. Puzzled, I removed the key and re-inserted it. The results were the same: nothing. I began jerking the key in all directions. The glass window in the door shook, the noise echoing down the hallway. I cursed and stepped back to consider my next move. My eyes moved upward and stopped at the number of the office adjacent to mine. I laughed then broke into tears.

Life had turned me inside out, with force, as if it was upset that I'd ignored it for so long. Thundering, disruptive life: breaking through the veneer of everyday reality to summon my heart. Sweet scented life: tender as a child's breath and her outstretched hand.

Melissa was a gift of grace, embodying the impossible and all possibility. She was mystery and revelation, darkness and light. Most of all, she was running and leaping!

At times my reaction resembled survivor guilt. Why me? I didn't deserve the gift. Doubt would seep in. The photos were convincing enough but perhaps the birth date wouldn't fit. I dug out my journal and re-read all the Costa Rica entries. I found the first mention of Gloria, the recounting of the day we met and the night which followed, and did the math. Melissa's birthday would need to fall somewhere between early November and December.

My travel journal also contained an interesting dream about the movie "Alfie," referring to pregnancy. Curiosity piqued, I went to my bedside, opened my current journal and re-read entries from recent months. There were many colorful dreams. One featured a stark red tree, beneath which I was digging down into the root system. Another consisted of three "performers" becoming one before separating into "a multitude." Interesting, but nothing special. Then I found this:

> *My wife and I are walking down a road. She tells me she's having a child. I immediately think that I need to work more to increase the*

family income. Then I rush home to our bedroom and begin arranging the flowered tree boughs which make up the insides of our comforter.

The journal entry was dated ten weeks before Laura called. A dream forgotten had become my life.

* * * * *

The next day, I stop periodically to picture Laura's whereabouts. She's boarding at O'Hare. She's transferring flights in Miami. She's snacking at 30,000 feet, ready for the descent into San Jose. We had figured out the time zone differences, her probable arrival time at Gloria and Melissa's house in Esparza, and the hour she would be at home to answer the phone.

Driving home from my office, I imagine Melissa and Gloria listening to Laura say that she found me. Melissa is smiling like she did in the photo. And her heart is beating fast like mine did when I learned about her, like it is right now as I dial the phone.

Laura answers and begins her story.

She walked to the house around sundown and sat with Gloria and Melissa on the front porch. She told them she had spoken with me, at which point Melissa trembled and her breathing became labored. She began coughing and went inside to clear the phlegm from her throat.

Laura tells me Melissa's birth date is November 9. My eyes close in gratitude.

In response to some of the questions I'd given Laura, Melissa reported that she enjoyed animals, especially her dog. She had a favorite place, by the river. She said she did not like school, a remark which her mother suggested she retract. Laura told Melissa and Gloria about my enthusiasm and passed along details about my life. When Laura stated that I had no other children, Melissa erupted. "Thanks be to God!"

I whispered, "My daughter!"

Laura's voice develops an edgy quality. She says she can't explain it fully, but something about Gloria didn't sit right. Before I can get anything more, she changes the subject to Melissa's medical condition. Gloria has to pound Melissa's back every day to clear the phlegm out of her lungs. She takes a handful of pills daily and gets hospitalized every few months for a week or two because she can't catch a breath.

I tighten. "What do they call her condition?"

"'*Fibrósis quística.*' It was first diagnosed when Melissa was six."

Cystic fibrosis. I remembered a newspaper story about a Petaluma girl who passed away from cystic fibrosis. It is a nasty, child-killing disease.

Laura and I talked a little longer, but cystic fibrosis was all I thought about. I watched the fading daylight outside my living room window turn rose red then ochre, until my house was enveloped in darkness. Two facts recycled through my brain. My fatherhood had been confirmed, and my allotted time to know and love my child was unmistakably limited. The latter was not some aphorism about the brevity of life or childhood. Melissa's body was badly flawed. How long would we have? Would we have time enough to meet?

My daughter had found me and, simultaneously, I knew I was going to lose her. The streetlamp gave my house its only light. I sat motionless for a very long time.

2. Southward—January, 1978

The sounds of an approaching car and crunching gravel yanked me out of a deep sleep. My eyes opened to blackness sprinkled with faint stars. I felt a burning where my shoulders and hips pressed against the truck bed. Next to me, bodies stirred slowly.

Sometime after midnight our ferry had docked in the warm darkness near Potosi, where northwestern Nicaragua juts out into the Pacific Ocean. The solitary *gringo,* I disembarked with a group of Latino men. We shuffled towards the single light visible in the night and formed a line at the door of a shed. This was the customs office, a table and a couple of naked hanging light bulbs. A man in an olive green shirt sat at the table, yawning. He checked documents with little more than a glancing comparison of faces and passport photos.

Still, I felt my chest tighten as I moved closer to the table. No one back home knew I was here, entering a country verging on civil war. The Nicaraguan borders — north and south — had been sealed periodically during the past several weeks. Pedro Joaquin Chamorro, a widely admired journalist and critic of the country's dictator, Anastasio Somoza, had been cut down by shotguns one morning on his way to work. For two weeks masses of people from all walks of life conducted demonstrations, most of them outraged, some of them violent. A vicious military response had solved nothing.

The official glanced at me, unseeing, and stamped my passport. If there were any enemies of the state in our group, he was not about to get involved. Taking a deep breath, I rejoined the group in the dim light outside and heard a man speaking in Spanish about a taxi which would arrive near daybreak. We walked into a clearing and six of us climbed into the back of a pickup truck to catch a few hours of sleep.

Now the automobile engine ran impatiently as we gathered our bags and relieved ourselves in the bushes. Eight adults crammed into a sedan built for five and long ago stripped of its identity. With barely a word other than *"Chinandega!"* our destination, the driver hit the gas and we peeled off down a dirt road into the predawn darkness. My companions dozed in silence. Pinched against the right front door, I gazed at a recurring stream of trees, bushes and fences briefly illuminated by the car's headlights. It was like a wild, fun house ride. Horses with bulging, fearful eyes, their heads and necks reaching over fence tops, would suddenly appear, then vanish into the night.

Half asleep, my mind drifted back to my recent passage through Guatemala and El Salvador, to the old man on the train, to the child singing to the birds, and to Yaneth.

*****

Sometime in 1977, my thirtieth year, a persistent disquiet settled into my life. It was boredom, lack of direction and listlessness, like a sickness that wouldn't go away. I figured it had something to with my hope for social rebirth and renewal which never materialized. Disillusionment felt as extreme as the idealism which spawned it. After the firing of my third or fourth supervisor in three years, interest in my job as a vocational rehabilitation counselor in Richmond, California, went away, and I followed. Someone recommended taking time to travel before settling into my next job and the idea of working as a deck hand on a cargo ship took root in my imagination. Memories of barfing my way across the San Francisco Bay on numerous occasions did give me pause, but the prospects of free travel to another hemisphere won the day. Machu Picchu, the ancient Inca city in Peru, would be my ultimate destination. Machu Picchu. Merely repeating the name stirred feelings of mystery, passion and spirituality, elements my life sorely lacked. I was not so foolish as to think that life's answers awaited me on a mountain in Peru, but this I knew: my workaday routine was breaking me.

I signed up for Spanish language school in Huehuetenango, Guatemala. After a month of classes I would search for a ship off the coast of Guatemala or El Salvador, or even Costa Rica. Travel books mostly ignored the countries south of Mexico, as if the region stretching to the Panama Canal was little more than an underdeveloped jungle sprinkled with coffee and banana plantations. I came across unsettling news of repressive governments in Guatemala and Nicaragua but found no descriptions of Central American ports of call. Somehow, I believed, it would all work out. In short order, I sold my VW bug, returned my Goodwill furniture to its place of origin, stored the remainder of my possessions, said good-bye to Jennie, my mostly off-again girlfriend, and bought an airline ticket to Mexico City, one with an open return date. I withdrew most of my savings, less than $1000, believing my expenses would be kept to a minimum by the room and board I'd earn working as a deck hand. A friend gave me a blank notebook to record my anticipated high times and finally, sleep-deprived from excitement, I headed south.

Living with an extended local family and studying Spanish in the highlands of northern Guatemala was just the beginning of a wonderful, disorienting month. Near Huehuetenango, rural villages such as Todos Santos sat like doorways into another time. Pungent smells, mud houses with thatched roofs, silent-eyed Mayans dressed in distinctive woven garments, all were daily reminders of an elusive, exotic culture with a history unimaginable to an Atlanta boy. Guatemala was mind-bending, like hearing Los Lobos after growing up on mariachi music.

When classes ended, I set out by rail and bus, searching for an ocean port on the Atlantic coast. Daily scenes and events wove themselves through me, creating a tapestry of memories. On a layover in eastern Guatemala, I drafted a letter to Jennie.

> *There's a half-moon overhead. Lots of palm trees laden with coconuts surround me as well as banana and lemon trees. A steady chirp of crickets mixes with assorted birds singing and playing in the trees; a woodpecker is over to my right. The air is cooler now, with a gentle breeze from the coast. The train ride was dusty and slow. It's good to feel the night come on and enliven my small backyard jungle with softening colors and temperature. I hear a little girl through the trees singing to the birds at the top of her lungs.*

Sitting across the aisle on the hot train ride across Guatemala's interior, a wrinkled, white-haired man dressed in a dusty black suit pulled a piece of bread in a napkin from his pocket. I guessed it would be his only meal of the day. I followed his movements from the corner of my eye as he broke the bread into two pieces. He pushed the napkin across the aisle and raised it in the universal expression for "Here, have some." With a bag full of snacks, I was the one who should have been passing food across the aisle, but sharing anything, especially with a complete stranger, was nothing I'd ever done. The old man's simple act stationed itself in my memory for a long while.

Guatemala gave new meaning to the term "other." No matter if I was standing on the crown of a volcano or at the edge of the outdoor market in Chichicastenango, the country enticed my eyes to open wide, then wider still, feeding me with wonder. Stepping off the train at Quirigua, I visited what had been a magnificent city twelve or thirteen centuries earlier. There, in the midst of a green forest, surrounded by towering stelae and round stone altars inscribed with images of turtles and jaguars, my imagination got its baptismal plunge into Mayan culture.

On the return to Guatemala City, my bus emptied beside an unmarked roadside shrine and I joined a line at the shrunken door of a hut. I stooped to enter two rooms filled with the smoke of incense and votive candles. The walls were layered in crucifixes, glass bead necklaces and hundreds of black and white mug shots with names etched in ink. Many of the photos were faded brown and slightly out of focus. In a far corner, people chanted in an unidentifiable language, lighting candles and offering money and gifts to a wooden puppet which bore an unmistakable resemblance to Howdy Doody. He wore a cowboy hat and was attended to by a young acolyte who monitored the puppet's shot glass of liquor and the burning cigarette between his painted lips. The scene made me dizzy.

Guatemala's cultural mix was tough to figure. Indigenous people appeared to go about their lives like inhabitants of a cocoon world, oblivious and invisible to non-Indians. Some were not ignored. In a ditch near my language school I saw the body of a murdered Mayan and heard stories of many more. I struck up a conversation with a woman on a park bench in Guatemala City. A doctor, she invited me to her home for coffee, too afraid to speak to me in public about the political situation. The intrigue and secrecy made me smile with excitement. I was too naive to know better- until she shared her gruesome stories of the government's violence against political dissenters and, mostly, indigenous people.

In the end Guatemala felt darker and more menacing than any place I'd ever visited. I knew little of its history or current events and had no real point of reference for my experiences there. My color slides from that month — mostly vapid, uninteresting and overexposed — reveal little about the country, but much about the young photographer: seeking, but not finding.

From Guatemala City air-conditioned buses took me further south to El Salvador and the coastal town of La Libertad. I was floating in the Pacific Ocean, happy to be away from Guatemala, when someone with a door key entered my hotel room. The thief, a kind hearted sort, took every bill from my wallet except for a single dollar. After discovering the robbery, I complained and even screamed at the poker-faced hotel manager, then stumbled into the street. It was Sunday, the banks were closed, and local restaurants wouldn't take a travelers' check. My stomach twisted over my shrunken bankroll.

Guileless, charming children had approached me daily throughout Central America like surf spooling around my bare feet. So I was accustomed to the group of seven which crowded me, shouting "Mister! Money?" They ignored my bad attitude and refusal of a hand-out and once they heard my Spanish, blithely accompanied me on my walk of pain. I couldn't resist them, couldn't help asking silly questions just to hear their answers. "Money, don't you make enough money going to school? Hey you, you're handsome, are you a movie star? That girl, is she your girlfriend?" I always loved the children's expressive faces and giggly answers. No more than fifteen minutes after descending into my funk, I was laughing with my companions. A foul mood never disappeared so easily. And I found a great fish dinner for 80 cents.

In the harbor town of La Union, my next stop, there were no ships to South America but by then, I'd just about stopped caring. Each day was rich and complete, better than any future could ever be. The journey had displaced the goal.

The only chance for travel by water involved taking an overnight ferry from La Union to Potosi, Nicaragua. Asking around, I had confirmed that the Sandinistas' long war against Nicaragua's dictator had intensified. But several men told me not to worry, I wouldn't have any trouble getting from Potosi to Chinandega, and then to Managua, the capital. The next ferry was scheduled to depart the following afternoon at 4:30. I bought a ticket for $1.60.

I walked the beach in near darkness save for the lights from the row of fish bars to my right. The air was rich with smoky odors as I wandered by groups of happy Salvadoreans in shorts and flip-flops, little more than shadows really, gutting and placing fish on make-shift grills. Laughter blended with the incessant bumps and sizzles of breakers rolling up the sand. To my left the sky had shrunk to a timid glow of pastel.

I kicked off my shoes and let the wet sand squeeze between my toes. I had done it, completed my initiation to Latin America. With rudimentary skills in Spanish and a vocabulary growing by the day, the door had opened to the cultures of millions of people, to the very tip of South America. Filled with an exuberant sense of freedom, possibility and confidence, I was a sparrow singing in the top of a tall tree.

Back at my hotel, The Rosales, with an entire evening to kill, I retrieved my Spanish notebook and returned to the humid lobby and its lone table, a four-top with two occupants. The lobby was nothing fancy but, in the manner of all things Central American, it made the most with what it had. The furniture and lamps were musty remnants of another era and stylish in a baroque, Goodwill-ish sort of way.

I smiled at the two little girls seated at the table. The eldest was doing homework. Her head did not reach far above the table top. She held her face close to her workbook, eyes devoted to the pencil moving across the page, giving it all the attention of a young artist. I sat down and showed the girls my Spanish vocabulary workbook, letting them know their table mate was a student, too. On the green cover of my *cuaderno* were Disney's Uncle Scrooge, Huey, Dewey and Louie, fronted by big black letters which read, *"Rico Tío Mac Pato"* (Rich Uncle Mac Duck). The girls smiled and, before getting on with our studies, I told them my name and asked for theirs. Yaneth was seven and Rosa four, almost five. They were daughters of one of the hotel clerks. I looked over to the front desk. A woman returned my smile and we both waved. Soon afterwards Rosa left. I figured the family had a room in the back of the hotel.

I peeked at Yaneth. She was a lovely child. She wore a tan uniform and her brown hair was immaculately combed into a braid which fell down her back. Her ear lobes were decorated with little gold studs.

I put all my attention into my vocabulary for a several minutes then excused myself and asked for the Spanish word for the bowl on the table. *"En español, cómo se dice, Yaneth?"*

"La frutera."

"Y este?" I touched the table cloth. *"El mantel."* I thanked her and returned to my studies, marveling over the open door of her azure eyes, clearer than crystal.

I again interrupted to ask what she was studying and, with that, Yaneth became my cheerful tutor. After exhausting all the items on the table, the body, clothes, etc., she pointed out objects in the lobby for me to name. I guessed wrong many times. Each time I slipped up, she shook her head, I exaggerated a grimace, and she laughed. The sound was so endearing that I attempted to elicit it as much as possible. It pushed through her nose in two little, fast exhales and was coupled with a wide grin which lit up her entire face.

After 45 minutes of this happiness, the Spanish lesson ended and I gathered up my things. I asked Yaneth to accept my ballpoint pen as a token of my appreciation, knowing it likely was the finest writing utensil she'd ever owned. She dug through her satchel to find a return offering. I politely refused a nearly new eraser, then a pencil. She certainly had little she could do without. I told her the best gift would be a photo, if she would let me take one of her and her sister after school the following day.

The next morning, I did laundry, wrote a few postcards and exchanged money into Nicaraguan *córdobas.* After lunch there was little to do but sit in the lobby, reading and waiting for Yaneth to come back from school. When she showed up, we joined Rosa outside. The sun was directly overhead and the girls found some shade beneath a tree. I could only hope the photos I took would reveal the exquisiteness of the sisters' smiles.

I retrieved my luggage and returned to find the children and their mom in the courtyard. I complimented the mother on her beautiful children and wished her good fortune. I thanked Yaneth for being a wonderful teacher. She reached out and, with a glowing face, placed her hand in mine. Caught off guard, I felt my heart open and fill. I returned her smile, aware of how fortunate I was to be me, there, in that moment. I dragged out the conversation. All the while Yaneth smiled and held my hand naturally, like she'd done it all her life.

Finally it was time for me to go. I bent to pick my shoulder bag and Yaneth's hand fell from mine. I backed away and we waved. I walked to the docks and found a seat on a bench outside on the upper deck, watching men load the small ship. I felt no regrets over moving on, but Yaneth's gesture merged with those of other generous, open-hearted people I'd encountered in Guatemala and El Salvador, and the cumulative effect was like the peak of a crescendo. My heart had grown vibrant during recent weeks. The unrest which brought me to this place had disappeared.

But I did not linger in these thoughts. Nicaragua awaited. As soon as the ferry left harbor, it began to roll sensuously from side to side and my mind drifted with the movement. I stretched out on the bench and fell asleep.

3. Costa Rica—August, 1990

An acupuncturist friend showed me into his office and dropped the bulky medical encyclopedia on a desk in front of me. I skimmed through passages on etiology, physical effects and courses of treatment for cystic fibrosis. "CF" arises from a combination of genes from both parents, corrupts and ultimately destroys a person's endocrine system. It invades lungs and the pancreas, blocking airways with mucous, and clogs up pancreatic ducts, leading to major respiratory and digestive problems. Nutrition, weight, strength, circulation — all are targets and nothing works well. People with CF live lives both demanding and painful. They never know when they'll begin to gasp for breath or how long before they'll feel bad or good, or have to be rushed to the hospital.

I'd found the information I needed. CF is a progressive disease, treatable but not curable. It affects each person differently and can sometimes be arrested in its progression. Life expectancy in the United States was under 20 years but there were instances of people living into their old age with CF. My brain seized upon every hopeful word and description, such as "can be arrested" and "treatable," and for the next several months I used them whenever describing Melissa's condition.

I closed the encyclopedia, convinced there was a purpose in being found by Laura and her parents. The United States' superior medical care and anything I could accomplish on Melissa's behalf and perhaps, most of all, my love would surely bolster her spirits and improve her physical health. Laura had told me that Melissa's condition was stable so it seemed plausible that she and I would have more than enough time to form a relationship. This was my conclusion even though serious chronic illness was a foreign subject to me. My feet had never even touched the soil of a cemetery.

I wrote Melissa for the first time.

Dear Melissa,

I am filled with amazement and happiness to know that you are the daughter of Gloria and me. I have received a great gift to learn about you and to know that you exist!

When Laura told me about you on the phone, I immediately sat-plop!-on the floor because my legs would not work! Then I lay back on the floor, because my neck and my back would not work. I did not talk too well either. Ask Laura!

There was no problem with my heart, however. It was filled with joy and wonder immediately. There was no problem with my eyes either. They were filled with tears of happiness.

Now I am happy to say my legs and neck and everything work fine again. And all of me looks forward to corresponding with you and some day soon returning to Costa Rica to see you and talk to you.

Laura told me that you like to go to the river. I love rivers. Perhaps you could take me to your river. I would like that very much.

I have many questions about you and your life: where you have lived, what kinds of things you do each day, special memories in your life, special things…the list could go on forever! I would also like to answer any questions you have for me and to exchange photographs.

I couldn't decide on a photo to send you. Finally, I selected a photo of me on top of a volcano, Mt. St. Helens, in Oregon….I chose the photo because that was a special day, special like the day that Laura called me. The day that Laura called me, however, was the most special day! I wanted you to see me in a special day photo. Also the volcano exploded near the time that you were born. A volcano is a big event, but your birth is a bigger event to me!

….Tell me how you would like it if I come to visit in November or December…

For now, be good to yourself. I think about you a lot!

With love, your father,

Olin

I took a calculated risk in delaying my trip to Costa Rica, but three months would give me time to take a Spanish refresher class and research the latest treatments for cystic fibrosis. I figured Melissa would benefit from any information or medicine I could bring her. In the public library I discovered the Cystic Fibrosis Foundation in Bethesda, Maryland. They provided the name of a Costa Rican doctor who had attended some of their conferences. I assembled a packet of CF materials in Spanish and read up on special diets and nutritional supplements for "cystics."

*****

Nicaragua, 1978. I braced for danger when the bus pulled into Managua. Along the road, in nearby Leon, we had passed walls and buildings freckled with bullet holes and revolutionary graffiti. I pressed my nose to the window, looking in vain for signs of recent fighting.

Managua seemed to spring up without warning. Suburbs, road signs, even billboards were non-existent. The city had a funky, disorganized appearance, like the bedroom of a giant teenage boy. Pot-holed streets led through grim neighborhoods. Stores and shops were little more than flea market stalls covered with corrugated tin over-hangs. People in the street wore tired clothes, their faces emaciated and dour. Where was the revolution?

Managua's heat and humidity drained my energy. With time running out before my bus departure to Costa Rica, I wanted to see the sights, assuming there was more than one. I hailed a taxi and asked the driver to take me to the center of town. Unlike the capitals of Guatemala and El Salvador, the city lacked business complexes, Dairy Queens and McDonalds. We skirted men on horseback and wood-wheeled carts pulled by bulls. Within minutes, the driver braked and half-flapped his hand. *"Aquí,"* was all he said.

He was referring to a mountain of rock, rubble and dirt, obvious leftovers from a killer earthquake six years earlier. The driver had misunderstood. I raised my voice. *"No, el centro."* The driver nodded and gestured again and I suddenly remembered another piece of Nicaragua's recent past. Entire city blocks of Managua had collapsed during the quake and never been re-built. Somoza had grabbed millions in world humanitarian aid for his own coffers. The people knew this and the lid on their anger was blowing off. The dictator had periodically closed the country's borders during my month in Guatemala and it was only a matter of time before I'd be trapped in a war zone. I had to get out immediately.

Two hours later motoring south of Managua in an air-conditioned bus, I stretched out in my seat and pulled out a post card I'd bought in the bus station. It had a photo of a four-lane street filled with dumpy sedans and a beat-up Volkswagen bus. At the top in red script were the words, "Managua rises from the ashes!" From all I could tell, it was the ashes which were on the rise, and I was glad that stable, prosperous Costa Rica was an hour away. Fellow passengers held palms and purses over their eyes to block the blazing afternoon light on our right. I glanced left and sat upright. Silhouetted against a curtain of dark blue was a pair of gleaming volcanoes. Smoke drifted sideways from the cone of the one nearest. The man in the aisle seat reached across me and pointed. *"Ometepe,"* he said, referring to the lake island from which the volcanoes emerged. They were like two breath-taking, beckoning women.

*****

My open-ended trip to Latin America in 1978 had not come about easily. The day after college graduation I drove across the country and established residency in experiment-with-everything, early 70s Berkeley, California. Three points on a triangle—Moe's Books, Leopold's Records and Peet's Coffee—demarcated the safe zone where I could retreat in adjustment to a strange town, life as a seminary student and uneasy target of my local draft board. Like many of my friends, I'd pledged myself to justice for all every morning for twelve school years and was raised to believe that all things were possible in America. How could I not be frustrated, even angry, towards a society so blasé and underachieving when it came to social injustice, hunger and poverty. Inspired by Bay Area poet Lawrence Ferlinghetti, I dreamt of a "re-birth of wonder," and a world beyond war and want. Throw in a bit of adventure and a regular sexual relationship and I would be a happy man.

Unfortunately, apart from a month-long hitchhiking escapade in the Pacific Northwest with a buddy, few dreams became reality. Any activity I couldn't master quickly was discarded to the junk heap. Consider the evening a friend invited me to join him for a city park volleyball game. Tall and agile, volleyball had been my game since high-school. But the limits of my casual approach to the basics—set-ups, serves and spikes—became apparent that night. Loud, biting insults from the testosterone-enriched players on both sides of the net punctured my ego. I toweled off early that night and never played again. Similarly, scuba diving seemed appealing until, courtesy of some unbalanced waist weights, panic overwhelmed me on my initial dive in the Pacific. I got my class fee refunded. River kayaking and hang gliding soon joined the list of Try Once, then Walk Away. I developed a way of lying to myself about what I wanted.

The persistent lure of mountains and rivers led me, in my late 20s, to sign up for an Outward Bound trip in eastern Oregon. The brochure promised Deschutes River rafting for six days, mixed with rappelling and rock climbing. Outward Bound was famous for its "solos," days and nights spent completely on one's own. In a masterful bit of self deception I sent in my check and registration, convincing myself that I could "do" alone in the woods without difficulty. This in spite of the fact that I'd rarely spent an entire night outdoors.

Mid-week was the time when the OB leaders escorted each member of the group to an isolated place in the woods for a day and night alone. We'd been given thorough instructions in how to forage for raw food. We were taught how to make fires using sap and needles from fir trees. When I was dropped off, the staff member told me how to find my way back to base camp and to return by noon the following day. My provisions were a tarp, a bottle of water and a little rubber container with six matches. My stomach felt a bit jumpy, but really, what was the worst that could happen? The night-time temperatures had been so pleasant a fire would be unnecessary. As for "solo cuisine," Miner's lettuce was plentiful. I would return to the campsite hungry for peanut butter and hot chocolate. So what?

I found a shady spot and prepared a mattress of dead needles. I curled up and fell into a deep sleep until the sounds of a breeze surfing through the trees awakened me. It was 4 o'clock. The sky grew dark, the air dampened, and then the rain began. I hastily spread my tarp over the lower branches of a spruce tree. I found a soft place underneath and scooped out channels of dirt to steer streams of water away from the base of the tree.

It rained heavily with no sign of letting up and the first chill of the week seeped through my jacket. It was time to build a fire but too late to cut saplings for resin. I scraped together a cone of dry needles and an assortment of twigs and fungus which had escaped the rain. With my first match, the needles didn't catch. I tried a second time. No go. My third match caught, went out. I sat back and considered my situation. I took a Kleenex from my jacket pocket, set it under the needles and, bending down on my elbows, touched the burning match to the tissue. It flared as I coaxed the needles to catch. In an instant, the flame turned to smoke and died.

I sat up and took a deep breath. Mean thoughts arose. I was stupid. I'd wasted four matches. I would have no one to blame but my own idiot self if I stayed up all night cold and wet. As anxiety sucked all the spit from my mouth, I fought to remember the group leader's instructions for starting fires.

Two matches left. I knew that if I couldn't light a fire, my inner critic would be unleashed, making for one hellish night. The week would end up in the trash bin of personal failure, like scuba diving and all the rest. I removed a paper receipt from my wallet and crushed it into a ball. I struck the fifth match. The paper ball caught and I set it under the needles. I waited, watched, then leaned close and blew. The fire wavered and went out. I sat up, my heart pounding with the force of a jai-alai ball hitting a wall. I tried to calculate if I'd blown too hard or not enough, too early or too late.

Everything rode on the one, final match. I took a deep breath, struck the match and put it to the paper. I bent over on my knees and blew gently, modulating my breath with my eyes focused on the flame. The needles smoked and caught. I blew a steady stream and more needles caught. I inhaled, throwing on more needles as the fire grew bigger and stronger. Finally I rose up, threw off the tarp and shouted. YES! YES, GODAMMIT! YES!

Starting that fire was *the* important event of my 20's, an accomplishment so tiny, so gigantic. It was years before I fully grasped that by giving my full attention to the task before me and facing failure and not giving up, my inner demon's powers had begun to erode. I signed up for two more Outward Bound trips in the following two years. When I quit my job and set off on another "solo"—to Latin America—in spite of waves of anxiety, I never considered backing out.

* * * * *

The crossing at Nicaragua's southernmost border happened quickly. Costa Rican customs guards climbed onto the bus and checked passports with smiles and friendly eyes, acting as if admitting people to their country was the best job on earth. Dance music blared from a café radio. A pleasant breeze fluttered through the windows. As beginnings go, it was auspicious. But the next morning I awoke to a stranger's snoring behind a sheet which hung from the ceiling and separated the room in half. Welcome to San Jose, Costa Rica, miles short of my intended destination of Panama City. I had no ticket <u>out</u> of Panama, so in the middle of the night, the driver had firmly escorted me off the bus in a dark neighborhood of the country's capital. I found a hotel and fell into a bed in the barren, shared room. Now, groggy and disgruntled, I squinted at some graffiti on the wall next to my head: "Oh that magic feeling, nowhere to go." I grunted.

The Panamanian embassy would be my first stop after breakfast. San Jose was a cute city with ornate old buildings, colorfully painted *pensiónes*, narrow sidewalks, and extraverted, handsome people. Its cool temperature was a welcome contrast to the heat of Nicaragua and El Salvador. From every store and car came upbeat rhythms fit for dancing. Huge political banners hung from buildings and street lamps, mementos of a recent presidential election. I had missed what was literally a nation-wide party, a celebration of the Costa Ricans' right to vote.

Suddenly a man stepped in front of me and asked me how long I'd been in the country. "Since last night," I replied. He smiled broadly. "This is a great country. Come, let me buy you a cup of coffee!"

We walked to a nearby café, me happy for the chance to practice my Spanish. I listened in amazement as the thirty-ish man, in a pale short sleeve dress shirt, used his fingers to tick off the reasons why Costa Rica was great. For starters, no standing army. A 98% literacy rate. The lowest debt in Central America. Massive acreage of protected natural resources. A functional democracy. In fact, he added, the president-elect, Rodrigo Carazo, had campaigned on a promise to expel Robert Vesco from the country. "You know who Robert Vesco is?"

"Yes, he's a friend of Richard Nixon. A financier, I think. On the run from the United States for embezzlement or maybe tax fraud."

"Correct. Our departing president gave him sanctuary here and it irritated everybody. Now Vesco will have to move to Cuba, or maybe Argentina!"

It was wonderful listening to this man, so proud and happy to be a *"Tico."* Back home there was an uproar because President Carter had on occasion lusted for women other than Rosalyn. Here the people were up in arms that the government had been harboring an international criminal. I began to wonder if Panama could wait.

And it did. A Panamanian embassy employee told me that I couldn't get a visa until I had a ticket out of the country. I tried to explain that I didn't need or want to buy a ticket out because I intended to find a boat to Colombia. The clerk smiled sympathetically, but in the end it was his way or no way.

Back at the hotel, I laid out my dilemma to Rich, the snorer from the other side of the sheet. He had left his job as a stock trader in San Francisco and circled the globe for four months. Perhaps his final good deed before returning to the States was patiently counseling the new kid at Camp Costa Rica.

"Ok, let me get this straight. You're heading to Peru through Panama and Colombia? Forget Columbia. Bogota is a *very* heavy-duty place. Thieves run up behind tourists in broad daylight and steal their purses and packs by cutting the straps then jumping into a getaway car. Panama is bad news, too. Best to find a way around those countries." He stroked his mustache. "Wait, you want to leave without even checking out Costa Rica? No wisdom there, man. I've just been around the world, and no place, I mean no place, has beaches half as beautiful as Costa Rica's. Plus the people are super kind and super mellow. Think it over."

I thought it over. It was Friday. I couldn't get a plane ticket and a visa in one day, so I thanked Rich and left the hotel to grab a bite. Over sandwich and a guidebook in a small café, I mused over how to spend a few days in Costa Rica, starting with a camera store and a post office. My guidebook wasn't much help, so I glanced around in hopes of finding a friendly face, someone to give me directions. A tall woman with kinky hair and creamy brown skin sat alone at a nearby table. I chose her. Her name was Gloria. I was not looking for a companion, but neither was I tempted to turn down her offer to show me around the city.

Gloria's face was carved with serenity, her voice was gentle, and her laugh came easily. She had picked up English in Miami where she'd worked for a couple of years. As we walked around San Jose, our conversation veered from language to language. Her reminiscences were like colorful short stories. Gloria was the youngest of a dozen or so brothers and sisters. They'd lived in poverty on the Nicoya Peninsula in western Costa Rica, but it wasn't a source of regret. Solidly grounded by the matriarch, Victoria Reyes Reyes, most of her children had built good lives for themselves.

I was perplexed at how content Gloria appeared to be, employed as a live-in housekeeper for a wealthy ex-pat. I admired the way she lined up her priorities, placing personal contentment above materiality. I was happy to have her company and pleased that she agreed to have dinner with me that evening. We agreed upon 8 pm although she said she might arrive a little later.

Gloria had recommended an open-air restaurant on one of San Jose's busiest streets. I settled in at a tiny linen-covered table and gawked at a stream of happy, handsome people. I nursed Coca-Colas, memorized the menu. I had nothing else to do. I remembered the words of someone in the hotel. "In Costa Rica, the expression 'on time' has no meaning." Two hours after I'd arrived, Gloria pulled up in a taxi. I greeted her with a smile.

We talked non-stop throughout dinner then strolled to a nearby club where the recorded disco music from the States was a few months old. Above us a rotating disco ball dotted the room with light. It was a corny touch but the dance floor was spacious. We danced and laughed until after midnight. Gloria knew of a little hotel within walking distance and we headed there sometime after midnight. The bed was too small for two people. It was just right.

The following day I left the city for a day trip which turned into three weeks immersed in a land of eye-popping beauty. The entire country had a magical, unexplored feel. "Ticos" were sweet and friendly. Babies didn't cry. Adults acknowledged others, even strangers, coming or going, with an *"Adiós." "A diós."* To God. A blessing perhaps? I liked it.

San Jose, sitting in the relative center of the country, became a natural hub for my comings and goings. On a whim, I rode an empty banana boat up the Rio Chirripo and spent a couple of nights in a shack at Barra del Colorado where the Rio San Juan, bordering southeastern Nicaragua, meets the Atlantic Ocean. I walked the beach crunchy with pieces of sea shells, feeling I'd been emptied and then refilled with beauty and wonder. The country was a bounteous spread from which my spirit could partake. My interest in finding a boat to South America expired completely.

Unlike life at home, my days were not marred by endless self-questioning about the direction of my life. There was no wrong decision. Simply put, one thing led to another. I merely had to keep going, keep looking, until I found a wonderfully cheap room, an unbelievably inexpensive and delicious meal or a place of staggering natural beauty. I was in love with life and the world.

I took a slow train to the west coast and lounged on a pristine beach at Manuel Antonio where a wild monkey was the only living creature in sight. I looked forward to the promise of day's end and every languid transition from day to night when the sky's pinks, golds and deep scarlet would fold around majestic billowing clouds touching the stratosphere. I stared at blue waters of every hue and fell into the depths of my soul. My journal was my constant companion and each morning I transcribed dreams. One involved the movie "Alfie," the 60's version with Michael Caine, which I had seen as a teenager. Alfie was a hound for women and a sexist pig of the first degree. In the dream,

> *I'm watching "Alfie" on television. There are various scenes with women, including one who is pregnant (just like in the movie). There is a young boy sitting beside me. I can't decide if he should watch this. Perhaps he'll misunderstand what is happening and get bad feelings about pregnancy.*

Each time I passed through San Jose, I phoned Gloria. With such little notice, she had trouble arranging her schedule to meet me. On one occasion her employer answered the phone and demanded that I identify myself. His tone pissed me off and I refused to give him an answer. I may have even insulted him in return. He began to shout at me and slammed the phone down. From that day forward, I asked the women desk clerks at the hotel to phone Gloria for me.

The next time I saw Gloria, I asked her what the man's problem was. She laughed. "Oh, Olin. He is Robert Vesco's son. He probably thinks you are a spy or something!!" She denied that "Junior" pressured or mistreated her, but I wondered. He made it almost impossible to meet again except for short dinners and once, a movie. We didn't have a romantic connection but our conversations were animated with comparisons of our different cultures and life styles. Over time it occurred to me that, since Gloria's questions frequently returned to topics like California wages, jobs and immigration laws, she might not be as sanguine about her life as she first appeared.

Living out of two shoulder bags grew wearisome as I neared the end of a month in Costa Rica. With a visa due to expire and a bankroll which resembled a used balloon, I decided to return home. I phoned my father, collect, for an emergency bail-out. The wire would take several days, so, in the interim, I decided to adopt a diet comprised exclusively of juicy Costa Rican pineapples. Dining in (in my hotel room) would cost less than a dollar a day. It seemed like just another brilliant idea until, overnight, the lining of my mouth ignited with burning canker sores. Gloria took pity on me and, with many giggles, treated me to dinner. I repaid her when I said good bye a few days later.

We met in a downtown café. Connecting with Gloria had given my weeks in Costa Rica a personal dimension. Egotistically, I searched her face for some show of sadness but she was merely withdrawn. We agreed to stay in touch, the way teenagers do at the end of summer camp. I was surprised by her request for my mailing address. She knew I had no place to live when I returned to the Bay Area. I handed her an old business card and told her my friends at the rehab center would have my forwarding address. I knew I would never see her again.

A bus took me to Guatemala City the following morning and from there it was an easy side-trip to Palenque, Mexico, before I headed back to Mexico City. My plan was to return home, find a well-paying job and regenerate the stash in my savings account. I would resume my travels, bypass Columbia, head straight for Ecuador or Peru and find a job teaching English.

Living with friends, I worked as a temp, managing a grout factory in Oakland, then gave in to the temptation to sample country life with a former work-mate and his wife on California's northwest coast. The Human Resources Department at the Georgia Pacific lumber mill, which sat at the ocean's edge in Fort Bragg, recognized my untapped potential to perform mind-numbing work in bone-chilling temperatures. They hired me as a trim sawyer on the night shift. I rented a small, below-code cabin with a loft, a broad deck and twenty-four windows facing state forest land. My days were spent experimenting with healthy foods and getting into the best physical shape of my life. I regularly biked down Highway One to Caspar and Mendocino and jogged forest trails and the frontage road beside the ocean. I ran the Avenue of the Giants Marathon and enlisted two friends to organize the first Mendocino Headlands 12K Charity Run. Practicing frugality for two years, I saved enough money to travel again. But fears of turning into a perpetual adolescent reined me in. A long-time dream to become a psychologist edged aside the South America plan.

Costa Rica faded into memory.

4. Letters and Other Presents—September, 1990

Melissa's first letter came in a standard grey air mail envelope, bordered in red and blue. I studied the delicate blue cursive writing on the envelope and slowly undid the seal. I removed the lined, onion-skin page of stationery folded around a photo of Melissa. A little black dog at her feet, she sits on a low, red-brick wall, neatly dressed in a school uniform: white shirt, blue skirt, dark socks and shoes. She looks happy and not skinny or sickly.

Hi, hello, Dad, [in English]

[In Spanish] For me it is one great pleasure to take in my hand this card in order to greet you and it gives me great satisfaction that you are somewhere in the world. What I want to know is what follows: Tell me when you are coming and how long you can stay.

I have a dog named Rosti and I love him a lot.

It pleases me to ask, if it is not too much trouble, if you could buy me a camera and when you come here I will pay you for it.

I am in the sixth grade. If God wishes next year I will be in secondary school. My mom wants us to go to San Jose, but I don't want to. I will send you a photo in which I am in the front yard of my house with Rosti.

I hope you will write soon.

I am 3 feet and 37 centimeters tall.

Respectfully,

Wendy Melissa Reyes Reyes

She calls me "Dad." It makes me cry, sadly, as if I could only now feel the parched nature of my life before her.

She wants to pay me for a camera. Ahhhh, she has no idea!

Soon I had my first dream of Melissa:

I walk over from my chair to the couch on which she sits. Our hands come together.

* * * * *

Laura and I spoke by phone. She told me that, in spite of her excitement about finding me, Melissa generally seemed depressed. My first letter, mailed more than a month earlier, had not arrived. I wrote again, responding to Melissa's letter and thanking her for the photo. I added, "I hope Rosti likes strangers!" Repeating some of my earlier letter, I also described her relatives in the State and provided the dates of my planned visit in late November. I included copies of my earlier photos and a few new ones.

In one of the photos you can see me sitting with my friend from the sixth grade, Britt, and I am wiggling the toes of his little daughter, Amanda.

I had two dreams about you this week. In these dreams, we sat together and walked together and talked. We were very comfortable, you could say peaceful together, as if we had known each other for a long time. I think dreams sometimes come true. I believe these dreams will, don't you?

Gloria's letter crossed mine in the mail. It began *"Hóla, Cariño,"* ("Hi, Dear One"). In large loopy script she described how happy she and Melissa were to find me. She asked if I could stay around for Melissa's grade school graduation, adding that she and I "had much to talk over." At the very bottom Melissa scrawled, "Daddy, send us a copy of the letter." The opening salutation was a bit unnerving but overall it seemed like a sweet, gentle letter.

A second letter from Gloria followed ten days later. It began, *"Hóla, Cielo."* "Cielo," in Spanish, means "Heaven" or "Sky." It is a term of endearment. Gloria asked if I could send money for Melissa's birthday party on November 9. In her brief letter, she addressed me as *"Cariño"* three times and *"Cielo"* once more. She signed it "Kisses from Gloria." My anxiety exploded. Was Gloria living in a world of romantic fantasy built up over the years? Was she hoping

I would marry her? Was this event more about her than Melissa? Would the police or a summons be waiting for me when I arrived? Laura had funny feelings about Gloria when she returned to Costa Rica. Now, I did, too.

Not lost in my little freak out was Gloria's request for money. It didn't take long for her to hit me up! A second reaction came quickly. I did want to help Melissa, and that was more important than my defensiveness about Gloria wanting money. Since wiring funds to Costa Rica could take weeks, I decided to bring them extra money for belated gifts in November.

The letter gave me a new slant on Gloria, one which raised more questions. She and I belonged to differing classes and cultures, with differing expectations, and my mind was filled with buckets of suspicion. Laura had told me that Gloria was already planning for us to go the beach when I visited. Was this an attempt to rekindle our relationship? Did it have something to do with my relative and supposed wealth? Did she fear I would use my financial resources to abscond with Melissa? I had no answers.

The next time we spoke I recommended she tell Gloria I had a girlfriend. I was certain this lie would demolish any illusions on Gloria's part. I could focus on Melissa confident that she and I would not have any similar dissonance.

*****

One day I told my story to a newspaper reporter who worked in my building. It turned out that she had recently written a local story on CF. She re-contacted a local couple she had interviewed while researching the article and asked if they would be willing to talk with me. It excited me to think they could give me tips for dealing with a CF child. I phoned the woman, Helen Dias. She told me she and her husband, Ed, had raised three daughters, two of them with cystic fibrosis. Their middle child, Diane, had recently died on her 12th birthday. When I heard that, my chest cramped. Melissa would turn twelve in a few weeks.

Helen and Ed lived a mile from my house in a modest, west Petaluma, ranch-style home. The interior was decorated with overstuffed furniture and ornate wall decorations. Looking around, I felt an overwhelming sense of the love and grief which lived there. It seemed unusually quiet, reflecting the contained personalities of the attractive late 30-ish couple who had met me at the door. We sat at the dining room table and talked about our daughters. Helen's voice had a flat quality, as if all emotion had been squeezed out of her. When Diane was 11, one of her lungs collapsed. She used a portable respirator for the rest of her life. Her parents were committed to their daughter living life as fully as possible. Helen described family outings to the coast, carrying Diane and her oxygen tank down to the water's edge.

Eventually Diane became worn down, her lungs and body exhausted from a long fight. She told her parents she wanted to be taken off oxygen. Helen and Ed disagreed wrenchingly, vehemently, with each other about what to do. In the end the respirator was put away. I searched their faces for any clue as to how they could have endured the outcome of their decision and the loss of their beautiful daughter. All I saw was a profound sorrow.

Diane was obviously an exceptional, loving young girl. She took on the challenge of living actively in a way which was far, far away from anything I'd ever done. It pained me to hear about her splendor and courage, really the entire family's courage, in the face of such suffering.

Helen invited me down the carpeted hallway to Diane's room. She opened the door into a room which sat in repose, softly lit. Stuffed pillows, stuffed animals and teenager decorations were everywhere. Helen kept it exactly the way it was when Diane had passed. I looked around the room, nodding, at a loss to say anything meaningful.

At evening's end I wept with Helen and Ed at their dining room table. My last request was to ask what advice they could give me. Helen did not hesitate. "Love your daughter with all you've got."

Not long afterwards, I had this dream:

> *I'm with another person and we're trying to locate a certain medicine man. We're in a desert town, in New Mexico, maybe. We drive up and down a street. The house numbers aren't ordered in sequence but we're in the right neighborhood, I'm certain. Finally I spot 107 (Helen and Ed's house number) and we go inside. The young Indian man there is called for by his mother. He gives us some vague instructions to locate the medicine man. He says to look for a building (with a name I can't remember). It's past a certain department store or mall. He won't give any more directions, saying, "If you want/need more explicit directions, it's not for you."*
>
> *I go and find the place easily. A young person greets us and we go inside. He shows us a man lying on a table of dirt, asleep or in a trance. The younger man calls his name and he raises up and acknowledges us. Right behind him my friend, Jeff, raises up, also from a sleep or a trance.*

Helen and Ed's house address. A desert town. A young Indian giving me minimal directions to find a medicine man and Jeff, who had lost a great friend in a terrible accident. They come out of trances to meet me. The dream seemed to point to old teachings and to another dimension where there was no clear path.

5. Behind the Veil—September-November, 1990

The autumn season in Northern California deepened and glowed. My ominous mood slunk to the sidelines, crowded out by the wonder of having a beautiful adolescent daughter. More than one friend noticed in me a new vulnerability, "cracked open" as one person put it. I was an expectant father even if my child was eleven years out of the womb. There were unexpected rushes of joy. A thrill flashed through me the first time a person spoke the words, "Your daughter." And when a new acquaintance asked if I had children, "Yes! A daughter!" came out like the blast of an orchestra.

A friend, Denise, and I spent a few hours together one morning at her house. She listened thoughtfully to my story, conveyed in choppy waves, one detail leading to another before overlapping yet another. She offered why the story so touched her—and everyone. "It points to purpose," she said, "and pattern—to what we believe in, or like to think is there, behind the veil. We see it so much more dramatically in this story than almost anywhere." I went home and wrote down Denise's lovely comment, just as I did with every other significant remark or event which occurred during those days.

* * * * *

Melissa's second letter filled me with delight.

Hi, hello, how are you,

I am very well, waiting for my day which is coming. It would please me if you would come and stay for my graduation. Send me a photo because the first letter did not reach me.

I have a friend who was born in November just like me. I don't know what to write, what it is you want to know.

Oh, Kuki is a little dog who comes to play with Rosti. It's fun.

What religion are you. Tell me in the letter that you send me.

Respectfully,

Wendy Melissa Reyes Reyes

The envelope was sealed with a red sticker of two hearts touching under the words *"Tú me perteneces."* (You belong to me)

Oh, God, how Melissa's unguarded grasp found a companion in my heart! Tender openheartedness and gratitude dug their roots in me. I knew happiness and closeness would soon be ours. If, as Laura had suggested, the light of Melissa's spirit had dimmed, I was certain it would strengthen from the power of love flowing within me.

Still there were the odd thoughts which bounced through my head. *This is too good to be true. It can't last. Why me? Something will ruin this.* Driving home from pricing cameras, tears filled my eyes. I felt overwhelmed, wishing I had someone beside me to help with all my feelings and decisions. An instant later I relished the days to come. *She's real! All the fun I've had with other people's children I'll have with my own!* I wrote in my journal:

Excitement and love swell within me and the wild amazingness of this event sweeps and rolls and lifts.

Laura sent me an exciting description of the preparations for my upcoming visit:

> *Well, hi there "Dad"....*
>
> *Melissa and I went to the hotel and pensione in town to check out the prices and facilities (ha ha) and we made an excellent decision! The rooms are about the same "quality" at each place: lumpy twin beds, a table, a bathroom—but the Pension Cordoba is cheaper, the people are friendlier and it's located right in the center of Esparza. Melissa likes it better, because "it's cheaper and it's on the same street as my house." So anyways, that's the rundown—400 colones a night, about $4.*
>
> *...She's so disappointed you won't be here for her graduation from the sixth grade. I explained that you're coming during a holiday and that you have to work, etc. Gloria asked if you lived in an apartment or a house, if you have a car or a motorcycle....She also asked me if you asked "by whom" when I told you that you had a child in Costa Rica. Because, she said, "he must have known many girls when he was in Costa Rica." To tell you the truth I think she has "butterflies" about seeing you! She's anxious about seeing your picture, etc...*
>
> *I was thinking more about Melissa's personality. Like I said before, she's a sweet precious girl. She's also a bit quiet and timid...It will be an emotional moment when you all first meet!! I don't expect that she'll be shy but I also don't think she'll be really out-going...*
>
> *Once again, I'm so glad to be a part of all the excitement, love and anticipation.*
>
> *Laura*

I pictured Melissa on the hunt for my hotel room and, soon, introducing me to her world. She and I inhabited a cosmos of imagination and anticipation, where physical distance did not separate us. I returned to that imaginary world as often as I could.

I chose the Thanksgiving holidays to go to Costa Rica, in part to meet and thank Laura's parents who would be visiting then. Laura's proficiency in Spanish would help Melissa and me greatly. Then I learned that Laura and her parents were planning on leaving town to sight-see two days after I arrived and I grew nervous about communicating with Melissa and Gloria. I pushed myself harder in my Spanish studies and decided to memorize a little "speech" to say to Melissa when we met.

*****

When your child is diagnosed with a deadly chronic disease, you take on a new relationship with Truth. You can't live without it. Good news is all you want at first, but eventually you learn that you must have the total truth about your child's condition and nothing less will do. No matter that the truth rips your guts out so often it seems like you will never heal.

I was thrown into the pool of truth's deep end when, in early November, I visited Cystic Fibrosis Research, Incorporated, in Palo Alto, for a parents conference. I eagerly drove the 90 miles that morning, anticipating a warm experience in a community of like-minded people learning about recent advances in treatment of CF. When I arrived 60 or 70 people were already in the auditorium, mostly adults with a sprinkling of young people. Two pharmaceutical companies had booths in the foyer and I grabbed the card of a woman whose company had a regional sales representative in Central America.

Researchers streamed to the podium to describe revolutionary advances in identifying the CF gene and ideas for "repairing" the gene and, with it, the disease's destructive effects on the body. Each made it clear that there were no major breakthroughs in treatment and CF remained incurable. The atmosphere in the auditorium grew thick even at the edge of the audience where I sat, close to the back door. I looked down the rows and stole glances at CF parents, my new tribe. Couples, seated beside and behind me, listened intently to even the most technical presentations. I saw creases bunched around eyes. I heard questions asked in voices with tones of worry and impatient intensity. My energy waned.

The lunch hour arrived and I squirmed in my chair next to strangers chatting about matters of life and death. I purchased a CFRI t-shirt and then lurched from the building. On the drive home, my entire body ached. I felt tired and terrified and a jumble of other emotions I didn't have words for. I didn't know whether I needed to talk to someone or be held or ram my car into a wall.

*****

Laura wrote again on Halloween.

Hóla Papá,

Cómo le va? Estóy pensando en usted mucho — solamente 20 dias mas hasta usted llega!! We all can't wait!! We still haven't received your letters — I think it's Costa Rica's postal system's way of making your arrival <u>*in person*</u> *even more exciting!!!*

I was talking with Melissa yesterday and get this!!!!! She asked if you were coming alone. "Of course," I said, "who would he come with *anyways??"*

"Well, my mom said that he was probably coming with his girlfriend. If he comes alone we can meet him at the airport, but if he comes with his girlfriend, "la novia," we can't.

"Why?" I asked. She just shrugged her shoulders and said, I don't know."

I told her that I can assure her that you are coming alone, because you are coming to see her and want to spend all your time with her!!!!...

We all can't wait to meet you!

See ya soon!

Laura

*****

I'm shopping at a camera store in San Rafael. Looking over the automatics, I find one I like and ask the clerk if it has instructions in Spanish. He looks offended and his voice rises in pitch. "Why in the world would you want instructions in Spanish??" As I glare at him, his impropriety takes hold and he mumbles something about never having had that request.

I'm too ragged to scream. I speak in a slow, measured, steel-fist-in-a-velvet-glove way. Guess what? I'm giving the camera to a Spanish-speaking person! We silently ponder his idiocy for a beat or two before I leave.

My tour of stores is usually successful, even triumphant. At every cash register, I proudly announce, "I'm buying this for my daughter!" At Macy's in Santa Rosa, I search for a watch and a golden locket. I'd never even looked closely at a locket, but I choose one I know Melissa will love. Its symbolism gives me joy: It is shaped like a heart, it opens, there are two inner chambers for photos, it glows in the light, and it is destined to rest near Melissa's heart.

Before the last-minute gift wrapping, my purchases sprawl on my living room floor, along with a stack of family photos, nutritional powders and vitamins, cards and little endearments from friends. Each day I sit before them, imagining Melissa's happiness as she opens each package. Alongside gifts for Gloria there is the locket, a purple and lime Swatch watch, a large box of art supplies, a little bear donated from my friend Sharon, a bigger teddy made for me by a client, and of course, the camera with Spanish instructions, batteries and boxes of film.

I wrote in my journal:

I sit here wrapping presents for my daughter.
The first ones.
I sign greeting cards "From Daddy."

I want to give thanks.
To whom?

To whom do I offer thanks?
Laura. Bob and Anne.
They were players in Someone's design.
Who designed this?
I wanted a child.
Did my wanting find its own fulfillment?
Am I just a player in love's own fulfillment?

Why make this more complicated?
A girl and her father are re-united.
They find love.
He finds love.
Love finds him.
That's it, that's the story.

Love enters a life.
A man interested in love,
is found by love.
A man unable to have a wife or a child to love
is found by generous people.

A child, not knowing the love of a father,
will soon find out.
She dreams.
She dreams of a man
far away.
She dreams.
She stirs in her sleep.
Only three more days.
They are endless, these days.

She worries.
Will he be what she dreams of—
and needs?
She worries.
She is sick.
Will he love her,
Sick lungs and all?
She worries.
Will he return her love?

She has watched men,
friends of her mother,
fathers of her friends.
These men are distant,
mysterious.
She longs for a father
She can really know and call Father.

Father, who will hold her.
Father, who gazes deeply on her.
Father, to be proud of her.
Father, to protect her.
Father, to introduce her
to new dimensions of herself.

He dreams.
What dreams they are.
This dream,
what reality it is.
The dream came over me, and
I could not but give into
its sweet fever.
This dream
became my life.
It chose me
and whispered to me
in my sleep:
You will forever long for love,
for a child.
You will ache for a child.
You will cry for a child.
A child will appear
and she will seem like a sign.
She is more than a child.
Your dreams are more, too.
They are summons.

6. We Meet—Tuesday

The dreams of Melissa and me were not shared by Pan American Airlines. My plane sat on San Francisco International's tarmac for ninety minutes. Electricians in tool belts jogged up and down the aisle looking to uncover the cause of the malfunctioning floor lights. The cabin rumbled with the mutterings of Thanksgiving holiday travelers. By the time some genius decided that the lights were not really necessary on a daytime flight, the chances of my making the connection out of Miami were in serious jeopardy. Once airborne, I vaulted from my seat and cajoled a stewardess to call ahead and get the Costa Rica flight delayed in the name of God, parents and children everywhere. But she didn't have the clout. It would have taken a miracle and for the moment at least it seemed that my quota had been used up.

In Miami a lone Pan Am agent "greeted" the unruly crowd denied the night in Latin America. He promised a free hotel room and a seat on the next day's flight, 22 hours later. The offer had barely left his lips before a small herd of people, me included, took off down the concourse in a mad scramble for a seat on an earlier flight. Lacsa Airlines held the best option. Although their desk was closed, the schedule board listed daily flights to San Jose at 6 am. I phoned their LA office and bought a ticket for $316. Since I had been planning on spending the night in San Jose anyway, this development meant that my arrival in Esparza would be delayed by only 3 hours. Still, I was angry, on the wave of a pisser that had begun hours earlier in San Francisco. I left a phone message for Laura about the delay and the approximate time of my arrival in Esparza.

Sleep was out of the question and at 4 am, I got up, showered and took a shuttle back to the airport. Two hours later we'd elevated out of Miami, over miles of reefs and azure waters south of Key West. The view of the sparkling sky and bulbous clouds mingled with the shore line of the Yucatan Peninsula and Belize. My frustration eased into anticipation and gratitude. I took out my journal and scribbled:

My insides dance
I want to commandeer the jet and
parachute into Esparza.
Yes, I feel like kissing strange women,
leaping down the aisle in pirouettes.
I'm a father!
My child is near my arms!
And when I cease
dancing, exhausted,

shadows on the wall
will continue the dance, never ending.

Multitudes could approach me today,
with their suffering,
and their souls would be restored.
"Today is the Day that the Lord has Made."
The writer of that line must have been a proud father,
a cheering, galloping, tumbling, jumping father.
Hey, maybe there's a
whole bunch of us new "papi's" on the planet,
singing songs and
loving the day,
her day,
my day,
The Lord's day.

*****

San Jose International's air conditioning, if it even existed, was out of order. But the building's steam heat took a back seat to the anxiety running through me. My luggage was filled with a dozen bottles of Ensure and boxes of protein powder. All that was needed was for a Customs Officer to unzip one of the bags and I could be whisked off to an interrogation room. I pulled my bags off the conveyor belt and took them to a customs official. He looked at my passport and waved me through.

A scrum of taxi drivers shouted at me. I shoved my way in the direction of a friendly face. He grabbed my luggage and I yelled "Direct bus, Esparza!" We tore through side streets for fifteen minutes before arriving at the end of a cobblestone lane lined with colorful *tiendas*. Young boys ran around crying out the names of distant towns. "Liberia!" "Quepos!" "Jaco!"

To the shouts of "Puntarenas! Puntarenas!" the driver stopped beside a bus which revved and rattled like it feared the open road. I dragged my luggage up the stairs and fell into a seat in the back. Up went my shirt sleeves and every nearby window. The bus lurched forward through invisible webs of humidity. The 30-hour marathon became a ninety-minute sprint to my prize.

The San Jose suburbs evolved into a hilly green freckled with berries and blossoms. The passing sights looked familiar, as if nothing had changed in twelve years. Single women, wary-eyed, stood motionless, always holding a half-full plastic bag in one hand. Skinny men in pressed pants and short-sleeved shirts carrying Bibles. Uniformed school girls in pairs. A boy in a baseball cap on a horse. An old man bent double by a load of firewood on his back. A long-skirted woman, erect like a fashion model, with a heavy bowl perched on her head. Their backdrop was an endless jungle of vegetation and trees, a natural botanical garden pastiched with shadows and blinding sunlight.

The highway's curves and twists sent my bags into the aisles. While the bus driver continuously honked the horn for no apparent reason, I leaned back and practiced my greeting to Melissa. We crested a small mountain range and the Pacific waters appeared in the distance. Traffic increased, houses and drive-in restaurants crowded the road. My senses perked up as Esparza approached. The driver caught my eye in his rear view mirror then pulled off at the *Bomba 76* gas station, just like Laura described it.

I pushed my luggage out the front door of the bus and saw a muscular, blond-haired man in his 20's walking towards me. He introduces himself as Scott, Laura's brother and says he's visiting along with his parents. They and Laura are at lunch awaiting me. We're scheduled to meet Melissa and Gloria in the plaza in twenty minutes.

All business, we throw the luggage into the trunk of the rental car and drive a few minutes to Laura's house. I blather to Scott, my voice sounding like it's coming from a tunnel. Melissa's little town looks like a bunch of little houses built on a boxey grid of little streets. A rush of blood pounds my eardrums.

We pull up to the house and I hear laughing voices as I exit the car. My chest explodes as if I'd just walked into a concert hall filled with thousands of screaming people.

The door opens and my three blonde angels stand in the entryway.

The mother, Anne. Straight hair, radiant face, glistening eyes.

The father, Bob. Warm eyes, strong face.

And Laura. Golden tan, blue eyes, sculpted features.

Their faces shine. I have a weird feeling of incredible size and strength, like I'm a giant dropped into a land of little people. One by one, we hug like long lost family. The din of our constant laughter is deafening. Someone says we are due at the plaza in five minutes.

We stumble out into the blazing noonday sun and stride up the street, giddy with purpose, bystanders staring at us from the shade of their front porches. We move, shoulder to shoulder, like heroes in a Hollywood western, marching to meet destiny.

Then I lose track of the Lees. Sound ends. I reach the street corner and the plaza's towering trees come into view. Sixty paces away, under a high yellow gazebo with a turquoise cupola, a woman and a thin child lean against a low

We meet. November, 1990.

cinder block wall. Gloria, in a print cotton dress, looking older than I expected, steps away from the wall, seeing us just as I see her. Melissa also moves, but slowly, wearing a frilly, floral pink and blue dress. It seems a size too big and accentuates her skinny arms and legs. She wears scruffy white Reeboks and carries an unopened umbrella which I briefly mistake for a cane.

Now I race-walk, my eyes riveted on Melissa. Gloria approaches, leaving her daughter several feet behind. I give her a happy greeting and pass her. I stop in front of Melissa and bend over with my hands on my knees and we say hello. Melissa grins broadly and I step forward and brush my lips on her cheek, then squat in front of her. She smiles with her lips pressed. Brown bangs cover her forehead, her long hair is pinned at the back. The Spanish word for "beautiful" comes to mind. *"Estás linda,"* I say, for she is even more beautiful than the photos let on. She says a tiny *"Gracias,"* and squirms shyly. I couldn't help myself. "Melissa, *es milagro"* (This is a miracle).

We gaze at each other for a long moment. The resemblance is astonishing. Almond-shaped eyes, high forehead, small chin. She stands beaming, a wondrous combination of the familiar and the different which makes me swoon. I reach forward and gently wrap my fingers around two of hers, as if cupping her very life.

It was bliss looking at Melissa.

A cloud passes over her creamy soft features. She scrutinizes my face before her eyes slant away. It is time to talk and I was glad I'd memorized my greeting in Spanish. It made the one point I wanted Melissa to hear in person.

"Melissa, I am very, very happy to be here and to meet you and to know that you exist. I am not here to decide if I want to be your father, but to say I am your father. I look forward to spending as much time with you this week and in the future as I can. You said in your letter that this would be your day. I want you to know that it is my day also."

Melissa looked at me intently throughout and pursed her lips together as if holding back something which wanted to burst out. But she said nothing. I feared I'd overwhelmed her.

Maybe Gloria and Laura had been there all along. When I noticed them I stood up and hugged Gloria and, though she smiled, that was the extent of her reaction. With Laura translating, we made small talk about my layover in Miami and the agony it caused for everyone, and now the relief and excitement we all shared. Everyone commented on the resemblances. Melissa saw them, too, bringing me happiness.

At moments, I didn't hear anyone. Melissa's face transfixed me. It would have given me great contentment to simply sit and gaze at her for hours.

The group of us set off for the hotel. Melissa had no bulk on her, her walk was more like floating. Neither of us spoke. I imagined that she, like me, didn't know what to say or do next. We stole glances at each other, trying to hide our keen curiosity. Whenever I could, I caught her eye and smiled.

After we ordered our soft drinks in the hotel restaurant, someone suggested that Melissa escort me to the upstairs room which she had chosen on the outing with Laura and Gloria. I gathered my bags and she led the way up the stairs in no apparent physical discomfort. I unlocked the door and motioned for her to proceed me into the room. I found the light switch and a low watt, naked bulb in the ceiling sprang to life. I was unprepared for what I saw: a dark, dungeon-like room. The metal bed frame held a caved-in mattress and a wafer-thin pillow. I leaned into the bathroom tinged with mold. The shower head was missing and the shower rod had no curtain. I nodded and smiled at Melissa. "Perfect," I said.

I gestured at my luggage. "I brought some gifts for you. Tell me, would you like them now or later?" Without hesitation, she replied, "Later." We went downstairs and rejoined the group.

It had been decided that we would take a tour of Melissa's school. The halls of the yellow stuccoed Escuela Arturo Torres were empty. We walked

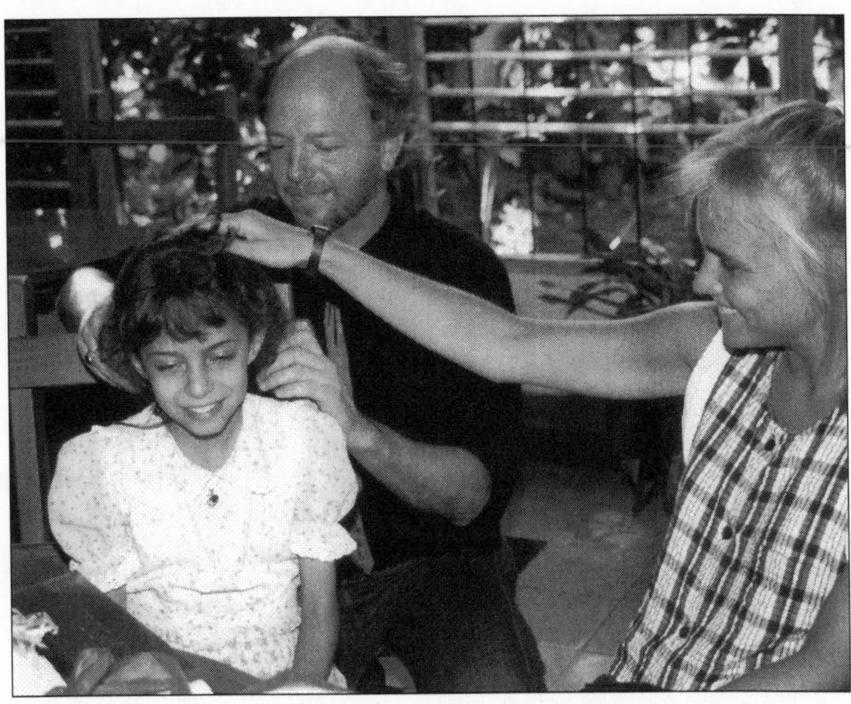

One of Bob Lee's many great photos from the party.

to Melissa's classroom. When her teacher learned who I was, her eyes opened wide and teared, and she hugged Melissa tightly to her chest. The teacher, Laura and Anne took charge as we toured the walkways of the school. All I could do was look at the classrooms and playground and beam like the proud father I was. Melissa and I hung back from the group. I asked little questions but her responses were short, in a voice I could barely hear.

We headed back to the hotel to get out of the smothering heat. After another round of soft drinks we agreed that the time for the party had arrived. I brought down a luggage bag of gifts, including two for Gloria. Around a large table we honored Gloria's persistence, the Lees' dogged efforts, and the glory of child and father uniting. Everyone's face glowed in the direction of Melissa. She looked engulfed by the stack of gifts on the table.

The unwrapping of the gifts must have lasted 45 minutes. Melissa opened each present in the same fashion: slow-slow motion. First she would carefully undo the tape, then make sure that the wrapping paper came off intact. Poker-faced, she would remove each gift from its box, thoroughly examine it on all sides, show it around the table, then replace it in its box. Even with the camera her expression remained one of extreme, controlled curiosity. When she came to the felt-tip pens, she uncapped every one to appraise the sharp points. Only when a gift was passed to her mom would she break into a smile. The rest of us watched, enraptured.

Melissa looking at me.

The only exception was the grey furry teddy bear made for me by a client. It was soft, wide-eyed and kind. Melissa never let it go. It sat on her hip, where she continuously patted and stroked it. I watched her in absolute delight.

Melissa offered a running commentary on the arduous task of opening gifts. "So many!" she sighed, and "Could there be more?" Later, with an exhale:

"Still, I must continue!" The rest of us laughed to the point of tears, blessed witnesses to the child, celebrating and being celebrated, with her loving father beside her at last.

Bob took photographs throughout the party. As I was to learn later, they show Melissa glowing throughout. One photo captures Laura holding Melissa's hair while I fasten the gold locket at the back of her neck. Melissa's eyelids appear to be fluttering. Our faces are flushed and full.

The ceremony ended with a silent pause. Then without warning, Melissa half stood, leaned over and touched her lips to my cheek. My insides gasped, crumpled, leapt. Bob, caught off guard, grabbed his camera and asked for a replay. Melissa agreed, he gave her the go-ahead and she kissed me again. Once again the camera malfunctioned. Bob muffled a curse and everyone exploded in laughter. Finally Bob got his shot as my face burned brightly from the three feathery, extraordinary kisses

7. Retreat—Wednesday

Melissa's new watch collapsed around her wrist and threatened to slip off. We set out across town to find a leathersmith to punch an extra hole or two in the band.

Esparza was a town with no discernible building codes. Houses, some with postage-stamp lawns, were constructed in idiosyncratic combinations of brick, lumber, poured concrete and cinder block. Each glowed in a different primary color so that every street looked like a giant paint set decorated with vegetation. The houses and lush greenery seemed to be in competition for space, with a slight advantage going to the flowering shrubs. Corner storefront *tiendas* featured candy, soda and chips in the front with drug store items on the back wall. The asphalt streets were lined with narrow, cracked sidewalks. Cloudy, foul-smelling water trickled through the gutters.

I walked in the street, dodging the gutters, so my eyes and Melissa's would be nearer to parallel. First my questions, then her answers, usually in a word or two, sometimes with only a shrug and a smile. Movies? Melissa had never been in a movie theater. Chatting on the phone with friends? Not much. Fun? Bicycling with a friend. Boyfriends? No!

We arrived at the leather shop where 30 cents got a hole punched. The watch still hung loosely but Melissa smiled. Her graciousness to the shop keeper made me proud.

Later, as the sky turned violet, she and her mother returned to my hotel.

They looked shy but glamorous in modest cotton dresses, especially Melissa in an over-the-knee, flowing green dress. Her long brown hair was pinned up in the back, showcasing the golden locket around her neck. I could have burst in happiness.

Melissa had selected the restaurant, a fried chicken joint named "My Father's House." It was a simple place with a wood counter, a grill, a soda dispenser and piped-in music. We took our seats at an unvarnished wood table, Melissa and Gloria across from me, and ordered three platters of chicken, the only item on the menu. Gloria talked continuously, carefully enunciating her Spanish, while Melissa did little more than swing her legs and giggle. I felt slightly drunk, the room seemed to swim in warm, frosted light. Every few minutes my trance was broken with the crack of a phlegmy cough. Melissa covered her mouth as her throat convulsed. Neither she nor her mom acted too concerned and I followed their lead, but the noise sounded real bad.

After we finished eating, they brought out a photo album which chronicled Melissa's development from infant to pre-teen. Pictures of friends, family and parties. The record of all the years I'd missed. It tasted bittersweet. I nodded appreciatively at a shot of Melissa posing like a glamorous model, holding her hair up, elbow pointed skywards, back slightly arched: a girl delighted to be on the verge of young womanhood. Melissa must have seen something in my face. She removed the photo from its binding and presented it to me. I protested briefly, just enough to be polite.

Gradually, Gloria's tone grew more personal and edgy. I tensed when she criticized Melissa for not finishing her small portion of chicken. She jarred me with memories of 1978. "Do you remember the Hotel Asturias? The Spanish teacher?" Sadly, I did not, and she was incredulous.

She asked why I had never married. I gave her a meaningless reply. She abruptly announced her wish to have many children. "In fact, 15," she said. I could have choked on my drumstick. "15??"

I checked my mental Spanish dictionary to make sure *"quince"* was "fifteen." Fifteen? It seemed like a good time to define my future fathering interests. "15? Not me!" I smiled and tapped the table. "I want only one… and she is right here." I pointed to Melissa. My insides pounded. After two sleepless nights followed by a major league curve ball from Gloria, it was time to call it a day.

I never did figure out Gloria's intentions that night, even after I learned she had undergone a hysterectomy. Perhaps I'd misunderstood and it was only her wish that she could have fifteen children. I did not know how my response was interpreted or if I had even spoken intelligibly in rusty Spanish. But that concern quickly evaporated. I lay on the bed, my head resting on a make-shift pillow created from my shoes wrapped in a t-shirt. With a full chest, I played and replayed the day until sleep came.

I awoke late the next morning to the burring of the table fan. The image of my fragile, lovely daughter filled my head, my thoughts shooting forward four days from now. How would I ever be able to say goodbye to her?

The image of Helen and Ed in Petaluma and their daughter, Diane, came to mind. I remembered my friend, Frances — whose husband John had died — and their children. I felt my heart's exquisite happiness and the pain of my aloneness here in Esparza and in my life in general. I thought about all these loves and losses. Tears rolled down my cheeks.

The Lees came by at 10 o'clock and we drove around the outskirts of town. I was happy just to be near an air-conditioner. Everyone was delighted to hear my dinner story and know that Melissa was so happy. We discussed my hope for Melissa to come to the U.S. for a medical workup. Gloria had expressed skepticism over the idea and I told them it was probably not good to push it at this point. Anne said I would have to bring my new family to Chicago should Melissa ever come north.

I returned to the plaza alone, at noon. Costa Rica's rainy season was at its end and the day was sticky hot. The shade of the overhanging trees had lured

Melissa, Gloria, and the Lees, Laura, Bob, and Anne.

many people to sit on the park's walls and benches. Mother and daughter awaited me, each decked out in colorful print dresses. Gloria's was blue, Melissa's pink, sprinkled with squiggly designs of blue, red and turquoise. On her feet were frilly white socks and polished white shoes. She carried the black camera bag on her shoulder. But the giggling child from the night before had disappeared. Her features were flat, even sickly looking. When I asked, she said she felt fine.

I turned to see a young policeman nearing us. He strode slowly but with purpose until he stopped in front of me. He asked to see my passport. I fumbled for it before remembering that I had left it in my hotel room. When the policeman heard this, his face stiffened.

I asked why he was questioning me. He said something about Costa Rican children being photographed then disappearing. I recalled stories of predators kidnapping Central American children and selling their organs on the black market. I pointed out that I didn't have a camera on me, but my mouth felt like cotton. Then from nowhere the Lees appeared and the attention shifted to Bob. He, too, was without passport. The policeman moved from foot to foot, clearly trying to figure out his next move. Then Anne pulled out her passport. The policeman looked at it for a long minute, handed it back and without a word turned and walked off across the plaza.

Gloria and Melissa, looking beautiful, just before my world came crashing down.

Bob ushered us to his rented car for a short drive to a restaurant on the highway west of town. Gloria climbs in the back seat and Melissa trails her. Seeing me preparing to enter the back seat behind her, she jumps like a scared animal to the other side of her mother. After we're all packed into the car and heading down the road, Melissa occasionally turns her head to look at me. Once she smiles, otherwise it's nothing but empty glances. She sits stone silent, staring out the window. It's as if my daughter has been replaced by an alien.

Over lunch she remains buttoned tight. The Mirador Restaurant holds 25 or 30 tables arranged spaciously on a concrete floor. The walls on three sides are shuttered windows, propped open so that breezes and scents from the nearby flowering trees can waft around us. We take seats under ceiling fans, Melissa and me directly opposite each other. It's nearly impossible to take my eyes off her. I fall into a rhythm of looking at her briefly, looking away, looking as if I'm not looking, then flat-out staring. Gloria shows photos while everyone feasts on blended fruit drinks. She passes around a photo ID dated the same day that she and I met and (our secret) the night Melissa was conceived.

I'm self-conscious like a teenager. Wanting only a simple chat with Melissa, I settle for sitting near her, anticipating the wonder I'll experience over every word she speaks. But while her mother enjoys the limelight of the lunch conversation, Melissa sits off in silence. I crook my finger and motion her to come and sit beside me. She makes a little grimace and shakes her head.

Behind the restaurant is a large tree-lined area where we go for a photo session after our meal. Melissa poses alone or with Gloria and me for many photos, smiling broadly for the camera. Someone convinces her to drape her arm over my shoulders for a couple of shots as I squat next to her. Before the second shot, I reach around her and lightly rest my hand on her thin forearm. Once the shutter snaps, she walks away.

The Lees are as perplexed as I about Melissa's dramatic retreat. Out of Melissa's hearing, Gloria tells me she might be preoccupied about a school exam the next day. I wonder if she really believes that.

We drive west to the ocean front resort near Puntarenas where the Lees are spending one more night before their departure tomorrow. The hotel is new but tacky, with the painted stucco already streaked with water stains. For Melissa, the grounds are a world she's clearly unfamiliar with. She stares at the beautiful floral landscaping around the building and the large pool with a sunken bar at one end. A large expanse of green lawn is filled with noisy tourists, both gringos and Latinos.

We find pool chairs under tree-like umbrellas. Glumly I sit near Gloria and Melissa, trying to figure out how I can connect with Melissa. I notice a German tourist in a polyester jogging suit walk up to Gloria. He holds up his camera and mimes asking permission to take their photo and Gloria agrees. She and my daughter are a frickin vacation photo op.

Gloria leaves for the bathroom and I seize the moment to go over and sit beside Melissa. Half-expecting her to get up and walk away, I hold the photos in front of me, hoping they'll pique her curiosity enough to keep her in her chair. She does remain seated and, nervously, I take her through photos of her new family and my dearest friends, most of whom contributed gifts to her. The alone time, our first of the day, is a great thrill, even though Melissa's expression remains inscrutable throughout. When Gloria returns, I tell her I'll show her the photos later and she sits down nearby.

When we finish the last photos, there is only a chilled silence. Melissa stands up and slides away like an ice cube, past her mom and towards the ocean. Gloria and I exchange looks and my insides fold. Hurt, fear, and desperation snake through my chest. I sicken over the possibility that, overnight, serious second thoughts have surfaced in Melissa and short-circuited any future we might have.

I approach Laura and ask her to talk to Melissa and try to determine what is driving her distant behavior. Bob and I slip into the water and, as we dog paddle around the pool, I share my confusion. He helps me make sense of my craziness, the reality being that I have no choice but to endure Melissa's rejection and try to sympathize with whatever she is going through. The thought sounds so right and mature, but hardly reassuring; the hours of trembling have left me exhausted. I'm still rattled when Laura re-joins us and says she got nowhere. Melissa is completely shut down.

* * * * *

That evening the Lees and I dined at a beach café on a spit of land near Puntarenas. The ocean crashed loudly, invisible in the darkness. Stiff breezes rustled palm fronds and carried the taste of salt spray. Over fish tacos and Imperial beer, we discussed the Melissa enigma until there was nothing more to say. It was near midnight when we arrived at my hotel and stepped out of the car to say our farewells. The Lees' job was complete and matters were in my hands.

In the glow of the automobile lights we embraced. Eyes moist, I thanked Laura for being both angel and intermediary. I hugged Anne, who repeated her invitation to visit them in Chicago, and then Bob. He recalled an incident recounted earlier by Laura. Melissa was off to herself, distant and dour-faced. Laura went out, sent by me to see how she was. She found Melissa with her new camera and asked what she was doing. Melissa told

Laura she had just finished pointing her camera to the heavens, "to take a picture of God."

I trudged up the stairs to my room and buried my face in the pillow so no one would hear my sobs.

8. Gloria—Thanksgiving Day, 1990

Gloria woke me with a knock on the door at 8:15. I cracked the door, mumbled a promise to meet her at 10 o'clock, then fell back onto the bed. I was a ball of frayed nerve endings. Gradually, I pulled myself up and wrote a few pages in my journal, trying to find some sense and solace.

We met in the plaza where the shade made the heat bearable. Gloria wore a faded skirt and blouse and plastic sandals. Her face reminded me of a photo I had once seen of Billie Holiday in her middle years. We sat on a low wall. Gloria looked at me and the words came out of her like a roaring river.

> *Melissa needed to study today, but promised that tonight she would go to church with us and then eat Chinese food afterwards. Melissa is so excited to meet you. She slept with her locket. She showed it to friends this morning. She only wishes you could stay at the house.*

"Excited"? I didn't know what to do with the word. The "excited" one had created a horror show. I dismissed Gloria's words as polite garble, nothing more.

She continued, jumping from one topic to another. I fought to keep up.

> *We've been living with Don Ramon for a year and a half. The doctor told me I needed to look out for Melissa on a full-time basis and this opportunity appeared, thanks to God. The problem is that Don Ramon is not a believer. He drinks Sunday to Saturday.*
>
> *Faith is very important because the medicines don't always work. Melissa doesn't like going to the doctor, and doesn't go at all unless she is really sick. She refuses to drink the high calorie supplements because the fluid looks like milk—which gives her a stomach ache.*
>
> *When Melissa was about two months old, she almost died. But God saved her. She's a miracle child. Unfortunately, Melissa doesn't like going to church.*
>
> *I never got married because Melissa has been my first and only priority. I give her physical therapy three or four times a day. I pound on her back to loosen the sputum so she can cough it up. When she has to stay in the hospital I sometimes find a room in San Jose. If I have work to do for Don Ramon, I take a bus back to Esparza for the night. The hospital room is big and grey and has six beds with coughing children,*

always younger than Melissa. They don't have CF, usually. They always get discharged before Melissa does.

She misses many days of school every year, but studies hard to make up her work and pass her exams. These final exams now, for graduation from elementary school, are very important to her.

Olin, I wrote five letters to your old address, but all were returned. I made copies of your business card so I wouldn't lose it. The copy shop made 500 copies, they wouldn't make fewer. Every time Dr. Gonzalez or someone else went to the United States, I gave them your card. I kept a post office box in San Jose for many years in case you wrote.

Finally, Gloria's face began to crumble. Her voice shimmied then grew tiny and high pitched until I thought she might wail. I pictured her many lonely, scared trips to San Jose. I imagined Melissa coming home from school, her chest heaving. Gloria hands her the inhaler and runs to pack a little suitcase. She calls a taxi to take them to the highway. A bus finally stops and Melissa pauses at every step up. A woman volunteers her seat. I picture Melissa sitting forward, head down, holding on to the seat in front. Her shoulders rise as she fights for every breath. Gloria stands over her for the next two hours as the bus lurches to San Jose. They arrive and grab a taxi to the hospital where they sit and wait for paperwork to be processed. Melissa is granted a bed. Laboring with every move, she changes into a gown and receives a shot, is hooked up to an IV and given some oxygen. Gloria answers the nurse's questions and looks on helplessly. She sits by the bed for an hour or so until she hears her daughter's breathing open up. Long after Melissa falls asleep, Gloria sits and watches. Late in the night, she shuffles across town to the house where she lets a room. Sitting on the bed, she eats a piece of fruit and prays to God to let her daughter live.

What was Gloria thinking when she opened the PO Box? It was the most hopelessly hopeful thing I'd ever heard. How hard had she tried to find me? What took her so long? I was short on answers, but my distrust of Gloria dissolved into deep sorrow. It made sense why she appeared so much older. I assured her that I would accept full responsibility for Melissa should anything happen to her. I explained my self-education about cystic fibrosis and the gene therapies being developed and the promise they held. I reiterated my interest in meeting with Melissa's pulmonary specialist the CF Foundation told me about.

Gloria repeatedly referred to God *("si quiere Diós")* as if He were dictating Melissa's future. I said, "God is important but medicine is too. Melissa's refusing to drink a protein supplement because she didn't like its resemblance to milk is not acceptable. It is your job to see that Melissa takes her meds and follows the right diet. It's a fight you have to win."

I didn't like the possibility of offending Gloria's religious beliefs, much less correcting her approach to mothering. I was dancing through minefields but I didn't have the patience to tiptoe when Melissa's health was at stake. To my relief Gloria nodded her head in agreement with my words.

* * * * *

The setting sun washes the horizon in purple as we convene at the gazebo with Melissa. The plaza is crowded with children still in school uniforms, running and screaming. Melissa's wearing a plain skirt, white blouse and tennis shoes. She looks around, avoiding my gaze. If anything she's more removed than the day before. Gloria walks to a phone booth to find out if we can talk to Melissa's doctor the next day. I sit down on the bench next to Melissa, she pops up and walks over to stand by her mother.

Gloria returns and announces our appointment in San Jose at 11 am the next day. We set off for evening vespers at the evangelical church on the far side of the highway. We stroll, like everyone else around us, as if we have nowhere to go. Melissa meanders apart, in an indifferent world. She offers nasally monosyllabic responses to her mother's comments, and none to mine. She seems both childish and powerful. I'm miserable. Trying to figure out something to do or say, I come up empty.

* * * * *

The church was a big concrete building with a concrete slab floor and rows of long wooden benches. Children cried, people fanned themselves and a dog trotted down the side of the room. The service began with live music from a band consisting of a guitar, drums, and electric piano. A miked singer led the congregation in simple songs everyone knew except me. A man gave a short sermon about love and *El Señor,* inspiring lots of murmurs and raised palms. Melissa sat on the other side of her mother and ignored me. After the service we headed for dinner, Melissa leading the way by 25 or 30 feet. Gloria's face pinched in irritation.

The Chinese restaurant was just a dark bar and grill managed by locals who took their best shot with stir fry and soy sauce. Melissa decided not to order, and I ended up wishing I hadn't. I gave Melissa the photos I'd shown her yesterday, a late birthday card and a little string bracelet. She looked at them with acute disinterest.

Groping for a connection, I asked her when would be the best time for me to come back to Esparza. She smiled briefly before stopping herself. Maybe she was delighted at the mention of leaving or perhaps at the thought that I would return. Maybe she smiled at her impulse to say, "Don't come back."

After dinner we walked the few blocks to the house of Gloria's brother.

The evening was humid but not unpleasant. The house sat near the end of the street across from a mechanic's garage. Ascension, lanky and dark skinned, awaited us in a rocking chair on the small front porch. His wife, Lesvia, or Bita, as she was called, emerged from the back of the house. She was round and short and, I could tell, not to be messed with. Both smiled and embraced me warmly. We moved inside to the wood-paneled living room and its fragrant traces of the evening meal. There was barely enough space for the five of us to fit between the dining room set, book case, table fan, television, and ironing board. Melissa, after barely acknowledging her tíos, disappeared into the back of the house.

She returned with her cousin Merilyn, a 20-year old with beautiful features and short dark hair. Merilyn talked faster than any person I'd ever met. And when she listened, her expressive face delivered her response without the necessity of words. Melissa stood at Merilyn's shoulder and, from time to time, whispered in her ear. Merilyn answered with cheerful, loud teasing. Soon Bita and Ascension joined in.

The conversation was over my head but I could see that the teasing was going too far. Melissa lowered her head and tears began to flow down her cheeks. I motioned to Gloria that it was time to go. The others grew silent as Melissa flew out the door and down the porch steps.

Everyone looked at each other in chagrin and after a few moments of uncomfortable silence, I walked outside to find Melissa standing in the shadows of the house next door. I knelt beside her. "Melissa, I know this is hard for you. It's hard for me. There are so many feelings, so many......I love you very much."

Fearful that she would get jumpy, I touched her arm and eased away. Gloria joined us and after hugs with the others, the three of us walked to the corner. I kissed Melissa on the cheek and wish her sweet dreams. I kissed Gloria and we said our goodbyes. During the night I had a long dream.

Laura says "I think I have this problem cured, but how do I know?" I say, "Buddhism, it is the only way I know."

The scene changes and I'm on a path made through a housing development. Drug dealers are proof that the neighborhood is in moral decline. I walk down a street where there are lots of fierce snarling dogs. One comes after me and starts to bite me. I put my head in his jaws to stop him.

I go uphill past another house where there are fiercer dogs. Soon a pack of dogs is following me but one runs ahead. At the top of the hill, I circle around and head down. The dogs all come together, with the ones behind me all running before me to lead the way.

9. Clouds—Friday

Gloria and I took an early bus to San Jose. I felt old and tired. Melissa had finished her exams but refused to join us. The night before, Gloria had warned me that Melissa was worried that the doctor would want to examine her if she accompanied us to the hospital. I tried to reassure Melissa, saying we wanted to go shopping for her and she could stay outside while we talked to the doctor. She hesitated then issued a definite "no." Her response gave me a chance to act detached. I almost convinced myself.

Once in the city we stopped for coffee in a crowded cafe. Gloria talked about events and places we shared in 1978, most of which were much more alive in her memory than in mine. I told myself she remembered them because it was the world she lived in. She asked if I ever wondered about other children I might have fathered in Central America. It was the second or third time she had asked that question. I repeated that there were no other women in Central America.

She asked how old my girlfriend was, asked if I would ever move to Costa Rica. I sensed that she liked me, perhaps romanticized and idealized me. I'd forgotten how gentle Gloria was, how attentively she listened to me. Occasionally she laid her hand on my arm or shoulder. I accepted her touch but did not reciprocate.

We had an hour before the doctor's appointment, so we went for a walk around the city. San Jose was barely recognizable from my visit in 1978. The Reagan administration had surely funneled big sums of dollars to Costa Rica as part of its war strategy against Nicaragua. The city was noisy, its narrow sidewalks jammed. Gloria showed me the site of the restaurant where we met. It was now a copy shop.

We sat on a bench in a little park surrounded by brown, water-stained buildings and the morning took a bad turn. Gloria said, "Olin, I must tell you that Melissa was upset with you over a couple of things." My heart sank like a stone tied to a boulder. "The first was the way you greeted us in the park, passing me to go to her. And then at the Lees' hotel, when you showed her your pictures without me."

I expressed my appreciation for her insights into Melissa's behavior, and apologized if I had offended her. I explained my intentions on both occasions, my excitement over meeting Melissa and beginning our relationship. Privately I felt an ugly self-revulsion. Here was the moment I had dreamt of and gone wild over and looked forward to for months, and I tripped badly. I was sick to my stomach. I said that I would talk to Melissa and apologize.

Gloria changed the subject to a story about Melissa's childhood but I couldn't concentrate. As Gloria described my offenses, her face looked peculiarly placid all the while. I wondered if Gloria was putting her feelings in the mouth of her daughter. Or did they feel the same?

We stood up and began the walk to the Children's Hospital on *Paseo Colón,* the widest, noisiest thoroughfare in town. Pedestrians dodged scary swarms of cars and buses just to cross a side street. Gloria rattled on but the din prevented me from taking in what she said. The truth was all I heard was an internal wail of remorse coupled with fear that the happy girl from the chicken shack was gone forever.

An armed guard let us through a gate into the hospital. Women and crying children filled the entrance area and hallways. The only men I saw wore hospital badges around their necks. I followed Gloria passively, too busy hating my bad decisions to fret over what the doctor might say. We took a seat in a cramped room in front of a nurses' station on the third floor.

Fifteen minutes later, Dr. Reina Gonzalez burst in and after an enthusiastic welcome, escorted us into a tiny room. She apologized for the broom closet appearance explaining that most doctors didn't even have a desk in the hospital.

A Honduran woman in her 40's, Reina spoke in a loud, instructor-like voice. She quickly got down to business, alternating between English and Spanish. She said that Melissa had a mild case of cystic fibrosis. Her lungs were minimally affected and her digestive system was getting along with simple pancreatic enzymes. Melissa had already passed the expected life span of a cystic in Costa Rica and was in relatively stable condition. I took big, slow, relieved breaths.

Dr. Gonzalez launched into a diatribe on the poorly funded health care system in Costa Rica, the low status of doctors and the unavailability of many good drugs. I brought her back to the subject of Melissa's check-ups. They seemed to be infrequent. She said that Melissa, and probably Gloria, feared that a check up would lead to a hospitalization. As a result Melissa had not had a check up since her last hospitalization eight months ago. In English, Dr. Gonzalez told me that Gloria let Melissa call the shots. We closed ranks on Gloria on this point with Reina taking the lead. I chimed in. "It's up to you to bring in Melissa for check-ups. You can do it, Gloria. You have to do it."

Dr. Gonzalez invited me to move to Costa Rica and work for her, but I told her I could do more good for Melissa in the States. Although Melissa did not yet need Pancrease, a strong pancreatic enzyme unavailable in Costa Rica, I promised to do what I could at home to get it marketed in Costa Rica.

Gloria and I left the hospital and went shopping. We picked up vitamins, supplements and high-carb food. People with CF have trouble gaining weight in part because of their bodies' difficulty in digesting food. So we loaded bags with pancake mix, bread, cereal, raisins and nuts. I purchased a set of scales, telling Gloria to weigh Melissa every week and for each kilo gained I would give Melissa a monetary reward.

We also bought new tennis shoes for Melissa, and mousse. As we shopped Gloria's mood brightened and in that regard, she was not alone. I was buoyant. My daughter was in good shape medically and I was contributing supplements and food to help her thrive. For the moment Melissa's treatment of me was insignificant.

That evening I joined Melissa and Gloria for dinner at the home of friends. The family's two girls, one of whom was Melissa's age, had lived in California for a time. Because they spoke English fluently we could speak freely without Melissa's understanding. They said that no one knew of me until three years earlier when Gloria had asked the girls' father, who was planning a trip to the United States, to look for me. In the girls' opinion, Gloria's religious faith had kept alive her hope of finding me. They said that Melissa was always "negative" about any man Gloria was interested in and non-communicative with everyone. They considered her entire extended family to be unaffectionate, a feeling I didn't share.

I told stories for them to translate, calculated to give Melissa more knowledge of me and my world. I related my dreams foreshadowing Laura's phone call and my beginning studies of Spanish since the phone call. My brush with a melanoma in 1983. My family's and friends' happiness about Melissa. My love of my friends' children and my excitement to learn about Melissa.

I may have been overdoing it, trying to obscure the disappointment I felt when I met Melissa and Gloria before dinner. Melissa had not commented on anything I bought her in San Jose. In fact the only difference in Melissa's behavior around me over the course of three days came when she spoke aloud to her mother in my presence. Such progress.

Later I traced my way back to my hotel on a country road lit every 100 yards or so by a dim lamp fixed to a telephone pole. Dogs barked helplessly in the night. My heart was despondent. With just one full day remaining in Esparza I was running out of time to establish any solid ground with Melissa. It was impossible to foresee that I would soon face my biggest challenge.

10. Touch—Saturday

The mid-day sun burned into my back as I approached the red iron fence which encircled Don Ramon's house. Compared to other Esparza properties in the neighborhood the corner lot was palatial, with a large yard fronting the street and a fake red brick well. A tiled porch framed the near side of the house with three gaudy plaster columns supporting a sloped tin roof. Quite upscale for a retired school teacher on a pension.

I rapped on the engraving of the palm tree on the front door, so thickly oiled I could almost see my reflection. After a decent night's sleep, I stood ready, like an eager door-to-door salesman. In my hand, today's presents: a puzzle, a San Diego Zoo baseball cap and a fancy coloring book. I hoped to spend the entire afternoon with Melissa, schmoozing and doing the puzzle. The door swung wide and there she stood in shorts and t-shirt. She stepped aside for me to enter and as I did Gloria helloed and waved from the kitchen on the far side of a spacious central area. Slat windows along two walls had been opened and there were angular shadows on the tile floor.

I handed the gifts to Melissa. She accepted them as if they were the day's junk mail. I recited my apology, composed the night before. She listened patiently. Later I guessed that Gloria prepped her for my recitation, but I was grateful that she stood there while I talked. A drop of water for a thirsty man.

I motioned to the puzzle and we moved to the large round table in the middle of the room. As Melissa unwrapped the box, I looked around at the décor. It was bare, save for several inexpensive metal chairs, several floor plants and standing lamps along the walls. A small room off to the side contained a couch and a television. A sewing machine stood in one corner.

Melissa slowly scooped puzzle pieces onto the table and we began the ritual of turning over all the pieces. She stifled a mucousy cough. I sneaked glances at her, now sitting next to me. Fine dark hair seemed spun onto her forearms. Symptomatic of CF, the nails on her fingers were rounded, while the tips bulged noticeably. I wished I could have held them.

The culturally appropriate puzzle, which I had devoted hours to finding, featured a water-colored scene of brown-skinned children playing in a bucolic landscape of lush trees, tropical flower bushes and horses. The 1000 pieces were smaller than I had imagined, making just the assembly of the border a tedious project. With Gloria coming out to work beside us, our successes were slow in coming and Melissa soon stopped and sat back in her chair. Don Ramon, his face bulbous from drink, blustered into the room. After announcing himself to me he remained standing and offered some irrelevant advice on puzzle-making. A few moments later, Melissa got up and left the room.

Gloria turned to me and crushed my heart. "Olin, Melissa is going to a party of a friend after lunch and won't be back the rest of the day."

Gloria must have known about the party before today. She saw my murderous eyes, gave an apologetic shrug.

We cleared the table and set it for lunch. Don Ramon, quite the windbag, commenced a lunch-long monologue while the rest of us, including his twenty-something son, politely chewed on chicken sandwiches. My appetite had vanished. Melissa excused herself as soon as she had cleaned her plate. I saw my time with her speeding towards a swift, sad conclusion. Minutes later she returned in her party outfit. A hand-made blue patched skirt extended just over the knee and buttoned up the front. Her short-sleeve white blouse had patches of the skirt material decorating the shoulders.

I thought of the few photos I had to show to friends and family and suggested, in my friendliest voice, we go outside to take a few more. Melissa shrugged and served up a disinterested expression. I fought to keep a friendly look on my face. With Ramon's son volunteering to operate my camera, Melissa joined me outside in the shade of the little roof over the well. I sat on the concrete foundation. Melissa took her position a foot or two to my side. She stuck an index finger against a tooth, unconsciously mimicking a mannerism of my own. We were told to smile, the camera snapped, and Melissa was halfway to the house before I could react.

In vain, I yelled at her to stop. My chest tore open and I felt my spirit puncture as if it were little more than a perforated parachute collapsing onto the earth. The hits had been hurtling at me day after day but this was the worst of all. I dropped onto the front porch.

I slumped there for a few minutes before the front door opened and Melissa stepped out onto the porch. She walked over to a concrete column and leaned against it, crying soundlessly. Gloria must have told her to join me on the front porch. I paused, then crawled over next to her and spoke in a soft voice. "I know this is difficult for you. It is for me. My bad Spanish doesn't help. I didn't expect this difficulty, did you? I know you have a party today, but I would like to spend some time together since I leave tomorrow."

I placed two fingers gently against her back, just below her shoulder blades. A stronger touch would have pushed her off balance. She allowed my fingers to remain there for a few seconds then took a step away, her face tucked down into her chest.

I follow her with a squat step. I tell her I love her and place a feathery finger against her back. She hesitates, walks to another column, then sits on the lip of the porch. She lays her head in her arms. I stare at her and try to think of something I haven't already said.

"Maybe we could meet after your party. I'm going to your aunt and uncle's later. Why don't you come, too?"

She doesn't speak or move. Nor do I. Five minutes pass and my frustration has grown. Why is she out here? She's unhappy. I'm unhappy. This is not good for either of us.

I go into the house and, muttering in frustration, jam the camera into my shoulder bag. Pens and journal scatter onto the floor. A whispered curse spills out. I sweep up my things, stuff them back into the bag and prepare to storm out. And then I take a deep breath.

I return to the porch and position myself in front of the door. In order to go back in the house, Melissa will have to acknowledge me in some way. I watch her back and wait.

A few minutes pass before she stands up. I look at her expectantly, but instead of coming towards the door she walks to the end of the porch and disappears around the corner of the house. I exhale slowly and offer a silent plea that her heart will soften.

A few minutes later, she returns to the edge of the porch, laying her head onto arms crossed over knees. A few more minutes pass before she leaves again, around the corner. I'm out of ideas. I decide to go through the house to the kitchen and stand in the back door. The back yard is almost dark from the thickness of plants and trees. The humidity tingles my nostrils. Gloria is washing clothes in a bucket and taking towels off the line and folding them. She looks up at me, expressionless.

Melissa sees me and bolts. I walk through the house, find her on the front porch and take a seat beside her. There is a pause then off she goes once again. I slowly stand up, pass through the house and stand in the back door. I adopt my best casual pose like I do this sort of thing every day.

When Melissa spots me, she heads for the front. On tip-toe, I move through the house. Then it's back and forth, back and forth, so many times that I lose track. Our metronome of movement slows until it's about a five minute stop at each end of the house. Our dance strikes me as both absurd and intensely serious, but I'm unsure what the point is. I look at my watch. A half hour has passed.

On one of my trips through the house I stop at my camera bag and pull out a package of gum. I sit down next to Melissa on the porch and offer her a stick. She takes it and, side by side, we chew. The gum has barely softened when she stands up and takes off around the corner.

Several cycles, maybe twenty minutes later, I retrieve a Baby Ruth candy bar out of my bag. Next to Melissa on the front stoop, I tear the wrapping and break the bar in two. I extend half into her line of vision which is locked downward. She accepts the offering and takes a bite. Rosti, who had been following Melissa since the beginning, jumps up from his shady spot under a tree, and takes a position of high alert in front of us. We feed him little pieces. He makes little snorts and chomps on the candy with his teeth showing. Melissa and I chuckle. Then she stands up and returns to the back.

I find her in the yard with her mom watering an aloe plant. They are talking and Melissa's spirit seems to be perking up. I sit in the doorway wordlessly. Melissa leaves and I follow.

We're in the shade but it must be 95 degrees. I look at my watch. We've passed the one hour mark. I sense that Melissa knows she is going to have to finish this business with me in some way before she can leave for the party. And I figure out what our dance is about. It's me delivering her a message: I am as strong as you are. I'm not backing down. I'm not going away.

Perhaps she gets the message. Perhaps it's why her spirits have improved.

Then she breaks the routine and we are alone in the back. Gloria has disappeared into the house. Melissa passes me on the door stoop and wanders off inside. Immediately she reappears, striding through the kitchen to where I'm sitting, my back to the door frame. She bends over and kisses me on the cheek. Then she turns and walks back into the house. I hear the front door open and close.

Gloria walks into the kitchen and laughs. "Try this for 12 years," she says, then sticks it to me with my words from yesterday. "It's important that you win."

I smile grimly.

* * * * *

Few Costa Ricans can afford to use copious amounts of electricity, so once night fell in Esparza, early was a lot like late. Alone on my way to Ascencion and Bita's for dessert, I became confused by the long, irregular blocks of houses and assembly of trees until I stumbled upon Ramon's house.

The artificial light and shadows bouncing in the darkened house told me the television was on and as I approached the fence I could see Melissa sitting alone in the little room. The front door was open but the gate was locked. I called out her name. She hadn't spoken to me in four days. Maybe she would draw me a map.

Melissa came out the door and slowly crossed the yard to the fence. A street light above us illuminated her tired face. I knelt so our eyes were nearly horizontal. "I'm lost. Can you give me directions to your uncle's house?"

She pointed. "It's over there. Go to the corner then three streets to the left."

She leaned her shoulder against the gate with her hands behind her. I slipped my hand between the bars and around her back and placed a finger in her tiny palm. Her hand was calm and pleasant to touch.

We were like wrestlers exhausted from an afternoon of pushing our full weight against one another. I looked softly into her eyes, joyous that I could touch her, joyous that she allowed it.

We lingered there on opposite sides of the gate for a minute, maybe less. I finally broke the contact, wished her sweet dreams and after watching her return to the house, I walked to her uncle's.

11. Breaking the Spell—Sunday

Departure day. Church bells announce morning Mass. It's sweltering, even though the sun has only been up for a few hours. I squat under a tree waiting for Gloria.

I thought about yesterday. The kiss. The evening interlude. I doubted their significance. Like a soldier attempting to secure a position, I had climbed the same hill four days in a row, each day falling back. The outlook for today seemed no more promising. As I shifted my body to follow the shadows' creep, my evaluation of the situation was clouded. I had not bargained on all the uncertainty, lack of gratification, exhaustion, and despair. Melissa's week-long indifference and antagonism told me that our relationship was tanking.

I took Melissa's rejection as a personal defeat. Beautiful fantasies of parenting her had played in my head for months. But she jerked me into another reality, with a jolt like a bridge diver coming to the end of his bungee cord. Every move towards Melissa ended with me no closer than before.

I couldn't fully accept the truth of what is now so piercingly obvious: Melissa and I did not share identical objectives. Only one of us wanted instant, joyful rapport. As for her, I couldn't really say. We were an asymmetrical pair, meeting on a bridge between worlds we'd never imagined.

On top of that, our differing native tongues eliminated the comfort of word play, suggestion and keen understanding. My mangled Spanish surely made me sound like a goofball. And then there was the disease. The fear of sand speeding through the hourglass was never far from my thoughts, but Melissa seemed to live, as teen-agers do, without fear of the future.

Dreams of meeting my daughter had been stirred with a big dollop of American naiveté and narcissism. Untested by reality, they lacked appreciation of Gloria and Melissa's cultural differences. The intensity of my needs prevented me from seeing theirs. Melissa's behavior confused me but in truth it was my confusion which led me to misjudge her behavior. My ignorance of our cross purposes drove me crying into my pillow each night, disguised the truth and meaning of these dark days, and blinded me to Melissa's struggles with herself.

Melissa, at a minimum, needed time to learn how her world would be affected by me, whether I would accept her world and her mother, and if I would even return to visit her again. In contrast to my heart, which could not have been more open, Melissa watchfully protected hers and moved through the world with her emotions in check. She had skillfully learned self-control by living with cystic fibrosis. Too much feeling, too much adrenaline in the blood stream, led to coughing spasms and a fight for breath.

As the adult it fell to me to extend my heart openly and genuinely, while remaining sensitive to hers. Instead I almost lost track of her need to hold back and to test and even doubt me. The pain of rejection, for a split second, tempted me to pull away from her. I may have loved more unequivocally at first, but Melissa carried a greater sense of the chasm we both needed to cross if we were to fully become father and daughter. As I sat under the tree, I acknowledged the gulf by hating and rejecting it.

* * * * *

Gloria and I walked to a fruit cart near the cemetery to buy a few things for a family picnic at the river. Melissa was waiting for us at the house wearing her new watch, yellow shorts and a blue and white striped t-shirt. We walked to the highway to find a bus and were almost there when Gloria remembered she had no knife for the casaba melon and turned back. Melissa and I found some shade next to a house and sat down at 90-degree angles.

I was ready with another ice-breaker for Melissa, created for quiet moments such as this. In spite of its cultural sensitivity, the table puzzle had been a failure. This time I had a structured set of questions, in Spanish, created in my hotel room and guaranteed to get Melissa to open up and have fun while she was doing it. Sort of a genial "Truth or Dare." Melissa listened as I presented the idea and she even appeared to give it consideration. Or perhaps she was only wishing she was anywhere else. In either case she shook her head no, then shifted her weight and turned her back to me. No response could have pissed me off more. I dug into my Spanish vocabulary and muttered a few pithy remarks on the topic of You've Got to Make an Effort. Melissa's back didn't move and we waited for Gloria, frozen like statues, except that I was shaking inside with no idea what to do next.

Minutes later Gloria appeared. I garbled my frustration and suggested leaving for San Jose right then and there, even though my plane didn't leave until the next morning. My eyes pleaded for an answer. She stared at me, hesitated, spoke. "Let's go."

* * * * *

We got off the bus at the far end of the bridge over the Rio Barranca. The sky was blue like a baby's eyes. Hoisting bags of picnic items, food, and towels, we marched down a steep bank of loose soil. Our little leader picked a spot on the river bank where the fast moving water churned and roared. We set down our stuff.

From time to time, Melissa glared at me like I'd stabbed her dog. I remembered my dream about Laura and Buddhism and shrugged her off. Gloria and I stripped down to our bathing suits and entered the chilly waters, talking and dog-paddling. I relaxed for the first time all week.

After the failure with the questionnaire, I decided not to risk anything which carried an expectation for a response. As Gloria and Melissa sat on the river bank with their backs to me, I scrawled a message on a piece of paper. It read, "I love you very much." I placed it in the top of her camera bag where she would be certain to discover it. We finished off the melon and sandwiches, then Gloria picked up my camera and ordered Melissa to join me on a large boulder which extended out into the river. To my surprise, Melissa climbed up the rock and sat beside me. Her long hair floated in the breeze.

Gloria looked through the camera and shouted something like "Whiskey!" but didn't snap the shutter. She yelled at Melissa, words I couldn't quite catch above the river's pounding. Melissa shouted "No!" Gloria shouted back and motioned with her hand. Melissa put her elbow on my shoulder.

Gloria took a photo I have looked at many times. It captured Melissa and me with broad smiles, briefly stepping out of time to experience a shared happiness unavailable to us in any other moment. The photo also captured the literal space between us and, gazing at it now, I still feel the dark streams of our fear and longing.

* * * * *

It is mid-afternoon when I drop my luggage on their front porch. Gloria, in a sleeveless blue top and skirt, lets me into the cool front room and I take a seat at the table. She brings me a fruit drink. I ask her when we should walk to the *Bomba 76* to find a bus. She just shrugs.

Melissa is in the side room watching an American sit-com, "The Odd Couple." I peek in as Jack Klugman and another character argue in dubbed Spanish. They cause Melissa to laugh aloud. I return to the table with Gloria where we sip on our drinks. My eyes fill. When Melissa crosses the room, I let her see my tears.

She emerges, freshly bathed, hair damp and uncombed, wearing the party dress from the previous day. She walks towards me, holding her camera, and stops at my side. She asks if I would unwind the film. I feel my face soften and break into a huge smile. "Of course. Would you bring me the instruction booklet?"

Melissa returns and stands next to me, almost touching, as I review the instructions. She presses her fingernail against a tooth. I look into her eyes then point to the rewind button and push it briefly. I hand over the camera and instruct her to push the button until the whirring noise ends. She does so until we hear it click. *"Bueno."* I point to the clip on the side of the camera. *"Va arriba."*

Melissa, chewing on her tongue, unlatches the back of the camera, hands it to me and exits to get more film from her bedroom. This is the moment I dreamed of without knowing it would be like this, head-swimming, breathless, nailed to the chair as if the faintest movement would break the spell.

When Melissa returns, I hand her the camera and she extracts the finished roll and places it on the table. She unwraps the new roll, fixes it into the well of the camera and snaps the cover. My chest fills.

We drift to the back yard. The trees and shrubbery give the area a cozy feel. Mom and daughter snuggle and giggle in the cool green grass. I tell them to look my way for a photo. Melissa peers directly into the camera. At times during the week, her eyes had expressed anxiety, indifference and anger. Now they glint with strength or maybe confidence, and a haunting depth. I take three photos, finishing off my one and only roll of film for the week. I see unused cannisters of film in my bag and ask Melissa if she would like more film. I hand her two to add to the four already given to her. Then, "Here, have another one." Her face lights up.

We leave the house walking three abreast. It's like my first day in town, but this time my companions are my very own child and her mom. People wave from their porches. Children call out to Melissa. We're a little parade marching down the street.

I turn to Melissa. "I love the photo you gave me. I want you to know that I will think about you all day on your graduation day. I'm very proud of you and the good grades you received." Without looking my way, she smiles and blushes.

We reach the road on the west side of town, where it curves through thick, tall trees. I had just set down my luggage when a honking bus zooms around the bend in the highway. Its air brakes engage. I see a "San Jose" sign in the window. A teenage boy leans out the door, waving a finger, indicating one seat. My hand raises weakly. The bus slows and I give Gloria a quick kiss on the cheek then turn to Melissa for a longer one. The bus is now rolling slowly behind me and the boy jumps to the ground, shouting impatiently.

He throws my bags in the stairwell and pushes me up the stairs. The bus lurches and picks up speed. I start up the steps, then hesitate. It was all too fast. I push the boy aside and jump into the stairwell. Grabbing the hand bar I lean out the door as far as I can. Melissa is standing motionless, arms by her sides. Our eyes catch. The bus takes me further away, until her features begin to fade. The wind tugs at my shirt and tie and I choke back a sob. Tears flying, I wave madly.

Melissa was in a relaxed mood in the hours before my departure. 1990.

Part Two
1990-1992

12. What Love—November-December, 1990

November 27, 1990

To my dear friends Laura, Anne and Bob,

I want to write you quickly so that you will receive this not too long after you return home. I'll be interested to hear what Laura learns from Melissa and Gloria in her last couple of weeks there. I want to pass along the highlights from the 4 days after you left. By the way I'm not very rested having spent Sunday night sleeping on some stairs in the San Jose airport. You will understand if the following doesn't completely hang together.

It was a wild week: wild exciting, wild emotional and wild difficult. Everything at the highest levels of intensity. Every morning I wrote for about two hours, not just for memory's sake but as a way of reflecting on the previous day's events and reminding myself of certain essential things I needed to be aware of when I went through the day.

The morning after you left, 7:30 or so, I was dead to the world when there was a knock at the door. It was Gloria "needing to talk." We met at 10… it was heartfelt, personal and open. I got a sense of where Gloria's been coming from and it set a positive tone for the rest of the week. I feel good about her and about our agreements and priorities and our ability to communicate. The content of our conversations was quite a bit about what their lives are like and how difficult it has been with Melissa's CF, with Don Ramon, etc. It didn't feel manipulative to me. I expressed my sorrow as well as my concern for Melissa's health and my wanting to visit the doctor in San Jose. Perhaps I missed some of the subtleties in her communication, but my overall impression was and is that she is just so alone with all of these struggles that she was glad to have me to talk to, glad that I was up on CF and glad that that I wanted to initiate some action with the doctor. It was an excellent Thanksgiving morning...

(Someone) later said that Gloria had been carrying around a wonderful love for me all these years. And yet even when she would spontaneously put her arm around me as she did a couple of times in San Jose, it just seemed like a natural spontaneous expression of her happiness. Gloria told someone (in front of me) that I had a girlfriend. It was said with acceptance, very matter of fact.

I grew to have great respect for Gloria's endurance and for her incredible hope; and with both of us centered on the same goal, Melissa's well-being, relating to Gloria and being with her, as in 1978, was extremely smooth and easy.

Unfortunately those words cannot be used to describe my interactions with Melissa…things became extremely difficult; in fact I have had very few experiences where there was emotional pain anywhere near what I felt there in Esparza. Yet she must have been overwhelmed and in confusion, too…There was really not much I could do except continue to affirm my compassion for her at points along the way. There was no response, hardly ever to anything I said or asked or even gave her during those four days. It was pure pain, that's the only way I can describe it; but I kept writing away and reminding myself to let go of my need for a response…….

It was a great, grueling week. I don't know how long before M and I will find a comfort zone with each other but this was a good and important first step. It was a week I'll never forget. One thing I forgot to mention. Melissa's doctor spent 90 minutes with Gloria and me and the doctor really socked it to Gloria: You've got to get Melissa to San Jose for an exam every three months (Melissa has refused to come since March). The doc half-seriously offered me a job. The bad news is the lack of availability of medicines in CR (tight import policies + politics= dying children). The doc gave me names of who I could write and I called Bethesda this morning and they are going to help me. Also in San Jose I bought diet supplements and powder, weight-scales, vitamins and shoes, etc. I offered to pay Melissa money for every kilo she gains and she seems on board with the plan.

…I'm running down, got to get to work and get this in the mail. I'll call you next month. I love each of you in a very unique and beautiful way. Thank you so much for all you've done for Gloria, Melissa and me. There could truly be nothing greater.

Love,

Olin

A week after my return from Costa Rica, the refrigerator was empty and luggage and travel clothes flopped around my house, just as I did. When I wasn't sleeping for long stretches, I was a moist cloud drifting through the day. Pumping gas one afternoon, I broke into tears. I sat with friends describing my time in Esparza, choking back sadness mingled with fear. I listened desperately to anyone who might offer an insight into Melissa's sudden change and resistance. Jeff had considered the matter with care. "This girl is smart, very smart. She has no way of knowing if she will ever see you again."

My letter to the Lees accentuated the positive. I didn't tell them that the CF Foundation-based on experience-was pessimistic about my dream of getting Pancrease, an effective CF enzyme, approved for use in Costa Rica. I left out the burn persisting in my heart over Melissa's glares and snubs. I didn't describe how my fingertips hurt from where I'd chewed the nails and cuticles.

The trip couldn't honestly be called a failure, but I couldn't fit the experiences together in a way which made sense or offered any serious hope. I was reduced to writing in my journal what could only be called a plea and a prayer directed to Melissa. It ended with the words, *Open and be secure in my love. Let my love grow in you.*

In my heart I was begging her not to die.

*****

I obsessed over whether Melissa would "86" me the way she had Gloria's male friends. I remembered two acquaintances who, as good teen-age Catholic girls in the 60's, had become pregnant and given up their babies for adoption. Years later both women had reunions with their grown children. In one instance, after the initial meeting, mother and son talked for a few hours and then shook hands and said good-bye. Their story haunted me.

For several cold December nights I laid wrapped in my feather bed and down comforter, reading a book entitled "Alicia: My Story." Before Laura's phone call I had travelled to Krakow for an international family conference and crossed Eastern Europe by train. Now, with Alicia, I was zig-zagging on foot through a similar landscape in the 1940's, after the Nazi's killed her father, her four brothers, and finally her mother. Alicia's story was filled with fright, separation, death, loneliness, horror, and despair, all of which gave me odd comfort in the dim light of my bedside lamp. Alicia's spirit, in unbelievably dire circumstances, never broke, while I could barely imagine mine prevailing. At present I seemed to be riding a treadmill into darkness.

Anne Lee wrote.

> *We will cherish the memory of being a part of your meeting with Melissa forever: your arrival at the Cruz home, the long walk to the park, the myriad of expressions, the gifts so thoughtfully chosen, the school visit, the endless butterflies and heightened awareness of all the senses and great multitude of emotional reactions...oh, we are so full of thoughts and feelings and <u>deep</u> love and joy for you all!*
>
> *You handled it all beautifully, Olin! We wonder if Gloria and Melissa will ever truly know how fortunate they are to have the mystery father be you!.... Our hearts go out to you, Olin. We've talked and thought about your situation so much. We must keep in touch as we'll always have a*

special place in our hearts for you all....

Our thoughts and love are with you! We love Melissa, also....

Hasta luego,

The Lees

One night I dreamt:

I stood alongside a friend, an old man, at the beach. We are looking at the ocean as loud, thundering waves tower above us. I tell the man to be careful. Then the fog parts and we see how staggeringly enormous the waves are. The tide rolls back and we look down. Below the exposed rocks in the shallows is an incredible scene: giant trees stretching up among the boulders below the water's edge. I look at the old man and he has tears in his eyes.

I did what I could. I sent a Christmas card with a letter and a cashier's check to Melissa and Gloria. I ordered a box of sourdough bread for the Lee family's Christmas. But I awoke crying one morning with the image of my departure on the bus from Esparza filling my head.

Bob Lee's photos arrive in the mail, sixteen in all. They reveal a prism of colors and moods on Melissa's face which I couldn't recall: shy, then tense; happy, then coquettish; vulnerable, then distant. The photos unearth my confusion — and my lingering exhaustion erodes into the flu. Within me, the crashing waves are not the ocean, but dread, doom and fear. Here is my beautiful young girl, her body carrying a critical genetic flaw. She's on a path no child should have to face, at an age when she should be dreaming without abandon of a beautiful future filled with school, travel, love and family. Does she give herself completely to her dreams? Or does a cough or a short breath recurringly remind her of the sword hanging above her head? Does she see the future as fearfully as I? Does she know that the disease can take her at any time? I try not to think that CF can destroy her before we have a chance to become father and daughter. In a flash of anger, I mutter a big fuck you to the Heavenly Father. Not that He cared.

On December 15, I talked to the Lees, mostly Laura, for about an hour. She had finished her volunteer commitment in Esparza and returned to Chicago to attend graduate school. She told me of several chats she had with Melissa and Gloria. Melissa persisted in her resentment about my social gaffes. But she expressed pleasure to her friends about the gifts I brought her, even the scales and the food. She was non-committal to Laura about writing to me.

Laura described how fanatical Melissa was about her privacy. One day when Melissa was reading one of my letters, Don Ramon walked in and Melissa quickly stuffed the pages underneath her leg. Laura confirmed that Melissa avoided her medical check-ups for fear that Dr. Gonzales would put her in the hospital for a few weeks. On top of that, Gloria said she wouldn't write me because of the "cariño, cielo" business which Laura took upon herself to discuss with Gloria. The decision seemed childish of Gloria and it made me surly. My reaction to Laura's stories was to dig in. I knew I could out-stubborn the both of them.

* * * * *

The days and weeks dragged along. I calculated the time it usually took for my letters to reach Esparza, and vice versa. If they were to respond to a letter immediately, the fastest turnaround I could hope for—from mailing to receiving—was six weeks. It seemed like an interminable length of time. Somewhere during that period I begin acting like a man with a mild obsessive compulsive disorder.

Each afternoon, at a time when I know the mailman has come and gone, I go to the vertical white mail box hanging beside the front door. A kind of voodoo protects me from possible disappointment. Some days I tell myself there is probably nothing in the box. Some days I try to act like I'm pre-occupied, or blasé the same way I acted as a little-leaguer standing in the batter's box, when my nerves had sapped all the spit from my mouth. Casually I remove all the mail from the box. Casually I thumb through the stack as my eyes search only for a blue international air mail envelope. Finding none, I insert my hand down into the box to see if there is anything I missed. I wiggle my fingers to make sure there isn't an envelope stashed in the bottom of the box or squished into a corner. Sometimes I peer down into the darkness as if by looking hard enough, a letter will magically appear. This was the mail box ritual; it continued off and on for several years.

By December 18, my anxiety explodes into a panic that my card and check will not reach Melissa by Christmas. I'm convinced she is not getting the treatment she needs. I hastily compose a three page letter and fax it to the office where her uncle Ascension works. The words pour out with a love which desperately needs to be received and reciprocated.

I begin by wishing her a very happy Christmas.

> *My Christmas will be especially happy because I met you, because you are alive and because you are Melissa: a strong girl with wit, intelligence and deep emotions. I look forward to knowing you better in the future.... Please tell me if you did not receive the three registered cards and letters I recently sent to you. If they did not reach you I will not send more letters, but will fax you instead. You are very important to me, Melissa, and it is difficult for me when I am not sure if you have received my letters.*
>
> *I hope you are enjoying your vacation. I thought about you on the day of your school party and your graduation, too. I'm sorry I missed them but I hope you took some good photos. The photos I took in Esparza are great.*

> *There are three of you and your mom which are absolutely beautiful....*
>
> *I talked to Laura and her parents on the phone recently for one hour. They were excited to talk about you and me and Costa Rica...Laura said that you showed her the scales. I'm sure your mom explained to you to weigh yourself every week. When you add one kilo, you will receive one dollar. I gave your mom some money to give to you when you add a kilo. I hope you will be very successful and become rich!! (Or at least, a little rich!!)*

I explain the importance of having quarterly check-ups. I acknowledged her fear of being hospitalized, but, I continued,

> *Regular check-ups will help the doctor stop a problem before it becomes too big. The doctor, your mother and I want to prevent those unhappy hospitalizations.*
>
> *Remember my story of the cancerous mole and how it was necessary for me to go to the doctor every three months like you??? It was very scary. But it is better to be scared each three months than to pretend there is no problem and then, find yourself very sick. I know it is very difficult to reach inside again and again for more courage. Sometimes the fear might be very strong. I hope for you to find effective ways of defeating the fear, the fear which wants to control you. I have seen you defeat fears of me, so I know you are capable.*
>
> *Enough serious words. My next visit is on my mind. Another choice to make. Is April a good time for you? Or would you prefer later? Sooner? Please tell me. Also when you write, tell me what your Christmas is like. Here in Petaluma there are many parties with good food and, sometimes, gifts....Because adults do not have enough holiday time to travel very far, my family and I send gifts in the mail and talk on the phone. I sent Laura's family a giant box of very delicious bread from San Francisco.*
>
> *My friends in Los Angeles have a 10-year-old son, Henry. He is flying here to visit for three days. Then we will drive to Los Angeles for Christmas with his parents. His father, Jeff, is my good friend who had the dream about you with my face. Someday I hope you will meet all of his family.*
>
> *Ok, it is time to end. Have a wonderful Christmas. I send my love to both you and your mother. I look forward to letters from both of you. Remember, I think about you throughout the day.*
>
> *Love,*
>
> *Papa*

That night, Melissa appears in a dream:

> *We are in France, playing. We're sitting on the floor; she's behind me, with her legs around me like we're rowing a boat. We're laughing. We sing the Stevie Wonder song for Martin Luther King, "Happy Birthday." We sing an extra lyric over and over, "I'm so glad you're alive." We play*

our fingers along each other's back as we sing and laugh.

Two days later, home for lunch, I find a phone message from Joseph at the business office in the building where I work. He says there's a fax from Costa Rica for "Dad." Joseph decided it can only be for me. I listen to the message several times then race downtown. I bound up the stairs, three and four steps at a time. Joseph hands me the fax. It's three handwritten, tender, lovely lines. Someone has helped Melissa write it in English.

Dear Dad,

I received your letter dated November 28 which arrived December 6. I have also received your check and your Christmas card. Dad, thanks for coming to see me.

Love,

Melissa

I run down the stairs and into the street, leaping up and down, whooping and punching the sky.

13. For Heaven's Sake—January-February, 1991

Over the Christmas holidays my spirits had been buoyed by Melissa's fax. But the follow up letter she promised never appeared.

January was devoted to mailing letters to anyone I thought could help, without really knowing who that might be. I wrote the Costa Rican ambassador in Washington and the United States embassy in Costa Rica describing the problem of getting essential CF medicines into Costa Rica. Both letters received prompt, sympathetic replies from the chiefs of staff promising investigation into the matter. I never heard another peep from either of them.

I wrote a thank-you to Bob Snowden at McNeil Pharmaceutical, maker of Pancrease, and expressed my hope that we could find a way for the enzyme to be approved and purchased for cystics in Costa Rica's public health system.

Reina had given me the name of an esteemed doctor in the CF world, Daniel Schidlow, Director of the Pediatric Pulmonary and Cystic Fibrosis Center at the Temple University School of Medicine. I wrote him about the Pancrease issue and received a prompt reply.

Dear Mr. Dodson,

Thank you for your letter dated January 9, 1991.

You are indeed quite fortunate to have Dr. Gonzalez as your daughter's physician, because she is a very dedicated and knowledgeable professional.

The difficulties obtaining prescription treatments that you referred to are quite common to most Latin American countries. The problem does not really originate in the US pharmaceutical companies, but rather with the local government agencies and authorities.

My perception is that the pressure has to come from within, primarily consumers and health professionals, upon the health authorities. To contact the Costa Rican embassy is a good idea and it may help accelerate things. The Cystic Fibrosis Foundation is also unable to put any pressure on local health organizations because each national reality is different....

Please do not hesitate to contact me if I can be of further assistance to you.

Sincerely,

Dr. Daniel Schidlow

I sent a letter to the Director of Hospital Nacional de Niños, Dr. Edgar Mohs Villata, and copied his deputy, Dr. Oscar Castro Armas. I introduced myself as Melissa's father and shared my appreciation for the fine work of Dr. Gonzalez. I offered to help both doctors in any way I could.

I also want to mention my concern for the lack of up-to-date medicines which could help my daughter and other victims of cystic fibrosis. Because my daughter's illness is in its early stages, the situation is not of critical concern for her individually but for her future and that of all the children of Costa Rica suffering from CF. I know you have as much concern as I. Thank you for your understanding on this subject. I hope to be making regular visits to Costa Rica. Perhaps some day I will have the pleasure of meeting you. Until then I send you my best wishes for your work.

Sincerely,

Olin Dodson

In mid-January, I received a Christmas card from Gloria, postmarked December 21. It contained a standard printed holiday greeting. The only words in her handwriting were, "Merry Christmas, Gloria." The sight of the envelope had sent adrenaline racing through me followed, after I read the card, by a crash of disappointment. I wished there was a dark hurricane to stare at from my living room window. Instead, January was sunny, spring-like and irritating, like a sappy song.

Still caught up in my interest in Eastern Europe, I read the prison writings of Vaclav Havel, the President of Czechoslovakia. Havel had been a long-time member of the Czech political underground, repeatedly imprisoned for a cause which held no realistic hope for victory: a democratic government in Czechoslovakia. At one point he wrote something like this: we either have hope within us or we don't. It is not a passing feeling. It is the ability to work for something because it is good and not just because its chances for success are promising.

I re-read the passage many times. Hope is not a feeling? Please, I wanted to feel just a shred of hope. I wanted to know where I stood, instead of feeling like shit, like I had for the past two months. Unequipped to handle Melissa's rejection and silence, I understood parents who were overly dependent on their kid's acceptance. It was pure misery.

My Spanish teacher at Santa Rosa Community College told me of a friend who was planning a vacation in Costa Rica. I phoned the woman, Nancy Friedlander, at her home in another part of the county. She offered to stop in Esparza and hand deliver a small package for me. I boxed a few small items: an assortment of children's animal stickers, a Judy Blume book in Spanish, photographs of my first visit, a cashier's check, and letters to Melissa and Gloria tucked into a colorful card of Noah on his boat with a dove and a rainbow. Nancy agreed to carry some medicine as well.

My letter contained questions to Melissa about her Christmas and clarified that the money I had enclosed was for school clothes and maybe a few extra things. I hoped to see her again in the fall.

To Gloria, I addressed a topic we had discussed in person.

> *I tried to find out how to give Melissa legal status as my daughter in the US. One question I need you to answer: Is my name on Melissa's birth certificate? If 'yes", the legal problems will be easier...If Melissa wants to use my name before the legal papers are complete, it's fine with me."*

Towards the end I added,

> *I made arrangements to take a class in a new kind of physical therapy which is easier than beating on Melissa's chest.*

The new therapy was called "PEP Mask." (PEP being an acronym for "Positive Expository Pressure.") It was a device a CF patient breathed into, at settings adjusted to their lung capacity, forcing the lungs to expectorate mucous. PEP Mask was a promising innovation, an alternative to the pounding-style of respiratory therapy cystics had every day to help expel mucous. I hoped I could learn it well enough to introduce it to Melissa.

*****

A friend phoned early one morning, his voice tinged with ominousness. A letter addressed to me had come through his fax machine. A real-estate broker who worked out of his home, Pete had offered his machine for emergencies and I had given the number to Gloria. Pete said he couldn't read any of the Spanish words except for "hospital." I jumped in my car and raced to his house in rural Petaluma, fifteen minutes away.

Pete opened the door and handed me the fax dated February 20. I read the first line aloud. "Melissa is again in the hospital." Then, "Melissa would like for you to come soon." I stood in the gravel driveway, ignoring Pete, poring over every word, struggling with Gloria's Spanish, trying to gain as much clarity as I could before driving home. The basic message was this: Melissa had arrived "purple" at the hospital on the 12th of February, her lungs filled with phlegm. Gloria managed to write four long paragraphs without mentioning Melissa's current condition or prognosis.

I gave a hasty thanks to Pete and jumped back in my car. I talked aloud, fighting fright as I drove, reminding and re-reminding myself how the letter sounded almost casual, without a hint of danger to Melissa. Between frantic and panic I spent the next few hours calling airlines, clients and friends. On hold with one airline, I remembered that Dr. Gonzalez had given me her home number in San Jose. Once I purchased my ticket I called her. There was the exotic, foreign-country phone ring, followed by Reina's calm voice, first in Spanish, then in English after I identified myself. She told me that yes Melissa had been hospitalized with an infection ten days ago, was doing quite well and would probably be released in a few days. Her words soothed me. I said I would be flying to Costa Rica and asked if I could bring anything with me. She replied in one word: "Pancrease." I requested that she tell Melissa and Gloria that I would come to the hospital within 48 hours.

Pancrease, a powerful enzyme replacement, was a staple in the daily regimen of many CF'ers in this country. I would have an entire day to track down a few bottles before flying out of San Francisco the next evening. Melissa had not needed the medicine back in November, so Dr. Gonzalez' request seemed to ominously contradict her report that Melissa was doing ok. I hadn't pressed for details. I didn't want to hear any bad news until I could see her face to face the day after tomorrow.

* * * * *

On February 16, several days before Gloria's fax arrived, I drove to a PEP workshop sponsored by Cystic Fibrosis Research Incorporated in Palo Alto. The class was designed to be a hands-on affair between parents and children, but I received permission to attend alone. I arrived at the class filled with hope, having somehow forgotten the difficulty I had there in October. As the instructor opened the class, my eyes roamed the room. It was filled with beautiful children of all ages. The adults appeared seriously anxious, but perhaps I was projecting. After all, I was in only my fifth month as a CF parent.

It was another sunny winter day in northern California, but the morning proceeded darkly for me. No one dared mention any feelings they struggled with, like the ones which filled my chest and tried to pull me to the floor.

Feelings such as "in over my head" and "scared shitless." I fought to keep my eyelids from closing in dread. At the morning break I approached one of the co-leaders and took him aside. I sped through a Cliff Notes version of my situation, vague and fumbling, not exactly sure what I wanted from him. I felt stupid. I asked for the name of someone I could talk to. Even a Cystic Fibrosis Parents Support Group would be a start.

As I listened to his suggestions, I thought to myself that a "Re-Uniting Families Group" would also be helpful. But something told me that, even two groups, if I could find them, wouldn't be enough. I needed a "Single Parent's Group for People Attempting to Develop a Relationship with their Severely Chronically Ill Child Who Speaks Another Language and Lives in a Foreign Country."

There was obviously no such group. I was on my own. I continued to ask what did I want or need? I could come up with only two clear answers: Someone to hold me and for Melissa to write me many, many letters.

* * * * *

Over a four-week period that winter, I recorded six dreams. The first ones centered on extraordinary scenes of nature and leaving my parents' house. The fourth dream was but a snapshot: me with my head against a tree, crying for the experiences of life I'll never have.

> *In dream five I was distressed to be in a competition, parrying knives in a gauntlet with a group of scary men. I finally got the hang of things by watching another man's prowess, and I exchanged my knife for a larger one. I pushed back persistently with one opponent, knife on knife, and broke free into a "victory zone."*
>
> *Finally I'm in a large house, visiting family, but not my parents. To get around-and especially upstairs- I must climb a wall and squeeze through a very narrow space. It doesn't appear easy to get a handhold, but I work at it and by the time I do it for the last time, I'm actually enjoying it. I find that the faster I move, the easier it becomes, until by the final time, I'm focusing my attention on every handhold, and it's peculiarly fulfilling.*

I was plagued by loneliness over Melissa's silence. I missed not being able to parent or mentor her. I saw parents with kids under the same roof, like the people across the street, having a precious, priceless opportunity. I described the sadness in my journal but resisted the temptation to sink into it or even to fight it. For a moment it didn't seem so horrible.

I did another round of phone therapy with friends and the Lees. Laura and Anne were just as baffled as ever. Jeff made one of those statements which seem less important for its truth than for how it stimulates a new way of viewing the situation. "She's more important to you than you are to her." When we finished talking, that single idea multiplied into three:

1) Our meeting, *by itself*, is not as important to Melissa as what happens over time.

2) What may have been awakened in her is not the same as with me.

3) Her pace for relationship is slower than mine.

That evening I gained a new and simple vision of what was being asked of me. Melissa just needed me to hang in. In other words, be hopeful.

*****

I sat alone in the dim light of the connector flight from San Francisco to Los Angeles, musing on Gloria's fax and the hectic events of the last 36 hours. After several phone calls and some anxious hours of waiting for pharmacies to contact their suppliers, I came up with a six-month supply of Pancrease, costing $400.

A letter from Gloria had arrived at the house as I packed the car to go to the airport. It was her first letter since my visit. Postmarked February 5, it described how Melissa had fallen ill after New Year's and been taken to Children's Hospital. She had remained there for ten days. Hospitalizations, I had learned from Dr. Gonzalez, were always beneficial because Melissa would receive medication, enzymes and more protein than she did at home. The letter contained a mild reproach telling me I needed to write more. I shook my head in frustration just thinking about it.

Blanketed by the low hum of the jet engines, I returned to the present and reflected on the date of this return to San Jose: February 22. It was the same day that I'd been escorted off the bus in San Jose in 1978, initiating a tidal wave which swept over me 11½ years later.

14. Children's Hospital—February 22-28, 1991

Hospital Nacional de Niños in San Jose, Costa Rica, is an imposing block-long structure of five stories, an unsightly architectural amalgam of every government office building ever built. The grassy lawn along the front of the building was bordered with a tall fence of thin iron bars along the street. There were signs warning of the potential for monstrous palm leaves to come crashing down on the innocent. At one side sits a guard's carousel and a gate where a crush of staff, patients, and visitors press together as if it were the entrance to a trendy night club. Inside the gate is a large open atrium which echoes with the voices of children and women who stand around like players of Musical Chairs, poised for the music to begin. They wait for their name on the loud speaker or drift to the pharmacy, phone, or bathroom. They are dressed in t-shirts, shorts and sandals; the privileged go to private hospitals or other countries.

Clutching my ebony-colored cardboard day pass, I took the elevator to the third floor. The tilt of a bird's whistle was the lone sound as I crossed a catwalk to the pulmonary unit.

It took a moment to adjust to the refracted light in the room. Melissa's bed, one of six, was at the far end by the windows. She saw me and her face broke into a smile which promptly disappeared. As I approached, she greeted me with an expressionless hello. I put down my shoulder bag, bent over and kissed her on the cheek. She looked thin and bony. Her face was drawn. I asked questions. She responded with shrugs or sometimes *"Si,"* or *"No."* Nurses and aides streamed in and out. They greeted Melissa like an old friend, serving as an irritating reminder that my daughter was spending large blocks of her life hospitalized. Some talked to her with a forced cheerfulness in an obvious effort to lift her spirits.

Dr. Gonzalez was not expected until later, if at all, so I practiced my Spanish with a friendly nurse named Inez Gutierrez. She explained that Melissa's lungs had improved, but the salmonella infection, which had also brought Melissa to the hospital in January, was slow to treat. A release date had not been set.

Walls of windows enabled me to see into all of the adjoining rooms on the floor. Each contained the same arrangement of six grey metal beds with grey side bars next to grey metal bed stands. A brown leather rocker at the foot of Melissa's bed looked comfortable but out of place. The five other beds in the unit held children much younger than Melissa, each hooked up to an IV and/or an oxygen mask. None had cystic fibrosis.

Gloria had yet to show, so I made myself comfortable in the rocker, surreptitiously alert to Melissa's coughs and movements. She, in return, scrutinized me on the sly. When I caught her looking at me, she would instantly turn her head.

In her grey knee-length gown, Melissa was free to roam the floor. One room was as boring as the next, though, and it was all a dismal scene. Like the others, Melissa lay in perpetual waiting: for her next IV, next physical therapy, next meal or bath. Her watery eyes hungrily scanned the windows into the hall. She coughed and the cough had an edgy crack. From time to time she'd place a tissue over her mouth and spit.

After lunch I saw her percussive therapy for the first time. A young female physical therapist sat beside her on the bed and with a cupped hand firmly pounded on her back. Melissa was polite and cooperative, but it looked like a rugged fifteen minutes.

I whiled away the hours doing, I suppose, what parents have done with their sick children for all time. I had arrived at a new way-station on the road to closeness with my daughter. She had wanted me there and I responded. She didn't welcome my attempts to help her, even the time I unwound her feeding tube. But for a little while, at least, I could accept that. I settled into my rocker and my new role of simply being there.

When the first-string quarterback arrived my importance and good feeling abruptly diminished. Gloria and I chatted briefly, but she was tired from work and her commute into San Jose. Since she needed to return home in the morning for another job, we agreed to catch up later in the week. I walked back to the hotel that night, as I would each night, mentally exhausted from speaking Spanish full-time and plotting how to make the best use of my time. It dragged me down to witness, however briefly, what cystic fibrosis forced Melissa to deal with. Although she gave just the faintest glimpse into her feelings, I felt her difficulty as if it were mine.

That evening I phoned Jeff in Topanga Canyon from the Public Communication Center where Gloria had sent her fax to me. It cost $21 for an eight minute call, but it was worth it to hear the familiar voice of my friend. He repeated his opinion that Melissa was very smart to be so committed to her own pace with me. I said "Not much seems to have changed with her but I know I'm doing the right thing." He replied, "I'm sure it's not lost on her."

The second morning I had to talk my way past the guard at the front gate because my day pass had expired. I walked into the room to find eight residents and Dr. Gonzales grouped around Melissa's bed. She was receiving percussive therapy and crying. Dr. Gonzales came over and told me how happy she was that I came to visit, then got down to business.

"Melissa will not be released in time to go to her school orientation. She's having trouble gaining weight; she's dropped to 56 pounds. Olin, is there any way you can get Melissa into a hospital in the States? It might be necessary to insert a feeding tube directly into Melissa's side. It's a procedure we can't do here; it would need to be performed in the US."

"Without question, I'll do everything I can to bring her to California."

"Olin, I've already asked Melissa. She said she would fly to the States if her mother can go with her."

Her words heartened me. "I'll work on it." Then the burning question. "Was Melissa's life in jeopardy when she arrived at the hospital?"

The doctor answered firmly in the negative but I knew that Melissa's frail condition would ultimately translate into more problems. Dr. Gonzalez returned to her waiting students, but not before we agreed to meet later in the week.

Melissa was somber throughout the morning and ignored anyone who tried to engage with her. Her veteran patient's demeanor, tough and impassive, was in fact, how she typically acted towards me whether we were in a hospital or not.

Almost daily I would see the residents waddle in like a flock of geese, avoiding contact with the children and mothers, and set about examining charts, conferring in low voices and honing their special style of detachment. At times, Melissa's face would look like she was placing a hex on them, but I could also detect a mix of fear and vulnerability in her eyes. When a nurse came in to draw blood from her skinny arm, she carefully supervised its withdrawal. At times she would offer a reaction to the needle, an almost imperceptible jerk of the chin or eyelids. I flinched myself whenever I saw one of the trolls, posing as a nurse, prepare to stick a needle in Melissa. I moved forward in the rocker and watched closely, as if it were within my power to prevent a bad stick.

I did what I could. On one occasion (Melissa was weary and unhappy from being away from her friends), one of the other mothers inched her way towards a tearful Melissa and Gloria in order to overhear their conversation. I got her attention, shook my head and motioned to a faraway destination with a flapping hand.

The unit was, without question, a woman's world. Rarely did I see another man. My approach would sometimes cause women's smiles to fade, giving me the same uncomfortable self-consciousness that arises when I pass a single woman on a lonely street. I wondered if Melissa found me strange. I figured she was uncertain and maybe frightened of me. How would I use my power?

In one of the beds was 3-year old, Jose, aka "Josetito," who didn't share Melissa's doubts. Unwrapped from his tubes and out for his morning stroll, he would stumble over to me, barefooted, as mom and relatives looked on. Our ritual consisted of my making various faces until he smiled and then, like a mime, reacting to objects he brought to me. One morning he was a bit teary and I picked him up and held him on my shoulder. His tears converted into an endearing, hiccupping giggle, until everyone in the room was smiling. When I looked Melissa's way, her face revealed NOTHING. She had perfected inscrutability, like the girl in high school who may have had a crush on you but treated you as if you were President of the Dork Club. Melissa would be standing at the nurses' station, see me approach and off she'd scurry like the Roadrunner. Once, sitting in bed and laughing with her mom, she happened to look up and see me watching. Instantly she broke off her smile in an astounding exercise in self control.

She did perk up when her mom and I talked. She would direct questions and comments only to her mom but on one occasion said good-bye to me in her own way. She was resting in her mom's arms and Gloria told her to respond to my *"Hasta luego,"* as I left for lunch. Without moving her head, she said a muffled *"Luego"* directly into her mom's neck.

Rocking in my daily perch, I observed the ways the two of them interacted. Gloria typically responded impassively to things. Melissa was extremely demonstrative, hugging and noodling in a friendly manner. Gloria would sometimes smile and talk but it was Melissa who most frequently initiated contact. Gloria was her main relationship model: quiet and distant.

That evening, I bent over her and kissed her good-bye as she lay on her side, getting an IV treatment. She hid her face in her hand. I spontaneously and lightly rubbed her back, and she squirmed. I walked out feeling good. I could live with unrequited love.

* * * * *

For six days, my world consisted of an eight-block area in downtown San Jose, bordered by hotel and hospital. It was a strikingly simple world: no phones, no television, no driving. I would pause before a television in a store window to learn of major world events like Saddam pulling his troops out of Kuwait, or Bush, Sr. starting a ground war. In my hotel room, one of my shirts disappeared, and there were night creatures in the walls, but I let it all go. My focus was on Melissa. I woke up at all hours to jot down ideas and the names of people to talk to.

I rarely spoke to anyone outside the hospital. One evening on my way to dinner, I stepped onto the hotel elevator and a small woman in a maid's uniform pushed a loaded cart of linens to one side. The doors closed and, uncomfortable with the silence in closed quarters, I fumbled for a friendly remark in Spanish. The scent of soap in the elevator was overwhelming so I took a pronounced inhale through my nostrils and commented on the sweet smell. *"Ah, el jamón!"* In my Spanish studies I had sometimes confused *jabón* (soap) with *jamón* (ham). When I saw the nervous look on the maid's face, I realized that I'd done it again. I'd blurted out, "Ah, the ham!" The maid and I were in convulsions when the elevator doors opened.

Over the winter months, I had re-assessed the importance of Gloria's involvement. Her fantasies of a relationship with me no longer concerned me. I was now fearful that she would withdraw and effectively scuttle my relationship with Melissa. When I learned she would be in San Jose on consecutive days, I arranged for a woman resident from Columbia, Dr. Nereida Arjona, to interpret a conversation between us. We found an empty room just big enough for three chairs. Gloria was dressed in a blouse which might have been white at one time, a modest skirt, with no jewelry or make-up.

Our conversation revolved around a list of topics I had made in my hotel room, among them our previous agreement to correspond regularly and ensure that Melissa went to San Jose for her quarterly medical exams. I described how to administer the dosage of Pancrease I'd smuggled in. I lightly chastised her for only sending only one letter and a fax in two months. In response to my question she said my name was not on Melissa's birth certificate and expressed no interest in my filing legal papers confirming my fatherhood. Her opinion made little difference to me at the time.

Gloria spoke with an economy of words, delivered in a measured pace and a soft, pleasing tone. Her eyes openly met mine, but repeated self apologies were unsettling. More to my liking was her wonderful braying laugh when I occasionally made a joke. Above all I was heartened to fully air my concerns and, for the moment, feel that we were partners on Melissa's behalf.

I was eager to learn what Melissa had done with the Christmas money I sent. It was likely the first big chunk of money she ever had to spend on herself and I hoped she had used it happily. Gloria smiled and said Melissa knew exactly what she wanted to do with the money. "She bought a Ken doll to be with her Barbie."

Gloria pulled out a stack of photos taken with the camera I had given Melissa. Many of the snapshots were taken at Melissa's grade school graduation and party, held just after my visit in November. There was but a single photo unrelated to the others. Melissa, in her party dress, sits on her bed, sideways to the camera, legs tucked under her. Her smile is soft and wide and her eyes glint with happiness. She's clutching to her chest the teddy bear I had given her. I drank in every detail of the photo. Gloria said that in the past Melissa would always go to the hospital with a frayed little teddy, which she called, *"Papi"* (Daddy). I said, "She has no bear with her this time." Gloria smiled and gave me a cryptic look, then handed me the photo to keep.

We thanked Dr. Arjona and strolled downtown to shop for a new school uniform for our daughter. We bought a blue skirt, while blouse, cotton socks and slip and a blue bow hair clip. We went for dinner, laughing and talking over a Pizza Hut pizza, Gloria's choice. She told me that Melissa was quite delighted with the ink pens and sketchbooks I brought to her. She recounted Melissa's tough treatment towards all men, even her Uncle Ascension and cousin, Marvin. She advised me to *"Que tengas pacíencia"* (Have patience).

Gloria said she would take the 90-minute bus ride back to Esparza the following day. I was excited to hear that Melissa had encouraged her to go, since it would give us more "alone time." Unfortunately, my alone time with Melissa was no different than any other. She disregarded my questions and comments and, with eyebrows furrowed, stared out the window or into some corner of the room, feigning ignorance of my presence. She looked at me like I was an ugly stain when I offered her the comics from the Sunday paper. They sat on her bed for hours untouched, before ending up on the windowsill when I stepped outside for a few minutes.

When I said I was going out for lunch, she asked when I would be coming back. I didn't know why she bothered.

In my luggage I had packed a Spanish translation of "The Wizard of Oz," purchased from a mail order house in the US. I had re-read the English version before my return and envisioned reading the translation aloud at Melissa's bedside. My Spanish pronunciation was quite good, so I knew it would be the perfect ice-breaker. I placed the book on her bedside table along with a little strawberry pastry and a pack of gum I bought on the street. All sat unmoved for an entire day, then vanished overnight.

The book re-appeared the next afternoon when Melissa's cousin, Merilyn, paid a visit. I walked in after lunch, surprised to see her, radiant as always, sitting in the rocker and reading aloud from the book. Another quarterback had rushed onto the field, sending me back to the bench where I could pick splinters out of my butt.

Dorothy discussed her predicament with the Tin Man and Melissa lay still, a soft, far-away look in her eyes. With resignation I decided to pull up a chair and enjoy what I could. Give it the old college try. Buck it up. Take one for the team. But my disappointment was too crushing. I pushed up from the chair and went out for an extended walk, up and down the hospital stairs.

A half hour later when the reading had ended, I entered the room and Merilyn turned to me in an enthusiastic deluge of Spanish. The scramble of words flustered and baffled me even after I asked her to repeat herself, *"más despácio."* Melissa broke into a giggle and leaned over to whisper something to her cousin. I could feel my face go red in embarrassment. By now I had moved near the bed and I reached over and gently tapped Melissa on the shoulder. *"Por favór…"* I began. With a jerk, she turned on me, her eyes burning into mine. I recoiled as if I'd been violently shoved. I felt my face heat up once more, my thoughts crackling in anger. I tried to carry on like a good sport, but my acting skills were insufficient to the task. I hurriedly said goodnight.

The setting sun blotted the city in shade and amber glows as I left the building. Tears in my eyes, the muttering began full-tilt before I was through the gate. *Cut me some slack!! I'm trying!!* My head bent low, I rounded the fence corner towards the city center, moving upstream against the crush of workers heading home for the evening. *At least she could say thank you!!* The words came out like little gun blasts. I must have looked like a street person on a rampage.

In my hotel room, I tore off my clothes and stomped into the shower where I continued to air my grievances. But as the hot water warmed my body, I softened and listened to myself. What did wanting "thanks" have to do with Melissa glaring at me? I tracked my anger to its source. I was resentful towards Melissa for not acknowledging my coming or the gifts or the school clothes or anything.

I knew what I needed to do.

* * * * *

The following day I began with my usual good morning kiss. Melissa's face wrinkled in disgust. I shrugged to myself and without a word angled the rocking chair towards the windows so she and I were outside each other's line of vision. I took my seat, opened my Spanish book and looked up only when someone came to speak to her. I didn't move when she had to squeeze around me to go to the bathroom.

I liked my new toughness but I couldn't resist buying Melissa a packet of chocolate hearts during my lunch break. She watched me set the candy on the dresser and said nothing.

Gloria and I met in the cool walkway outside the ward. I looked into her eyes and slowly enunciated my words. "Gloria, just one time before I leave I want to hear Melissa say, 'Thanks.' Just once."

Gloria's eyebrows shot up towards her hairline, as if I had just demanded ten acres of prime Costa Rican beachfront. "I don't know, Olin." She shook her head. "That's very difficult for Melissa...."

I touched her arm. My voice was firm. "Just once, Gloria... Just once."

Our conversation continued on to other topics, like their projected expenses for the next several months, including school books, nutritional supplements and emergency funds. I had $80 in US currency in my pocket. I gave Gloria $70 to pay for a few things for the new school year, including a day pack. I told her about the boxes of Ensure powder and Pancrease resting on the floor next to Melissa's bed. I promised I would cash some additional travelers' checks for her. She accepted the money and looked down, her face frozen into blankness. I waited for a response, then broke the silence, "Gloria?" I leaned over and put my face in front of hers. She shook her head and smiled weakly as if coming out of a trance. Was she embarrassed? Shocked? Grateful? She never said.

Appointments filled my day, the first with a respiratory therapist to discuss PEP and to share printouts from the Palo Alto workshop. Next came the Assistant Chief of Hospital Services. I solicited his commitment to securing governmental approval to import Pancrease. Following that, I briefly met with the local Cystic Fibrosis parent's group followed by a longer consultation with Dr. Gonzalez, who said there was still no set discharge date for Melissa, but it would probably be another two or three days. She reported that as a 12 year-old Melissa was doing fairly well, 12 being the life expectancy of most children with CF in Costa Rica. Finally I searched for the children's psychologist to discuss the possibility of counseling sessions for Melissa, but learned I couldn't see her until the following day.

In the middle of the night, my brain stirred with dark thoughts. I wondered if Melissa resisted me because she didn't really have any hope that I would hang in with her. Perhaps she lacked hope for herself. Then I remembered the Ken doll. Wasn't that a symbol of a future love? And the bear. Didn't the smiling girl in that photo have hope? I turned my head to the glow of the city lights through the curtains. The Beatles tune, "Blackbird," came into my head. I imagined Melissa in the dead of night, waiting for her moment—just to breathe fully once more.

* * * * *

Thursday arrived, my last full day in San Jose. On my morning walk to the hospital I saw the latest news headline on a giant electric board overlooking a downtown plaza. It read, "War in Iraq Ends." My mood was upbeat as I entered Melissa's room and greeted her with a kiss on the cheek. She accepted it without turning away as she usually did. I left her in order to track down Maritza, the social worker. I told her that Gloria would be contacting her for an appointment. I made a joke about being the only guy on the ward upstairs. "Most Costa Rican men aren't involved in child-rearing," she said. "Melissa has no cultural role models for you."

I caught Doctor Arjona walking down the hall and told her I hadn't seen Melissa receiving any physical therapy for two or three days. She said there weren't enough physical therapists on the hospital staff to cover all the patients, then promised that she'd try to get PT scheduled later in the day. She assured me that she would look out for Melissa after I left.

When I returned to the room, Melissa was laying in her bed, crying silently. I figured the residents had come by and told her she couldn't leave. I felt my face fill with sorrow. I leaned over and kissed her on the forehead. She looked me in the eyes when I told her I was sorry she had to be in the hospital so long. I sat down in the rocker and began looking at Gloria's photos one last time. I raised my head to see Melissa, legs dangling over the bedside, smoothing out wrinkles in the plastic covers in a photograph album. She spoke.

"Does your flight leave tonight or in the morning?" Her voice sounded genuinely curious and casual, as if we were old buddies.

I gulped in shock. "Um, actually I leave in the morning." I go into an excited description of bus schedules and customs procedures. She nods her head as I talk and makes appropriate hmms and ohs. It is truly the loveliest little conversation of my life. When my answer runs out, I sit silent, uncertain what to say.

She helps me out. "Thanks for the medicine."

"De nada," I reply, and notice a light rain has brought a sweet wet scent into the room. I sink into a feeling of bliss.

Then from the corner of my eye I see Melissa approach. For some reason I don't turn towards her. She kisses me on the cheek then retreats to the bedside where, with her back to me, she busies herself with the photo album. I feel the touch of her lips on my cheek and then, trapped by my limited Spanish, I speak the absurdly irrelevant. Instead of thank you Jesus, or thank you Melissa, or how nice of you to kiss me, I tell her I gave her mom money to buy her day pack, school books, nutritious food and postage stamps. She graciously follows my lead into the mundane and corrects my mispronunciation of day pack, *"mo-kee-la."* I thank her. "Do you need shoes or anything else?"

She shakes her head. "No."

Then Gloria walks in with the new pack. It has a modern girl look, blue with red hearts on the outside. Melissa lights up and carefully examines it from one end to the other. My eyes tear. The tiny flower opened. I can return home now.

When I return from lunch, Gloria is gone but Merilyn is back. I sit by the bed and watch as Melissa carefully shows her cousin copies of Bob Lee's photos which I gave to her. I glance past them and, swear to God, I see a rainbow out the window. I hear Merilyn's excitement over each of the photos. *"Qué bonita!!!" "Muy línda!!"* Melissa holds back the photo of her kissing my cheek. It's okay with me.

The next morning, I hand Melissa a get-well card with Snoopy on the front. The card contains a note that I worked on each night in my hotel room. I tell her how happy it makes me to be near her, but sad that she is sick. Seeing her with all the needles and doctors, and in a strange room for two and a half weeks, I write, gives me great respect for her courage. It's amazing that we met only three months ago. We are building a new relationship. We don't have twelve years of living together like most children her age have with their fathers, but I know that, through writing and visiting regularly, we can make a special relationship. I believe this because we are special people.

I wish that California and Costa Rica were closer. But I am happy that you are in the world. I will always be interested in you and your life. Whatever may happen—-earthquakes, hurricanes, floods or illness — I will do whatever I can for you, so that you can have the happiest and most beautiful life.

Melissa, take care! Write me when you get out of the hospital.

I look forward to seeing you again soon.

I dream with you. I love you a lot.

Dad

Melissa accepts the card without looking at me.

At the foot of Melissa's bed I have my final talk with Gloria. Take care of yourself, get rest, make sure the therapy is done daily, here's 1,000 *colónes*. I give her a warm embrace. We look at each other for a long time.

Gloria leaves and brings back the respiratory therapist. I present her with the PEP materials from Palo Alto. She is delighted. We discuss a plan for me to raise money and bring a physical therapist from the states to Costa Rica. We exchange addresses.

Melissa, looking towards the door, says, "Here is your friend." Dr. Gonzalez has entered with her team. She greets me and reaches out to shake my hand. She says Melissa will go home today if her test results come back negative.

It's time for me to leave. I kiss Melissa. Gloria asks me to tell the Lees to come visit again. She says, "Thank you, Olin." Tearing up, I gather my bags and start towards the door. Near the door, Reina stops me and takes my hand. "Your daughter is in good hands," she says. I wipe my eyes and go back to kiss Melissa again. Then I'm gone.

15. Love and Darkness—March, 1991

During those demanding days at the hospital I'd felt like a real life dad for the first time. I began to understand that, lacking any early formative years together, our biological connection was only a beginning. Our relationship would be a thing to figure out, create and re-create, for however many days were allotted to us. For now our relationship was a knob-kneed baby giraffe wobbling in all directions, searching for upright and forever poised to collapse. I knew that fostering Melissa's trust was critical and I made a secret pledge to never make a promise to her I wasn't sure I could keep.

All the positive experiences in San Jose were offset by other, darker ones. The agony of seeing Melissa in the hospital bed. Melissa's pissy behavior. Dr. Gonzalez' admission that Melissa needed a treatment she could not provide.

I sent Melissa a postcard.

I am happy that I was able to see you last week. I hope that you left the hospital soon after my departure and are now happy in school and back in Esparza. To be very far away is difficult for me. Do your therapy regularly. I am going to talk to some doctors here about your health.

You are very special to me, Melissa, and I love you. I will write you and your mother soon.

Love,

Dad

I had work to do. My mind ran like a lab rat racing through a maze, sniffing around corners, looking for doors of opportunity. No longer would I fill my days pining away for a letter which never came. I needed to establish my paternity, acquire residency for Melissa, enroll her in the state's health plan, Medi-Cal, and arrange a medical workup in one of the fine Bay Area hospitals.

I moved into a new gear with a new mission, feeling at times that I was fighting not only for Melissa but for every child who'd been dealt an unjust hand with a crippling health condition. There was no one governmental official or businessman to scream at, sue, or lock up, but fury was unmistakably part of the fuel which ran me.

I stopped at the main post office in Petaluma to send the postcard and pick up a week's worth of accumulated mail. The long building was rock solid and ornate, with wrought iron rails running alongside the front steps and around the porch. The high-ceilinged lobby and marble floor discouraged secrets, since the faintest whisper, zipper or footstep echoed long and loud. I thumbed past the junk mail as I turned from the window and removed a single ebony card with a blue border. "Nancy Friedlander" was embossed at the top of the back side. She had appeared in Esparza several weeks before I flew to San Jose.

Dear Olin,

I'm just back from Costa Rica, very pleased with my visit to Gloria and Melissa. Gloria is very friendly and easy to talk to and welcomed us into her house. I was glad you sent along the photo because someone recognized her and pointed out where she lived.

Melissa seemed quite ill, I'm afraid. I was struck by her detachment even in our short visit. It took Gloria so long to bring her out of her room and then there seemed to be a great deal of passive resistance to participating in the whole present opening business. She held your gifts on her lap without opening them. Later while I was chattering with Gloria, my friend Anita observed Melissa peeking at your letter which made her cry. She had to go into the kitchen to gain control.

I hope you will be going there soon.

With kind regards,

Nancy

I moved to the farthest corner of the lobby. Other than the teddy bear photo, Nancy's card was the only evidence that Melissa's heart had been touched by mine. I lowered my chin and let the tears flow down my cheeks.

* * * * *

Dear Melissa,

I hope that you are 100% better now. I have beautiful memories of my visit with you. I am happy that I could contribute with your school stuff, backpack, etc.

It is important that you go for your examinations when necessary. Dr. Gonzales believes that there is a treatment for you here in the States. I will write more about this in the future.

Laura Lee and her family called me on the phone after I returned. They were so curious how you are. They are like family.

I'm working a lot, especially in the afternoons and evenings, since those are the best times for people to go to counselors. My support group for parents of soldiers in the Iraq war ended because the war ended.

In school we are studying the imperfect verbs. It's hard to know the difference between the imperfect and the preterite.

Melissa, I hope you are very happy in school and at home too. I love you very much and I am happy that you are my daughter.

Love, Dad

Dear Gloria,

I am happy that we were able to talk so much. I understand you better and I am happy that we have a good relationship. Thanks for your patience with my Spanish! I know that I speak very strange at times.

Did you receive my card of March 5? Also a card from Laura Lee?

Please write soon. I am curious, what is new?

Also, Happy Birthday, Gloria!

Love,

Olin

I spent my days on the phone, working the angles. The first call was to Children's Hospital in Oakland to someone who knew someone I knew. I told my story to three people before I reached a high-ranking social worker. Everyone expressed concern but none had a clue how to obtain treatment or financial coverage for a Costa Rican. The social worker referred me to CCS, California Children's Services, a state agency which serves children with chronic illness, and recommended I push CCS by getting Stanford to first accept Melissa as a patient.

I phoned my health insurance company. They couldn't add Melissa to my plan until my paternity was "certified." I tracked down a retired immigration officer. We met for coffee in a North Beach San Francisco café. He, too, advised me to establish paternity in Costa Rica. He warned me that my plan could become a very expensive proposition, involving a lawyer there and one in the States. His mention of the expense was discouraging. I was still paying off my student loan and carrying a large sum in credit card debt.

Social Services in Sonoma County told me that Melissa's eligibility for Medi-Cal would require her and her mom to establish residency in the county for six months. But immigration was out unless I married Gloria, and Melissa would still need medical attention in the interim. Marrying Gloria was an option for about a nanosecond. Layers of misery would result for Melissa and her mom if they were to live apart from their family and culture. It was the strangest thought of my life: there was something I wouldn't do to save my daughter's life.

I resumed the phone calls, feeling like I'd lost my car keys and was running around the house ransacking drawers. I phoned California Children's Services, an office in the Sonoma County Public Health Department. After a brief conversation they sent me a handwritten response.

Dear Mr. Dodson,

CCS would be glad to review medical reports on Melissa Reyes Reyes. Cystic Fibrosis is an eligible CCS condition medically.

However financial eligibility includes residency in California and in a particular county. CCS will need documentation of residency, visas, and parentage/legal guardianship. From the information we currently have Melissa would not qualify for CCS.

Please send any information you feel would be helpful.

Next drawer, Stanford, allegedly one of the best CF hospitals in the country. Applying the strategy from the woman at Oakland's Children's Hospital, my hope was to somehow get Melissa admitted for a work-up in order to pressure CCS to accept her case. Another friendly voice listened to my story and I was given an appointment to speak to the Chief Financial Officer by phone several days later.

An air mail letter arrived in an envelope decorated with a large stamp of a scarlet red parrot sitting on a branch. I opened it to see Gloria's familiar handwriting, round and irregular.

Olin,

How are you? Melissa is very well now. She has more weight, very active. She is very happy in school. Everything is going well for her. We received letters from Laura. She sent two pairs of socks to Melissa. Olin, I will write you when we get passports.

Regards,

Gloria

Then, in Melissa's bumpy script:

Hello. It's going well for me in school. We have many teachers, and Rosti is well. I hope you are well.

Passports! Perhaps after a talking to by Dr. Gonzalez, they were preparing for a medical trip. I was stunned.

More weight! Unbelievable.

Melissa's little PS was not so impressive. My own childhood thank-you letters to my grandparents were surely slight, but her lack of a signature seemed discourteous, at best.

At some point I had committed to sending monthly faxes via Gloria's brother, Ascension, but the blandness of typed pages could never convey my love to Melissa. I hatched an idea to inundate her with beautiful post cards. It would give Melissa proof I thought about her all the time. I scavenged for cards everywhere. Melissa had such a small window into my life, perhaps the cards would tell her a little about me and inspire dreams of her coming to visit.

Dear Melissa,

How happy it made me to receive the letter from you and your mother. It pleased me to know that you are happy in school and also that you are gaining weight. In your next letter tell me about your classes. What subjects are you taking and which do you like the most? Are you going to school all day or half day?

I am very busy. It often rains during the month of March, so I read a lot and see many movies. I like foreign movies. I saw one entitled, "Ay, Carmela" filmed in Spain. It is the story of love and courage during the Civil War in Spain.

I recently went to Chinatown in San Francisco, ate Chinese food and went to a Chinese action movie. I bought postcards to send to you. Some are beautiful, others funny and others of special people. Also I will send you a fax the first week of each month.

Eat well, take care, and enjoy yourself. I love you,

Your Dad

Dear Gloria,

How are you? Thank you for your letter. I read it often. Don't hesitate to write me again!

I sent Melissa three or four postcards a week with brief personal notes on the back, a total of forty cards in twelve weeks. The first one had a photo of puppy faces sticking out of a back pack. It was followed by (among others):

puppies in a drawer
puppies in a flower box
a dog in a floppy cap

a cocker spaniel with eyeglasses
a girl and a cat sleeping in a chair
a smiling baby
a dancer holding a baby
a baby elephant hugged by a boy
a mom and baby penguin
a man and a dolphin
whales in a pool
Snoopy
Mickey Mouse
Pooh Bear
Dorothy and her friends from the Wizard of Oz
outlandish, lip-sticked lips
outlandish eyes (by Man Ray)
cat's eyes
Half Dome in Yosemite
San Francisco in the sunlight
San Francisco in the fog
San Francisco trolley cars
the Golden Gate Bridge
San Francisco's Japantown
my office building in Petaluma
Frida Kahlo
Martin Luther King, Jr.
a Human Rights poster
the man blocking the tank in Tiananmen Square
the Earth photographed from space
the young Beatles, and
the John Lennon memorial in Central Park.

* * * * *

The weekend was wasted in miserable agitation, courtesy of my upcoming Monday morning telephone appointment with the financial officer at Stanford. I woke up slowly that day, startled by the memory of a dream that I was being treated for cystic fibrosis. My chest felt sore for no apparent reason. At 10:00 a.m. I phoned Stanford and the receptionist put me through to my latest best hope, Ruth. She listened to the summary of my situation, followed by my plan for CCS, a sort of simultaneous hospitalization and qualification for eligibility. I put it to Ruth to help me figure how to manage this stunt. She answered with a big bad blunt broadside. "How can you say that Costa Rica, with its universal health care, is 'inadequate,' Mr. Dodson?"

I began to respond as if she were asking a sincere question. "Well, in this case…."

"And why would you expect California to, in essence, pay for your daughter's treatment?"

"Well, since she is my…."

"We cannot be expected to treat the sick children of other countries!"

When there is a power differential in a conversation like this—and Ruth clearly had all the power—no matter how much you feel like yelling, you suck up the impulse. You take a few deep breaths because you don't have a card to play. But you stay in the game and watch carefully, in case the creature opposite you lays down something you can pounce on: information, leads, suggestions, uncertainty, or a hint of compassion.

I spoke respectfully, keeping my emotions in check and practicing a lesson I learned in graduate school. It is often the impulse you don't indulge which counts. I managed to talk to Ruthless for about an hour and grew to accept what everyone else had been saying: Melissa had to be a resident of California in order to receive public medical assistance.

Less than forty-eight hours later, between 2 and 5:30 a.m., my acceptance and expansiveness had disappeared. I lay on my bed staring into the darkness. Social Services, CCS, Stanford, none offered the faintest glimmer of encouragement. I had expected someone other than friends and family to care about Melissa's fragile situation. I felt like a stranger in a strange land, crushed in disappointment and full of rage at the world.

The ecstasy of last autumn had once again become today's agony. A future together required a living Melissa and my mind contorted in an effort to find an idea to improve her health or bring us closer in whatever time we had left.

Consolation came by way of fantasies. Melissa smiling at my postcards. Talking with me as we stroll on a beach. Me living in Costa Rica. Best of all was a dream.

> *I'm in a Brooklyn hospital. I ask for directions to the Cystic Fibrosis unit. Melissa is there, but perhaps not a patient. She's gained weight and she has a different, round face. "Hello, how are you?" I say.*
>
> *She smiles. "Fine, how are you???" She's animated and friendly.*
>
> *Gloria appears and we make plans for where they can stay now that Melissa has been released.*

I awoke, pleased by Melissa's visit.

16. Opening Doors—April to May, 1991

Desperation builds. I phone pulmonary specialists in San Diego and Philadelphia who perform pro bono operations for children from other countries. I'm not precisely sure how tube feeding works, it's learn as I go. I soon find that these doctors work on a cash-only basis with hospital expenses waived. The expense is out of my reach. The Philadelphia nurse adds, "Mr. Dodson, you should keep in mind that there is nothing sacred about the medical interventions we do. Even the tube feeding is not the answer in every case."

An idea springs into my head. "Let me run something by you. It might sound crazy.... but what do you think about me sponsoring someone, a nutritionist, to fly to Costa Rica and evaluate and treat Melissa right there?"

"Sure, I don't see why not."

I ask her if she knows a nutritionist herself. "As a matter of fact, I do. A wonderful dietician who worked here for years and now teaches at Drexel University."

And with that, an idea becomes a project. I'll scrape together money, hire a professional to go to Esparza for a week to teach nutrition to Gloria and Melissa. The next evening I phone Dr. Gonzalez at home. She loves the idea. I ask her how many Costa Rican children does she know with CF? Around thirty, she answers. We discuss offering nutritional consults for all of them. She suggests I call Bob Snowden at McNeil Pharmaceutical and ask for a donation. I figure he should be generous after all the lobbying I've been doing to get Pancrease approved in Costa Rica.

"Gloria wrote me that Melissa is putting on weight."

"Yes, that's right," Dr. Gonzalez says, "four and a half pounds."

"How did you know? Have you seen her?"

"Yes, twice."

"Is something wrong?"

"No, she's simply come in for check-ups."

"I was just wondering, she hasn't come in the past."

"Perhaps you're having an effect, Olin."

Early the next morning I phone Bob Snowden in New Jersey. For starters, he tells me the Pancrease application papers have been filed in Costa Rica and it shouldn't be too much longer before it's approved. Surprised and delighted I thank him profusely then change the subject and pitch my plan. I ask if McNeil will foot the airfare for the nutritionist I've yet to find, perhaps $500. He says, "I won't know my annual budget until next week." He paused. "But that shouldn't be a problem."

Eventually the stress built up again and I came down with the flu. I rented "Ikiru," a Kurosawa movie recommended by a friend years before. The story revolves around a government bureaucrat named Watanabe, a drone who never missed a day of work in 30 years. His nickname at the office is "The Mummy." He learns he is dying of lung cancer and struggles to truly live for the first time.

A wistful Japanese folk song is used as a backdrop for Watanabe's story. He sings it twice during the film.

Life is so short.
Fall in love, dear maiden,
While your hair is black
And before your heart withers,
For today will not come again.

"Ikiru" haunted me for days. In spite of the awareness of my heart's needs during my journey to Central America, I had reverted to a Puritan-ish fear of personal fulfillment. The scene of Watanabe confessing that he did not truly know how to live made my neck tighten. It stirred up a feeling of guilt that I had turned my back to life for a long time. Now the obsession on building my counseling practice seemed somehow out of balance. Once found by Melissa, my heart came out from hiding for the first time since 1978 and asserted its place in my life.

"Ikiru" does not paint a pretty picture of a man striving to save his life. It combines sadness, agony and beauty, reflecting my life since I met my daughter. In the two hours it took to watch "Ikiru" I began to let go of a naïve vision of an idealized relationship with Melissa, and to embrace something more real and bitter.

* * * * *

I phoned the nutritionist at Drexel. She was skilled and experienced in all sorts of pulmonary issues. I asked for her resume and references. By this point I had realized that Spanish fluency was a must. It was also clear that the project must be geared to all Costa Rican kids with CF, not just Melissa. I phoned Pacific Presbyterian Hospital in San Francisco, having learned that they were hosting a CF Caregiver's conference. A woman named Carol, the Pac Pres nutritionist, told me that she would love to go to Costa Rica and would introduce me to other nutritionists if I came to the conference.

The Cystic Fibrosis Caregivers conference convened during the last week of April. Fog-tinged sunlight edged its way into the Pacific Presbyterian Hospital auditorium where it mingled with an energetic buzz of conversation. I found Carol and she escorted me on a tour of introductions to clinical dieticians and physicians. I summarized my story repeatedly as if it were a speed-dating event. One of the dieticians spoke Spanish, but she had less than a year of work experience and seemed neither highly knowledgeable nor confident.

The conference was a helpful Intro to Nutrition and CF-101. Young women at pharmaceutical booths answered my most basic questions. But the best experience was an hour long panel presentation by CF patients in their late teens and early twenties, speaking about their hospital experiences. One of them, a black woman, entered in a wheelchair, hooked up to all kinds of electronic monitors. She looked like someone from a science fiction movie, half human, half machine. She sounded upbeat telling her story, but it was difficult to completely believe her. The young woman's body was a wreck and her life dependent on a machine. I noticed I wasn't listening to her. My mind whispered silent judgments about her cheerfulness. The judgments kept her at arm's length, fiercely pushing away the nightmare that Melissa could someday end up like her.

Two other young women on the panel take the mike and my tension subsides. They are twins, Anabel and Isabel Stenzel, freshmen at Stanford University with smiles which seem genuine and warm. They laugh easily. Their soft manner and thin frames remind me of Melissa. I can see clearly in them what I try to avoid thinking about with Melissa: the awareness that life hangs by the slimmest of threads.

I stare almost desperately at Ana and Isa as if I could absorb their positive attitude, their young wisdom and perseverance. I wish Melissa were here to see them. They speak about their commitment to exercise to help their bodies stay strong. They do percussive therapy on each other every day. They create written summaries about CF to hand out to their college friends and dorm mates so they will understand their limitations. They appear full of life. On this day, at least, they are not discouraged. Today, they don't cough or fight for breath.

I observe how the audience falls into hysterics over Ana and Isa's humorous hospital stories. They describe their years of hospital visits, making friends and seeing old friends, both patients and hospital staff. At 14, they even wrote an autographical "book" about their hospital experiences. As the audience breaks for lunch, Isabel suddenly calls out to the audience, to tell them something important, something a doctor told her which has stuck with her year after year after year. The room hushes to hear her words: "Hold on to your dreams."

A week later I phone the twins at their dorm and ask if they will send me a copy of their "book." We talk about Melissa. They are excited I want to read their book and decline my offer to send them a check for the postage. Their voices are high-pitched and effusive, leaving me warm-hearted. In a few days a large envelope arrives. Inside is a flowery card with a handwritten note.

Dear Mr. Dodson,

Here is a copy of the "book" you requested. I hope you enjoy it. Please excuse the simplicity and primary nature, but we wrote it when we were 14. I hope you find it useful for your daughter.

I hope all is well with you and your daughter. Please let me know if I can ever be of any other help. I'm always eager to help others since I myself have been helped so often. If you ever need any advice from a cystic's perspective please let me know and I'll do my best to accommodate you.

Best wishes and kind regards to your daughter. Thinking and praying for her and hope she is well.

Love always,

Anabel

Anabel and Isabel's book, entitled "Life at Kaiser Hospital, Volume 1," is a little over twenty pages in length, xeroxed, typewritten and stapled. Their brief introduction explains that they had relatively healthy childhoods until the hospitalizations began at age ten.

What follows are sixteen short chapters, including drawings of an IV and other medical procedures, a map of the hospital, and lists of all their doctors, medications, medical terms and guest visitors such as Michael J. Fox and Ricky Schroeder ("!!!!"). The book itself is an example of the twins' approach to their disease.

Ana and Isa did not develop a mastery of cystic fibrosis, as if anyone could. But they met the disease directly, head on. However their lives had suffered and been shaped by CF, they refused to let it be the ultimate definer in their lives. They disproved any notion that human beings require total freedom, excellent health and unlimited choices in order to flourish. Their incurable disease did not touch their will, thoughtfulness, or their love of life.

* * * * *

Over time my list of prospective nutritionists ballooned. I lost track of the numbers of phone calls I made. Proficiency in Spanish was the perpetual obstacle but the supportive response from every stranger buoyed my spirits. My life had gained cohesion and meaning. My heart had dropped its protective layer and become like a doorway to a universe of generous strangers.

May arrived and in spite of the many post cards flowing south, there had been no more follow-ups from Melissa or Gloria since mid-March. I faxed another letter to Melissa on May 5.

Dear Melissa,

It is the first week of the month again. It seems like a long time since my last fax.

I hope that you, your mother and your family are doing well. Naturally

I hope that you are happy, healthy and gaining weight. I imagine that Dr. Gonzalez explained to you my new plan, but I want to explain it to you in my own words.

For three weeks I tried to find financial assistance for specialized medical treatment for you here in the US. But the law demands that you live here. I will continue to look for a solution.

For now, we are going to do something different. Because weight is such an important part of your health, I decided to bring a nutritionist to Costa Rica. I am trying to find a nutritionist with experience in cystic fibrosis and who speaks Spanish. I called Texas, Arizona, Florida, Pennsylvania, Maryland and attended a conference in order to locate such a person. This person will meet with you and your mom and me, also with other children and their parents. The meetings will last one hour or so. Perhaps there will be two meetings, I don't know.

For this reason I want to know when is your school vacation this summer so when we meet you won't lose time from school. Let me know so that the person I find can confirm their trip as soon as possible. Dr. Gonzalez believes that this project will benefit you and many children in Costa Rica. I feel very happy when I work on this project.

I hope that you are receiving the post cards. Yesterday I sent #15. Some are funny don't you think? I especially liked the ones with the dogs.

At the CF conference, students from the University who also suffer with CF talked about their experiences. Two were girls 19 years old. I wish that you could have heard them. They have some problems but are doing well. They give each other physical therapy. They said that exercise is very important. It doesn't make them happy but they understand that it is very beneficial. The exercise causes the lungs to expel the phlegm and at times they do exercise instead of PT. Also they feel very good at the end.

All of the students believed that it is very important to do things that make you feel happy. They had different opinions on things. For example, one of them told everybody she knew about her lungs and medicines. But others told no more than a few people. There was so much information that I could write 5 pages, but I should end for now. How I wish that you could have been there.

Melissa, I think about you all the time. In my imagination I see you in school, or talking with your friends, or hugging your mom. Every day I send you happiness in my thoughts.

Take care!

Your Dad

The next day, May 6th, was surprise time once again. The mailman brought an envelope from Costa Rica with the name Merilyn Reyes Araya, Melissa's cousin, in the upper right hand corner. I tore open the envelope. The letter was typed and in English.

Dear Olin,

Hi! Mr. Olin, sometimes I wish I could explain to you their behavior, but it's hard, sometimes they show that they're scared that you will find out they love you and they don't know how they are going to act. For Latin women, the mother's role is so important and in Melissa, it's double, because she always saw her mother like a big love and like everything in her life.

When you came you changed their relation. Another problem is that Meli thinks that you only have plans for her and not my aunt. That makes her be that way.

You tried to win your daughter first and, I think, excuse me please, that you should win my aunt with Meli at the same time; that you are interested in her mother; I understand your position, you made your life and all this is new for you.

Don't stop fighting for what is yours and what you love. Don't surrender in spite of their behavior. It's necessary that you insist in a delicate way.

See you soon!

With respect,

Merilyn Reyes Araya

Excuse me please but Meli is very important for me. Bye!

I sent thank you's to Merilyn into the stratosphere. Melissa's closest friend was my advocate! I read the letter repeatedly in order to extract every shred of insight and comfort. The more I read, the greater my perplexity.

They "love" me?

I should "win" Gloria?

Does Melissa want me to marry her mother?

I faxed a response to Merilyn the following day.

Dear Merilyn,

Thank you very, very much, I received your letter yesterday. I am so happy to hear your thoughts and I appreciate your words of support!

You raised many important subjects. I would like you to explain in more detail. For example, you said that I changed their relationship. How?? I am curious. You said that Melissa believes I have plans for her that don't include your aunt.

I would like to know exactly what you were saying. Please write me again and don't worry about writing me in Spanish. I understand Spanish although it is difficult to express myself in it.

I want to give you thanks again for your letter and I hope that you will continue writing!

Sincerely,
Olin

* * * * *

Three days later the alarm woke me at 6:00. I made coffee and awaited a call from a Sheah, a dietician in Miami, Florida.

As it turned out, Sheah said what everyone said. The project is a great idea. I wish I could go, but I don't speak Spanish. Good luck, I'll pass the word along.

Three hours later the phone rang again. "Olin, this is Sheah. Your nutritionist just walked in the door. Would you like to speak to her?!?"

17. It Never Entered My Mind—May to July, 1991

Mirta Rios' voice marched through the phone with authority. She summarized her qualifications: a dozen years as a licensed childrens' clinical dietician, an experienced educator, and, most recently, a presenter at an AIDS conference in Panama. She was a soldier in the only kind of war I liked. I asked for her resume and references but my instincts told me the search was over. I immediately faxed Reina.

Dear Dr. Gonzalez,

I found a nutritionist who speaks Spanish. She works at Jackson Memorial Hospital in Miami. She will be able to work at your hospital from a Monday through a Friday. I will come with her....Please write me as soon as possible, as we need to confirm the dates of the trip in order to make airline reservations, etc. Please confirm that she will have a house to stay in with breakfast and dinner, I hope. Also we need to know what to bring...We are very excited about this project. We hope that many CF patients will benefit from this visit, and we hope to gain public attention for CF in Costa Rica.

Hope to hear from you soon.
Respectfully,
Olin

She promptly faxed back.

Dear Olin,

I have just received your fax of 14/5/91.

Congratulations! I am very excited because you could get from McNeil support for the nutritionist to fly to Costa Rica. I will be very happy to offer my home for the stay of the nutritionist....

If it is possible please write an agenda and send it to me by fax. I think she can offer a lecture for the staff of the Hospital and spend one day with the parents and also with the CF Association. It is possible also for you to meet with the parents....

Please bring all the educational materials that you consider useful, also books on nutrition and if it is possible PANCREASE!!! and samples of supplemental foods.

Best regards,

Reina

That night a memorable dream:

I'm posing with Melissa for a photograph by Jeff. We are standing beside a large swimming pool. Suddenly, large, furry white whales surge powerfully out of the water and onto the sidewalk next to me. Water pours everywhere. They look up at me with big searching eyes and I tenderly scratch the top of their heads.

It wasn't the last appearance of whales in connection to Melissa.

* * * * *

The weeks fly by in intensity. I live on the phone, soliciting donations for an honorarium and airline tickets for Mirta. We exchange faxes and letters about the project and I encourage her to let her ideas flow. A flood results. She researches typical Costa Rican diets and puts together a list of CF related products available in Costa Rica. She prepares a detailed 3-day diet chart for parents to fill out and bring to her with their children in August. Dr. Gonzalez and I also exchange faxes. I put her in touch with Roche, International (in their San Jose, Costa Rica office!) They sell a water-soluble Vitamin K, useful for cystics. The project monopolizes my interest. Friends poke fun at the number of movies I walk out of, either bored or distracted.

By phone the secretary of the Cystic Fibrosis Foundation in Bethesda tells me that the Foundation does not usually fund small projects but asks for a one-page description about the project. I write a letter to them and another to CFRI in Palo Alto. I receive prompt replies with promises of $500 from each organization. Joanna, a woman in my Spanish class, donates $500.

Helen and Ed agree to help me start a support group for parents of children with CF. We decide to hold our first meeting in Petaluma just prior to my departure for CR in early August. We obtain an address list from CFRI and send out invitations.

Then Merilyn's second letter arrives, four pages, in Spanish. It takes me some time to get used to her hand-writing and her missing punctuation, but the slow translation process gives me time to take in her intriguing observations.

Hola Olin,

Thanks for giving attention to my letter, I trust God that you are in good health.

I will try to explain to you what I wished to say: you changed a bit the relation between Auntie and Meli. What I tried to tell you is what I perceive and think, at least Auntie feels in part jealous; she wants and doesn't want for Meli to accept you, but she knows that if it happens Meli will give you attention, affection and pampering that has always been there for her; on the other hand Meli feels this fear of her mother's, they don't talk about it but it is obvious; they are not accustomed to someone knowing too much about them; always they have been accustomed to receive the minimum and then arrives your heaping of love for Meli. It is logical that Auntie thinks that you want to move her aside, or at least win the affection of this capricious little girl; but they don't say anything, they don't talk about their fears anxieties or plans for the future.

She believes that you have plans for her and not for Auntie because of the following: each time you say that you want her to meet her grandparents or aunts in the States you don't say that you are going to bring Auntie to meet them also and that you are interested in the well being of both, try to write more to auntie and ask her to write you how Meli is and say to her very modestly and discreetly that you are interested in how Auntie is as the mother of your child. Meli believes that when one person doesn't show affection to another it is because they don't like them.

For Meli, this is <u>important</u>, her mother is the only one of value that she has had and who has loved her, cared for her and spoiled her until now, Auntie is not interested if she acts good or bad, she always loves her the same; what I'm trying to tell you is that for mothers, her child can be good or bad they always love them and encourage them to go forward, the bad thing is that Meli is very capricious and stubborn (hard-headed) and more than once you can tell her what is advisable, she lends a deaf ear.

Merilyn's words about Gloria's ambivalence sadden me. It is true that I have focused my attention on Melissa and not only because she is the one I love. Gloria's fantasies and fabrications and her stepping ahead of her daughter that day in the plaza had made me extremely wary. But I feel guilty for my rudeness to her and Merilyn's words point out how I am partly to blame for the pot in which I now sit.

It is necessary that she feels the moral support of a father, she doesn't know how it feels when someone wants to treat you badly and your father steps forward to defend or protect you, it is a feeling so great, when they sit you in their laps and tell you that you are the most beautiful thing that has happened to me. She doesn't know what she is losing and so she can't realize that life gives us only one opportunity to be happy if we want it.

I admire you, you know, it is hard when someone that you didn't know existed appears, your hopes are built up, she treats you with affection and when you meet her, it all goes to the contrary. But you know one thing I would call it self-defense, to close oneself to that person, you don't believe that you need him, a self deception because they want you to pay more attention and rejecting that person, it is logically you will try to make a good impression and do everything possible to help her; therefore the little girl feels satisfaction to know that she has dominated everyone all around her, I don't know if you understand me, but I ought to emphasize that this is how I think and feel, how do they say because of my feminine intuition or because I have done the same thing as her.

It is painful to be reminded of Melissa's emptiness from not having a father to grow up with. She begs for then closes her heart to love's gifts. People back off from her demands or they go overboard. It somehow works for her, but she loses out on the big prize.

I will continue writing you and I hope that you understand that there are life stages for children that are difficult to understand and only by living with them can you adapt and comprehend them. She is going from being a child to become in every way a "senorita." And this makes her pass through unstable and emotional time, I believe that you understand all these problems that one goes through, but she doesn't and therefore it makes for a big conflict in the head, it seems as if the whole world is coming down on you and everyone is against you.

Please don't be downhearted, but life is beautiful but filled with stuff that for some are little, and for others enormous. And this situation is difficult for Meli, also delicate, and it requires lots of tact understanding love and comprehension.

Thanks for doing so much on your part and continue having patience with them.

I say good-bye for now,

Merilyn

I lowered the letter onto my lap, suddenly depressed to think about Gloria's power and how her jealousy might defeat my dreams for Melissa. I could hardly blame Gloria, I might feel the same in her shoes. Still unsolved was the problem of whether I could provide a feeling of inclusion to Gloria. Then there was Melissa, whose MO seemed to be high control in relationships, uninterested in relationships when she could not keep the other person at arms' length. It was a grim picture.

I wondered what Merilyn had seen or heard which prompted her to write. I pictured her in the hospital observing Melissa glare at me, then looking at my shattered expression. Perhaps she imagined the possibility that I might be driven away and wanted to prevent it. In a culture where women are expected to wait on men, Merilyn's initiative to advise me seemed remarkable.

The weight of my aloneness had often been crushing, so Merilyn, I hoped, would be an ally. She was Melissa's closest friend. Her mom, Bita, had shared a story of how, one night, she looked in on them in Merilyn's room. They lay side-by-side in bed, asleep, but, Bita insisted, still talking. Merilyn's letters told me more about Melissa than anyone else had in nine months. By comparison, Gloria seemed to have no interest or ability in interpreting Melissa to me, typically shrugging her shoulders in response to my befuddlement. I wondered if she had found me more for her own sake than for Melissa's and was disinterested in Melissa and me ever growing close.

A letter from Gloria unexpectedly arrived the following day. I was overjoyed to see the large brown envelope, and eagerly pulled out the thin page inside.

Olin,

How are you?

Here everything is fine. It's going well for Melissa.

The point of the letter, in two additional lines, was that Gloria wanted **me** to tell my parents, **for Melissa**, that they had received letters from them, and "many thanks." That was it from Miss Gloria.

Underneath Gloria's curious message was one from Melissa. Her handwriting was scrawny and slight, as if she had barely pressed the pen to the page:

Hi,

It's me, Melissa. I would like to say hi and tell you we received the post cards.

Ok, bye.

A meager message. I suspected Gloria had ordered it.

*****

Anne Lee wrote to say she had called around for the pharmaceutical company which manufactured the high-protein drink, Ensure. She gave me the name of Ross Labs' chief nutritionist, Dr. Susan Finn, in Columbus Ohio. I wrote Dr. Finn, describing the Costa Rica project and asked for samples of Ensure which Dr. Gonzalez requested.

I received the news that McNeil's donation had been officially approved. The Pancrease samples would be shipped to Mirta. I sent a fax to Melissa and Gloria, putting Gloria's name first on the heading. I began by telling them about a Memorial Day picnic.

I was happy to receive your letter of May 24. It was the second I had received since February. You know I want to know if my letters reach you and perhaps you want to know also. I have not been able to determine if you have received all my cards. Recently I sent you card #25 and a check on the same day.

As I said in the card, I will bring a nutritionist with me the 5th of August. The plan will be to talk with the patients of Dr. Gonzales who have CF and their parents. I imagine that the office of Dr. Gonzales will communicate with you so you can come for an appointment that week. I hope to stay two weeks in Costa Rica, one week in San Jose helping the nutritionist.

I am sorry that the plan for you both to come to California has not had any results. But I want you both to come for a visit, next December or January are good, but it is cold at times, even in Disneyland or Arizona. Perhaps the school vacation in July of 1992 would be the best time. We can talk about this in August. I look forward to the time that I can see you both again. I will send you more information when I have it.

Take care. I always think of you both.

Love,

Daddy

Melissa's cousin, Merilyn, with her family's adopted son, Jose.

If hearing me say I think of her all the time rekindles Gloria's love, it's a risk I have to take. I faxed Merilyn on the same day:

Dear Merilyn,

Great thanks for your letter! You have a profound understanding, so intelligent, and I give thanks to you for adding to my understanding. I agree completely with what you say and it makes me happy that Melissa has you as her cousin.

With different languages and cultures and because we are strangers, we have big obstacles to overcome. You make me realize how difficult the situation is for Melissa. It is ironic, because I want to make her life more easy and happy, you know? When I say this I include Gloria also. And of course I want this to succeed eventually but I know that relationships can be difficult. They require time and effort.

For this reason I want to tell you how much I appreciate your letter's honesty and support. I believe that clear and direct communication is necessary in order to make understanding flower as well as trust and love. People like you help me to overcome the discouraging times. So I hope you understand when I end this letter to you, "with affection."

Olin

PS Write whenever you feel like it!

* * * * *

My first Father's Day arrived. No presents, no coffee in bed, no special dinners, just phone calls from friends, a few cards and an emotional bounce every time I thought about being a father. I spoke with Frances' teen-age daughter on the phone. Heidi's father had suddenly passed away when she was only a child and I think she was especially interested in the Costa Rica soap opera. I was touched to hear that she'd purchased fashionable barrettes for me to take to Melissa.

Over the months of spring I began to read books by contemporary Latin American authors, like Eduardo Galeano. His "Memory of Fire" trilogy kindled my interest in Latin American history, food, music, and movies. I watched the Miss World pageant on television and applauded enthusiastically when Miss Costa Rica appeared. I saw author Isabel Allende interviewed on television. One of her remarks jumped out at me. "We can construct reality in the image of our dreams." I spoke to the image on the screen. "Isabel, you should hear how my reality has become a dream!" The next day I wrote to her.

Dear Isabel,

I asked the Chronicle to forward this letter to you. I have a story which I would like to tell you in person.

The story began last August when a stranger phoned me to tell me

I have a 12-year old daughter in Costa Rica who desired contact with me. Naturally, this story is rich and beautiful. It involves dreams, premonitions and longing. It is a dramatic story complicated by our differing cultures and expectations, as well as Melissa's cystic fibrosis.

When I saw you on "The Creative Mind" I heard you describe your love of stories. This is a story to end all stories. I want nothing from you. I gain immeasurably from re-counting this miraculous story to my friends. I know you would love it as does everyone. The story continues to unfold. On August 5 the third trip to Costa Rica in a year will take place. This time a bi-lingual dietician from Miami will accompany me. At the Hospital de Niños we will meet all of the clinic's CF children and their parents for important nutritional evaluation and counseling.

While my only wish is to make Melissa's life richer, my presence has complicated her life. Her spirit glows dimly. Life and hope have never been strongly embraced. And so she watches and passes much time in retreat from me, as if she had a precious secret. An often heart-breaking effort to establish common ground with Melissa and her mother is currently taking place.

I believe we will do it.

I know you are a busy person, receiving many requests and invitations. However I could not shake the idea of writing you. If your interest and time allows you can contact me at my business number listed above. I hope we might have the opportunity to talk.

Sincerely,

Olin Dodson

The story was bursting out of me. If I owned CNN or knew Oprah, I would have told the entire world. Three weeks later I received a response with a Marin County return address in the upper left corner. It was a large orange card with a Santiago, Chile, stamp on the back. The entire front of the card was a wool weaving of a landscape, three trees with red fruit, and stars on a gray sky.

Dear Olin,

Thank you for your kind letter. It was very moving. I hope that Melissa is doing well and that you'll be able to give her the love and care that she needs. You seem to be a very special person!

I am in the middle of writing another book, locked in a room with no social life but I will keep your invitation in mind for the future.

Good luck,

Isabel Allende

I purchased Mirta's airline ticket and did some shopping for gifts. In one final letter to Gloria and Melissa before my departure. I told them about Mirta, the project and my fundraising, and assured them I'd bring Pancrease.

I expressed my enthusiasm about seeing them again and suggested we take a day trip together.

I returned from a medical appointment on my birthday to find a letter in the mailbox addressed in Melissa's handwriting. I couldn't help but smile and thank the heavens. Unfolded, the letter revealed color photos of various Costa Rica scenes including the National Theater, the Atlantic Oceanside and two shining gold turtle jewelry pieces.

Melissa's note was a little wave of the hand beneath Gloria's message. I noticed that, since her first Christmas fax, Melissa had never addressed me as "Dear" Anything. Obviously, "Dad" was not a term she could bring herself to write. Nor did she sign her name at the end. The omissions made her comments seem altogether impersonal.

> *Olin,*
>
> *How are you? Melissa is very good. Olin, I have used the money that you sent for some things for Melissa. She received the check and all the cards. The cost of the passport is 16.782 colones. Everything here is going well. I am happy that you are coming in August. Thanks for the cards.*

In Melissa's handwriting:

> *Hi, how are you, school is going well for me. I am taking a course in handcrafts, on vacation we are going to go to San Isidro and to the monastery. I have received all the cards and the check.*

It was their second letter in six weeks and contained actual responses to my questions! Mention of the passport gave me great joy along with relief that my cards and money had reached them. Melissa's note did not cheer me as much as the one five months earlier. Maybe I expected more of a response to my post cards. I didn't know why she bothered to write.

As my departure date drew nearer, thoughts of losing Melissa would eat at me then fade as my insides filled with anticipation. The possibility of another rejection never entered my mind.

Once again I found myself on the living room floor gazing at a row of gifts lined up on the floor. Pens and notebooks, two boxes of rubber-molded stamps and inkpads, a shoebox of 50 knickknacks, including Heidi's barrettes, a necklace for Gloria and more.

In late July, the CF Parent's group had its inaugural meeting at Helen and Ed's house. Fourteen people showed up. The event never became too heavy for me because I was so focused on watching the flow of conversation and ensuring that everyone participated. I phoned Helen the next day and asked for her reaction to the meeting. She said she liked it but Ed woke up in the middle of the night, crying.

18. The Cold Hard Facts—August, 1991

My luggage bumped along the frayed conveyor belt in the bowels of San Jose International Airport. One bag contained gifts. The second was stuffed with clothes and personal items to last fifteen days. The third held Instant Breakfast, Vitamin K and enough Ensure and Pancrease to feed a family of four for a month. This was the bag, I now realized, which could lead to trouble. Denial, or perhaps the notion that God was on my side, had led me to ignore any previous thought of being fingered for undeclared medicine and food.

There were three lines of people standing in front of a row of customs officials. I was overdressed in a blazer and perspiration dampened my shirt. The officials seemed unusually active this day and most of the arriving passengers were asked to unzip a bag or two. I tried to let my facial muscles sink into a bland, bored expression. A guard reached out for my passport, glanced at my bags and waved me through.

I stepped off the bus at the roadside in Esparza at mid-day, near the spot where Scott Lee had met me eight months earlier. The sun peeked around a massive cloud of black. Drenched in sweat I crossed the highway as the sky began to open up. Slow, heavy droplets increased in speed until they hit me like pebbles. I ran the final two blocks to the hotel.

A cold shower and a nap were followed by a bowl of soup and a beer in the hotel café. As the sky turned to crimson, I strolled to Ramon's house, little flowers on every street sweetening the evening. Across the gate came the sounds of a man's voice and people laughing and clapping. Through the thin curtains were the silhouettes of Melissa, seated, and Gloria, standing behind her, bathed in the light of the television.

I called out. Melissa peeked through the curtains and spoke to her mother. Gloria came to the gate smiling. I kissed her on the cheek and we walked towards the house. She told me Ramon was asleep and put her thumb to her mouth to indicate he was soused. I stepped to the doorway into the rec room. Melissa turned and smiled, then returned to her program, "America's Home Videos," dubbed in Spanish. I gave her a little kiss on her cheek and told her how happy I was to see her again. She stared straight ahead at the TV, frowning, unresponsive to the people on the screen running from ducks and falling out of trees. She responded to my questions about school, her class trip to Panama and the recent solar eclipse in monosyllables: *Bien. Bien. Bien.*

I turned to Gloria for more engaging conversation and could almost see Melissa's ears cup to overhear our words. Gloria told me that they had just returned from church. I noticed their flowery but modest dresses, their hair pinned up. Melissa held an umbrella by her side. I glanced at the watch on her wrist. It was not the one I gave her and my mood soured. The program ended and Melissa turned her back to us and faced the dark window.

Gloria escorted me back to the gate. She looked worried. "You and Melissa need to talk." I wondered how on God's green earth she could imagine that happening. I could have laughed, instead I nodded. "We will." We agreed that they would come to my hotel room at 11 the next morning to open the presents I'd brought.

Jet-lagged, humidity-dragged, I went back to the hotel and slept for twelve hours.

*****

My hotel room was on the lean side, just a double bed, a small table and a straight-backed chair. We took our places. Gloria in the chair, Melissa at the end of the bed and I atop the pillows. The presents lay on the bed between us.

Melissa announced the ground rules. She wouldn't open a present until her mother did. But as soon as Gloria began pulling the paper off her first gift, Melissa set to work on hers. This was my first opportunity to study Melissa in the light. I had not lost the joy of merely looking at her face, no matter what her condition. There were dark pouches under her watery eyes and her pallor was pasty. She was boney, a strong wind gust could have knocked her over. Still, she appeared to be in better shape than when she was hospitalized 6 months earlier. I yearned to reach out and hold her in my arms.

Gloria gushed over her bead necklace while Melissa, in super slow-mo, was still opening her first gift. At last, tape un-taped, paper un-wrapped, Melissa held two boxes of rubber stamps in her clubbed fingers. Her frozen expression forecast what I was to see for the next half hour. Bewilderment was all I felt as she mutely pulled forth each present from its ribbon and paper: more rubber stamps, ink pads of different hues, sets of colored ink pens and pencils, a box of assorted stationary from my sister, Jan, cards for stamping from Frances, barrettes from Heidi, a box of glue pens, fancy shoe laces, Garfield Post-its, hair ties, packages of gum, Pop Rocks and more. She tried out the pink and purple pens on a Post-it, then listlessly scratched out a simple portrait of a girl with green hair. I stole glances Gloria's way, but mostly I searched Melissa's face for a reaction. I searched in vain.

I had never met a child so emotionally hidden as Melissa. Her frown conveyed more than a hint of ferocity. Her gaze, flat at times, feral at others, offered no clue as to her next move. She could be planning to bite my neck, scamper off into the rain forest, or climb into my lap. I bet it wasn't the latter.

Melissa began to cough. She went out to the balcony while Gloria and I listened to her sputum erupt with a crackle, like loose parts dislodged. The sound made me shudder. Melissa returned, her face drained of color, and refused her mother's offer to use the bathroom.

When the final gift was set aside, Melissa looked at her mom, who told her to thank me. She did not. I brought out six months worth of Pancrease and an envelope of money. I gave Melissa a copy of Eduardo Galeano's "Book of Embraces" to pass along to Merilyn. We agreed to meet later at the church and then go to Bita and Ascension's. They stood up to leave and I kissed Melissa good-bye. She said, "Grácias."

They walked out and I bent over in defeat. Then, suddenly curious, I bounced up to watch them from the balcony. Gloria briefly walked alone in front of her daughter before Melissa passed and left her behind. I thought she is either confused, or ambivalent, or, God help me, uninterested. I fell on the bed, like a bag of bricks. I imagined that if I were Melissa, if I had her life, I might not want to open my heart, but I wouldn't want Dad to give up.

Dad, staring at the hotel room ceiling, remembered the Avenue of the Giants marathon in 1979, mile 19, when his energy vanished and his calves cramped and he wondered if he would make it to the finish.

*****

One of the stories in Galeano's book was entitled "The Flowers." It tells about a lonely man who meets a woman and falls in love. At her apartment building each morning he sends her a bouquet of flowers, never the same kind, never the same colors. Each day he stares up at the woman's balcony and each day she drops them from the window into the street where they are run over by passing automobiles. Finally, after many, many days, the flowers are not thrown into the street. The man goes to the floor where the woman lives and knocks on the door. It opens.

The story described my life with Melissa and the life I hoped for.

*****

The next morning before hopping on a San Jose bus for a meeting with Reina, I stopped by the house with grocery bags of Ensure and Instant Breakfast. Melissa sat on the front porch chewing on a mango peel. Esparza schools operated in two shifts and Melissa's was in the afternoon. She was wearing shorts and t-shirt and furry blue house slippers. Her eyes were puffy and she had a serious case of pillow hair. Gloria, in her usual off-white skirt and blouse, brought two chairs onto the porch. She began to complain about Melissa's refusal to eat more. It was a conversation I didn't want any part of, but I listened. Occasionally Melissa made grumpy comments, variations on the theme of "I'm not hungry." I noticed ink on her thumb and stamp-marks on her forearm. Before I left Gloria agreed to meet again the next morning. On the way to the bus stop, I dropped by to see Merilyn, but she was in class in San Jose at the University of Costa Rica.

At the Hospital de Niños I ground my teeth for an hour near the Costa Rican Screaming Infant Chorale, waiting for Reina. I had looked forward to finalizing the details of Mirta's upcoming schedule but Reina greeted me in a clipped tone and fed me a diet of grievances: disagreements with the hospital nutritionist, the lack of involvement from the CF Parents group, the probable failure by some official to meet the deadline for getting approval on the Pancrease application, and a hospital official who blew off a visiting pulmonologist from Denmark.

Gone was the sparkle from Reina's eyes. They smoked in a mix of fury and defeat. The Danish visitor had described Costa Rica as "an underdeveloped country" and his comment had brought to the surface Reina's deep bitterness over a health care system which was supposed to be a model in Central America. My commiseration was paltry; I had my own problems at the moment. But I volunteered to talk to the nutritionist and the CF parents when I returned the following week.

I didn't like thinking about the dark side of Costa Rica's health care system any more than Reina. I slumped in defeat as the bus rolled and rattled back to Esparza in the warm dusk, the only visible lights the occasional dimple of a yellow bulb outside a house nestled in the trees or dangling on a cord over a soda stand. The driver accelerates past slower vehicles, honking frantically to warn oncoming traffic. I grip the seat and slide into a fantasy where the bus careens off the road and tips over in a terrible rolling mass of metal and screams. Bodies fly in all directions and when the dust and noise settles, many are hurt or dead. The survivors are helpless to do anything. They are haunted for the rest of their lives.

*****

The next morning, Gloria escorted me into the shade of the front porch. The fronds on the palm trees rocked gently in the breeze. Gloria avoided my eyes, so I asked her how she was feeling. She explained that she had been giving Melissa her physical therapy when I arrived. I imagined pounding on Melissa's back for a half hour two or three time a day was difficult, even frustrating, when there were no visible improvements. Gloria interrupted my thoughts to say that she was upset with Melissa. Was it again about her not eating? She wouldn't say.

I told her I was going to the beach for a couple of nights but I would be around all day and tonight and hoped she and I could talk. This would be my major surge to "win her." I waited eagerly for her response, then waited some more. But Gloria was a woman struck mute. She would not meet my eyes or speak, and my insides boiled. At a younger age, I might have stood up, maybe kicked my chair or hit the table. I likely would have stormed off the porch. I definitely would have slammed the gate on my way out.

I did none of these things, but was pissed, out of answers, doing everything a man could think of and getting nothing, no help, no action, no encouragement, only passivity and rejection. This was the crowning touch, the death blow to all of my expectations for this visit, for Gloria and myself, and why not throw in my expectations of life, as well. And the belief that good intentions and good works produce results and that I can do anything I set my mind to and love conquers all and people are desperate for connection, and all that .... crap.

No, I didn't pout or make a scene. I gradually, so sensitively, so nicely eased my way up and out, told Gloria I'd see her later and, oh, on her idea of Melissa and me talking, why didn't she try and arrange for Melissa and me to be stuck together, running an errand or something when I returned. Gloria said yes, good, she'd work on it. She was hardly convincing.

* * * * *

On my way back to the hotel I stopped by to see if Merilyn was at home. She wasn't. I cooled down at a bakery, sipping Pepsi through a straw and observing the absence of all life forms in the blazing street. There was a brief shower but the humidity only worsened the heat. A nine-year-old girl with matted hair and smudged clothes rode by on a mini-bike. She balanced an umbrella in one hand and a baby on her thigh. I felt sad for her. I felt sad, too, for Melissa. Her delight in finding her dad fizzled into anger and misery.

I finished the soda. The saddest person, really, was me. I'd been given the greatest gift a man could receive, but the gift was not mine to keep. Only now had I noticed the fine print. "You have been given this most precious life, but there's a catch. It's really not yours. The precious life has to decide if she wants to claim you and sorry, pal—she might not want to."

God, I hated this set up. The mere thought of leaving our relationship in Melissa's hands terrified and confused me. Somehow I equated letting go with giving up. It would be a concession that my power was severely limited, that I might not get my way, that this glorious story was headed to a pitiful conclusion.

* * * * *

At 4:30, Ramon meets me at the gate. His short stature and bushy silver mustache give him the appearance of a gnome, and a drunk one at that. He says no one is home. I turn to leave and see Gloria coming up the street carrying a plastic bag of groceries. She droops after cleaning houses all day. Yes, I'm not the only one who struggles. I walk to the house with her and we stand on the porch. There's probably a Ramon Rule prohibiting Gloria from sitting around, especially with me. The shadows lengthen and we watch, beyond the iron rail fence, children in white shirts and dark blue skirts or pants walking home from school, laughing and calling out to each other.

Something about the man of the house bothers me. "Has Ramon has ever touched Melissa inappropriately?"

"Oh, no," Gloria answers.

"Did you ever visit the hospital social worker?"

"We met once but Melissa didn't like it."

"Perhaps the three of us can try to see her next week when we're at the Hospital."

"Ok."

Melissa comes through the gate dressed in her school uniform and carrying her day pack. She gives me a little smile when I greet her. I crook my finger and she comes closer, looking at ease.

"Let's go for an ice cream." Melissa shakes her head and slowly trots into the house. I look at Gloria with an "oh, well," shrug. In spite of all the pain she puts me through, my affection for Melissa has never diminished. And I never can predict when I'll be angry or merely smile like a fool lucky to have a proud, tough daughter.

On my way back to the hotel I wander past a public park with an Irish green soccer field and a cracked cement basketball court. It's still too hot for dogs to bark, but shirtless teen-age boys in ratty tennis shoes are playing four on four. I lean against a tree and watch their game. Something catches my attention, I turn my head. Melissa and another girl are racing down the street on mini-bikes. Hair flying, face frowning, Melissa zooms past, her eyes locked on the road. Her friend, pedaling madly to keep up, must know my identity because she smiles at me as she speeds by. It thrills me to see Melissa enjoying her body, letting loose like I had never imagined.

My body gradually rotates a full 180, my eyes never leaving the girls. The friend keeps looking back until the two of them disappear in the distance. I laugh and walk briskly to the hotel.

*****

Playa Tamarindo by bus, including a layover in the airport-hanger-style Liberia bus terminal, was a 9-hour day trip from Esparza. The bus ride offered intermittently scenic vistas of volcanoes and *fincas* in northwestern Costa Rica, but not enough to keep me from chewing over the week's disasters. A quarter of a mile from the ocean I found a quiet *cabina* on a piece of well manicured lawn claimed from a grove of trees and thick vegetation. $26 for two nights.

I walked beside the ocean at dawn. The sky was faded blue-jean blue. Grey pelicans rolled above breakers thumping the beach. Like a sanitarium resident, I ambled past bouquets of butterflies, through natural gardens of hibiscus and periwinkle fragrant with tiny flowers. An afternoon rain shook giant leaves and palm fronds as if they were blankets on a clothes line. I worked to drill it in my head that I was doing all I could do and there was nothing more to do. I couldn't quite believe it.

At the *cabinas,* I met some friendly people in their 20's, Bruce, Libby and Beatrice, on extended vacation from New Zealand. Over fried fish and Imperial beer we swapped Costa Rica travel tales. Bruce and Libby were fascinated by my story, but Beatrice had a slightly different take. "Did you ask Gloria if it was safe to have sexual relations?" Beatrice knew the answer, she was only making a cynical moralistic point, one which pinched a guilt button and incidentally assumed that my maleness somehow overwhelmed Gloria's say in the matter. I was pissed at her importunity and, even more, pissed that I couldn't get away for a brief beach excursion…without getting pissed.

When I returned to Ramon's house on Saturday morning, Melissa spotted me at the gate and scooted around the side of the house. I squirmed patiently in the sunlight, believing she had told someone of my presence. When I felt my shirt wet against my back, I decided to call out. Gloria let me in and I sat on the porch while she finished some chores. Ramon took a chair and regaled me with stories of his greatness. I feigned interest while wondering if Gloria came up with a clever scheme, like we talked about.

She came out and said they were fixing to leave for Puntarenas and would be back late. There was a possibility we could meet tomorrow after church but she couldn't commit. Paranoia struck. I wasn't sure if Ramon hadn't joined in the obstruction, trying to monopolize their time in order to win his personal pissing contest. Fuck it. I told Gloria I had to get to San Jose early on Sunday, before the homebound beachgoers clogged the highways to the capital. Melissa peeked through the door then disappeared without saying a word. I stood up and told Gloria I'd see them in San Jose.

I walked to Ascension's. No one was home.

19. Not Now—August, 1991

It was daybreak. Bus fumes and noises floated through downtown San Jose. I maneuvered down pencil-thin sidewalks, past vendors setting up street-corner carts of fruit and vegetables. I passed a man, a stone pillar in a suit, his eyes staring into no tomorrow. His outstretched hand held two AA batteries and a Kleenex packet for sale.

I found a seat in the rear of the hospital auditorium just as Reina finished her introduction of Mirta. Uniformed hospital employees filled half of the room. Smartly dressed in a dark skirt and white blouse, Mirta took the microphone and paced the stage like a big cat. She made children's nutrition, in Spanish, interesting.

Afterwards I went down to meet her. She sized me up through oversized glasses and shook my hand with the grip of a carpenter. Reina escorted us upstairs, beaming over Mirta's successful speech. Amidst crying babies and oxygen tanks, Reina launched into another round of attacks on Costa Rica's health care system. Tapped out in my own despondency, I excused myself to look for the hospital social worker.

Maritza Orlich had a comfy office and looked relaxed in a short sleeve cotton top. She invited me to take a seat and, in a soft alto voice, told me about the one occasion she had met with Melissa and Gloria. She thought Melissa seemed angry and far more powerful than Gloria. As trained counselors we both understood that when children gain power over their parents, depression usually results. Maritza offered to keep the next day's lunch hour open to facilitate and translate a family meeting. I should have poured out my problems to her. Instead I simply thanked her and returned to the pulmonary unit. Distracted and agitated I rolled through the day in meetings with Mirta and the pulmonary unit staff.

In the evening I found a popular restaurant, complete with low lighting, table cloths, a decent wine list and a friendly wait staff. Decent and friendly, this was San Jose. I tallied up my accomplishments in Esparza. It took all of thirty seconds.

Merilyn. Saw her once, briefly, at her parent's house.

Gloria: Short, unmemorable chats. Didn't react to my invitation to talk. Didn't arrange for me to be alone with Melissa.

Melissa: Spoke twenty, maybe twenty-five words, tops.

Pathetic failures, every one.

My glum reflections were interrupted by a quartet of Ugly Americans seated at a table nearby. A brown-haired woman held center stage, her voice whining like a dental drill out for a test drive. She carried on, oblivious to the stares from other diners, the most offensive act many Costa Ricans will commit in public. I wanted to yell at her. I wolfed down my food and hastened back to the hotel.

* * * * *

The Children's Hospital building was a fitting symbol of the health care system: monolithic, unpleasant and impersonal. Inside its walls, boredom reigned. Patients, families, staff and their uniforms, the paint, the signs on the walls, even the air seemed heavy with monotony. No one, no thing was immune. But at 9 o'clock on Monday morning, in a distant administrative wing of the hospital, I heard something different: an animated mix of childrens' giggles and adult chatter. Somehow I'd never pictured this moment, the gathering of all the country's poor and middle class families who had children with cystic fibrosis. It was like a church social after a rousing sermon and, in the center, my glittering, lovely Melissa pressed against her mom's arm. Hard to believe they had spent two hours on a bus that morning, so fresh and clean did they look, Melissa in a crayola red top, Gloria, a starchy white blouse. Melissa gave me a smile which probably meant less than I wanted it to. I smiled back.

The children in the hall appeared healthy and vibrant and I guessed they were overjoyed to be in the hospital for something other than involuntary confinement. Melissa's face turned red when one of the medical staff fawned over her. She allowed me to stand beside her and the pride of fatherhood was mine for a moment or two.

An hour later, 35 or 40 of us piled into a classroom and took our seats at little desk chairs. Windows on either end let in fresh air and sunlight. Reina, wearing a bright red top and black slacks, welcomed everyone like a happy evangelist, then introduced a real one. He invited everyone to stand for a prayer and, except for Melissa, we did. Holding a Bible he intoned fervently, then asked that we take our seats. Reina introduced me to a round of applause from everyone, except Melissa.

Mirta, in a sea blue floral print dress, walked to the front. Even Melissa listened intently as she talked about the importance of nutrition and passed out information sheets and diet charts. She summarized the purpose of the individual appointments and how all the children from outside the city would be seen that day. Locals would return later in the week.

When Mirta finished, refreshments were served. Reina asked all the children to gather at the front of the room front for photos. Melissa, the oldest cystic in the room, remained glued to her chair, looking angry. Soon she drifted to the far window where she remained for the duration, staring out the window.

When we broke for lunch, Gloria and I left to see Maritza. Melissa stayed behind with Mirta, who was making a special effort to bond with her. Instinctively, she took the same aggressively attentive approach that Merilyn did and Melissa clearly enjoyed it. Melissa agreed to come for her mom and me at 1 o'clock.

Maritza, Gloria and I pulled chairs together in a small circle in the center of Maritza's office. There were a few toys on the floor and colorful prints and posters on the walls. Gloria fidgeted. I jumped in, expressing my happiness that Gloria was doing such a good job monitoring Melissa's health and ensuring that she saw Reina more often. I brought up the topic of "our" irregular correspondence, requested more letters and direct answers to my questions, the kind of thing I was always saying to Gloria.

Gloria offered agreeable, compliant responses and asked if I was bothered by how little Melissa wrote. I ducked the question, fearing that Gloria might use a "yes" answer later to criticize Melissa. In return I asked if she was hurt that I gave Melissa so much attention in postcards and the letters I'd addressed only to her. Gloria answered cryptically: "It doesn't bother me, but Melissa doesn't understand it or like it." I said I wasn't sure when I could visit again, because of my limited means, but said I would fly them to the States if I could arrange some low-cost medical treatment. I offered to pay for Maritza's services twice a month. I told Gloria that I would always be connected to her and her family, that they were a part of my life. I don't know exactly how Maritza said this in Spanish, but Gloria reacted like a statue. Me: big gesture. Gloria: freezing. It had become a pattern.

Gloria had a few discussion items of her own. She returned to the subject of Melissa's treatment of me and said she felt bad about it. I said, "It makes me feel bad too, but there is no need to feel guilty about it. I wonder if Melissa is treating me this way in order to get Gloria's goat." Maritza translated this and then they both, simultaneously, turned their heads to me and nodded.

Gloria went on, "Melissa has things to say to you but she has said more than once, 'I don't need him.' Gloria imitated Melissa in a sarcastic tone. "I don't need the enzymes and other supplements either."

"At one time Melissa had fantasies of one day sleeping between her mother and father, but she now understands that we won't marry." Maritza translated Gloria's words to me, then whispered her first observation, in English. "If Melissa had those fantasies you can be sure Gloria did."

There was a faint knock at the door, Melissa's cue that our time was up. The three of us headed back to the third floor for the 2:15 appointment. Gloria stepped away for a moment and I reached into my shoulder bag. I knew Costa Rica's Mother's Day was coming up and pulled out a card for Gloria.

I asked Melissa if she would give it to her mother when the day arrived. She shook her head and looked away. I felt my face flush in anger, gazing at the now familiar back of Melissa's head.

*****

Mirta and Celina Guzman, a young resident from Venezuela, invited me in for a consultation shortly before Melissa's appointment. Celina's long hair was wrapped atop her head and she wore a friendly, bemused expression. We sat in a 12x14 room with no windows. It resembled an old storage closet. Fluorescent ceiling tubes dimly revealed rows of medical journals lining three walls and a foam day bed along the fourth.

Mirta took a deep breath and pushed her glasses up the bridge of her nose. "We've reviewed Melissa's chart. Nutritionally speaking, Melissa is one of the worst cases here. She's very underweight which prevents her from quick recovery when she becomes ill. Her physical growth has been stunted and that will become more apparent when she reaches adulthood." She paused and took another breath. "Melissa could use a week in a private wing of a hospital. If you can get her to Miami, we could give her a 24-hour IV, no problem and I would donate my services." She smiled. "Bring her to Disneyland and she'll want to move to the U.S."

It was Ugly Truth Time. All I could do was nod my head and take a few deep, shaky breaths. I'd become accustomed to thinking Melissa was "doing fine," just as Reina had told me in November. Somehow she'd gotten worse or maybe I'd dozed when I should have been on guard. I tried to ignore the noise of fear in my head and give all my attention to Mirta and Celina.

They held a brief discussion about feeding Melissa through a nasal tube and concluded this would be the best course of treatment. Celina left the room briefly and returned with mom and child. We gathered around a heavy table covered in brown plastic, the kind with a cheap wood grain pattern. I sat to the side between Gloria and Celina. Mirta was directly across from Melissa. There were a few opening beats of silence, then Mirta asked a series of questions about Melissa's daily eating habits. Celina weighed Melissa, measured her height, tape-measured her bicep and measured something with a caliper. I watched everything keenly, taking notes and wondering when the hammer would drop.

Melissa seemed to enjoy the experience. She listened thoughtfully to every question and was pleasant in her answers. Gloria offered useful details about Melissa's diet but mostly sat in silence, watching with worried eyes.

After Melissa's average daily caloric intake was calculated and announced by Celina, there was a pause like the silence between movements in a concerto. Then Mirta leaned forward and gave Melissa an earful about eating more food, getting more calories and taking her enzymes. Tag-team style, she and Celina described types of high-calorie, high-fat food and the amounts Melissa would have to eat daily. They made their points respectfully but in such a take-no-prisoners manner that everyone in the room sat frozen. I peeked at Melissa, frozen-eyed. Without warning, she pushed up from her chair and squeezed herself between Gloria and the back of her chair, digging her face into her mother's back. I felt a surge of satisfaction that Melissa's defenses had been pierced. She could use a dose of hard truth.

I looked at Mirta and Celina, who continued as if nothing had happened. Now speaking directly to Gloria, they described the best ways to prepare different foods for Melissa, easy to digest and maximally nutritious. Gloria's mouth widened in a show of surprise and perhaps, protest. "I've always been told to avoid high-calorie, high fat food!"

Mirta was curt. "That's wrong."

The nurse named Inez entered. She hooked up a little breathing apparatus to Melissa and measured her exhale. She took out another piece of equipment designed to analyze sputum. Melissa labored to take a series of deep breaths, which wheezed and crackled. Her face tightened and turned a dark color. She cleared her throat and spit into a jar held by Inez. The heavy breathing must have broken Melissa's emotional defenses for she burst into tears and began to cough uncontrollably. Gloria stood up and led Melissa from the room.

Gloria, looking shaken, returned with Reina a few minutes later. Dr. Gonzalez listened to Mirta's observations then said she'd put Melissa on steroids, for her lung infection, and if that did not produce results, she would hospitalize her. Gloria waited until Reina finished then spoke.

"Melissa has the idea that she's going to die."

"Not now, not yet!"

Gloria changed the subject "None of her friends know that she has CF, but one father refuses to let his children have anything to do with her. Getting her to take enzymes at school is impossible."

Mirta responded. "As long as Melissa keeps her CF a secret, her denial to herself and to her mother retains its grip." The five of us brainstormed how Melissa could tell a friend or a teacher, maybe come to a group for CF teens at the hospital.

Gloria stepped out and returned with Melissa, face puffy and eyes red. They took their chairs at the table. Mirta brought out a nutrition chart, showing where Melissa's nutritional levels fell compared to most kids. She made little jokes in Spanish, too subtle for me to understand. Melissa began to giggle, then laugh. Mirta stood up and walked around the table with her arms outstretched, as if to hug Melissa. But Melissa, now crying or laughing, or maybe both, jumped up, pulled open the door, and ran from the room. Mirta grabbed a little instant camera and chased her down the hall. The rest of us moved to the door but Gloria, still seated, began to talk. Apropo of nothing we had discussed, she described Melissa's lack of appreciation for all the sacrifices she'd made and the difficulties she faced. The three of us listened but what could we say? Reina spoke. "Hang tough, Gloria. She's a tiger."

We looked down the hall to see Mirta pleading to take Melissa's photo. Melissa was having none of it and was, once more, fully in tears. Mirta stood up, and walking towards us, shrugged. "She thinks she's ugly."

When Melissa rejoined the group, everyone was talking and saying their goodbyes. I squatted in front of Melissa. Her eyes briefly touched mine. "I'm leaving on Saturday. I love you……" She turned and raced back down the hall.

*****

Mirta, Celina, Inez and sometimes Reina and me, met with children and parents continuously that day. It was only the beginning of a busy week of appointments. After Melissa's appointment, she and Gloria returned to Esparza. Mirta and I composed a letter to all the parents urging them to stay active with their children's nutrition and to inform the hospital staff if they were unable to afford the necessary foodstuffs. Reina and I drafted a thank you to McNeil Pharmaceutical on her behalf and a separate letter from the parents. We sent an appreciative fax to Dr. Robert Beall at the CF Foundation.

Once home, I would send Dr. Beall my own letter.

> *On behalf of everyone involved with cystic fibrosis in Costa Rica I want to again thank you for the Cystic Fibrosis Foundation's support of the recent nutrition project….*
>
> *Dr. Reina Gonzalez, who was the Costa Rican liaison for our project, is the primary physician for the majority of the country's CF patients…. Her work has been an uphill battle for a variety of reasons. Hospital space and financial resources have been so limited that Dr. Gonzalez has neither a desk, office or secretary. There is no coordinated CF clinic. Out-patient consultations with respiratory therapists, nutritionists, etc., typically require separate appointments. For most Costa Ricans, multiple hospital visits on a quarterly basis are a sever hardship. We found that this fragmented system discourages patients and children alike so that supplemental appointments and follow-up visits go unscheduled or missed altogether….. Case notes go unnoticed and needed referrals for tests are often overlooked. We encountered families who lacked the financial ability to purchase any of the supplements recommended for their child. Here is a summary of some of our week's activities.*

Mirta Rios conducted a nutrition class for parents and their children who have CF. This was the largest CF meeting ever held in Costa Rica. Following the instructional segment of the class, a letter was drafted and signed by the parents urging McNeil Pharmaceutical to step up their efforts to make Pancrease available in their country.

Mirta delivered a lecture to 35 physicians, interns and other hospital staff. Complete with slides and research summaries, the lecture provided a through medical analysis of CF's nutritional effects on the body and why nutritional consultation is necessary.

Mirta and I had several lengthy and profitable meetings with hospital administrators and clinicians. We were told that the hospital would begin purchasing Pancrease once it becomes approved. At a second meeting, we discussed the nuts and bolts of setting up a multi-disciplinary clinic with Dr. Oscar Castro Armas, Chief of Pharmacological Services. The outlook for such a clinic, to offset the need for multiple appointments over the course of several weeks is promising.

We arranged contacts with local sale representatives of Vitamin K, water-soluble vitamins and nutritional products such as Ensure.

More than 20 children, some currently hospitalized, received team consultations which one or more parent attended. These meetings lasted from 1-2 hours. Individual physical assessments were performed on each child and enzyme usage, caloric intake, diets, etc. were reviewed. Growth histories were charted and specific recommendations and nutritional goals were set. When it was determined that poverty was an obstacle to the purchase of food, vitamins and/or supplements, referrals to social workers were made. For three pre-adolescents facing CF-related social problems, a child psychologist at the hospital agreed to conduct a support group… In every instance, modifications were introduced to each child's daily regimen and without a doubt, these children's live have been significantly affected and the general state of CF patient care in Costa Rica impacted in a substantial way…….

Best regards,

Olin Dodson

On my last full day in Costa Rica, shortly before sunrise, an earthquake rocked the city for about twenty seconds. Two aftershocks rolled through around noon. I was dining in the hospital cantina when the room began to sway. The ceiling fixtures circled ominously. The lunch crowd grew silent until the walls' shifting sandpaper sounds came to an end. I was already at the stairwell, trying not to look panicked.

Mirta and I had one final conversation. I hugged her and told her how much I appreciated the way she had given the children and parents such clear instructions and, more importantly, hope. She gave me an angular look.

"Don't you think I feel like crying sometimes?"

I took a walk with Reina through a private children's ward, hidden away in a wing I'd never seen. The hallway was serene and decorated with colorful murals. "Reina, a trip to the States for my daughter seems no more than a distant possibility. Her life is in your hands."

"Olin, you have done more in three months than we did in fourteen years. We still need more medicines and equipment. But you know I'll do everything I possibly can."

* * * * *

I left San Jose the following day, continually replaying memories of the nutrition project. Many of the twenty families who came to the consultations lived in great poverty and I knew would struggle to purchase the essential vitamins and proper foods for their children, whether they had cystic fibrosis or not. Every child I met touched my heart and I worried for them. But I had to think that they were better off because of what Mirta had taught them, their parents and the hospital staff.

Melissa was in Gloria's hands now, even more than in Reina's. I had done all I could do — at least, until my next idea came along. As for Gloria and me, I couldn't be sure that I was any closer to "winning" her. I hoped that, for a brief time, she felt a little less alone as a parent. And Melissa? I knocked but she never came to the door.

* * * * *

The sparkling, new air-conditioned airporter, the biggest, heaviest bus I'd ever seen, neared San Jose International. Rather absent-mindedly I stood up and, with my foot, pushed my luggage across the aisle towards the steps leading down to the back exit. I didn't anticipate the driver making a sudden sweeping left turn into the airport access lane. The centrifugal force threw me violently over the luggage at my feet, head first into the stairwell. My bags followed me and propped my body in a vertical position, my face mashed into the dirty bottom step against the door, arms pinned beneath me, legs floating straight above. I couldn't move. The bus stopped and two men pulled away my bags and holding my legs, tipped me slowly towards them until they could pull my upper body out of the stairwell. I felt the wetness of blood on my forehead as I straightened up. A crowd of people stared at me with breathless concern, but I knew I was ok. I had suffered a public embarrassment, but nothing worse than I experienced every day with Melissa. For the first time in two weeks, I laughed. And everyone joined me.

20. About Time—September, 1991-January, 1992

Autumn is a spectacular season in the wine country of northern California. The fog mostly retreats to a winter resting place in the Pacific while overland, cool breezes mingle with the warmth of the sun. West of the river and the old railway station, Petaluma's big oaks rattle their mustard and maroon leaves.

I carried my grey Schwinn 10-speed down the front stairs and shifted my day pack until the water bottle and snacks lay flat against my back. I jumped onto the seat and coasted down Cochrane Way, waiting until I hit the corner of I Street, checking the cross traffic before I pressed my shoes into the toe clips. I turned left and wound through the neighborhoods, angling progressively westward, until I reached Western Avenue. The loud shift of gears signalled the familiar, reassuring climb up the hill.

This was another ritual during my years in Petaluma: solitary meditative rides into the countryside. Several miles on, with muscles oiled and breathing eased, boundless ideas and images entered my mind. Negative thoughts would glide by like the landscape, arriving, disappearing, arriving, disappearing, as if linked to the rhythm of the bicycle chain.

I arrived at the crest of the hills west of town to find my initial distant view of the ocean sky. Even in October and November, a line of fog could surprise, but more often there was a coal-blue emptiness in the distance, as there was today. It told me that Tomales and Pt. Reyes Station near the coast were dry and pleasant.

As I biked, memories of dreams often floated to the surface of my awareness. The tree bows of my marital bed dream returned one lyrical night. Another time I was in a hospital taking a sputum test and I began to hack, just like Melissa.

Melissa appeared in one dream.

> *She and I are riding a flat river boat, like the night ferry I took from El Salvador to Nicaragua. We're on a long bench, like the one on which I fell asleep that moonlit night in 1978. Melissa crawls along the back of the bench, like a cat. She flops onto the bench and says, in Spanish, "I'm having a good time."*

I regretted waking up.

Several miles outside town, hills and gullies of golden grass, manzanitas and live oaks were dry and dusty. Bodega Avenue turned into Spring Hill Road and my body grew accustomed to straining briefly then relaxing as I hit a series of rises alternating with short straightaways. This stretch of road was always a reward, even with its fruity waft of cow pies.

The most powerful dream that autumn featured my first love, Barbara Johnson, a sparkling-eyed California brunette. The summer of my nineteenth year, I'd taken a job as assistant crew chief at a Colorado dude ranch where Barb worked in the laundry. Our connection was instantaneous and she, me and our clothes were always extra clean and nice smelling. Over the next two years, Barb and I corresponded, talked by phone, traded visits, then agreed that, upon college graduation, I would move from the east coast to Berkeley, near her home. A prolonged silence on her end surprised me during the spring of my senior year. After many failed attempts to reach her by phone, it took me several frantic days to track down her parents. They told me Barb had suffered a nervous breakdown several weeks earlier while sitting at their kitchen table. Her mother remained distressed in spite of the fact that Barb seemed to be fully, or nearly, recovered. She had lost out on an entire semester at college, but sounded fine to me when we finally managed to talk.

I knew nothing about serious emotional problems so a re-evaluation of my decision to move across the country never entered my mind. When we met again after my drive across the country, it took about one second to see that her medication had a near knockout effect, making her eyes and speech fuzzy, like she'd just awakened from a deep sleep. I had my first inkling that maybe love couldn't conquer all.

In the fall of that year, there was a second episode. We were "taking a break" from each other at the time so I was unaware that Barb had been committed to Herrick, Berkeley's all-purpose city hospital. Late one evening, she somehow escaped from the locked psych ward and walked across town. She appeared at my north campus apartment door, barefoot and wearing just her hospital gown. She outlined her plan to hitchhike to Washington State and asked me to drive her to Highway 101 near the town of Novato in Marin County. I persuaded her to return to her parents' home in Orinda.

A day or two later, sitting with Barbara in her parent's living room, I discovered the destructive effect of her electro-shock treatments at Herrick. I mentioned a funny incident we had shared in Colorado. Barbara looked at me blankly. "I don't remember that." Stunned, speechless, I stared at her. She began to cry. "I really don't remember much about you." We tried to rebuild our relationship for a time, but falling in love with a stranger was beyond our reach. We drifted slowly, feebly, apart. In the dream

> *I learn that Barbara has passed away from a disease, possibly AIDS. I walk into the crowded mortuary where the memorial is being held. There is a long table at the front. On it sits a Bible. I open it. In the back pages are inscriptions, funny ones, from high school friends, like you find in a yearbook. I turn to the beginning of the book and find a series of photos of*

> *us at the beach. One shows us nuzzling.*

Tears awakened me briefly before I fell back and returned to the dream, in the same room as before.

> *Barbara walks through the door into the gathering, having returned from a conference of some sort. She tells us that a doctor there announced that a cure (for AIDS? for CF?) had been developed, effective in 80% to 90% of the cases. The room bursts into sounds of joy.*

The dreams of a playful Melissa and a resurrected Barbara were way out of sync with my day time experience. I would have liked to know where they originated.

I turned left off onto the Tomales road and coasted past the Coast Guard Academy. The buildings always appeared deserted, miles from any coast to guard. Thoughts arose about recent mail and faxes. I had adopted the habit of regularly sending cards and checks to Gloria and Melissa, including five faxes in two months. I had written Gloria an impassioned letter with eight questions about Melissa's progress. I reminded her to contact Maritza about the CF children's group.

Two months after I left San Jose, Gloria mailed her first letter, a two-pager, apologizing for being too busy and too tired to write. She said that Melissa was taking her vitamins and supplements and would be voluntarily checking into the hospital sometime later in the month. She thanked me for writing and caring and lamented the fact that I was too far away to talk to regularly. She asked for 3,000 *colónes* so Melissa could take a tile painting class. Melissa did not contribute anything to the letter. At the end, Gloria wrote, "Melissa sends greetings." She was being nice.

I sent enough money to cover the tile class and Melissa's thirteenth birthday. My birthday card carried love wishes from Laura and her parents. I reminded Melissa that I was there to support her in any way I could and I was happy to be her father. I expressed pride in her for choosing to go to the hospital. My negative feelings about her snubs were not included. My disappointment was not hers to hear. I spent less time looking at the early photos of her smiling. They made me miserable.

Bending low, I leaned into the pedals and my thighs burned with lactic acid. Passing solemn redwoods and eucalyptus, there was only silence apart from the spurring of the bike chain and the roll of tires on the pavement. I sat up on the seat to relieve my back and felt the sweat on my face drying in the rush of air. Clouds, fuzzy with moisture, streamed across the silver sky.

There had been a flurry of mail with Reina and Dr. Beall. I had sent Reina several faxes, a mixture of cheerleading and questions. Dr. Beall responded generously to my update on the project. He wrote that the CF Foundation was developing a generic brand of Ensure which he hoped would be made available in Costa Rica. A second letter mentioned a pancreatic drug being tested. Both products would be much cheaper than Pancrease and Ensure. I passed along this news to Reina who made arrangements to fly to Dallas for a CF conference and to see Dr. Beall.

Reina's response angered me. She wrote extensively about the parents group, and the ongoing problems getting Pancrease into Costa Rica, her surprise at not hearing from Mirta, and Maritza's being on vacation. There was but one line about Melissa, describing her unchanged condition. I wanted to scream, "Is that all you can say??!! Did I fail to convey to you my concern for my daughter?? Have you forgotten our walk and the promise you made??

In my return fax, I tried to soft-pedal my fury.

> *I was upset that there has been no change in Melissa's condition. I was under the impression that you were going to admit her into the hospital if she did not improve. I do not understand why this did not happen. Please write soon and tell me what your plan is for Melissa. I will not sleep well until I hear from you....*

I reached an area several miles shy of Tomales where I dismounted in the shade of a eucalyptus tree. The change in my brain chemistry and the gradual downshift of my heartbeat were pleasing. I sat with my back to the tree and loosened my shoes. Here, a peanut butter and jelly sandwich with water was a delicious meal. Here, Costa Rican dramas seemed far away and life was good.

However, life was not good for many people and I seemed to notice them everywhere, especially Latinos. One evening I sat in my office, reading and waiting for my next client. The door was slightly ajar and the hallway was dead still. So I was startled by a little girl who peeked her head in the door. She was six maybe, a small six. She had brown hair and tan skin, and a faint sheen of grime on her face.

"I need to use the bathroom." She spoke in clear English and without apology.

I gave her the warmest smile I owned. "Sure, I'll show you. It's down the hall. The door is locked but I'll unlock it for you."

The girl, tiny at my side, seemed totally comfortable walking beside me. I wondered what she was doing here on the second floor. Perhaps her parents were in another part of the building. I looked at her faded shorts and t-shirt and scruffy sandals.

I smiled again and chose my friendliest tone. "So, what are you doing here?"

She looked up at me and giggled. "We came to get food." She giggled again and broke my heart. "We don't have any food."

We arrived at the women's room. I unlocked the door and, hiding my true feelings, said a cheerful goodbye. The bathroom door clicked shut and an overwhelming sadness pinned me against the wall. I wanted the girl to never lack food—or nice clothes—or anything. Puzzling over where I might find her parents, I looked up to see my client walking down the hall. I followed him to my office.

*****

In mid-December, praying that the Christmas season would soften Melissa enough to write me, I exchanged cards with the Stenzel twins from Stanford.

Dear Ana and Isa–

...I just finished re-reading your book and was moved all over again by your spirit and courage. I hope all goes well for you in your health, academic pursuits and relationships...I should enclose a local newspaper article which describes a little of what has been going on in my world.... On the trip which the article describes I tried to have a child psychologist at the hospital organize a support group for the pre-adolescents with CF. Since then I've learned that an initial meeting was held with two girls, including my daughter. For the first time each got to meet another girl their age with CF... You both inspired me to create this opportunity for Melissa and the other girl. The doctor told me by phone that Melissa is gaining weight and participating in her treatment more fully....

I hope we can see each other again sometime soon....

Olin Dodson

It wasn't long before I received their response.

Dear Mr. Dodson,

Thank you so much for your letter and the interesting article... It's funny to me, how people without CF always tell people with CF how "strong and courageous" we are. It sounds to me that generous and loving people like you, without CF, are just as strong and courageous. I'm glad you enjoyed our booklet and please let me know if I can ever do anything....

All my love and best wishes,

Anabel

Mr. Dodson,

Thank you so much for your enlightening letter! Sometimes I get so caught up in petty complaints about Kaiser and their medical services, yet when I hear about the situation in Costa Rica (no Pancrease!), I feel so fortunate to live here in this day and age. Although CF has its obvious drawbacks, we are very lucky to have CF affect our lives today. Let's all pray that 1992 brings further advances in CF research to give us more hope for the future...Next quarter I will be trying the new DNAse drug at Kaiser in Oakland. The drug seems very promising and I really hope it works well for me...

Good luck in the upcoming year. Hope your daughter continues to gain weight and stay healthy.

With lots of love,

Isa

For two girls whose lives had been interrupted with chronic health problems, Ana and Isa were full of optimism and love. They seemed to know something I didn't.

*****

Christmas cards from Costa Rica arrived in early January, first from Merilyn's family, then a few days later from Gloria. Inside Gloria's were the words, *"Feliz Navidad,"* and, underneath, "From Melissa and Gloria," in Gloria's handwriting. Nothing more. My eyes closed tight in pain, as if a soup can lid had cut my heart.

Grudgingly, bitterly, I conceded Melissa's implied point, which she had made repeatedly. She was not interested in communicating or interacting. There would be no playing on the beach with a little girl thrilled to find her dad and embraced in his overflowing love for the rest of her life, however brief. We were still father and daughter in biological name only. Whatever the explanation for her behavior, this was not the dream I had held and caressed for two years. My arms were empty, my heart crying, my spirit drained, as Melissa went about her life, seemingly unmoved.

Biking in the hills one morning, I remembered a bite-size dream about a dog, a blue healer, chomping down on my hand just enough to hold but not hurt me. The image, I concluded, was a visual joke about being caught in the jaws of unconditional, disillusioned love. I could not escape a moaning, bereft feeling each time I thought about Melissa.

I had utilized my entire "Love Thyself" arsenal to neutralize the misery. I leaned on friends and a therapist. I practiced acceptance and patience. I reminded myself of the grand gulf in geography, language, and culture. I listened to music, wrote in my journal. I diverted myself in charitable acts. But the bleeding never stopped or even coagulated, any more than Melissa's lungs were cured by her hospital stays. Merilyn's words about Melissa's love for me felt like the pathetic wish of an onlooker with poor vision.

My need for acceptance and understanding kicked in and with it a new approach designed to end the ambiguity. Although I could not imagine a life without the agony of a relationship with Melissa, the rejection was killing me. I decided to offer her and her mom the option of escorting me out the door.

Part Three
1992-1993

21. Brush Strokes—January-July, 1992

No brush stroke is in vain.
—Isabel Allende

Dear Melissa and Gloria,

I received your Christmas card today, a happy and sad occasion.

I'm happy naturally that you sent me such a beautiful card. My sadness....well it requires more of an explanation. I don't know exactly how to say this. I feel more and more that you do not want me to be very much in your lives. I have tried to do everything that I can think of to demonstrate that I care for both of you and that I would like to be an active part of your lives.

And yet most of the time I feel that you are not interested in a relationship where we take time for each other, share our thoughts and feelings, share our worlds actually-and gradually know each other. I feel sad to say this. And this is why it was difficult when I opened your Christmas card. With only your signatures and nothing more at the bottom, I felt almost like a stranger.

I have tried to understand and accept that each of us is different and could want different things from the relationship, but it is very hard not to feel rejected, even discouraged. I am certain that you have reasons for being so silent and writing so little. Maybe you want more also and you don't express it, I cannot say. It does seem that you do not want what I describe as a more active relationship.

I still love both of you and your family. I will still study Spanish, send money every month, write you and do what I can medically for Melissa.

Perhaps I have misinterpreted you and am wrong in my impressions. Still I believe it is better to be wrong than to keep my impressions to myself.

I hope all is well for you both.

Love,

Olin

I copied the letter in Spanish, softening my question about whether they wanted me in their lives. I carried it to the post office with only a faint hope that they would respond. I dropped it into the mail box thinking that the dream was over. I wondered if Melissa, having met me, had moved on to other goals. Did she dream? She certainly had little reason to think that her future held much more than a turnstile of breathing problems and hospital admissions. If she had fantasies of college or marriage or children, did she suddenly stop and say to herself, "Get serious. I won't live that long."

I doubted that Melissa put much time into dreaming of a cure for cystic fibrosis, as Anabel and Isabel did. I took them to dinner in Palo Alto in January, where they enthusiastically described joining a clinical trial for something called DNAse. It was one of a new type of experimental genetic inhalants which were all the rage for the future of CF treatment. Every stride forward with gene therapy gave cystics and their families great hope as well as dread of disappointment. Ana and Isa had signed up for the experiment scheduled to begin in April. They were full of hope.

My new girlfriend, Ahria, took me to an all-day workshop in Oakland with Steven Levine, one of the recent generation of spiritual teachers sprouting up around the Bay Area and affirming the suffering nature of life. Ahria and I had met one weekend at Wilbur Hot Springs while I was flirting with her friend. Our relationship had developed quickly. We sat in front of an elevated stage on a carpet brought by six people Ahria shared a house with. Steven stood and spoke while his ill wife Andrea sat by his side, in meditation. His powerful presence and genuineness supported the strength of his message about compassion. He spoke persuasively about the importance of cultivating a soft heart, one which dares to feel pain and the suffering of others. One of his remarks stood out: "The enemy is lovelessness." It was a day of meditation on Steven's thoughts. I came away with the idea that to merely stand in a world of hurt, as I was, no running, no fixing, was something of value.

I had to look at my motives for "saving" Melissa. Was it more important for me to love her and be with her, as opposed to pressuring her to be a good patient? What was the best approach to winning her heart? My answer changed from day to day.

* * * * *

After their Christmas card, it was over three months before I heard from Gloria. She mailed a letter in March which ended up in the international postal system's spin cycle until it finally popped up in my mail box in late April. The letter contained no response to my ambiguous offer to leave them alone. It relieved me to know that my suffering would not end. The big news was that Melissa had added a couple of kilos in weight. "For me," Gloria wrote, "it's like [I won] the lottery." She went on to say that they had received my checks and spent the money on school shoes and a *"coqueta,"* (a dressing table) for Melissa. Melissa contributed nothing to the letter.

My spirits were bolstered when my long-time friend from Seattle, Sharon Felton, connected me to the family of one of her friends who were planning to vacation in Costa Rica. They agreed to take a box of Pancrease to Esparza. This time I managed to obtain a newer, stronger Pancrease, MT16.

Dear Gloria and Melissa,

I hope everything goes well for you. I think of you often. By the time you read this Senor and Senora Felps may have visited you. When they left California they were not sure they would be able to come to Esparza with the Pancrease. But I hope so. Also I hope the camera they brought works perfectly. I had it repaired but I did not try it out.

The Pancrease MT16 is stronger than the other pills. One pill is the same as 4 of the others. So Melissa should perhaps only take half of the new pills each time she usually takes one. Whatever she does, she should not chew the little granules. See how this works and also consult with Dr. Gonzalez.

I was happy to learn that Melissa had gained weight. I hope she was able to avoid spending hospital during her school break. There is very exciting news about gene therapy. I am sending you an article from the San Francisco newspaper. It is too complicated for me to translate but I hope there is someone in Esparza who can, or take it to Dr. Gonzalez.

There is not much change in my life since my last letter but I have been hired to teach three classes for adults in May, which I am very enthusiastic about. Spring has arrived here the weather is warm and sunny and everyone is happier. Many people are becoming hopeful that President Bush will <u>not</u> win the election in November.

So much for now. Please give my best wishes to Merilyn and her family, and write soon.

Love,

Olin

Another letter from Costa Rica arrived in May. My heart rose over Melissa's name typed in the upper corner of the envelope then dropped when I found only Gloria's writing inside. My disappointment grew stronger as I read the letter.

...Melissa had a crisis and remains very thin. Last month I took her to see the doctor. I received the check in April and a few days later the camera and the medicine. Thank you for everything for Melissa. Last month Rosti passed away. Melissa has been crying a lot. She had him since he was two months old...You know at times I can't sleep because I worry so much about her.

Olin, write me and tell me about Laura and her family.

Best wishes,

Gloria

I tossed the letter on the kitchen table in frustration. With Melissa's health, it was always two steps forward, two steps back. What bugged me more was how little Gloria passed along about Melissa's current condition. It was almost impossible to imagine her being any less communicative or helpful. I faxed Reina my questions. How is Melissa? Can you identify other needs I can help with? Did the Vitamin K and E help her? Is Pancrease available? Did you receive the enzymes and supplements from the CF Foundation?

I busied myself with CF-related activities in my spare time. Helen and I sponsored more CF parents meetings. I clipped out an article from the SF Chronicle about a Bay Area woman race car driver with CF. Perhaps Melissa would meet her someday.

"In the Absence of Angels" was my new bedtime reading. Written by Elisabeth Glaser, founder of the Pediatric AIDS Foundation, the memoir described how the author and her newborn infant had contracted AIDS through a blood transfusion received during delivery. At age 44, I had never experienced the death of someone close to me, much less a child. The book provided a horrific glimpse of what the future might hold. One image, in particular, refused to leave me alone. After their child died of AIDS, Elisabeth and her husband, Paul, would lay in bed at night, their backs to each other, separately dying in grief.

*****

Dear Melissa,

I hope everything goes well in your life. I was sorry to hear about Rosti. I know you loved him very much.

I hope you are enjoying school this year. I recently finished a psychology class which was very interesting!

I am looking forward to two weeks of vacation in June when my girlfriend and I will travel to Hawaii.

Everyone in my family is fine and sends their greetings.

Write when you can.

Love,

Your Dad

In late June, another communication from Laura arrived in the mail. She enclosed a letter she'd received from Gloria. It was nearly identical to my own letter from Gloria, except for a remark about me and news that Melissa had a new puppy

Laura-

....I wrote Olin in March. I'm writing a lot because at times I feel very depressed. You understand that it's not easy to see children that enjoy good health while Melissa languishes.

Olin does not understand because he's always far away, he's never seen

Melissa very sick...

Gloria

I dismissed her comment about me and moved on to Laura's letter.

Happy Easter and Happy Spring, Olin–

Spring is slowly but surely approaching the Chicago area. Amidst the rain and clouds, we watched some flowers bloom and birds build their nests this weekend. My body and soul are ready for nice weather. I guess one of my favorite aspects of this time of year is the feelings of hope, rebirth and just being alive.

My mother passed on your feelings of joy about the woman in your life. I'm interested in knowing more about your relationship with her and so hope that things are going well. My mother also relayed your feelings of frustration with Gloria and Melissa. I too am pretty fed up and can't imagine what <u>*you're*</u> *feeling. You've invested your heart into developing a relationship with them and have received so little in return. It's not only hurtful and frustrating but confusing as well. I share your feelings of desperation and uncertainty. I wish there was some way to get inside both of them and know what they're feeling and thinking.*

I've written them a letter and in broken and grammatically incorrect Spanish have expressed the following. I explained that we all think of them constantly and are very worried because no one has heard from them in a long time. I expressed our need to hear something about their lives–primarily, how they are! I also refreshed their memories about our long and emotional search for you, Melissa's father. I reminded them of our happiness and hopes when we found you. I explained that you and I both believed that they wanted to form some type of relationship with you but that they have done very little in the way of building a relationship. I shared all of our feelings of concern confusion and hurt. I specifically pointed out that you are a person with feelings and you have doubts and wishes and are very confused. I explained how you care so much and how difficult it is for you to continue this "manera de comunicacion." I begged of them to please write either you or me and explain what they are thinking and feeling. I also asked them to let us know if they have been receiving your letters and if Melissa needs more medicine. I explained a number of times that we are concerned and confused and not mad. We just want to hear from them and know that they are okay. I hope that this all makes some sense to you and more importantly I hope the letter makes some sense to Gloria and Melissa. This is a confusing situation for all of us and I imagine that you are especially feeling hurt and frustrated. Hopefully I will hear from them soon but, if not, I will follow up on this letter. You are an incredible person Olin and they are so blessed to have found you. I hope so much that time and understanding will enhance your relationship with your daughter.

Well, I've sent the letter and I hope for the best. We'll be in touch soon!

Take care!

Laura

*****

One morning at a downtown coffee shop, a guy strolled in looking familiar. It was John Strong, a member of the local Rotary International, the service organization which regularly sponsored assistance projects in Central America. His photo had appeared in a local newspaper article about his volunteer work. Photo and article travelled around in my back seat until it turned yellow. I had stopped by his office once but he was out.

John listened to my description of the nutrition project and the needs of the CF kids in Costa Rica. Remembering Costa Rica has a Rotary chapter in San Jose, he invited me to collect some information for an idea I created on the spot: Nutrition Project #2.

I rushed home and composed a fax to Reina, although she'd never responded to my earlier one. I asked her for a list of the CF clinic's needs for a letter to John Strong. I threw in a few questions about Melissa's health and requested an immediate answer. Even if I couldn't have a relationship with Melissa, I could still try to save her life.

Melissa and Gloria visited me in a dream, speaking in both Spanish and English. Just before I awoke, I was tickling Melissa's feet, both of us shrieking with laughter. If only Melissa and I could spend our days in a world such as that.

Dear Gloria and Melissa,

Thanks for your card. I hope when you receive this card, it finds you happy and in good health. I apologize for not writing sooner. The woman who helped me with Spanish translation moved away. Fortunately a woman from Guadalajara moved next door with her husband. She helps me with my Spanish.

...I sent you a newspaper article about a young woman who has CF and races cars for a living. I hope you enjoy her story.

Take care, I think about you all every day.

Write!

Love to you and your family,

Olin

I was invited to two parties on Sunday, July 19. I drove first to the home of Pete, my real-estate friend, for his birthday barbeque. Ahria had to work, so I went solo. I was in a buoyant mood. My practice had grown and I was close to paying off one of my student loans. When I arrived at the house, Pete shocked me by handing over a lengthy fax which he had just received. It was written in Spanish, an ominous reminder of Gloria's February fax. My heart thumped with anxiety. Seeing Reina's name at the bottom, I wondered why it had taken her weeks to respond and moved into a side room to study the message.

> *Dear Olin,*
>
> *First of all I would like to tell you that I had received recently a letter from you requesting a letter requesting the health status of Melissa. Unfortunately for a long time I do not follow her.*

Help me out, Reina! Who *does* follow her?

> *Recently, she was admitted to the hospital because of an exacerbation of her lung disease. . During her stay I was out of town, but I reviewed her chart and her last exams, including chest x-rays. My feeling is that the disease has been progressing and her prognosis is not good.*

I read the ugly words again. When did her prognosis go bad? I thought she had gained ten pounds. Confusion turned to a sick feeling.

> *I talked to the psychologist and she told me that she does not come to the appointments. Also her nutritional status is not good. As you know it is important in this disease to come to the clinical appointments and follow the instructions. I told the mother that it is important that she comes to the appointments, if she wants other doctor to follow her I will help her, because the most important thing is to be in consultation with our team. I think you have to help her in this matter.*

"I have to help her"? Reina understood nothing.

> *In regards of your request in your recent fax I think that the Rotary International could help us a lot, would you please let me know his address and fax number in order to…*

Where was Gloria when Melissa needed to keep appointments? This shocking news began to sink in as I read on. A weight crushed my chest until I couldn't feel, lost the desire to feel. I tumbled down to a place where the darkness welcomed me and everything was futile and nonsense and hopeless and I wanted to fall further and further into numbness and blackness, unmoving, unawake.

> *In regards to your questions: At present we have Pancrease available. The CCSS finally agreed to help us in this matter. But I think this will not be forever and as you know the policies change with different governments…*
>
> *With regards to antibiotics, we have available very good ones but at present not in our Social System. Tobramycin is a very good antibiotic and if we could have this available it would be a lot of help… Also any supplements like Ensure would be very welcome. In Costa Rica we have*

Ensure but it is very expensive for us to buy. Also we need urgently the influenza vaccine, not all of our patients are vaccinated with this vaccine and it is very important that all of our patients get it.....

I am sorry not helping a lot with Melissa. I am very worried about her health and I think it is a priority for you to help.

Best regards,

Reina

I dialed Ahria's number and peered through the blinds at the partygoers on the patio. They were worlds away. Ahria agreed to come to my house in the morning. I apologized to Pete and his wife and crept to my car.

Well before the sun went down, I lay in bed, dispirited, almost catatonic. Angry at Gloria who seemed to have given up on getting Melissa regular treatment. Depressed about Melissa's resistance to the doctor visits. Repulsed by my own helplessness.

My face felt as if it had been in the same knot for about six hours. I stared at the ceiling and called to God. My heart was breaking.

"Why were Melissa and I brought together if they are going to give up?" It all seemed pointless. "I don't understand. I just don't understand," I repeated to the room's shadows, until tears ran down my cheeks and eventually brought on sleep.

The next morning, fueled with anger, I threw on some clothes and headed downtown for breakfast. I stomped down the street like a guy with untreated Tourette's, barking "Fuck it!"

Then I decided to call Merilyn.

22. Gifts—July-September, 1992

Ahria drove up from Mill Valley the next morning to join me and Tina, the young Mexican woman who lived next door. A tingling breeze off the Pacific accompanied her through the front door into the living room where we gathered around the phone.

I dialed Ascension's number as Tina held the phone next to her ear. I had no clear plan in mind, just desperately needed to hear an understanding voice, hopefully some reassurance from Merilyn or her parents.

I chewed on a fingernail like it was an offering to heaven for no bad news about Melissa's health. Sitting next to Tina, I heard several faint, lonely phone rings. They stopped and there was a muffled voice. Tina identified herself, then listened to the other speaker. She whispered to me, "It's Merilyn." I smiled. Through Tina, Merilyn and I repeated the ritual greeting: How are you? Good, thanks to God. And you? Good. How is your family? Good. And yours? Good.

Tina moved the phone away from her mouth. "Melissa is there. Would you like to speak to her?"

"Melissa is there?"

Tina nodded.

"Yes, of course!"

Ahria grabbed a pen and paper and I took the phone. "Hi, Melissa! It's me, your father. How are you?"

"Fine," she said, politely.

Now what do I say? "Melissa, what's new?"

"We're moving." Her voice was tiny and flat.

Mine was cheerful, inquisitive. "Moving? To where?"

"We're staying in Esparza, just moving to another house."

"Oh, I see. How is school?"

"Good."

How is your health? How are you feeling?"

"Good."

Breathless, my mind fumbling, I gave the phone back to Tina so I could think of more questions without worrying about my Spanish. *Quick, back to the topic of school.*

I fed Tina a question. "What courses are you taking?"

Tina looked puzzled by Melissa's answer. " 'Nothing.' "

I was losing her.

"Have you seen Dr. Gonzalez lately?"

Tina shook her head, telling me there was no reply.

"Tell her I love her and to put Merilyn back on the line."

Tina said, "Melissa?......Melissa?........Melissa?" Melissa had either frozen or put the phone down.

I had been holding my breath. I inhaled and exhaled several times, trying to release the tension that had tightened my entire body.

Merilyn came to the phone and said Melissa didn't want to talk more. I gave Tina the description of Reina's fax. She listened to Merilyn's reply. "She said she will pass along the news to Gloria. Everyone has to speak gently to Gloria because she has a quick temper when anyone talks about Melissa."

Tina frowned. "A spot has appeared on one of Melissa's chest x-rays." My insides tightened as I listened to the rapid cadence of Merilyn's voice in the earpiece. "Merilyn doesn't know what it is. She suggests you ask Reina. She can't talk more freely because Melissa is standing beside her, listening to everything."

I didn't know what to say. I changed the subject to Merilyn's course work at the University and later my work, the Rotary Club and so forth. She asked when I was coming back, it had been almost one year. I wasn't sure. I answered, "Soon, I hope."

We said our good byes. I asked her to pass along my love to her parents, her brother, Marvin, and to Gloria and Melissa, who didn't want to get back on the phone.

Tina placed the phone back in the cradle and I expelled a heavy breath, emotionally spent from the 15-minute adrenalin rush and the new worry about the x-ray. Ahria hugged me.

I paid Tina and she left. Ahria offered to stay around to help me de-brief. We talked through everything we could remember, beginning with Melissa's willingness to talk to me. I wondered if Gloria's absence had anything to do with that. The big topic was the mystery spot on the Melissa's lung. Anger and powerlessness gnawed on me. I would need to fax Reina again, pull more information from her.

Before she said goodbye, Ahria wanted to share her most powerful memory of the phone conversation. She said there had been one moment when the expression of yearning on my face was so intense she had to look away.

*****

I drove to Pt. Reyes National Seashore and parked near the trail head of the Bear Valley trail, a coastal site of extraordinary beauty in all seasons. The groves of towering eucalyptus trees and the mix of silence and sunbeams often gave the area an ancient, fairy tale-like ambience. When there are few hikers, as there were on this day, it's easy to sink into dream worlds.

The trail was wide and easy, rolling through serene glens as it meandered to the ocean. I flipped through my scrapbook of mental images from Costa Rica. Melissa, giggling and swinging her legs at the chicken shack the day we met. Her three kisses and the unabashed glow on her face at the hotel party. Her kiss in the hospital. Her hand cupping my finger as we pressed our faces to the front gate.

My mind created a scene of Merilyn talking to me on the phone. Melissa was leaning on the arm of the chair, listening to every word. I pictured a Melissa no one knew, perhaps not even Merilyn, a girl intrigued by her father, who considered letting go and trusting him. This was the girl who appeared in my dreams at unpredictable moments, the one who held my heart and delivered to me a new life.

I spoke aloud, working things out in the morning's stillness.

—Maybe the frequent trips to San Jose are too much for her.

—Maybe she'd rather spend more of her life at home, half-sick, since she has already spent so much time in the hospital.

—She could be deep in denial or fear.

—Perhaps she sees her path, her destiny, more clearly than anyone gives her credit for.

—She's 14 and if her decisions mean she's departed this life two years from now, so be it. It's her life.

—Melissa has the right to die as she chooses. If that is the decision, Gloria, Merilyn, Melissa's *tios* and I must do the loving thing and help her face her end.

The unexpected thought of releasing her to death when we had barely begun a relationship caused me to double over in sobs and I stumbled off the trail and crumpled in the wet earth behind a fallen tree. My insides heaved in pain until exhaustion set in.

I rolled over and looked up at the canopy of tree branches, like dark tendrils against the sky. Their swaying motion calmed me. Once again I let go of the idea that Melissa should live her life according to my blueprint.

By mid-afternoon a curtain of fog filtered the light over the sweeping shoreline south of Drake's Bay. My back against a boulder, I gazed down upon miles of metallic lines of breakers. The distant, pounding surf was like the heartbeat of a cold universe, one in which my fears were immaterial.

I understood that fatherhood, Melissa's life, my dreams, all of these could end badly.

*****

John Strong and I met in his office to discuss my idea for the Petaluma Rotary to collaborate with the San Jose Rotary. He requested a formal letter he could take to his chapter. The next day I sent him an article about me published in the Santa Rosa Press Democrat with a cover page summarizing the need for medical products which Reina had described in her letter.

*****

Late August. A letter from Gloria. There is no mention of my phone call in mid-July. She said Melissa was doing a little better after receiving a hospital "treatment" in July and had a follow up appointment soon. There was a lung infection. The doctor treated it.

> *Olin, we received the checks for June and July. Many thanks for this help for Melissa. Write soon. It's been many days since we've received anything. I know I haven't written much. At times I am very depressed. I ask God to heal Melissa from this illness. In my mind always are the problems of my little girl. I ask for forgiveness because for me it is not easy to see other children enjoy good health while Melissa is held back by sickness.*
>
> *Greetings from Melissa.*
>
> *Gloria*

Gloria's letter filled me with frustration. I wanted her to be tireless about Melissa's medical care and forget about God healing Melissa. In spite of acknowledging that she was emotionally overwhelmed, I lacked an appreciation that she was reaching out for hope and forgiveness in the only way which made sense.

I had been working on a major letter to Gloria for several weeks and now translated into Spanish, it went out the following day. It was my tears, my scream, my plea, in six pages.

Dear Gloria,

I am sorry that you were not at your brother's house on the day I called. I did not have time to advise you of my call. I only decided to call the day before after I received a fax from Dr. Gonzalez. I was happy to speak to Melissa and Merilyn.

Again I am sorry that you were not present. As I told Merilyn, the doctor is extremely concerned about Melissa. Gloria I know the illness has gone on for a long time and has been very, very difficult for you and Melissa. Like you, I frequently experience sadness, fear, anger, worry and frustration. I feel great when I get positive reports from you and then after news of a setback, I sink into the worst feelings. I know it is harder for you both since cystic fibrosis is something you have to live with every day. I want to say again that I always want to help in any way I can. I feel bad that I cannot do more since I am so far away.

It seems like I spend a lot of time encouraging you to take Melissa to the doctor regularly. Doctor Gonzalez said that Melissa has not been going for her regular check-ups. This makes me very worried if it is true. The only way to stop CF is through nutrition, exercise, medicine, prayer and visits to the doctor. The time to see the doctor is before problems arise, not after. I cannot say this enough. Gloria I wish I could directly help you with all these things because I know it is very hard. You have very little emotional support. It is too much for one person. This is no time to avoid reality. You deserve and need support to fight. We don't want CF to do any more destruction in Melissa's body.

Gloria, I also want to make it clear how it hurts that I cannot be in Melissa's life and yours on a regular basis. I miss seeing her grow and change. I miss helping you to parent her. Sometimes I become very sad thinking that I did not know her when she was a baby or a young girl. CF takes up a lot of my attention but I would still be as involved as I am if she did not have CF. Melissa is someone I am interested in, who I receive happiness from–to see, to hear about and think about. I am afraid she will never feel good or happy or secure knowing her father. I do not like to face it but I fear that I may never be important to either of you when I am so far away. Nevertheless I care. I am affected deeply by both of you. I hope that someday Melissa and I may know each other as you and I are beginning to. Do you talk about these things with each other? What do you say?

There is so much you and I do apart, without discussing it. I am an idealist in certain ways, someone who works to make the world better, who believes the world doesn't have to be just the way it is. Even from a long distance I am trying to do as much as I can. I lay in bed some nights thinking and planning. I go to CF information meetings 80 miles away. I am presently working to convince the local Rotary club to give financial assistance to Hospital de Ninos. I have been organizing and teaching classes for parents of children with chronic illness. I have been invited to lead a discussion at a hospital meeting in San Francisco in December. I am studying a videotape on CF with the idea of putting a Spanish sound track on it. I have been searching for good books which Melissa might enjoy. These projects take hours and days of time. I feel so helpless, but still I am busy as I can be with things that relate to you all. I have even spoken to the company which is going to manufacture the CF gene therapy so it can be available in Costa Rica as soon as possible.

I know Melissa hates going to Dr. Gonzalez. I'm sure I would be angry and resistant if I were her. At the same time we know is essential for her life to have her check-ups. On one hand it is her decision. If she accepts the consequences of infrequent visits: more illness, more damage to her lungs, well, she has the right to take her chances, knowing it is a gamble she cannot win. But if she is avoiding the doctor out of fear or anger, then it is up to you and your family to help her to deal with those feelings.

Whether or not it is true, I <u>guess</u> that you both have anger towards me. It would not surprise me. Perhaps I have been a disappointment to you. And I can imagine that it is difficult for both of you to open up your lives to someone after those 11 years alone. It surprises me a little bit is how stuck things seem. Soon it will be two years since you first contacted me. Two years. Gloria you have become more and more open in your letters. I thank you for that, but truthfully, I wonder if you want Melissa and I to know each other. Apart from health matters you tell me nothing about her. You've never mentioned art school or what she is studying in school. I know nothing about Melissa for this past year and how she is changing. It would be nice to have a recent photo for example and to learn what activities and interests she has presently.

Gloria, you have your hands full and I understand that. And I hope you see that I have all the feelings a father has—love, willingness, openness. You cannot expect me to be invited into your lives and be happy with no details of your lives, no clarity about your feelings, no word of your discussions, no encouragement.

I am trying to be a father the best way I can, but I need your help. You are the central person here. Unless you sincerely allow, actively assist and encourage Melissa to have a relationship with me it will never happen. I know this for a fact. A young person so close to her mother will not risk endangering that relationship. The mother must go to great lengths to assure this child that is it safe. It is important for you to speak honestly to her about your wishes and fears as much as it is necessary for you to get support from others. Of course I too want to hear your concerns and wishes so we can talk about them.

I end now. I hope I have been clear. If not tell me.

I hope you will talk things over with Melissa. Discuss it with your brother and his family.

I write and act from love. This has been a surprising, world-shaking experience for all of us. It really is a miracle, but the story is not finished. It is up to us to decide what we do with it.

My best wishes to Melissa.

Love,

Olin

I knew the letter was strong, more direct than Costa Ricans tend to be. I had tried to cleanse it of my harshest feelings, but bluntness had worked when I demanded that Melissa thank me for visiting her in the hospital. Any strong reaction by Gloria would be better than the soppy kind she usually sent.

* * * * *

In the meantime, along came Merilyn.

Dear Olin,

I trust in God that this finds you and your family enjoying good health. Thank you for calling Meli. A few days ago she was very bad. When they admitted her to the hospital, I went to see her and she had purple fingers for 8 days, a sign that she was not breathing well, so they had oxygen (for her) for several days. I don't want you to worry too much but I know that you are her father and she is as important for you as she is for me.

Please don't stop writing or calling her. I know it is very hard for you that they don't write you, but try to be insistent. Meli is entering a very difficult time of life, emotionally as well as physically and she needs to be surrounded with love and support from the people who love her.

I know that Aunt Gloria is being egotistical with you but I hope you understand her. She's never shared the love of her daughter with anyone and now you are here and she feels threatened and for that reason they don't write you. I don't know if you understand me, please don't tell Auntie I wrote you. I have not written because I thought it was too much involvement in something outside my life but I realized that no, Meli is like a little sister I never had. I love her so much, more than any person I can imagine. If God was my servant I would have healed her, but since he has not done it, it is for a divine purpose.

I find it hard to understand that Meli is sick but at the same time I think: God permits me to share with her a beautiful relationship and while she lives I will be present in her life for whatever she needs me. That makes me smile.

I hope you understand me and that you struggle to achieve the demonstration of the love that she feels for you. I know it is difficult for you to give the most without receiving a little love in exchange but this is what it means at times to be a father, not only do you feel this feeling but also many other fathers love their children, give them life, money, and don't receive anything in exchange. Mothers always give them their love and very few times do they complain that they don't tell them they love them, for this reason theirs is always compared with the love of God.

Greetings to all of your family. And greetings from my family to you.

Hasta pronto,

Merilyn

I sent Merilyn a response as soon as I could get it translated into Spanish.

Dear Merilyn,

Thank you very much for your letter. I was deeply moved by it.

..Like you I do not know the mind of God in this difficult situation, but I try to allow Love to be my guide.

Like you I only want to do what I can. I can endure the pain of the silence from Melissa, but the silence from Gloria is unnecessary. Without her assistance I absolutely cannot determine how to best express my love and concern and to know what is useful and what is not.

I am only guessing about how to help Melissa <u>all of the time.</u>

Being kept at arm's length, my love has more obstacles to overcome and is probably neutralized. It is sad.

Gloria also needs support and there is so much she could receive but does not.

Melissa's life is the important thing. I do not mind if they know that I write you. The pot needs to be stirred, you know?

Again let me say how happy it makes me that Melissa has you and your parents and Gloria, too. Each of you is in the circle of my love.

Best wishes,

Olin

Merilyn and I had never discussed the depths of my frustration with Gloria, but her letter's tone told me we were comrades. For the second time Merilyn had referenced Melissa's "love" for me. I wanted to believe her, in spite of the absence of evidence. I half suspected that Merilyn was attempting to prevent me from becoming fed up and bailing out.

Perhaps in her heart of hearts Melissa felt something for me but fear prevented her from expressing it. Fear of her mom, maybe fear of vulnerability. Hell, it could have been a cultural thing. All my wondering about Melissa's reasons for treating me like gum on her shoe never gave me a solid place to stand.

Not once had I considered that being a father would involve persuading Melissa to come running to me. With her damn near un-persuadable, I figured that my default course of action was to be true to my heart, regardless of her response. I needed to make my love so concrete, so obvious, so unwavering, that should Melissa suddenly pass away, she would leave this life knowing in her heart that her father had totally embraced her.

My getting no love in return was excruciating, but beside the point. I was her father. Her need trumped mine, the need to know she was loved by me. With time my direction became even clearer. All that counted was, as Helen had said, loving Melissa with all I had, relentlessly, like the surf pounding the shore.

Besides, I'd already received an embarrassment of gifts. A fiery, unconditional love for my child was a wondrous thing. It was accompanied by events which seemed other-worldly. How could it be that a "chance" encounter at the county fair with a co-worker from 10 years prior had led to my reunion with Melissa? How to explain the precognitive dreams, Jeff's included? And the involvement of the perfect family to take on the task of finding me?

As if that wasn't enough, my life had taken on a razor-sharp focus. I was no longer dabbling with life, like a cat batting a toy. Definition had arrived instantaneously when I knew that I had no choice but to fly to Costa Rica. A few friends disputed the point. "You are choosing to do what many men would not." But there was nothing to argue. I was unable to resist the summons. Love had freed me from musty self-preoccupation and a calculating heart.

And finally, my early thrill about Melissa had been transformed into a commitment which would not be deterred. For forty-plus years I had somehow avoided the big challenges. When the United States Selective Service drafted me for Viet Nam in 1970, I'd resisted them for more than two years but when the war wound down, they gave up on me. There had been a scary melanoma in 1983, promptly removed, with no hard road to recovery.

My life had been lived on many sidelines. For Melissa, I ran repeatedly onto the field of contest and had my ass kicked every time. I looked into her future and saw life's biggest ass-kicking in waiting. I kept running onto the field.

This was, perhaps, the greatest gift of all. How blessed I was to love.

23. Communique October, 1992-January, 1993

My relationship with Ahria took a nosedive over the course of the summer. In her words, "it dissolved right in front of our eyes." With Ahria I'd broken the spin cycle with mismatched, off-center women I'd been so fond of. She was a professional woman, thoughtful, vivacious and funny. Simply looking in one another's eyes could send us into peals of laughter. But as our relationship deepened, Ahria found herself caught in the middle between me and the spiritual community that had nurtured her for several years. Her associates weren't Jonestown types but my interest in becoming a regular participant in their spiritual circles and meetings was less than zero. What began as "Ahria in the middle," became "Our relationship at an impasse." We looked for compromises but there were none to our liking. Although snippy bickering became common near the end, we parted respectfully. She had been my closest ally and stalwart through the travails of 1992 and her absence left me listless for weeks.

*****

Shortly after Ahria and I uprooted another letter from Costa Rica arrived. The envelope was addressed in Melissa's handwriting. My hopes were not raised. I pulled out three pages, hand-written, the longest letter Gloria had ever written me. The opening gave me a hint of what was to come.

> *Hola, Señor, (Hello, Sir)*
>
> *How are you. We are better. I'm sorry I haven't been able to respond to you before but I was very sick and afterwards I had to take Melissa to the hospital on September 30 with another crisis. She left the 7th of October.*
>
> *Olin here I am answering your letter. I'm very sorry that you never saw Melissa grow up nor saw her when she was a very beautiful baby. I am the mama and I never saw a more beautiful vixen. Well you never saw her grow because you never sent a card, even out of friendship. You had my telephone number where I lived. Esparza is a little town where people can be found very easily.*
>
> *Well, that is a thing of the past. When you came to meet Melissa two years ago I thought you didn't care about the child very much, because you didn't ask anything about her. Olin, neither my friends nor your friends can imagine the things that have happened with Melissa first to be three weeks in the hospital with her so she could receive treatment.*
>
> *Olin, I understand what you said about the pain of not being in our lives, but it's too late.*
>
> *Here there are people who work to see that Melissa has food and tranquility.*

I had hoped that Melissa would grow up with her parents but it wasn't to be. God never left us, He's always helped us. I believe strongly in God. When there are appointments with the doctor, Melissa goes.

Olin I'm very sorry for this for Melissa: She told me one time that her friends had their parents with them. I told her that not everyone has their family together.

I wish so much for God to have a miracle for her. Melissa was very depressed to be in the hospital but now she has returned to school again.

I always desired a beautiful world for Melissa but she has had a very hard life. She almost never communicates with everyone.

Olin, thanks for the cards to Melissa. She likes her new dog.

Regards,

Gloria

"It's too late" was the line which stuck like dry ice. Key sentences seemed to make no sense, so I waited for Tina to verify that my translation was correct. We went over the letter line by line and then I said, "What do you think?" The silence was so pronounced I knew what she would say. "Gloria's shut the door."

Tina's words sent my stomach on the verge of convulsions. Blindly I'd invited Gloria's ogre to come out. No, I provoked it, somehow thinking we could talk "like mature adults," across the great cultural divide. I'd risked a future with the woman I should be trying to win.

Still, I could hardly believe the untruths in her response and I ranted for a while.

I never knew Gloria's address and did not know how to reach her by mail, even if I had wanted to.

If she had told me she was from Esparza, it was a detail I'd long forgotten.

As for my not asking questions about Melissa, I thought back to all our time together in Esparza and in San Jose. When we shopped and visited Dr. Gonzalez, what *did* we talk about, if not Melissa, *all the time*?

It took several days for acceptance to show up. So Gloria was not being rational. Any expectation that she be rational was a waste of time. Besides, Gloria's "truth" was between the lines, not in their literalness. She was saying, "Don't bother me with your regrets." And, "You abandoned me." Did she really think *I knew* she was pregnant? Perhaps she did. I would never know. As for the accusation I hadn't asked about Melissa, I never could put a clear spin on that one. But I gave her this much: she was entitled to throw garbage.

Not that I was so heroically sympathetic towards her. I was pissed off at the self-pity and the fatalism and the ignoring of my plea for her assistance with Melissa. The insinuation that I didn't care about Melissa was so ridiculous that it glanced off me without a scratch.

I summed up my thoughts in a letter to the Lees:

> *I can't tell if Gloria is completely closing the door or is just trying to hurt me by expressing herself in a totally unfeeling manner. I believe from the way her feelings are so primitive and unbridled that I can't really look to her for support. And worse that Melissa cannot; that Melissa is really trapped in all this; and Gloria can not, will not, help her have a father...*
>
> *As far as hopes and expectations, I just don't know anymore. The picture has become clearer and yet cloudier, too. Having my suspicions confirmed about Gloria is not what I most desired. But there she is. As always, I'll keep hangin' in unless Melissa should ever tell me to exit. And that's where it stands for now.*
>
> *Can you <u>believe</u> this?*

Gloria's reply was all about Gloria. True, she had made unbelievable sacrifices, she had operated alone. But where was Melissa's wellbeing in all of this? Nowhere. "Melissa doesn't talk." So there, Olin, suck on that. Gloria was the gatekeeper and Melissa was the obvious loser. There and then I understood that, even if Melissa invited me to back off, I wouldn't abandon her. I couldn't leave her to her mother.

I looked at the schoolgirl handwriting on the envelope. It seemed like the most hopeful sign in months from Melissa, as if she were a mute child unable to communicate in any other way than addressing envelopes to me.

I spent hours laying on the living room floor, listening to solo piano music of Thelonious Monk and Charlie Mingus. They felt their way in improvisations and I played with possible responses to Gloria, scribbling ideas in my journal.

*****

In early November, the day after Melissa's 14th birthday, Isabel Allende gave a free lecture in San Francisco at Fort Mason on the edge of the Bay. Acting on instinct, I drove to the City, to hear her, really to talk to her. The room was packed with 70 admirers who sat reverentially waiting for her entrance. She took the podium, adorned with a gorgeous scarf draped around her shoulders and killer earrings, the hanging, beaded, silver kind. Isabel's English was decorated with music and sensuality and intelligence. She spoke at length about the writing process and about rituals she observed, such as beginning a new book in January of each year. She discussed her motivation for writing: "So people will love each other more." She described her outlook on life, referring to cycles of up and down, light and dark and the effect of personal actions which "ripple" outward in the world. I'm sure I was not alone in being seduced by her language and physical beauty.

I waited around after the lecture as a line of people sought Isabel's wisdom or blessing. I constantly smiled in an innocent way, trying not to look weird, which must have looked extremely weird. The last to leave, I introduced myself and Isabel visibly brightened. She immediately remembered my letter from over a year earlier and graciously asked about Melissa. She told me her daughter was quite ill and, in so doing, revealed a person the audience and I had not seen. We chatted briefly about our daughters, discussed getting together some day and then parted. A few minutes later, heading north, I passed her car on the Golden Gate Bridge. Looking in the rear view mirror I noticed she was driving in the slow lane with only her parking lights on. I flashed my lights to try and alert her, but her brights never came on. Feeling protective, I drove just in front of her until my way home took me in a different direction.

A week later I was back in San Francisco at California Pacific Medical Center on Russian Hill. The CF Specialist, Dr. Karen Hardy, had invited me to preside over a Cystic Fibrosis Patient-Parent panel. Afterwards Helen Dias came up and handed me a flower. She introduced me to Margo, another mom from Petaluma with a teenage son, Aaron, who had cystic fibrosis. Margo and Aaron had heard the story of Melissa from Helen, about finding her dad and dealing with CF in a country where the treatment was not so good. Aaron was moved by the story and talked to his mom about Melissa for days and tried repeatedly to think about ways he could help. I began to understand what a remarkable community of people there are in the CF world: parents, doctors, researchers and not least of all the children and adults with cystic fibrosis. I'd been grafted onto a family tree where you grew a big heart, regardless.

* * * * *

In mid-December I returned to my house from a long weekend with my father and step-mother in Sun City, Arizona. Going through the mail, I noticed a small ivory envelope crisply addressed in fine black ink. I recognized the handwriting and return address.

My dear Olin,

My daughter died three days ago, peacefully in my arms.

I am very devastated and very tired, but I believe she is finally resting.

Love, Isabel

She had drawn a long-stemmed flower beside her name.

Isabel knew me too superficially to call me "my dear" but I understood the profound need you have to connect with others when your heart feels weak.

As Anabel Stenzel once said, "Love and pain come from the same place in the heart."

I sent Isabel a brief personal note of condolence, offering to share my company or help in any way I could.

* * * * *

Christmas and New Year's passed without a word from Gloria and Melissa. The holidays had been another teeth-grinding experience since I looked for a Christmas card to tell me that I had not completely blown my future with Gloria and Melissa. I intended to delay mailing a response to Gloria's letter until I had received their Christmas card, but on January 6, tired of waiting, and fast approaching basket case status, I sent it off.

Gloria,

Thanks for your letter in October. I'm very sorry to hear Melissa had to return to the hospital. I hope she's very much better now.

I am writing this letter after Christmas, thinking about you and Meli. I'm curious what you bought with the money I sent you for Melissa's birthday and Christmas, too.

Communication is so difficult by letter, in different cultures and with different languages. I want to be sure that I understand your letter with as much clarity I can.

First I understand your feelings when I didn't make contact with you after I returned to the US. You maintained hope for 11 years while raising Melissa alone. I tell you sincerely that I would have returned to Costa Rica before if I had known, but this doesn't change the fact that I never made contact and that you took responsibility to be everything for Melissa.

The other point that I understood in your letter is how alone you are and how no one understands what you and Melissa have gone through.

The third point that I understood from your letter, touches upon Melissa's relationship with me — that it is too late, there is nothing you can do.

I want to know if I am correct in understanding these three points, if this is what you were saying in your letter.

I want you to know that I felt sad for many days afterwards about your letter. I am grateful for your honesty even if the words are so sad to read.

I don't know why we have been presented with circumstances which contain so much suffering. Whatever the reason, I am in agreement that what happened is in the past. But I am with you both in spirit and action always.

Love,

Olin

I had taken Gloria's "feedback" to heart and adopted a simple four-part response. First, keep my emotional reactions to her letter to myself. Two, don't rebut. Three, let her know I heard her main points. Four, ask her to confirm that my understanding was accurate.

I could only hope her door wasn't closed too tightly. It would take several months for me to find out.

24. Isabel—January, 1993-February, 1993

Isabel wrote again over the holidays.

Dear Olin,

Yes, let's meet in January, anytime after the 10th.

Love,

Isabel (Allende)

Her last name was in parentheses, as if the return address and her handwriting weren't enough. She was laboring.

There were several days of attempts to reach her by phone, getting only busy signals, before she picked up.

"Oh, yes, Olin, how are you?" Her voice was thin.

"I'm doing ok. How are you?"

Every piece of her answer ended in silence. "The same... Every day is different... Some days are very hard... I'm very, very busy... How are you?"

"Up and down. I didn't receive a Christmas card from Costa Rica. That was hard."

Hard? Jesus. I felt a stab of shame for complaining about a missed Christmas card to a woman who'd just lost her daughter.

"Have you tried calling them?"

"No. I've thought about it."

"We can call them from my house."

I told her that would not be necessary. We compared our schedules and made arrangements to meet the following week. She gave me directions to her house. I felt the generosity in her offer, but it seemed backwards. I was the one who should be giving. It didn't occur to me that a person could, or needed to, give at a time like this.

I received a letter from a Rotary Club in San Jose, officially requesting financial assistance for the CF Clinic at the Hospital de Niños.

Dear Mr. Dodson,

We received a request of Dra. Celina Guzman of the Gastroenterology Center of the Hospital de Ninos, asking for the intervention of our Club in order to obtain, from another USA Rotary Club, support for a project to supply medicines for children under special treatment in their center.

After boilerplate descriptions of the Club and their plan for monitoring any donations, the letter concluded with a line item description of the request, for 24 children with cystic fibrosis.

ENSURE 200 cans, $870

KANGAROO Enteral Infusion Pump, 1 unit, $1,090

SCANDIPHARM (multivitamin/Zn. supplement), 40 boxes at $580 per box, $2540

Yours truly,
Federico Lachner,
President, San Pedro-Curridabat Rotary Club

I sat in my front room looking out the window at the gray winter scene. An all-night rain had soaked the ground and birds nearby were calling all worms. My eyes returned to the letter. Six hundred dollars for multivitamins. Costa Rica had the strongest economy in Central America and they couldn't afford a basic multi-vitamin for 24 chronically ill children!

The letter felt good, like a hand reaching for mine. I pulled out my Costa Rica photo album and carried it back to the chair. Scared of sinking into depression, I hadn't looked at the photos for months. The shots of Melissa's smile enchanted me and I felt a moment of joy before a wistfulness set in. I studied her frail arms and legs, the clubbed fingers. My face moved close to the photo of us side by side on the boulder in the river, Melissa's elbow on my shoulder. I close my eyes. *I imagine cradling her in my arms and carrying her through the water to the riverbank. She nestles against my chest. She breathes easily and deeply. Her body releases in relief and peace.*

* * * * *

I parked my Honda across the street from Isabel's house. It was a wealthy neighborhood, not too splashy, with lots of shrubbery, stocky trees and houses like old bank vaults. I walked up the short set of stairs and knocked, then once again with force when I sensed how thick the door was. I was close to miserable, the way I get when I don't know what I'm doing. The original plan of sharing my story seemed inappropriate and I didn't know what else I could offer.

Isabel opened the door looking smaller than I remembered her. She smiled warmly and beckoned me in. The house was still. I trailed her into a modest kitchen and sat at a table by a window while she checked on the coffee. Sunlight speared at a low angle through the trees to my left. We were two grieving parents, but I was the only one whose child was alive.

Isabel set our cups down, asked if I wanted milk or sugar. She lowered herself slowly and we small talked about the weather and the new administration in Washington. When I asked how she was, she replied "I'm trying to write, but… "

I stared at my coffee. I was ignorant of death.

I answered several questions about Melissa before Isabel said, "Let's call them." Gloria picked up the phone at Ramon's house. Isabel introduced herself and translated as Gloria and I had a skin-deep conversation. Gloria was fine, Melissa was fine, I was fine. Melissa had a doctor's appointment in a couple of weeks with Reina. Gloria thanked me for the Christmas money. She had yet to receive my latest letter. The conversation wound down and we said our good-byes. Isabel touched the telephone's off button and looked at me. "You're like an alien from another planet." It was not what I wanted to hear.

Shadows had lengthened and covered the table. I offered to pay for the phone call. She refused. I insisted. She refused again, saying she didn't even let her husband buy dinner the first time they went out. She invited me to come back, we could call Gloria again. As I stepped out the front door, I asked if she knew an expert Spanish translator for a story I wanted to write for Melissa. She promised to find someone.

A dream of black ants woke me at 3am. I was sad that I'd offered Isabel so little, sad over the discomfort between us and her comment. She sent me a note several days later, "I hope you are feeling better." She asked me to contact her if I was still interested in hiring a translator.

After a week-long jumble of thoughts and feelings, I drafted a response.

> *Dear Isabel,*
>
> *The darkness intensified when I said good-bye to you. That night I dreamt of ants swarming everywhere in black shaky lines and clusters.*
>
> *I woke up bloated and anxious, like the night my friend Helen talked about her daughter with cystic fibrosis who was tired and wanted to be unhooked from the respirator.*
>
> *I'm still sorting out the emotional confusion from when I met you. I kept blathering in your kitchen about how I wanted to offer you something, dimly aware of feeling overwhelmed and impotent. And angry. Angry about your daughter. Angry about the chronic limitations Melissa feels every day and the impending deadlines on our possibilities together and my constant craziness about what to do and what not to do.*
>
> *Even angry about the horrible loneliness of missing her and the chasm I feel when I call her. The chasm swallowed me during the call from your house and I'm writing you, in part, to pull myself out.*
>
> *Your remark about my being an alien may be true but I grew discouraged when you said it. I fight to maintain hope when all seems*

hopeless. I realized I wanted you to give me hope when it is not yours to give. You gave me your truth and I needed it, however painful. Rarely do I plunge into the dark so quickly with someone I barely know, but given the circumstances...

My hope will not die, dreaming of them coming to live here with me, many dreams other than ants swarming. Isabel, I'll think about you on your travels. I hope there is love and solace with you.

Until next time,

Love,

Olin

The next morning I read my dark words and decided it was a journal entry, not a letter for Isabel. I never sent it.

A few nights later, a dream soothed my jagged spirits.

Serene and happy, I'm talking with Melissa. She's bigger than I've ever seen her. She's curled up on a couch and we're talking in English, discussing a trip in the south, Florida, perhaps, and what we can do.

The dream reminded me of how much I missed Melissa. I investigated the prices of flights to Costa Rica but couldn't see any value in going there right now.

Meanwhile, my counseling practice had grown and I was close to paying off the credit card debt from my Costa Rica trips and my graduate school loans. My work was solid. I had three clients who had worked with me between seven and eleven years. These clients and their therapist had grown up together.

Whether I was reading psychology or novels or watching a movie, everywhere I noticed the central themes of my life: daughters, dads, family struggle, grief and loss. My waking thoughts of Melissa began to morph. I had daydreams for Melissa. I wanted her to have a boyfriend and realize her goals in school, work and marriage. I never prayed much but I begged God to let her hang in and have a future.

February 27 was a sparkling, breezy day. Accompanied by Toots and the Maytals, I cleaned house, paid bills and wrote out a check for Gloria. I was changing clothes for a bike ride, when I heard the mailbox shut. There was just the one letter in the box and I gingerly opened it. I read the long page. Even without Tina, I was able to understand the choppy handwriting and the punctuation-less sentences.

Olin,

I hope that when you receive this you are in good health. Melissa apparently is good, thin as always.

She now has a new bicycle and is very happy. She says it is very cool. Some things happened to her. Her other dog got sick and died on Sunday.

We took it to the veterinarian and gave it medicine that he sent us. The dogs always die. She is very happy with her animals now. She has three chickens. There were 4, but one had its head cut off by another chicken's talons so we are left with 3.

Olin I am going to send you photos of Melissa in another letter. Olin, it pleases me greatly that you understood me in the letter from October. Olin you can imagine how much I have suffered about everything with Melissa's illness. And when you came the first time to Costa Rica, you arrived bothered by the first letter I sent to you and by the word I said, "cariño." I request that you pardon me. Pues, here people are friendly in this way. Pues, I didn't have personal interest. When you came, you didn't ask anything about Melissa. I didn't understand it.

Greetings from Melissa. I hope that you will write us.

I received the check. Thank you.

Best wishes,

Gloria

Gloria's friendly tone and acknowledgement of my letter was encouraging. It re-affirmed my belief in love, positive intentions, persistence and honesty. It underscored the value of offering understanding to her even if wasn't reciprocated.

I was impressed with Gloria's apology for the "cariño" misunderstanding. As for her insistence that I had not asked questions about Melissa, it could only mean that she needed to be right or I had not asked the questions which were important to her and perhaps culturally meaningful.

My happiness surged with the sense that Gloria seemed interested in making things work. Perhaps Melissa's "greeting" was genuine. I could only hope.

I ditched my plans to go bicycling. I stayed home and resumed cleaning, karaoke style. I played a Stevie Wonder album with songs which nicely summarized the past three years.

"Isn't She Lovely"

"Joy Inside My Tears"

"Love's in Need of Love Today"

* * * * *

Dear Gloria and Melissa,

It gave me great happiness to receive your letter three days ago. I wish they came every day. I am glad that everything is going well for both of you.

Gloria, thank you for being so clear and direct. Regarding the letter you wrote before my first visit, perhaps it is best if we discuss that when I visit again. However I am confused by your comment that I did not ask about Melissa. My interest in both of you is the reason I visited with so much enthusiasm. I remember talking very much about you and her the morning you came to my hotel room and on the bus ride to and from meeting with Dra. Gonzalez. It is true that because I was having so much difficulty comprehending everyone in Spanish I did not talk or ask as much as I wanted to. Also I had so much stress about Melissa's silence, getting the report from Dra. Gonzalez, etc., that I am not surprised if my behavior confused you. We need to discuss this more when we visit. I hope I can return in late April or May this year. It depends on my financial situation, but I very much want to see you both.

I will bring what I can. If you want Pancrease, please send me soon the number: MT 4 or MT 10, whatever. I am enclosing money for Mucomist. It is difficult for me to buy it here.

I look forward to your photos. I am happy to know that Melissa has a new bicycle.

Write soon.

Love,

Olin

PS The candy bars in the package I sent are high-calorie, for Melissa. Greetings to your family.

25. Celia—March-April, 1993

Sometime during the winter of 1993, I read about the parents and grandparents of a Native American family who annually recounted the events surrounding their children's births. Their ritual storytelling included descriptions of the time, weather, season, and unusual occurrences around the day or night of the birth. In this manner, the family and perhaps their tribe celebrated the lives of their children and connected them to the universe. It was so simple, really. A child needs to hear the fundamental family stories tied to the larger world, and have her/his life affirmed and re-affirmed by elders. It gave me an idea.

I once heard author Luis Alberto Urrea say, "we don't come from cultures, we come from stories." My parents were not big on sharing family history, and in fact, were not good tellers of tales. Their East Tennessee childhoods were lonely and deprived, they were only children, and, in their respective families, talk was sparse. I doubt many stories were shared, much less listened to. It could have been the absence of ancestral stories in my family which led me to place a value on these sorts of things.

When I left home after high school, my family disintegrating because of alcohol and its companions, I sought out experiences which would give me stories to tell. Hitchhiking to Canada. Hopping a freight train in Montana. Working on a dude ranch in Colorado. Taking Outward Bound trips. I needed more than stories, but I did need stories. I figured Melissa could use one, too.

The translator Isabel referred me to was named Celia. We met at a mom and daughter coffee shop in an east San Rafael strip mall. Celia was brimming with energy, a mother twice over, with a third on the way. She was also Isabel's daughter-in-law. Celia's dark hair covered her eyes as she bent over my photo album resting in her lap. Without raising her head, she posed questions with a lyrical Venezuelan accent. I provided a running commentary, taking her through my knockings at Melissa's door, past and present. Celia lingered on the final photo, closed the album and looked up, all glistening eyes, before she spoke. "Go for it!" With that, Celia joined Melissa's extended family which included Mirta, Nancy Friedlander, the Lee family and everyone who understood what I was trying to do. I handed Celia the story I wrote for Melissa.

Another letter from Gloria showed up several days later, three-plus weeks after the one which had offered so much hope. The envelope was addressed by Melissa.

Hola, como está,

This morning I received the check. Thanks for the letter. You said that you are confused because I said that when you came you did not ask any questions about Melissa. Yes, I thought that you would ask everything about her, a bunch of questions that fathers want to know about their children. I thought that I could talk with you about Melissa because she is the daughter of us both but it wasn't so and so I was cold. I didn't understand anything. When I worked for a company I had an associate, a very special friend. I could tell him everything and he always consoled me. He is a good friend. We always talked by telephone and with him I talked about Melissa. At this moment, she is drinking coffee at the table. She has a little cough. Olin I would like you to tell me something about the research for the drug for CF.

Forgive me but I also want to know if you could do me a favor and buy me a pair of tennis shoes that I can use daily in the house. They are with elastic in the front and are very cheap. Here they don't have size 11. Thank you. Olin, the son of Don Ramon went to Miami. I am happy for you to come because that way you can see her this year.

She doesn't want to go to school because last year she lost out on three exams. Today she went first to sociology, Thursday she has to do mathematics and afterwards science. When they did the exams she was hospitalized to receive medicine. Olin, don't bring Pancrease. The Association has it.

Melissa wants to know your birth date because she doesn't know it.

Melissa sent a post card, without a date. Melissa wants a tape recorder but she wants to ask you for it. I hope that she is going to write you soon. There is no Mucomist here. Ok, see you later, tell me about your work and your family and everything.

Best wishes,

Gloria

Another chatty, stream of consciousness letter from Gloria. It made me happy that Pancrease was now available in Costa Rica. I couldn't quite figure out the purpose behind the story about Gloria's "amigo." Nor did I understand what questions she had expected me to ask, but I was glad she told me about Melissa's school.

The parts attributed to Melissa were another story. I tried to picture Melissa voluntarily asking about my birth date, but it seemed unlikely. I continued to believe Gloria was pressuring Melissa and even fabricating her questions. Perhaps my skepticism was a protection from becoming optimistic and getting crushed again.

When a post card arrived four days later I was happy again. The front of the card was an aerial photo of Poás Volcano, near San Jose. The handwriting on the back side was all Melissa's.

We received the vitamins and the check, books, etc.

Best wishes, please write.

Gloria Reyes

Why had Melissa signed it "Gloria"? It must have been dictated by her mom. Melissa had "written" it, the only direct anything I'd received from her in almost two years. I wanted desperately for it to be a sign that she was reaching out, that she was inching closer to me. But I doubted it.

Maybe the story Celia was translating would budge her, even if budging her wasn't the point. I only wanted her to know I loved her. My love was bull-headed, sure, but something else motivated me: my basic belief about life; maybe it was a need about life. I refused to concede that the extraordinary events of the past two years had unfolded to no ultimate benefit for Melissa. For it all to dead end would be the ultimate in absurdity and meaningless. The defeat of love would break me.

I wrote back as soon as I could.

Dear Gloria and Melissa,

I'm sorry that I did not respond to your letter more quickly but I have been sick for two weeks. Even now I feel a little fuzzy.

Your letter arrived so quickly this time only three weeks after I wrote you. And then soon afterwards I received a post card about the package in Melissa's handwriting. With so much mail from you, I thought I had died and gone to heaven!

Gloria you wrote so many interesting things and I look forward to talking with you in person. I can only respond briefly in a letter of course, but I will try. First the new treatment for CF has not been approved yet in the US but I think it will come this year. I will try to find out about its availability in Costa Rica before my next visit. I will bring Mucomist then. Gloria I am still concerned about Melissa's weight as I know you are. One time, Dr. Gonzalez discussed feeding Melissa through a tube. Would you check on that with her?

As far as shoes are concerned, I will be happy to look for some. Everyone here from Latin America tells me that the sizes are so different here, so the best thing is for you to trace the shape of your foot on a piece of paper and send it to me. Also if there is anything more I can bring, let me know.

I recently learned that I have much to pay in taxes so I must postpone my next visit until July or August, I regret to say. God willing, I will come this summer.

It's time to stop but I want to say that I hope Melissa did well on her exams.

Take care. Give my love to you family.

Olin

PS. My birthday is July 8.

* * * * *

On a slow work day, I went to a movie matinee, "This Boy's Life," featuring Leonardo DiCaprio and Robert DeNiro. In the nearly empty theater, sadness crested over me when the father began slapping the boy around, even when the boy stood up to him and ran away from the family. There were echoes of an evening when, irritated by something I said, my father escorted me to the garage and undid his belt. I jerked with each slap of the belt but I gritted my jaw and refused to cry as I always had. In response to my 11-year old defiance, Dad kept whipping on me until I could no longer hold back my cries. My father and our relationship crossed a line that night into the land of distrust and disrespect.

The next day I sat on the deck of a coffee house overlooking the Petaluma River with a friend. He was another son of an intermittently cruel father and had become one himself, his anger both medicated and unleashed by a terrible alcohol problem. We talked about the movie and our childhoods of anger towards our fathers for the repeated stories they told us about what disappointments we were. Our memories eventually left us silent as stones, staring across the water. We laid down a few dollars and walked back across the bridge to the center of town. The conversation left me wondering about the connection between my childhood loneliness and my obsession for Melissa to know she was loved.

* * * * *

Celia and I met at the coffee shop. I opened the perfectly typed pages she handed me and looked at key passages. It was a simple translation, beautifully worded. I searched for the line referencing the night Melissa was conceived. It was missing. Celia said it was not such a proper thing for a father to say to a Latina daughter. I handed her a check and an extra thank you, an antique glass plate I knew she would appreciate. She smiled and asked me to stay in touch so she could learn how Melissa responded. I said I hoped to find out the same thing.

That night, I finished the final chapter of "Their Eyes Were Watching God" by Zora Neale Hurston. It had a simple passage which offered some solace. *"Mah love didn't work like they love, if dey had any…Love is lak de sea. It's uh movin' thing, but still and all, it takes its shape from de shore it meets, and it's different with every shore."*

26. My Story—April, 1993

Dear Melissa,

Recently I decided to write for you the story of how your mother and I met. It is a special story and perhaps there are parts of the story which you have not heard before. I hope you enjoy it, along with your mother.

The story begins in August, 1977. I was working as a vocational counselor for handicapped people. We trained people and helped them to find jobs. I enjoyed my job, although it was very hard work. I did not respect the people I worked for. It often seemed that they did not really care. After three years of frustration, I quit the job. I was 30 years old and uncertain what to do next.

A friend suggested that I take time before finding a new job. Another friend told me about a Spanish language school in Guatemala where the students lived with Guatemalan families. This sounded very appealing: a chance to travel and learn Spanish and live with a family. I had some money saved up so I enrolled in a school in Huehuetenango, Guatemala. I planned to study there for one month and then proceed on to South

America by boat. I planned to have a great adventure in an unknown part of the world. I was excited and scared.

I stored all of my possessions and my car with a friend near San Francisco where I had lived since I was 22. It was January, 1978, when I said good-bye to friends and family. First I flew to Mexico City. I spoke about 20 words of Spanish, enough (I hoped!) to find my way from the airport to the bus station. There I bought a ticket for Guatemala, thinking I would change buses at the border and take one to Huehuetenango. But to the ticket seller, "Guatemala" meant "Guatemala City," so the bus took me all the way past the road to Huehuetenango in the night and into Guatemala City. I arrived at the school late the next day three hours after classes began, late, but better late than never!

I loved Guatemala. The mountains were dramatically beautiful and the people so kind! Unfortunately there was a great deal of poverty, violence and repression towards the native people. There were also news reports of increasing fighting in the civil war in Nicaragua. I was hoping that the government of Somoza would be overthrown but the borders were closing off and on, so I began looking for a ship out of a Guatemalan port instead of travelling through Nicaragua. After spending January in school, some North American friends invited me to travel with them in their van. We spent a short time near Lake Atitlan. We climbed Volcan de Agua, near Antigua. We borrowed some cheap sleeping bags and spent the night in a hut in the crater on top. The freezing temperature and some very active mice in the hut kept us awake all night. After thawing out the next day I decided it was time to say good-bye to my companions…

(I briefly summarized my travels through El Salvador and Nicaragua and finally getting kicked off the bus in San Jose.)

The next morning I finished breakfast at a restaurant near my hotel and prepared my list of things to do that day. There was a pretty woman sitting alone nearby. After I excused myself I asked her if she knew the directions to the Embassy of Panama. This woman was, of course, your mother.

Gloria was extremely kind. She told me that she had some free time so she personally escorted me to the Embassy, the post office and a few other places. Not only was she friendly and patient, but she had a great sense of humor, too. By this time, in early February, I was able to make conversation in Spanish, but Gloria needed to have lots of patience with my language "skills" and didn't laugh too much at me!

She accepted my invitation to meet that evening at a restaurant. I was unfamiliar with Costa Rican customs, so for 2 or 3 hours after the time we agreed to meet, I sat there miserable, thinking Gloria had let me down. But I waited and she eventually arrived. We walked to a disco and danced for hours and stayed together all night. Originally, I had planned to be in Panama City that night. But through circumstances beyond my control, there I was in San Jose with this very nice woman.

Many people encouraged me to remain in Costa Rica and see its beauty. In fact, one man walked up to me on the street and said, "Where are you from? Isn't this a great country? Let me buy you a cup of coffee!" It did not take me long to decide to stay in Costa Rica for a while and soon I decided to remain as long as my visa would permit: 30 days. I travelled all around: by boat to the Rio San Juan, to Limon and Puntarenas by train, and to Manuel Antonio, where monkeys came up to me on the beach. I was very happy, happier than I could imagine. It was during this time that I had that vivid dream about a pregnant woman which I wrote down in my journal and previously told you about.

Every time I was in San Jose, I called your mom. I remember that it was not easy to arrange times to meet because of her job responsibilities. Another obstacle was her employer who did not like me telephoning her. One time, in anger, he hung up on me! After that I asked a woman in the hotel to call Gloria for me. When it was possible, she and I met for dinner or coffee, and one time for a movie. We talked to each other about our lives, asking many questions and always laughing a lot. After a few weeks in Costa Rica, I realized I was running out of money, a serious miscalculation on my part. While I waited for my father to send me a loan, your mother bought me a dinner, although I don't think she had much money.

Near the end of March, with only a limited amount of money left, it was time to return to the U.S. and go back to work. I was sad to leave Costa Rica and to say good-bye to Gloria. I gave her my old business card as a mailing address, because I did not have a place to live when I arrived back in California. I am sorry that I did not give her my parents' address because soon after I returned, I moved to a small town in the far north of California and I lost touch with the people I knew at my old job.

I kept the idea that I would travel again to Central and South America after I saved enough money at a saw mill where I took a job. But after a year or so, I decided to commit myself seriously to a profession. I took the money I had saved and enrolled in a post-university school in psychology.

In 1983, I graduated, then trained for three more years and passed my state exam in 1986. From 1986 on I developed my business and finally by 1990 I had saved enough money to travel again. That was when Laura Lee found me- as I was preparing to go to Eastern Europe for a conference on families in other cultures.

So, Melissa, that is the story of my trip and the unseen hand which brought your mother and me together. For years I believed that my happy time with her was an isolated event in my past. Now I see that it was a wondrous event, one which has influenced my heart and my beliefs about life in powerful ways, and completely changed the direction of my life.

I hope you have enjoyed this story, Melissa. Sometime, I hope you'll write me one (or more!) about you.

Te quiero mucho,

Tu papá

27. The Great Plan—April-June, 1993

Springtime brought more dreams and letters and another encounter with Isabel. She gave a reading at a Corte Madera book store in connection with her new book, *The Infinite Plan*. The title, from a woman who'd lost her daughter, had a hopeful vibe. The early evening sunlight cast a glow on the room of books and Isabel who looked elegant in a dark dress imprinted with patterns of flowers. She beamed at the audience and generally appeared to be in better shape than me. Celia appeared at my side and greeted me with a prim hug. She introduced me to a friend who mentioned a wonderful Spanish tutor named Rosana. I later contacted Rosana for lessons and, much later, for an important telephone translation.

I had a dream on May 13.

> *A friend brings me a stack of mail. In it I find an envelope in Melissa's handwriting. Inside, there is a simple birthday card, signed by Melissa, her mom and an unknown woman. I begin to read the card and suddenly Melissa is sitting beside me. She begins talking to me in English, seven or eight sentences. I am surprised and delighted, and begin to cry in joy. The scene shifts and I'm in a reunion with all the people I had met in Costa Rica, and I listen to stories of what had happened in everyone's life.*

That same day, I received a letter from Gloria.

> *Hola,*
>
> *Como está, I hope that when you receive this you are in good health. Melissa is well. I see that the Doctor Gonzalez has written you and told you how Melissa was. She is now very good and doing well in school this year. She is in the third year, at last passed her exams.*
>
> *She was interested in the letter that you sent and I never on purpose made you wait 3 hours that time. You are lying. That time yes you waited. That time, it's past.*
>
> *Olin I am always interested in treatment. Here there is no Mucomist. Melissa is gaining weight.*

About the shoes, it's that here there are no big sizes. For that reason I am bothering you with this. These shoes are very cheap...

I will tell you something, Melissa is already thinking about the party of her 15th birthday. If God permits it to take place, she says that she wants to invite all her friends from school and they are around 40 students. A good party with food and party favors costs money.

Best wishes, respectfully,

Gloria and Melissa

PS–I didn't send photos of Meli, because I don't know if they would reach you but if you want I will send them in another letter. Greetings to Laura and the family.

Melissa had not signed her own name, but the letter strengthened my belief that Gloria and I were approximating normal in our communication. The news about Melissa's health and weight and her dedication to school relieved and delighted me. Meager and disappointing as the feedback was about my story, it was hardly surprising. I figured Gloria was teasing me about lying and surely Melissa's reaction was more than "interested," but how could I be sure of either?

Dear Gloria and Melissa,

This morning I dreamed about you all. I dreamed that I received a letter from you all, signed by you all and another unknown person. And so I woke up very happy. A few hours later, I received your letter. It was incredible!

I am happy that Melissa is well. By the way, perhaps you are right, Gloria. Perhaps I only waited for you for two and a half hours! Also I am happy that Melissa was pleased by my letter and is doing well in school. I am proud that she passed her exams.

Regarding the letter from Dr. Gonzales, the last letter I received from her was in July 1992. I don't have any recent news from her.

Everything is good with me. I am going to visit my father and his wife in Arizona next week. I still don't know exactly when I am going to visit you all. I am trying to make reservations for the first week of August. Gloria, I am going to bring shoes for you but you ought to send me a drawing of your foot. I am going to bring Mucomist also. Melissa, I hope that you will soon write me a list of wishes, things that you would like to have for yourself. It is easy for me to buy gifts here and there are things here that I don't know if you have in Costa Rica.

Gloria, if there is something else beside the shoes that you would like, tell me. I need your suggestions for buying something for the family of your brother.

With respect to CF, a friend is translating the latest information about treatments. I will send it to you as soon as possible.

A little while ago, I began to study with a Spanish teacher, Rosana, in order to prepare myself for my visit with you. I still have so many problems understanding Spanish, but I plan to study with Rosana for two years (unless she gets bored with me!) However I suggest that the three of us find a bi-lingual person in Esparza, because I want to hear your thoughts about Melissa's future, if she has planned to go to the university and other things. I want to help her financially, as much as I can, if she wants to continue her education. If this is so I want to plan it in advance.

So, Gloria, if you know someone who is bi-lingual, ask if they can help us. Otherwise I will find someone in San Jose, when I arrive, perhaps Maritza again.

Ok, I believe that is all for now.

Love, Olin

PS Perhaps it isn't necessary to send the photos. You can give them to me in person!

By now I was eagerly dreaming about Melissa's approaching 15th birthday and her high school graduation only two years later. I hoped that my pledge to assist her had boosted her mental, physical and spiritual health and implanted a certainty that I would be around for a long time. God, if only she would be there with me.

Two weeks later I received Gloria's fourth letter in four months. The envelope was again addressed by Melissa, again with Gloria's name in the upper left corner. Inside was the big surprise: the entire letter in Melissa's handwriting! I danced across the room to a chair and stuck my face near the page. Such beautiful lettering! Such evenly lined sentences! Then I saw "Greetings from Melissa" in her handwriting at the bottom and my heart pranced. My eyes returned to the top and, as I read down the page, confusion and disappointment set in. The letter was nothing more than a request, engineered from Gloria, for immediate financial help.

Hola, Como está,

I hope that upon receiving this you are enjoying good health.

I am in good health. Mommy wants to ask you a favor, which is the following, that the doctor had sent me oxygen for the nights at home, and the cylinder rents for $40,000 colones, but my mother obtained it from another hospital (in Puntarenas). My mother now needs a percussor. There is a woman here who has a company that told mother that she can send off to bring one from Miami. The price for this percussor is $85,000 colones.

What my mother is asking is if you will do a favor to send this sum of *money. The price in dollars here is $1,388.*

I hope that you will answer me as soon as possible. The woman will bring it next week.

Greetings from Melissa. *Gloria Maria Reyes*

I grumbled to myself. Ok, there was the sentence, "I am in good health," written by Melissa. And she did sign her name. But Gloria dictating the letter for Melissa to co-sign seemed weird, manipulative of us both. And then there was the request.

Where was I going to come up with $1400?

How was I going to get the money to them in a week?

What would Melissa think if I didn't come through on the request?

Why the sudden need?

I grew a bit panicky before Rational Mind took charge.

First, the percussor, an electric device which mechanically performs chest physical therapy. Who knew if the Miami percussor was new and of high quality? How much of a cut was the woman taking? What was the cost of percussors in the States?

Second, the money. I didn't have $1400.

Third, the money. I couldn't get $1400 to them in a week even if I had it.

The puzzle popped up each time I awoke that night. Some part of me continued to work the next morning until an old saying, a remnant from a cave in my brain, bubbled forth. Don't take the mountain to Mohammed, bring her to the mountain. Forget the percussor. Fly Melissa to San Francisco. I had it! Creating a plan obsessed me. For a couple of nights running I couldn't sleep until after midnight. I made a phone call to a social worker at California Pacific Medical Center and ran some ideas past her. I asked friends for fund raising suggestions. I phoned my father to remind him of his earlier offer to help pay for Melissa's medical expenses if she ever came to the States. The initial idea was to bring Melissa by herself, but my friend Frances convinced me it would be a mistake, surely resulting in Gloria, if not Melissa, turning me down. I revised the plan to include Gloria and took the written version of the proposal to my new tutor, Rosana, and we translated it together. The offer, nicely typed in Spanish was mailed to mother and daughter in early June.

Dear Gloria and Melissa,

Thank you for your letter concerning the percussor. I was impressed with the quality of Melissa's handwriting. I received the letter only a few days after I sent you my last letter. Gloria, I remembered that you mentioned the percussor when I phoned you in January. I am sorry, perhaps I did not respond clearly on the phone.

Unfortunately I am not able to afford the cost of a percussor. Recently

I have not been able to build up any savings. My trips to Costa Rica and to see my father are possible because of my credit card which I can later pay off, little by little, over the months.

However, there is good news. A percussor is not the best alternative to therapy by hand. I've also learned that percussors do not work well for everyone. The most popular and effective method is pep mask/autogenic draining which Melissa could learn to do for herself in 2–4 hours of easy training. (In fact, I went to a pep mask class for young adults 2 years ago and all of them liked it very much). This method, popular in Europe and now in the US is unfamiliar to the hospital therapists in San Jose. I know this because I asked around during my second trip to see you

The only way really for Melissa to learn this method is to come to San Francisco. So, instead of me coming to Costa Rica in August, I am willing to buy you both a round-trip airline ticket to come here for a week or so. Melissa can receive the training in Spanish in a couple of sessions.

After I made the decision to offer this trip to you, I called California Pacific Medical Center. This is a modern hospital in San Francisco where several of my friends take their children. The CF unit has an expert and a warm staff of 6 or 7 people. I asked if the doctor would examine Melissa while she was here and give her some pills and inhalants which would be more effective than what is available in Costa Rica.

They were interested in being of help and said that they would like to obtain some specific data on Melissa from Dr. Gonzalez. So I will fax her tomorrow their questions. Her answers will give them a clearer picture of how to help. They are especially interested to see if they can do something to prevent Melissa from going to the hospital so often. This was exactly what I wanted to hear.

The more I think about this idea, the more it makes sense. One of the biggest advantages of you finding me is that Melissa might be able to have access to health care in the US. And then in your free time there are a million things to do near San Francisco: Sea World, Great America (a park like Disneyland) etc, etc, etc, etc. We could play tourist and buy shoes for Gloria, too!

The final decision about the date of your trip would depend on you and the doctor in San Francisco. But the first step is for the hospital here to collect the information from Dr. Gonzalez. Then I will call or write you to pass along their ideas. There would be many details to work out, so the earliest that this trip could happen would be September.

As I said, for now, I will postpone my trip to Costa Rica. It is clearly more important for Melissa to receive this medical care here than for me to visit there. Please let me know your thoughts on the matter by letter or fax.

Take care. Give my regards to your family.

Olin

PS For sure I will give you help with Melissa's 15th birthday celebration.

Simultaneous to the mailing of the letter I faxed Dr. Gonzalez:

California Pacific Medical Center has agreed to see Melissa. CPMC would like some information from you or the physician attending Melissa. They have requested that you call or fax as soon as possible with the following:

Melissa's height and weight

Pulmonary function results

Oxygen saturation results

Last hospitalization: When? How long? What for? Oxygen? Antibiotics?

Antibiotics at home?

Broncho-dilators?

Daily Pancrease?

Associated problems with liver pancrease heart?

Blood sugars

Liver functions

Bacteria in her lungs

Hemoptysis?

Pneumothorax?

Last TB test

Muconeum ileus

Spot on x-rays?

Thank you Reina. I hope you will call or write soon.

Best Regards,

Olin

Waves of excitement carried me through the days. I knew Gloria and Melissa could not turn down an all-expense trip to America, one which would offer Melissa the best in medical treatment and maybe save her life. They had passports, all they needed to do was obtain visas and step on a plane.

I floated in visions of Melissa being near me. It was unusual to have such a period of quiet anticipation. In a week or two CPMC would receive Melissa's records and they would contact me, and soon afterwards, there would be a response from Gloria. My bliss was cut short one morning with a sudden remembrance of a requirement of CPMC's that I'd failed to mention. I dashed off a quick postcard.

Dear Gloria and Melissa,

I forgot to mention something important in my last letter. For Melissa's medical examinations, it will be necessary that you obtain and bring a revised birth certificate for Melissa with my name as her father.

What you will need to do is go to the office of Registro Civil and ask for a new certificate. I sincerely hope that this will not be a difficulty for you but it is necessary. Also it would be very good if Melissa had my name on her passport. This would ease things greatly and I recommend it in order to assure that Melissa is accepted for medical services here in the US.

Take care,

Olin

I didn't spend much time thinking that this forgotten item would impede the golden plan. My third Father's Day arrived with cards and phone inquiries about my recent invitation to the Costa Ricans. Life was good and looked to get much better.

28. 31 Kilos—June-August, 1993

"The $2,500 for the Hospital project in San Jose has been approved. All that remains is for the clubs to exchange confirmation letters before Hospital de Niños gets the money." John Strong, the Rotary guy, saw me downtown and gave me the news. Finally! I felt that things were working my way and I could now turn my attention to the next big event: the arrival of Melissa's medical records.

But a month passed and nothing arrived at CPMC. I re-faxed the request to Reina and received nothing in return. My anger increased day by day until it seasoned every mood. I was even bitter that I would have to confront Melissa's primary physician about her irresponsibility.

It was mid-July when I dialed her number. Reina answered and sounded happy to hear from me. We began a cordial 20 minute conversation, cordial on my part because she had the power to continue delaying sending Melissa's records. Reina confessed straight up, admitted she'd not responded to my faxes, said she'd been ill for two weeks. She didn't explain what had happened to the other three weeks. Listening to an excuse would be pointless so I didn't pursue it.

"Have you seen Melissa?" I asked.

"Yes, she was admitted to the hospital 3 weeks ago, the first time since December. She had a lung infection. We took care of it, but I prescribed for her oxygen in the nights."

"Did you all discuss my plan to bring them to the States?"

"Gloria said nothing. I guess she did not know about it. Gloria and I have not had a chance to talk. You know she is not good at following up."

Reina's criticism of Gloria opened a door into her warehouse of grievances.

She described her worsening relationship with the hospital then referenced a malpractice suit, Miami, and Mirta in a blur of puzzling connections. I interrupted her and asked, in my best no non-sense tone, to please fax the records to CPMC. I suggested she have Dr. Guzman help her. Reina liked that idea.

I hung up the phone, my anger somewhere off in parts unknown. But Reina had given me all I could hope for: a promise.

Laura, Jeff, Frances and others phoned me to learn the latest developments. It looked certain that Melissa and Gloria would not come to the States anytime soon. I offered a defense of Reina, that she was not being irresponsible, at least not terribly, or passive/aggressive, at least not horribly. Maybe she'd become stuck in a vortex of guilt. She was overworked and perhaps subject to a cultural time clock different than my own. I could imagine Gloria and Melissa also responding in their own time: months, maybe years. My irresistible plan was proving to be pretty resistible.

For the next seven days, I made daily inquiries to CPMC. I slept erratically each night and by the final day's "No, nothing," my anxiety turned into feeling duped and angry. Seven days became ten and my anger evolved into despondency. I grew weary of responding to friends' inquiries with the same words CPMC gave me: "No. Nothing." It was like we were all waiting for my water to break.

Reina was not the only mute correspondent. Six weeks had passed since I sent a letter to Gloria and Melissa. How could they not respond? I could feel my spirit erode from the double shun. My idea, the best and biggest lifeline for Melissa, meant nothing to them. Nothing. I wondered if Gloria's silence could have stemmed from a fear of putting my name on the birth certificate. As much as I was operating out of anxiety and aggression, Gloria seemed to live on an opposite pole of caution and fear.

I turned to Celina Guzman in a fax on July 26, hoping Reina had spoken with her.

> *Dear Dr. Guzman,*
>
> *Greetings. I hope you are well. I think about you at times and your generous contributions during my visit two years ago.*
>
> *I wish to appeal to you for your assistance once again. Seven weeks ago I sent a fax to Dr. Gonzalez requesting medical records for my daughter, Melissa Reyes Reyes. There was no reply, so I sent another fax and then Called Reina at her home ten days ago. As of today the doctors here have still not received any information. The doctors and I wish to fly Melissa and her mother but we are not able to make definite plans because of the wait for the records. Seven weeks is a long time.*
>
> *I write to you in hopes that you can investigate the problem. I do*

not know what else to do. I am hopeful that you can talk with Reina. If necessary could you fax the information to the doctors or to me, as quickly as possible, perhaps tomorrow or Wednesday.

I am sorry if for any reason, Reina feels insulted because I contacted you, but I cannot wait any longer where my daughter's health is concerned.

Thank you very much, Celina.

Sincerely,

Olin Dodson

That night I dreamed I was a passenger in a truck.

The driver, a young man, drives through thick masses of trees and foliage so dense there is no light. He drives without hesitation. We come to our "destination," a lake surrounded by trees, a house on either side. The truck plunges into the lake and I feel the water rise up my body to my waist, but I feel nothing. I wake up.

I waited three days for a reply from Celina. Nothing.

I dreamed of Melissa. We spoke in English and Spanish and played patty cake. I woke up momentarily happy. I sent Gloria a check along with a reminder that I was waiting for a response.

I checked with CPMC, got the usual "No fax today," and blasted another fax to Reina.

Dr. Gonzalez,

We are still waiting for you response.

At the bottom, I listed the names of the CPMC doctors and their phone and fax numbers.

I took my hatchback for a respite at the Pinnacles National Monument on the San Andreas Fault, south of the Bay Area. I left town late and ended up stopping in Salinas for the night. The town baked like a bad sauna. The motel manager recommended a nearby Mexican restaurant with the dubious name of *La Fogata,* Spanish for "The Bonfire." I puttered down Main Street and studied the facades of the empty buildings in the late afternoon sun. They looked pretty hopeless, like something out of Dorothea Lange's Dust Bowl photographs. I found comfort in those dilapidated exteriors. They fit with a radio tune I heard on the drive down Highway 101, Ry Cooder's version of "I Can't Win (Your Love)." It was a weekend for the blues.

I passed Soledad Prison the following morning, arriving at the Pinnacles around mid-day. But it was 3 p.m. before the heat of the day eased sufficiently for me to leave the shade of a sycamore grove and begin the hike into the park. The castle-like formations of volcanic rock had been split and slashed by centuries of water and wind until they gained a rough beauty, like a pock-marked face. The trail took me along rock shoulders, by tiny caves, spires and scars.

I couldn't avoid thinking about the weeks of bad news, no news, day after day. Over breakfast I had stared at a story in the Chronicle's sports page. A pitcher for the New York Mets had finally won a game almost two years after his last victory. Twenty-seven losses. It had been almost three years since Melissa had written me. Maybe she never would. At a younger age I might have looked to that hard luck athlete for a lesson but he surely knew nothing I didn't. I would continue faxing Reina until the machine broke. I remained in the park until late in the day. The moon's ebony face rose and illuminated my path back to the car.

I sent Reina the same fax as I had a week earlier. I was ready to send the "I'm still waiting" fax every goddamn day for a year, but I needed something more, a strategy which would produce the medical records. Two months after my letters to Reina and Gloria, my excitement about the plan had waned as my anger boiled. In my journal, I spit it out. *"Thanks, both of you. Your frozenness chills me and pains my heart for Melissa."*

*****

"Are you ready?" I asked. She smiled. "Yes, ready." Rosana had agreed to come to Petaluma for the morning to interpret on a call to the Hospital de Niños. She wore a blood red sweater and her wavy brown hair almost touched her shoulders. I had briefed her on the frustrating history of my plan and how I hoped in the next hour to find someone at the hospital to give me a hand. I could hear the tightness in my voice. I picked up the telephone.

We tried calling International Information for about 15 minutes but the lines were jammed. Rosana, an immigrant herself, explained that "this happen sometimes." With the emotions of the past two months caged and hungry, I stifled a curse. Finally, we reached Gloria's house. A relative of Ramon's answered and I asked for Gloria before handing the phone to Rosana. An image crossed my mind of calling Gloria in 1978 and talking to her through the hotel desk clerk.

Gloria came on the line and Rosana identified herself and they exchanged pleasantries. Rosana repeated what Gloria said. "The teachers are on strike so Melissa is home today, she hasn't gone to school all week."

How is Melissa?

"She's getting good medical care, is doing better since coming home from the hospital. We rented a percussor and it works well."

Did you receive my letter? I sent it many weeks ago.

"Yes, we received it."

What was your response to my idea to come to San Francisco?

"I think it is a good idea, but Melissa doesn't think so."

Why not?

"I don't know. She is very stubborn. Melissa will only come if she can be cured."

Well, you know we aren't talking about coming here for a cure, since there isn't one. You do know that?

"Yes, but that is the only reason she will come. You know how she is."

As I said in my letter, we are interested in improving her health, helping her to live longer. The doctors in San Francisco are some of the best in the world.

There was a long silence as Gloria spoke. Rosana covered the phone and whispered to me, "She's repeating the same thing. Melissa won't come."

Ask her, "What do *you* think, Gloria?" Rosana translated my words and listened patiently before speaking up on her own. "So, Gloria, are you letting Melissa make the decision??" Looking at me, Rosana gave a small shrug and nodded her head.

I rolled my eyes. Ask this: "So are you telling me to cease my efforts to help Melissa from here?" Rosana repeated my words, then listened quietly for a couple of minutes before placing her hand over the mouthpiece once again. "I think we should hang up and discuss this and call back." I nodded and Rosana explained to Gloria that we would call back in five minutes.

Rosana set down the phone. "Melissa has been beside Gloria the entire time. I heard Gloria tell her to go get something at one point. Gloria said that the two of you had talked about putting your name on the birth certificate in 1990, when you initially met Melissa. Since that time, Melissa has seen television programs about fathers stealing their children and she is worried that changing her name on a birth certificate or putting it on a passport would make her vulnerable to being trapped by you in the U.S. once she was here."

I said, "I bet Gloria is worried about that, too." Rosana nodded her head.

We strategized for a few more minutes then dialed the phone.

Rosana began. "Gloria, I am going to tell you a few things which you should pass along to Melissa. First, I can tell you as an immigrant myself that your rights will not be compromised once you are here. There is a Costa Rican embassy here in San Francisco and they intervene if there is any trouble for Costa Ricans traveling here."

"Second, kidnapping would be a criminal act, and Olin is not a criminal! Third, separating Melissa from you would make Melissa unhappy and Olin would be unhappy if Melissa was unhappy."

Rosana's head nodded up and down, her voice warmly encouraging. *Sí, claro. Claro. Perfecto.*

"Claro, you can bring any document you want. I think the hospital doesn't care as long as you have something." That was Rosana's idea. She described

a Latina friend who carried a forged birth certificate in order to show her fiance that she was five years younger than she really was.

Rosana whispered to me that Gloria had changed the subject. "She's talking about going to a lawyer who is a family friend."

"Does she think that by talking to him, Melissa's fear will disappear?"

Rosana listened for Gloria's answer to my question and nodded up and down.

"Gloria says that Melissa has an appointment with the doctor on Friday."

"Dr. Gonzalez?"

"No, an endrocrinologist."

"Tell her I've asked Dr. Gonzalez five times for Melissa's medical records. The doctors here must have a chance to review them before you come."

Rosana: "Gloria recommends you talk to Dr. Castro. Do you know him?"

"Dr. Castro? Yes, Mirta and I talked to him two years ago."

"She says that while Melissa meets with the endocrinologist, she will talk to Dr. Castro and get his phone and fax numbers. Is there anything else you want to say to her?"

"Tell her 'thank you.' Oh, and tell her when she doesn't write it is very difficult. I worry all day."

"Gloria apologized. She said that when Melissa was in the hospital for three weeks, she had to take the bus every day to San Jose and then return at night. It was very hard."

I thought Dr. Gonzalez had said Melissa was in the hospital three weeks ago, not for three weeks. No wonder she could not reply to my letter. I felt like such an imbecile. My ignorance had fueled my anger towards Gloria.

Finally we reviewed everyone's assignments, in truth, mostly Gloria's, and agreed to talk in a week. Rosana hung up the phone and made big eyes. "Man, that was draining!"

* * * * *

I heard nothing from Dr. Guzman. Unsure if she had received my request, I decided to fax Dr. Castro at the same hospital number I had used for Reina. I included news about the Petaluma Rotary Club's upcoming donation.

Two days later, I received a fax from Reina.

> *Olin,*
>
> *I am sorry for the delay in sending the information you had requested concerning Melissa's health status. I must tell you that, unfortunately, because of difficulties in locating the medical records of the patient, it is not until now that I am able to do it.*
>
> *Dr. Castro Armas handed me the fax in which you informed him*

about the donation our CF center will receive. I am very happy because our joint effort on this matter was successful.

I hope this information will be useful. I am sending a fax to the doctors of CPMC, by mail, enclosing a weight/height curve, pulmonary function test results and a Spanish summary which a resident performed. I am also answering the questions you requested and giving my general impressions of Melissa's health condition.

If you need any more information, please do not hesitate to contact me. (I had problems with my phone and fax but at present they are OK)

Yours sincerely,

Reina Gonzalez, M.D.

Two days passed, then Rosana returned to my house for our follow-up call. Gloria picked up promptly and the two women went through their greeting ritual.

"Claro," Rosana would reply, then listen some more. *"Claro."* Then, *"Un momentíto, Gloria."* She held the phone in her lap and smiled. "Gloria sounds a little hyper, very nice. She says that she did everything we discussed. She talked to Dr. Castro, who received your fax, and he said he would take care of the medical records. Melissa saw the endocrinologist who recommended that she eat more vegetables and cereal. Melissa doesn't like vegetables. Gloria is looking for new recipes. Melissa is thin, she weighs only 31 kilos." On my notepad where I was writing pieces of the conversation, I scribbled "31" and multiplied it by 2.2. 68 pounds.

Rosana was listening once again. *"Claro."*

"She says they will return next week to San Jose for a clinic Reina is holding for the children with CF. She still has to make an appointment with a lawyer. Gloria had a long talk with Melissa but she still does not sound too excited about coming to the States. But Gloria has high hopes she will convince her."

I said, "Tell her if everything works out, can they come during Melissa's school break?"

"Yes," Rosana said, "January or February. She hopes Melissa will sweeten up."

"Tell her they only need to stay for one week, more or less, for the medical work-up, and if they want, for fun, they could stay another few days. And tell her I sent her a check for $50 for Melissa's *quinceañera.* I will send another $50 next month."

"Gloria says 'thank you.' She wrote you a letter on Friday."

The conversation wound down. I told Gloria I sent my love to them both and all the family and she said the same for my family and Laura Lee and her family. Rosana hung up the phone and, letting out a long breath, looked at her notes. "Sixty-eight pounds, that's not very much. My niece weighs 68 and she's only six years old. But she's a big girl."

"Yeah, but 68, that's an improvement from before. Low, but not horrible. Not horrible at all." I was pleading for Rosana's agreement. "Seventy is ok." Now I was fudging. Ignoring me, Rosana looked down at her notes. "Let's see…" Here she gave a little laugh. "Melissa wrote you a letter on Friday……"

"Melissa did??" I shouted.

"You didn't hear that? Yes!"

"I thought you said Gloria wrote to me!" Still shouting.

"No! Melissa! She sent you a letter last Friday!" Rosana was shouting, too.

"Yes!!" I yelled the word.

"At least you made her react, even to say 'No.' No matter what she writes."

"I don't believe it! Holy Shit!"

"It seems that they had a long talk….."

"Holy shit."

"I said to her, maybe you won't need to change her name or do anything…."

I barely heard Rosana. I let out a huge exhale……..Nothing, nada, for almost three years. How did this happen?!

The letter. Gloria's upbeat tone. I knew they would come, I knew it! I motored through the day and didn't go to bed until after midnight and woke up at 2:30. I slept from 3:30 to 7 and was up for an hour before going back to sleep from 8 until 9.

Lovely mental images began to appear, as if they'd been stored in my heart waiting to be released. Gloria and Melissa meeting and greeting my friends. The three of us riding the Sausalito ferry across the bay, staring up at the Golden Gate Bridge. Rolling through the City, grinning uncontrollably on a clanging trolley car.

Sixty-eight pounds wasn't good. Forget Rosana's niece, 68, nearly 70, was good enough. Something to build on. I wrote Melissa, knowing my letter would cross hers in the mail.

> *Dear Melissa,*
>
> *How are you? I hope that you feel better now that you have returned from the hospital. It worried me to learn about your hospitalization when I spoke with Dra. Gonzalez at the beginning of July and I am happy that you are back home.*
>
> *Things are going well here. My friends gave me a very enjoyable birthday party last month and also friends from LA, Jeff and Marnie,*

and from Seattle, Sharon, visited me.

After speaking with your mother yesterday, it made me happy to know that Dr. Castro will take charge of following up for sending your records to the hospital here. Also I am happy that your mother and I are acting as a team together and can obtain positive results.

As I told your mom, I sent 5 faxes to Dr. Gonzalez and I called her once, and still 9 weeks passed without a response. What do you think? I was truly very worried all the time because of the lost time, because I think that as soon as we can do this it will be best for your health. After talking to your mom, the first time, I again called the hospital here in order to find out exactly what documents we need. Now they say that it is not so important that you have a passport or birth certificate with my name. At this time they are still deciding what they need. I hope that they decide before the end of the 20th Century.

Bueno, now I want you to know that I am doing all these things for you because I believe firmly it is going to help you. I will do nothing that will impede your return to Costa Rica at the agreed upon time. Remember what I put in the last letter—that the three of us can have lots of fun. Melissa, I also want you to know that I have no interest in controlling your life, nor do I have the right or the power to do that. I only know that I can help you if you will allow me. I can do so much for you, but the decision will always be that of you and your mother.

Now let's change the subject, you know that I am very pleased after speaking with Gloria and even more happy to know that you wrote me a letter. Now I anxiously await it. I say good-bye with a big hug for the two of you, and send greetings to your family.

Dad

PS I am enclosing $50 for your quinceañera and $35 for the lawyer, and $50 more next month.

29. "Saludos, Melissa"—August 21, 1993

From the beginning I'd had regular conversations with the financial office and a social worker at California Pacific Medical Center concerning Melissa's admission. Two months down the road, the social worker had some sort of ah-ha experience, one that wasn't so good. She said she'd been under the assumption that Melissa was going to be a California resident when she came from Costa Rica. When I said no, she let out a groan of disappointment. That sound told me Melissa's fortunes had changed. Not even my name on her passport would provide her financial assistance.

The day after I called Gloria, the hospital left a follow-up message on my answering machine. I did not return the call immediately. My emotional bowl was already overflowing with dread. The more real Melissa's visit became, the more real grew the fear that the dream would somehow derail. In my state of emotional dissipation I couldn't handle more bad news from the social worker.

My friend Sharon related that she had only weighed 85 or 90 pounds in high school. As a nurse, she assured me that Melissa's weight, by itself, was not a singularly critical factor. Margo, the Petaluma woman I'd met after the hospital panel, said her CF son's weight wasn't so different at age 15, either. I held on desperately to their encouragement but I was slowly sinking into a pit.

I sent a plea heavenward in my journal, one which, as I wrote, petered into confusion.

> *I pray that Melissa lives to at least 28, the median age for CF'ers here in the US.*
>
> *Maybe I should ask for more, but 28 years will allow her to have a husband, maybe a family.*
>
> *But, then if she died, her husband and, maybe, children would lose her. What do I want?*
>
> *Fuck. This disease sucks.*
>
> *I have to live by a different assumption.*
>
> *She will live and be okay.*

It's the parent's dilemma when your child has a life-threatening, incurable condition. You dream of their future, knowing that at any moment death can crush the future like a cigarette butt. You say it's the same for everyone? You are wrong. Death hovers over every cold or odd cough, every doctor's visit, and you are never far from sleepless nights and biting your fingernails to the nubs. You live as if your child will live until adulthood and as if she could die any day. You swing from pole to pole, from hope to discouragement. And once hope arrives, it's attacked by fear. You project a positive attitude to others even if you feel like collapsing on the floor. You lose track of how genuine your optimism is. You're a social schizoid.

On Saturday, August 21, almost three years to the day after Laura's first call, Melissa's letter arrived. I looked over the envelope with the familiar red, white and red striped border and the customary name of her mother in the upper left corner. But there was a difference. My name was written in script for the first time. I peered closely at the stamp in the upper right corner and smiled. It depicted a ship with sails, celebrating the 500th year anniversary of the discovery of America. In tiny letters was the ship's name: *"La Niña."* The Little Girl.

I removed the contents of the envelope like an archeologist unearthing an intact Mayan treasure. The stationery inside was unlined but Melissa's words rolled out evenly across the page with nice wide margins on either side.

Good day.

I hope that this finds you in good health. As for me, my health is good. And that of mommy is also good, thanks to God.

The Reyes family is good. As for travelling, I don't wish to travel. As for your wish to help me, I feel very happy. Perhaps in the future I will travel.

The vibrating apparatus, the percussor, which my mommy rents, cost 85.000 colones. You asked my mom about a gift for the Reyes family. They would be pleased by a camera. Greetings from them.

It would please me if you will send me the addresses of my grandparents.

Regards to all your family.

Please respond to this letter.

Respectfully, Melissa

The letter stirred up three year old emotions: delight, admiration, and the lovely, wondrous pride in my child. A new person was unveiled to me. Not a child, not yet a young woman. Merely by signing her name, Melissa owned her words. Every sentence was polite and straightforward, with no sign of the author's earlier tentativeness, no evidence of her mother's hidden influence. I smiled at her "no" even as she left the door open for a change of mind. I loved her request for a camera for her family. It thrilled me that we were conversing on paper.

I felt like a new person, born of my daughter reaching forth to grasp my outstretched hand. For a week my dreams of a relationship had become reality. There was the conversation with Gloria on Monday, the letter to Melissa on Wednesday, her letter on Saturday, and a letter to them both the following Tuesday.

Dear Gloria and Melissa,

How are you? I hope everything is going well for you.

Do you know who wrote me? Dr. Gonzalez. She says she is going to send the records! Dr. Castro must have been very convincing!! But I know that much of it is due to you. Thanks for your support.

I still don't have a definite reply from the hospital social worker. However I am sure that I will know more the next time that I write you. Even if they won't pay for the assistance, I will get the money some other place.

Please give my greetings to your family. With regards to Melissa's remark about a camera for them, I am going to buy one. By the way, how is Melissa's camera working?

I told Melissa in my letter that I am proud to see such positive aspects of her personality. This comment is also for you, Gloria, since you raised her.

Please send me a photo of you all, because I don't know when I am going to see you. I will write you soon and I hope that you do the same.

Affectionately,

Olin

If the State wouldn't reimburse me, I didn't see how I could raise thousands of dollars for a hospital stay. But I had to believe I could make it work. A realistic appraisal meant that massive debt would await me, eliminating future visits to Costa Rica. I couldn't dwell on that possibility.

Dear Melissa,

I am very happy to receive your letter. My father, his wife, and my older sister were visiting me when your letter arrived. They were happy to be here and share my joy. Each of them says hello to Gloria and to you, and sends you best wishes.

One of my first impressions of your letter was how different it was compared to the early letters you wrote to me. In English, when a person begins to develop their individuality and maturity, it is called finding or developing her "voice." This aspect of your letter stood out immediately. You expressed yourself with consideration and clarity. For me these qualities are admirable and I am proud that you possess them. Also it pleases me that you always say what you want.

With regards to my offer to help you, I am very glad to see that you are happy that I want to help you, because I love to help you. I take it seriously. Even though it will be a little more time before we visit in person, I am committed to helping you. Also I want to say that I respect your desire not to travel at this time and I look forward to a time that you will want to travel here.

I hope that you continue to feel good and continue learning lots in school and having lots of fun.

Please respond to this letter.

I am enclosing addresses of your grandparents.

Affectionately,

Papa

It wasn't more than a week before my father and his wife received a letter from Melissa.

Dear Grandparents,

I've gained weight, a kilo, and continue keeping track.

I hope you enjoy good health. I don't know English so I hope you will find someone who can translate this letter. School is going well not counting English and math.

Best wishes. I hope that you answer as soon as possible in Spanish.

Respectfully,

Melissa Reyes Reyes

Melissa's radical turn sent me soaring with confidence, relief, joy, enthusiasm and inspiration. My friend Frances, who had taken clown lessons, exaggerated a dumbfounded expression with a dropped jaw. "Gosh, I always thought her opening would take five or six years. How did she change so quickly?" The first thing which came to mind was the stream of cards, faxes and letters I had mailed into the emptiness. Melissa's letter reinforced the need to listen to my heart, that harsh teacher, and continue sending those bouquets.

* * * * *

Imagining Melissa, I picture her sitting at the kitchen table when no one is around. She writes carefully, then hesitates at the last line. She wants me to write again but fears rejection. She summons courage. "Please respond to this letter."

In my reverie, she has been secretly happy for some time. She re-considers medical treatment. She's always hated the hospital, but she acknowledges that she sometimes feels better from the Mucomist and the Pancrease. She has read the two articles I sent on new medical advances in the U.S. She is curious about the country she sees on television. And she is drawn to a new world of more relatives. There is the hope of more love, protection, opportunity — and being around father. She hides her feelings from others, but her cousins, Marvin and Merilyn, aren't deceived. This pleases her, too.

I had to see her soon.

* * * * *

While the decisions by Melissa and the hospital sat in limbo land, I continued poking around for new paths to Mohammed and her mountain. I attended the annual conference of Cystic Fibrosis Research, Inc, in Palo Alto, where I searched for people with medical or Costa Rica connections. I met a young sales rep from Scandipharm, a maker of nutritional supplements with a Central American office. I recommended her company develop their Costa Rica market. She agreed to put me in touch with their Central American regional rep. I also made arrangements to hustle projects and ideas with a couple of other people, including Ann Robinson, Executive Director of CFRI. I bumped into Isa and Ana Stenzel, who were now almost 21. They looked pretty healthy, thanks to their discipline, rigorous exercise and continued use of DNAse after the clinical trials in 1991. (DNAse had received approval by the FDA and was being sold under the name of Pulmozyme). Ana and Isa renewed my belief that Melissa, having already passed the median age of life for cystics in Costa Rica, could have a long, bright future. The entire conference imparted optimism.

That night, my dreams weren't so positive.

While out of my house for a day, I walk outside to see all the trees are barren. There are not even leaves on the ground. The same is true for all the trees as far as I can see. I'm incredulous.

* * * * *

Reina, for unknown reasons, sent Melissa's medical records to my house. I undid the envelope then stopped, terrified of reading the reports without Dr. Hardy there to interpret them. A few days later, I dropped off the envelope at the hospital in San Francisco and walked downstairs to see the social worker who I'd never called back. She gave me the final verdict and apologized, taking responsibility for the misunderstanding. It was confirmed: the State wouldn't pay for Melissa's treatment and CPMC wouldn't admit her without a hefty down payment and proof of assets to cover her costs. I obviously had neither.

I couldn't totally blame her or even feel much anger over what was, essentially, a dream that was fated to die. The harsh reality had arrived like slow paint dripping down my forehead. Perhaps I had obfuscated, adding to the misunderstanding because I so badly needed a plan. Perhaps I only heard what I wanted to hear and my reluctance to return the phone messages was an admission of what I had suspected for weeks.

I went home and sat on the expensive oak futon couch I had purchased for Gloria and Melissa to sleep on when they came to the States, purchased out of much hope and little realism. The $1800 had gone directly to my credit card account where it began accumulating interest. I felt like a poor person at a rich person's party, all because of "residency." That some people get great health care and others do not seemed more absurd than ever.

I attended a matinee of "Lorenzo's Oil," the Susan Sarandon movie about the parents of a child with an incurable disease. It was scarier than "Aliens 2." I didn't know what awaited me in the future with Melissa. The worry hadn't left me for three years.

I remembered telling the saleswoman at the futon store that my daughter had a "terminal illness." I had never used the term before. Was I trying to obtain sympathy or was it merely the truth suddenly bursting out? I told the woman Melissa and I had lots of time left. Why would I say that? How much more time did we really have? I didn't know.

All I knew, really knew, was what it means to love no matter what.

30.Spinning—September-October, 1993

"Melissa's health, as I'm sure you know, is not good. She's not declining rapidly but she can't be considered healthy, either. Looking at her height and weight, she is below the 5th percentile in both. Her pulmonary function tests score well below normal. She has the standard CF lung infections which are difficult to treat because of her resistance to certain antibiotics. She's been admitted to the hospital thirteen times in... let's see... in the last ten years."

Stiff and sweaty, I sat across from Dr. Karen Hardy in her Pacific Heights office in San Francisco. She looked to be mid-30s, with straight strawberry blonde hair and keen eyes. From my previous contact with her at CF conferences, I'd come to respect Karen as a straight-shooter who could string together a series of medical observations and recommendations without a blink. Today we had exchanged little more than brief hellos. Neither of us was there for the pleasantries.

"On the plus side, she's not having lung bleeds. Her heart and liver appear to be doing well. Her pancreas is, surprisingly, pretty small. She would definitely benefit from an admission here. It wouldn't be the answer, but, then, nothing is. We could boost her up with antibiotics and a solid nutritional program. She'd leave in better shape than she is now." She paused so I could speak, but my jaw felt like it was wired shut. She continued. "How is it looking, as far as bringing her here?"

"Iffy, at the moment. Can you determine what kind of care she's receiving in Costa Rica?"

"Well it's a bit hard to know. Dr. Gonzalez appears to be quite knowledgeable, but there are obvious limits to what she can do, in terms of the treatments and meds available. The recurring admissions, the low weight, the lung infections...it's quite serious. The body gets worn down. It would be ideal if your daughter could live here for awhile."

"I don't think that's going to happen. She's not eligible for state assistance. And she's very resistant to come here even for a week. I hope she'll change her mind and come up this winter, but...."

In the end, there was only so much we could talk about. I asked if Melissa could be admitted to the hospital's CF program as an outpatient. Karen nodded, saying Melissa could receive intravenous nutrition with IV's for a week and go home each night. Still expensive, but the best possibility under the circumstances.

I walked to the parking garage with my throat and stomach in knots. Every passing day is a day or more erased from Melissa's future. It's a cruel circus. I'm in the gallery, eyes skyward, frozen by Melissa and Gloria and their innocent, high-wire act, biting my nails, shaking my head, kicking the seats in front of me, screaming.

Despair led me to hatch another scheme to take the mountain to Melissa and others with CF. At the annual CFRI conference, I described my idea to Barbara Palys, Chairman of the International Association of Cystic Fibrosis Adults (IACFA). She surprised me with the news that Reina was holding a CF conference in Costa Rica next year. Barbara later wrote me a cordial letter filled with names and addresses of people she knew in the field of CF throughout Latin America.

I called my latest idea "The Bridge Project." The project would bring two, maybe four children to Northern California from Latin American countries. Each child would receive medical work-ups and lots of information to take home. I would organize the services to be delivered in San Francisco. I just needed money, always money. I had solid ins with the Hospital de Niños, CFRI, the CF Foundation, and was working my contacts with Scandipharm and the IACFA. I phoned and made an appointment to see the Consul General of Costa Rica in San Francisco.

*****

The futon couch sat unused in my living room. It had been sold to me by a stylish Polish woman with a wry smile and honey in her accent. She was 30-ish, and her pitch black hair framed generous eyes and a lovely, freckled face. Her name was Nika and I was smitten. I called her at work to invite her to join me for a hike on her day off. She counter offered: come to her house tonight for fish and wine for two. Several hours later I knocked on her door.

Nika's house was situated in an old neighborhood in north Santa Rosa. She looked fetching in a colorful apron, broiling fish. Dinner was tasty, a tad more formal than I was accustomed to, with cloth napkins and no talking with food in my mouth. During spicy conversation, mostly centered on the new Poland and Central America, Nika's face held a perpetually gentle, bemused expression. I smiled each time I looked at her.

As I was preparing to leave, she asked if I wanted to see the rest of the house. She showed me her bedroom. I leaned in through the doorway. "Nice," I said. She invited me to try her bed. I masked my surprise with an exaggerated expression of shock, then lay on the bed. Our eyes met and we sort of laughed as she came closer.

In the dim light from the street, before we fell asleep, Nika made a comment on my stories of Melissa. "My heart goes out to you." I pulled her close.

I barely had time for a relationship, but we began seeing each other several nights a week. Nika would often call late in the evening to wish me a sensuous beddy-bye. When I initiated the call, however, I encountered another Nika, tight-lipped and removed. I had an odd sense that someone was listening to her. It made me uneasy, as if I had set foot in David Lynch country.

*****

Gloria's letter arrived in late January and I sang a wordless song when I saw it. The top page contained an outline of her foot while the ones underneath looked like they'd been written in the back of a bus on a bumpy road. I peered at the nearly indecipherable letters and words. I pieced together the important parts. Melissa is doing very well. She liked the letters you sent her. I'm happy that you understand Melissa. Melissa's dog *"Cuqui"* (Cookie) had a litter of puppies and Melissa wants to keep all of them.

The letter was noteworthy for what it lacked. No mention of a trip to San Francisco. No mention of the money I sent for Melissa's 15th birthday. Gloria had returned to her previous penchant for avoiding the big things. I spoke aloud. "Forget the shoes, Gloria! Time's running out! No trip this school vacation and we'll end up waiting another year!" They were living in a dream land.

I tried to apply a measured tone in my next letter.

Dear Gloria and Melissa,

I hope everything goes well. Everything is good here. I was happy to find your letter waiting today when I returned home from bicycling. I am glad to receive all the good news about you all. Melissa, what are you going to do with all those dogs?

Dr. Hardy received the medical records of Melissa. She expressed concern about Melissa's digestion and the recurring infection in the lungs. She said she could provide a more effective treatment and would need to see Melissa for 4 or 5 days, but that Melissa could go home to sleep every night, she wouldn't have to stay in the hospital.

The Doctor also said it would be best if Melissa would come to see her in January or February and she said that if she waits until the next vacation in early 1995, it would be impossible to predict how her health would be then.

Because Melissa is so well, I can understand that you might want to stay away from doctors as much as possible. But you know, the most effective approach with CF is to act before further damage happens to the cells in the lungs and pancreas.

So I will phone you later in October and discuss this in more detail. Gloria, thank you for the tracing of your foot. When I know that someone is coming to Costa Rica I will send shoes with them. In the meantime I am enclosing the other $50 for Melissa's 15th birthday. I hope it will be a great event.

I wondered what would happen if Melissa maintained her refusal to travel. What would her condition be a year from now? Or would Gloria exert her authority and force her? In addition to my steady companions of dread and worry, a series of colds and ear infections hit me. Stress had turned my immune system to crud. I felt my resolve weaken and questioned the value of Melissa's visit, should it occur. What long term benefits could be gained from six days of outpatient treatment?

The breakthrough in my relationship with Melissa allowed me time to focus on her health. At the same time, I felt emotionally drained. I had ignored the loneliness of the past three years which had weighed on me like the wind bends a tree. I longed for an alternate life where I could simply enjoy Melissa and not deal with the life-threatening shit forever hanging over our heads.

One night, a young girl named Polly Klaas was kidnapped in a neighborhood a mile from my own. A predator had broken in through the bedroom window and abducted her while her mother was in the next room. In the coming days, volunteers sprang forth and hunted for Polly throughout Sonoma and Marin counties. The balance of evil and good in the world seemed even more out of whack than usual.

The following night, I woke up to another dream of a tree.

> *My house is under a giant tree. At first I'm out front with a friend discussing tree-trimming. It's dusk. I see the tree as if I've never really looked at it and I see the limbs are long and powerful, like one of those classic African trees. The long limbs spread horizontally and down so that they are touching the house at the corners and other spots. I am filled with curiosity, even wonder, when I see for the first time that the limbs encircle the house. I walk back and forth to see it all. I feel a slight concern that the limbs might be pushing against the house, but my examination shows me that there is nothing to fear.*

It was a transcendent scene, a visual opening to another dimension of life, at a time when my days were nothing but drudgery. Go figure. When I'm high on life, the tree is barren. I'm down and the tree of life appears. I was reminded of a bumper sticker, *Don't believe everything you think.*

There seemed to be no let up. My practice dipped slightly for several weeks, bringing financial worries. And there was Nika. We had known each other for less than a month when, one night, she whispered into my chest her longing to be a mother. The sadness in her voice lacked all self-pity. Her heart seemed to be caught in giving and not receiving, something I understood perfectly well. But her words scared the bejesus out of me. As I heard her sink into sleep, I wondered what kind of relationship I'd gotten myself into, where I would need to monitor my girlfriend's menstrual cycle like a spy and never, ever be enticed into unprotected sex.

I dream once again of Barb Johnson, my girlfriend who'd had an emotional breakdown.

> *Dark-haired, Barb resembles Nika in some intangible way. We are newly involved. We speak and she comes over next to me. I look closely at*

her freckled shoulders and neck. I feel drawn to pull away and leave. I am aware of some history we have. I stay.

I awaken, panicked. My world is going places I don't want to go.

One Saturday night at my house after dinner, the evening took a bad turn. Nika told me of an older man, a widower, she sometimes slept with. And there was an ex-boyfriend she also slept with, non-sexually. I took my best non-therapeutic approach, saying something like what the hell are you doing? Her tears turned to anger and she grabbed her coat. It was late and I talked her out of the thirty-minute drive back to her house. We slept together, not touching. It was another eyes-wide-open night in the dark. Nika was perpetually crawling in and out of holes while I was hardly the model of balance and emotional health. I was agonizing over Melissa and Gloria, juggling interviews for extra jobs, Spanish studies, a men's group, the CF parents group, a social life, an upcoming phone call to Gloria, a meeting with the CR Consul General. Polly Klaas had been missing for 12 days. I was sleeping in fits and starts and filling up on junk food.

A few days later I called Nika's house and a man answered. Nika took the phone and told me it was only her ex, whom she didn't really love. In spite of my hesitation we made plans to get together the following evening after I finished work. She appeared at my door, golden in the porch light, holding out two embroidered decorator pillows and a box of persimmons. The gifts delayed my plan to end our relationship but my loneliness was the bigger reason I kept my thoughts to myself. Chewing a persimmon, Nika said, "You can't put your life on hold for Melissa." I answered, "Anyone who gets involved with me inherits a potentially traumatic situation." I didn't see it then, but we were marking our territory and preparing to part.

* * * * *

The rep from Scandipharm called to say she had seen Reina Gonzalez at a CF conference in Dallas. Reina told her that Melissa was doing well. Dad and Shirley sent a nice letter in Spanish to Melissa. It was filled with warm, grandparent-type words of encouragement and love. They expressed a hope to meet her some day in California.

Two years had passed since I'd seen Melissa and my need to be with her was overwhelming. It would be foolish not to seize the opening she'd created. It no longer mattered if it was "a good time" to see her, her *quinceañera* was just around the corner. I pictured myself in the room at Melissa's party, standing beside a beaming Gloria. I would see Melissa, surrounded by friends and family, smiling for the first time in three years. It would be the first of many major events in my daughter's life. It was well before Thanksgiving and a few phone calls informed me the airlines were lowering fare prices.

I called Gloria on a weekday morning, when I figured Melissa would be there. I knew Gloria's English was good enough that we could communicate about me visiting in three weeks. Fortunately she answered the phone. We said our hellos and asked about each other's family. I inquired about Melissa's health and her latest thoughts on coming to San Francisco.

Gloria's answer did not surprise me. "She hasn't changed her mind. She doesn't want to travel."

"Gloria, I've decided to come to Esparza for Melissa's *quinceañera* and I just want to check to be sure that would be ok. I'm planning on buying the tickets tomorrow." Gloria asked me to wait and I heard a clunk, as the phone was set on a table.

"Meli!" she called. "Meli!" There was a pause and I pressed the phone to my ear but could barely make out Gloria's muffled words. They talked for some time. I sat, poised and alert, until they finished. The phone crackled and Gloria's voice came through once again.

"Olin?"

"Yes, what did she say?"

"She says 'no.'"

31. So What—October-November, 1993

Ten years earlier, an ugly melanoma mole was excised from my back. During a follow-up appointment, the surgeon walked behind the examining table on which I sat and, without warning, ripped the taped bandage from my back. The sharp pain caused me to curse and weep involuntarily. Melissa's unexpected refusal had a similar effect: Pain compounded by anger over Gloria's apparent concession to her daughter. But my motivation to go to Esparza was unquenched. I waited a day to put together a plan before phoning Gloria. In a brief conversation, I told her I would fly down in late November, several weeks after Melissa's *quinceañera*.

Nika and I met at my house to for a quiet night in front of the TV. We watched "Nova" on PBS. The subject was organ transplants. During that hour, my imagination bloomed again with a dream of giving a lung to Melissa.

It was the last time I saw Nika. We confirmed the mutual decision a few nights later. I lay down the phone, feeling a terrible aloneness, but I didn't have room for relationship drama or my own ambivalence.

A few afternoons later I drove south, sneaking peeks at San Francisco's magnificence as I crossed the Golden Gate Bridge. I picked up airline tickets in North Beach and bought a camera for Melissa's *tíos*, then jumped on the Powell Street cable car to Union Square. From there it was a short stroll to one of the elderly, ignored buildings on Market Street. I glanced at the directory in the lobby before entering a gold-trimmed elevator. On the 5th floor, my footsteps echoed on the marble hallway as I passed doors with smoked glass windows and brass knobs. It was a scene straight out of *The Maltese Falcon.*

I entered the office of the Consul General of Costa Rica. Following an introductory phone call, I had sent a letter to Natalia Jimenez Carvajal:

Dear Madame Consul General,

Over the past several years, I have been very active in assisting Costa Rican citizens who have the disease of cystic fibrosis. My involvement in this work began in 1990, when I learned that my daughter Melissa, a Costa Rican herself, had been diagnosed with CF...

One priority has been to hold discussions with major US-based pharmaceutical companies in order that more effective medicines could reach those Costa Ricans with CF. I also drafted a grant proposal for a local Rotary Club chapter, which donated $2500 to the CF Center at the Hospital de Niños.

I am writing to you, Madame Consul General, to express a sincere interest in meeting with you in person. I have an idea which I think could easily develop into a tremendously significant event for the lives of Costa Rica's CF citizens. I would find your thoughts and input on this idea tremendously valuable.

I am enclosing a letter of endorsement from Ann Robinson, Executive Director of Cystic Fibrosis Research, Inc., who can attest to the seriousness and depth of my commitment. I will be happy to follow up this letter with a phone call after November 1, and I look forward to our meeting together.

Very truly yours,

Olin Dodson

Here I was, chewing on my lip, hoping Natalia would be the kind of woman whose heart sat on her sleeve. She invited me into her modest office and motioned for me to take a chair beside her desk. Natalia was half my size, and like every Costa Rican I'd ever met, subtly charming and unpretentious. She mixed up her English tenses and meanings and I met her halfway by speaking slowly and minimizing my slang and contractions. She informed me that Dr. Castro Armas at the Hospital de Niños had been her daughter's doctor and she'd phoned him after reading my letter. I was encouraged to learn he'd spoken well of me.

I briefly reviewed my circumstances and crescendoed to a request that she write a letter to Melissa and Gloria, guaranteeing their safety while they were in the US. I offered to compose the letter and Natalia consented to signing it. Spirited by this quick achievement, I moved on to bigger fish: The

Bridge Project. Natalia was game to support the idea and shared my hope of persuading Genentech to make a nice-sized contribution. But, in the telling, I realized the absurdity of trying to organize a large international project when I was the only staff person. A second realization distracted me even more. Natalia had no political clout. I was such a naïve 46 year-old.

Then came another innocent little bomb from Natalia. "Do Gloria and Melissa have visas?"

My face grew hot. I'd failed to achieve even that first step in my attempt to bring Melissa to San Francisco. Self-recrimination set in, like daggers. Further discussion was impossible. Natalia made small talk about having lunch sometime and my appreciative good-bye was overdone. Going down the elevator, then stomping up Grant Avenue, I felt foolish and angry, some of it misdirected at Natalia for puncturing my various delusions. I frothed in mad-dog mode. *"They have to do this or else....or else I don't want to be involved! Here I am out of my mind, planning giant plans while Melissa and Gloria haven't even applied for visas! They brought me into this, for what? For nothing! I refuse to play games while Melissa deteriorates. I can't do it all. I can't do more than I'm doing."*

* * * * *

The next day was Melissa's birthday. I would call Gloria after I spoke with my father. He had forwarded me their second letter from Melissa.

> *Shirley, Olin,*
>
> *I was happy to receive the letter from you. I had imagined that it had been lost or that you had not received mine. It makes me glad that you like to travel. I hope that someday you will come to Costa Rica.*
>
> *Greetings to my Aunt Jan. It would please me if you would give me her address so I could write her.*
>
> *Soon I will be 15 years of age, "Supuestmente la edad mas dificil y bonita de una mujer" (Supposedly the age most difficult and lovely for a woman). It appears they are giving me a party. It would please me if everyone could attend, but I know it is difficult for you. If they give me a party they could not give me what I want, it costs $175 and Olin only sent me $100 for the party, which is to say that they can't buy me what I want, "una grabadora" (a tape player). I am wondering if it is possible that you present to me as a gift, part of the cost of a boom box, even though I don't know if I ought to ask you. In the end I'd be happy if you could help me to realize my dream.*
>
> *Until next time,*
>
> *Wendy Melissa Reyes Reyes*

Dad and I discussed the letter. He and Shirley were put off by Melissa's hitting them up for money and I couldn't blame them. But I defended Melissa, certain that Gloria had put her up to the request. Melissa would not ask for

$100 from *abuelos* she hardly knew. Privately I was embarrassed for Gloria and Melissa. Dad and Shirley knew of my pain over Melissa's silence and understood her less than I. Gloria had reason to want financial assistance but her approach was wrong.

A bigger difficulty for me was Melissa's openness and interest in Dad and Shirley. In a way I was happy, but still in a piss that she didn't want me to attend her birthday party. Why does she invite them and not me? Then there were the larger issues. Here I was trying to save my daughter's life; they were focused on a boom box. I wanted a relationship; they weren't so sure. I'm working my ass off, they don't seem to care. Briefly I wondered if I shouldn't try to find a woman and child who could appreciate the love in my heart. I was confused about the true nature of my so-called unconditional love for Melissa. I still loved her unconditionally but I needed something in return.

I looked at Melissa's writing on the page in front of me, and her reference to me as "Olin." It was the first time I could remember her calling me anything in three years. One little word, but not "father." It saddened me.

I wasn't in a great mood after speaking to Dad, but I still had to phone Costa Rica before heading downtown to my first appointment. Gloria answered and we made small talk. I was cheered to learn that no one had bought Melissa a boom box, since I'd found a nice one I wanted to bring her. "Before I go to work — I know Melissa is at school — tell her I called to say 'Happy Birthday' to her."

"She's here. You can tell her." Adrenaline flooded my blood stream.

Melissa came on the line and I wished her a Happy Birthday and quizzed her for a couple of minutes, getting little in response. I asked her when her party was and where, how many people had been invited, if there would be music, things like that. I was pulling teeth. I told her I would see her in a few weeks. It was brief and very matter of fact, like we're in business together.

Hello. I'm Olin, your dad.
You're the teenager whose life I'm trying to save.
I hear you're having a birthday party.
Well, it's been nice talking to you.
See you soon.

* * * * *

I met with my therapist, Anita. I told her Gloria's attitude seemed like madness, even neglect. Her and Melissa's inaction were self-destructive. I made manly threats like guys do when we feel weak or threatened: I won't be quiet about this! I'm not going to keep doing this! As the session went on, I dropped the bluster and puffery and sank into feelings of sadness and aloneness and, finally, terror that the story could end soon, not with Melissa dying, but by my withdrawal.

Three years had passed since I learned I was a dad. Had anything significant happened? Melissa had Pancrease and Mucomist. She'd gained a few pounds. I didn't want to be saying this a year from now.

That night a bad dream woke me.

> *A child with a skull's face stared in the window at me. I tried to hide in the corner.*

A few nights later Melissa appeared once more.

> *I entered a doctor's office. I sat down and began talking to the women in the room in Spanish. An adult Melissa came out of a door. She sat down and we spoke in Spanish. I asked her about the latest test results on Melissa, our child. Adult Melissa did not like the subject but agreed to retrieve the most recent results for me.*

Was the dream reminding me to talk to the adult in Melissa? Or telling me that the child in Melissa was hidden from me?

In a few days, I adopted a greater acceptance of their attitudes towards Melissa's health care, even as I disagreed with it. I would go to Esparza, register my feelings and see what developed. I could get the door slammed in my face one more time. So what?

I would appear in Esparza without heroic pretensions. Not as Lancelot or Che Guevara, just me. I would match their commitment, stop knocking myself out, maybe spend a day enjoying Costa Rica, something I'd done only once in my first three trips. As for my latest stack of gifts, they no longer dripped with emotion or expectation. They were merely nice things I hoped Melissa and her mom would enjoy. My conversation with Melissa might go like this:

> *"Want to shop for tapes for your new boombox? No? Fine."*
>
> *"Want to ride the ferry across the Gulf of Nicoya? No? Okay."*
>
> *"Want to take another picnic by the river? No? No problem!"*

If they want it to work out, it will.

* * * * *

I nurse a cup of coffee in Aram's, a Middle Eastern restaurant in downtown Petaluma. I'm outlining strategy in my journal when Miles Davis' "Sketches of Spain" comes on the sound system. I raise my head to the mournful trumpet. It cries and my insides bundle. Images of what I missed hijack my thoughts. I missed Melissa's infancy, her baby smile, her little fingers reaching for my face, holding her against my chest, burrowing my nose in her neck and smelling her sweet fragrance, feeding her, wiping food off her chin and those millions of miracles of new life. Now I will miss the one birthday I want to attend. The dream is over. I can't think of anything more to do for them. Perhaps it's time to get on with my life.

Part Four
1993 - 1995

32. Secrets—November, 1993

This was the plan. Raft the Rio Pacuare. Hire a translator. Travel to Esparza for the summit with Gloria and Melissa. Visit Merilyn and her parents. Confer with Dr. Gonzalez and Dr. Castro. I would be in country for six days.

The Guatemala City airport, backlit by morning sun, was a brief touch down on the red-eye to Costa Rica. The airfield had been swathed from the jungle and edged with olive hangars and dormitories. Khaki-garbed soldiers milled around, their dark faces pinched in the horizontal light. In the fifteen years since my last visit, the country had witnessed a protracted civil war. The evangelical Christian president, General Efrain Rios Montt, led the army's effort, generously supported by guns, funding, and a look the other way from the United States. Within a 10-year period, 600 villages had been destroyed, 75,000 indigenous and/or anti-dictatorship people killed, and countless others "disappeared."

I couldn't make sense of the relationships with my daughter and her mom apart from the history of the convergences of our cultures. A tug of war had been played out for centuries between the United States and Latin America, each trying to figure out the other and get its way. For 150 years, the United States had treated Latin American countries like children, always doing what was "best," even when it attempted to overthrow legitimate governments in Guatemala, Chile, Panama, Haiti, Nicaragua (twice) and so on. The list of our military incursions seems never ending.

I, too, was convinced I knew best. The more Gloria and Melissa resisted my plans, the more I wanted to force them. I grew judgmental. Gloria was weak. Negligent. Stuck in her ways. But I was also suspicious of repeating my country's paternalism and that suspicion helped temper my self-righteousness.

At San Jose International, immigration police once again ignored me and my bottles of medicines. I checked into a colorful B&B downtown, the Pensión de la Cuesta. After a cool shower, I phoned several language schools in search of a translator and reserved a place on a guided river trip the following day. I wandered downtown and spotted two blind street singers I'd photographed in 1978. Back then, they'd been a threesome. Now the duo stood on the same sidewalk, one on guitar, the other on mouth harp, attracting curious crowds, from businessmen to young couples. Missing from the musicians' faces was the preciousness they had in my memory.

I flopped on a concrete bench in Morazon Park across from the Holiday Inn. The building was tall and brittle-looking. A security guard approached a man sitting on a low wall near the hotel entrance and ordered him to move on. Passersby in business clothes wore tense faces. Costa Rica had changed. The buildings seemed more paint-pocked and water stained than before. The tourism industry was thriving but the country's economy teetered. A drug-corruption scandal tainted the government. Street crime was on the rise. I thought about the man on the street in 1978 and wondered when he'd last stopped a stranger to brag about his country.

Central America's rainy season peters out in November, so the Rio Pacuare, winding through the mountains east of San Jose, was low and short on thrills. However, no running river is a bad river. My little party put in around mid-day, surrounded by echoes of bird song. In a t-shirt and swim trunks, I lay back in the trailing raft and handed myself over to the river's spell. Lianas dropped from lofty branches and circled languidly in the current. Sunbeams speared through the forest canopy. Rocking gently in the roll of the water, I dozed off.

On the drive back to San Jose, Enigma's exotic rhythms thumped through the van's speakers. I stared into the darkening landscape, fine-tuning my strategy for Gloria and Melissa, well, less strategy than directive: Get On Board. That and a wish to demonstrate to Melissa that I was a kind man and a loving father. The following morning, I joined a couple of congenial fellow rafters from Manhattan traveling west in their rental car. They dropped me off in Esparza.

I walked north on a dirt road in a neighborhood of dappled light and brick houses, generously spaced. Straps of two gym bags filled with medical products, the boombox and Gloria's shoes, criss-crossed my chest. The heavy air soon had me sticky with sweat. Their stucco house was easy to locate, ten minutes from the highway. It was green with a tiny porch and a small yard in front enclosed by a low, gated fence. Iron security bars, painted white, covered the windows.

I stopped at the gate and shouted hello. Gloria came out of the front door, dressed in a modest cotton print dress. Stylish rimless glasses were not flattering but gave her a well-to-do appearance. Maybe Ramon had given her a raise. I kissed her cheek. She stood aside as I stumbled through the doorway and entered a large room with a dining area set back from the door. A sparsely decorated living room with a television sat to the right. Lace curtains covered the windows.

Gloria showed me to a circular table covered with a thin table cloth and walked to the kitchen to get me a glass of water. Her hair, faintly streaked in grey, was gathered in a bun atop her head. Sitting down, she told me Melissa was in her room, then turned her head and called out. "Meli, your father is here." I looked to my left and, down a short hallway, Melissa poked out her head from behind a screen door. My heart quickened. I smiled and waved, and she retreated.

Melissa at her quinceañera. 1993.

Gloria was explaining Melissa's plans to visit a friend when the screen door popped. Outfitted in shorts and tennis shoes, she looked different, all legs and arms. Brown curly hair fell over her shoulders. Her face had a wan, almost ashen cast, absent its childhood cuteness. Her eyes were bruised and watery. Still I could have held her and gloried in her features for an hour.

She came to me and offered her cheek. I kissed it lightly, felt its softness on my lips. In response to my question, she said she was fine. I waited to see if she would sit at the table. She glanced at the box with the tape player resting on a chair next to mine. This is for you, I said. She looked at it, chewed her finger, looked at her mom, and then turned around to leave. I watched her walk down the hall and told myself not to be discouraged. Gloria looked at me but said nothing. I said, "What?" She shrugged.

Gloria and I talked in a Spanish-English mix for a half an hour or so. The tone of her voice sounded unhappy, even fearful. I complimented her on the nice house and told her of my plans for the week: to return with a translator in two days, visit the hospital, and, I hoped, come back to Esparza a third time at week's end. Gloria nodded her head. She thanked me for the shoes and boxes of medication.

How is Melissa??

"She's well," she answered, lacking conviction. "She uses her inhaler and percussor every day. She's stayed out of the hospital, thanks to God." Her expression brightened. "She's started going to church. Twice on Sundays and once during the week."

I raised my eyebrows. When did that happen?

"Oh, she's been going for a while. Maybe a year."

And school?

"She's doing well. When she can stay out of the hospital, she is able to keep up."

What else does she do? Does she have a boyfriend?

Gloria laughed. "No, no boyfriend. She doesn't go out much except for church. She listens to religious music on the radio. She reads. She reads the Bible sometimes." Gloria's eyes brightened. "She likes catalogs of women's clothes."

I smiled. Do you ever go to San Jose just to shop with her?

"No. She doesn't like San Jose."

A real country girl.

How was her party?

Gloria's voice grew wistful. "Oh, it was beautiful. She had many friends there, and everyone had a good time."

Do you have any photos?

Gloria stood up and sauntered down the hall to Melissa's room. The door behind the screen door was locked. Gloria's knock got no response. She crossed the hall briefly into another room, but came back empty handed. "She has them," was all she said.

We heard a rumble of thunder, a warning that I should walk back to the highway to look for a bus before a downpour began. Gloria agreed that a heavy rain could arrive at any minute. She said she would be around all week, come back any time.

Our initial meeting had gone well, I thought. "Gloria, I'm very glad to see you again!"

She managed a faint smile. "*También.*" (Likewise)

I requested she give the medicine and tape player to Melissa and to tell her I looked forward to seeing her tomorrow or the day after.

It was drizzling when I stepped onto the bus to San Jose. The air inside was humid and there was a thick smell of warm bodies. Condensation masked the windows. I held onto an overhead bar for the next two hours, looking at the tops of people's heads. The chill between Melissa and Gloria surprised me. Three years earlier they had moved around inseparably, resembling a mare and her foal. Now Melissa was like a colt and the power differential had tipped in her favor. Her non-reaction to the tape player disappointed me, but it also served as a reminder that I'd not exactly been welcomed into their lives and that I couldn't carry the relationship on my back.

* * * * *

There was a message waiting for me at the *pensión*. I phoned the number and a woman named Xiomara answered. She easily passed my little interview. Summarizing her education and experience in translating, she spoke English with precision and intelligence. Her price was modest and she was available to travel the day after next. We set a time to meet at the car rental office.

The following morning, I walked to the hospital. Reina was not at work but I tracked down Dr. Castro. He invited me to his office. I remembered his kind eyes from our meeting during the nutrition project. He stated that he was now Melissa's primary doctor. With typical Costa Rican courtesy, he masked the reasons for the switch from Dr. Gonzalez, but I was sure the decision did not leave Melissa unhappy. He confirmed that Melissa had not been hospitalized recently but was due for a check-up. He and I discussed the Rotary Project and my visit with Natalia at the consulate. I asked that he pressure Melissa to come to the States for treatment and re-assure her and her mom that they would be safe in the US and able to return to Costa Rica without difficulty.

During our conversation, my stomach began to cramp up. The doctor wrote out a prescription which I filled at a pharmacy across the street from the hospital. I returned to the hotel, encouraged by Dr. Castro's support and appreciation. Except for a short dinner excursion, I slept all day and through the night.

*****

Xiomara Cubillo de Hernandez impressed me just by arriving on time at the rental lot. Though her maiden name was Arabic, she was raised in a traditional Costa Rican Catholic family and married into San Jose money. She was decked out in a modest black skirt and a crisp white blouse as if poised for a sudden confession should the need arise. I was happy that, given her recent interest in God, Melissa would be exposed to a young, attractive, religious girl who was ambitious and well educated.

Once again I called from the gate in front of Ramon's house and Gloria escorted us inside to the table. There was a vase of mixed flowers offering a faint but pleasing scent, and a box of tissues in the center of the table. The open door and windows invited in a pleasurable breeze. Gloria served us water and introduced Xiomara to Melissa, who had come out of her room to stand and lean against the corner of the hallway, some six feet away from the table. I invited her to sit with us but she shook her head of matted hair, eyes pointed to the floor. Her face was like a dirty window. She wore a t-shirt and light blue pants with flowery decorations. I paused to look at her until she raised her head and caught my eye. I knew that Melissa was self-conscious about her appearance, so I limited my sneak peeks.

Relying on Xiomara to translate, I began by asking questions about the current state of Melissa's health, her medications and daily regimen, and her meetings with the doctor. Gloria described her dissatisfaction with Reina and the hospital, the long waits and skimpy information, which she took as a lack of basic respect. I was happy to hear about her spunk, knowing it would benefit Melissa. She welcomed the transfer to Dr. Castro, even if Melissa only tolerated him. As she talked I tried to make it obvious, especially to Melissa, that I was interested and understanding of their ordeals, which I was.

At some point, Melissa drifted over to the table and sat across from me, between her mother and Xiomara. The vase of flowers blocked my view of her. When I adjusted my chair, she scooted sideways in hers. She ensured that the flowers always blocked my view. She stifled a watery cough from deep in her chest, then spit into a tissue.

I described the Cystic Fibrosis clinic at the California Pacific Medical Center in San Francisco. I used their experience with the Hospital de Niños to contrast with the personal treatment Melissa would receive from Dr. Hardy and her staff. Out of nowhere, Melissa, still looking at the table, blurted out, "*Yo no voy!*" (I'm not going!) In mid-sentence, I stopped. I glanced at Gloria, received a blank stare in return for my trouble, and resumed my description.

Ok, Melissa might have been pissed, thinking her letter had ended my efforts to bring her to the States, but I wasn't inclined to detour into a Why-don't-you-want-to-go-to-San-Francisco? cul-de-sac. I had asked enough teen-agers in my life the "why" question to know it was wasted breath.

At the conclusion of my pitch, I was surprised and encouraged by Gloria. "Would this be one of many trips?"

"Great question. Not necessarily, every patient with CF is different. That's why we want Melissa to have a thorough assessment." I proceeded to describe my meeting with Natalia Jimenez, her connection to Dr. Castro, and her guarantee of their safe return following their treatment.

"I'm not going!" Same defiant tone, eyes now forcing themselves on Gloria. *Pretty rude*, I thought. Gloria's face showed irritation. I pulled out Natalia's card from my shirt pocket. I displayed it to Melissa like an ace of hearts before handing it to Gloria. "Everything is set. All you need to do is obtain visas and decide on a date. I'll take care of everything else."

"I'm not going!"

On the drive to Esparza, I had explained to Xiomara my intention to ratchet up the pressure on mother and child. But, given Melissa's hard line petulance, I knew this was not the time to get into a fight.

Gloria apologized and said she had to run to the store and would return in five minutes. When she left, Melissa, surprisingly, did not move. My mind raced to think of something to keep her at the table. I turned to Xiomara. "Tell her I forgot and left the instructions to the tape player in my hotel. I'll bring them, the tape cleaner and the batteries with me tomorrow."

Melissa faced Xiomara. I stared at her bony hands and forearms, occasionally stealing a glance at her face. I never caught her looking at me. It was wrenching to converse with her, inches apart, our eyes never meeting.

I asked Xiomara if Melissa had any special plans for her school vacation. "No." She coughed and swallowed.

I reported on my trip down the Pacuare. "It was a lovely river, with beautiful birds. It was so relaxing, I fell asleep. I'm just glad I didn't roll over and fall in the river! Melissa, I know you like the river we went to in 1990. I bet you would enjoy taking a raft trip. Have you ever boated down a river?"

I saw her slightly shake her head after Xiomara repeated the question.

I asked what had happened with her litter of dogs. She said, "I gave away all but one. Its name is Ruby." I smiled to myself. Ruby was the name of my paternal grandmother.

Melissa got up from the table and walked through the kitchen door leading to the back yard. Xiomara gave me a sympathetic smile before Melissa returned carrying a little red dog. Ruby was a squirmy quasi-dachshund with a hint of rodent lineage. Sitting on the floor I scratched her chest and let her lick my face. Her coat was fresh and soft. I glanced up to see Melissa's poker face. She didn't look away when our eyes met. We spent time playing with Ruby and making little jokes, like how different from my grandmother she looked.

Gloria came through the front door with a plastic bag filled with fresh fruit, and Melissa left the house with Ruby. The breeze had died and the room was now quite warm. Gloria blended melon *liquados* and joined us at the table. I repeated the story of Helen and Ed Dias' daughters, Diane and Mandy, who both had cystic fibrosis. Although Diane had a virulent type of CF and passed away at age 12, I offered Mandy as an example of someone who was living a healthy life due to the best medical care. Then I turned up the heat.

"Gloria, parents have to be forceful. I've repeatedly made you the offer to bring Melissa to San Francisco. I want to be clear that there's no expiration date on the offer, but I'm not going to keep bringing it up. To be perfectly honest, I can't take the repeated pain of hearing 'No'."

Gloria's face cracked like a tea cup and tears came to her eyes. "Olin, I pray to God every day for Meli. Many, many people are praying for her. A woman from the church was told by God that Meli would be cured this year."

I thought, "*He'd better act fast, it's November.*"

"The drugs don't cure her, Olin. One is the same as another. Only God can heal Meli."

I started to speak but thought better of it. This was a repeat of what she'd told me on the phone. Gloria's beliefs had made her mind up.

I looked for a segue to our departure for San Jose—and learned more about the mess I was in.

What did you think of the story I wrote for Melissa? I asked.

"It was good."

And Melissa, what did she think?

Gloria shrugged. "I don't know."

You don't know?

She added, "She has it locked up in her diary."

Is she scared of me?

She shrugged. "I don't know."

Nervous?

"I don't know."

Thanks, Gloria. You couldn't be less helpful.

We knocked on Melissa's door to say goodbye.

No answer. I guessed she was asleep, overwhelmed or, like me, angry.

*****

Xiomara and I stopped at a roadside restaurant across the highway. An odor of old grease and chicken filled the room. I ordered cold sodas and sank in my chair. The sun was dipping low, meaning we would arrive in San Jose well after dark. "I doubt that Gloria is giving the trip to California serious consideration." Xiomara nodded in agreement but her kind smile saved me.

I had an idea. "Do you have time to visit Melissa's *tíos* for a few minutes?"

We found Ascension, Bita and Merilyn at home. After I introduced Xiomara, they each embraced me. Bita brought a round of watermelon drinks into the room and set them on the table. Their sweet perfume filled the room.

Merilyn joined Xiomara and me at the table while Ascension sat in his rocker and Bita stood over us. Merilyn asked Xiomara a question. When I heard the translation, my jaw and eyebrows jumped. I repeated her words. "Gloria married Ramon?" Merilyn gave a loud "*Sí!*" Bita, dish towel on shoulder, smiled and made a throaty sound which I interpreted as, "*That's right, girlfriend!*" Ascension merely rocked his chair and chuckled.

Merilyn said she was shocked Gloria hadn't told me. I shook my head, trying to let the news sink in. I thought back to yesterday and understood why Melissa now had her own room. Merilyn continued on, changing the subject. She described her and her parents' persistent encouragement to Meli to write me.

I said, "Well, I owe all of you lots of appreciation for your great success."

Xiomara offered her translation and Merilyn's face screwed up. "She wrote you?"

It was my turn to grin. "You didn't know?"

"No!" She looked at her parents and everyone laughed.

That revelation set Merilyn to talking as if she'd been freed from a lifelong vow of silence. After Ramon and Gloria married, they made plans to move to a little town called Palmares, a 45 minute drive from Esparza. Melissa's response was "*No Voy!*" and she asked Bita and Ascension if she could live with them. Ramon and Gloria's moving plan was abandoned without explanation.

Merilyn and her parents had encouraged Melissa to travel to the U.S., reminding her she could visit her friend, Jessica, whose family had moved to California. "Olin, Gloria is the one who is afraid to come visit you. Although Melissa may be resisting in order not to upset her mother."

"What is Ramon's place in all this?"

"Ah, who can say? But I know Melissa won't let him tell her what to do."

My mind buzzed with the revelations but Merilyn wasn't finished. "Melissa was extremely resentful towards Gloria after you first visited. You see, Gloria never told her that you did not speak Spanish. And she told her misleading stories." I remembered Gloria's fiction about my "girlfriend" but was too caught up in my thoughts to ask Merilyn what else Gloria had said.

"Lately, Melissa has been pulling away from affection and interest with everyone! I think she was unhappy with her mother's marriage to Ramon. "

My heart filled with appreciation for Merilyn. I was glad she had returned to the subject of the nuptials. "How did the marriage happen?"

In a world class nasal tone, she snapped her reply. "Gloria never talked about it." She changed the subject. "Melissa is confused and doesn't know who to be angry with. Sometimes she cries she is so confused." I shook my head.

Melissa's aunt and uncle (Merilyn's parents) Bita and Ascension. He is Gloria's brother.

I told Merilyn about the tape player I brought for Melissa and her non-reaction when she saw it. "Melissa is always that way with presents. At her *quinceañera*, only three people were allowed into the room when she opened her gifts. She is very, very private. At times she comes here to our house and talks to no one but me." She changed the subject. "Did Gloria tell you about Melissa's birthday party?"

"A little, why?"

"Did she tell you about Melissa crying?"

"Oh, no. Why was she crying?"

Merilyn's face broke into a victorious grin. "She was crying in happiness, telling everyone the party never would have happened without her daddy."

* * * * *

We drove back to San Jose and I gripped the wheel for two hours, my stomach feeling like it was filled with a brick. Trucks and buses made death-defying passes, filling our little sedan with diesel odors. I asked Xiomara what she noticed while translating my table conversation with Melissa.

"Melissa's eyes brightened when you mentioned the tape cleaner and the instructions. She smiled when you made the joke about falling out of the boat, and also when you told her she would enjoy rafting." Xiomara paused. "Melissa's responses were very polite, but she seems very angry."

I was angry, too. Gloria and Melissa had blown off me and my plan, while Melissa's mortality clock ticked away. I tried to set aside my feelings. *I need to keep a clear head, focus on convincing Melissa that I love her. The quinceañera story tells me she might be getting it. Why hadn't Gloria told me that story?* Headlights in the face interrupted my thoughts. From behind an oncoming truck, a Jeep accelerated towards us. I braked to let the idiot circle the truck and return to his lane, then exploded. "Jesus!" I turned to Xiomara and felt my face flush. I made a brief apology but she said nothing.

The entire trip felt like a bust. I would return home in three days with nothing but holes in my pockets. I wanted God to make Melissa's health improve, wanted us to have time to know each other, wanted us to talk and do father-daughter stuff, wanted her to have a long, full life, wanted to give her a lung or anything else I owned to make that happen. All were dreams falling from my grasp.

A sorry platitude comes to mind: Live Like There's No Tomorrow.

Oh, man, if there's no tomorrow, I got nothing.

33. Darkening Road—November, 1993

I dodged speeding diesel trucks to cross the highway to Ramon's house and jogged to the nearest tree. It was mid-day. A lone woman in flip flops, holding a plastic grocery bag, stood in the shade and smiled as she touched a handkerchief to her upper lip. I carried low expectations for my final meetings with Melissa, with about the same level of motivation. Merilyn's stories had perked me up and Xiomara's faith in me was nice, but my failure to budge Gloria and Melissa outweighed everything. I thought of the letter I would send Melissa from home. A part of me was already there.

Early that morning, I had driven to Esparza like a mad man. In the mountains, a police officer standing beside the highway blew his whistle and gestured to me as I sped by. I found my lodging for the night, hardly a crown jewel. The A/C grumbled in the window and gave the room a damp odor. In the shower stall a scummy, uncovered drain appeared highly infectious. I got out of there and took the sedan south to Orotina on a rolling two-lane where emerald grasses waved at the starchy sky. Aging clapboard *casitas* shared the roadside with modern stucco homes fronted by gated gravel driveways. Sunlight and the scent of moist earth lifted my spirits.

Esparza sits near the edge of a lush plateau above the Pacific coastal plain. Famed explorer John L. Stephens mentioned the town in his 1841 travelogue, "Incidents of Travel in Central America, Chiapas, and Yucatan," but found little to say. The town had not exactly surged into the 20th century. Wherever I drove, a man on a three-legged horse would have received less attention than my compact rental did.

I stopped into a small café for lunch, but the discovery of animal parts in the soup caused me to put down my spoon. Minutes later, Gloria offered me a second chance for a meal. She cleared a place at the table across from Melissa who offered her cheek to me, mumbled "*Hola*," and returned to her sandwich. The previous day's anger was gone from her eyes; they drooped. She finished eating and went to her room. Gloria brought me chicken and tomato on toast. We exchanged small talk about my visit to Ascension's which she had already heard about. Perhaps she knew her relatives had informed me of her marriage, but neither of us mentioned it.

She brought out some trinkets and placed them on the table. They were gifts for me to take to my family, little replicas of farm carts and plaques painted with Bible verses and heavenly vistas. She began to wrap them in colored paper. Melissa returned and leaned against the wall at the corner of the hall, head down. Every few minutes our eyes met but her expression was like cold oatmeal. I tried to ignore the pain in my heart and act cheerful.

Gloria finished her wrapping and made noises about going to the bank. I was unsure if she meant for me to leave as well. I still had another group of gifts from me, a friend, Crystal Hishida, and my sister, Jan. I left and hastily retrieved them from my hotel room.

*****

For the unwrapping of the gifts, the three of us gathered in the living room in front of the television. Gloria looked on from a chair across from Melissa and me on the couch, sitting side by side, only inches apart. I offered a running commentary on the givers of the jewelry and art supplies, and Gloria chimed in now and again. Melissa opened, she looked, she said nothing.

Gloria turned on the television and went to the kitchen. The gifts sat in a pile of wrapping paper on the floor. The curtains hung motionless and the room was now quite warm. It was the first time that Melissa and I had been alone together in nearly three years. The adrenaline kicked in as I searched for a way to take advantage of the moment. We watched the Road Runner speed across the screen. When a commercial began, I composed my voice to sound friendly, but not overly eager. In Spanish I said how happy I was that she was healthy, that she'd been able to avoid hospitalizations for the previous four months. I asked her to let me know when she ran low on medicine or Vitamin K. Little side-ways eye movements told me she was listening, but her face stayed fixed forward. She coughed. Sweat dripped from my armpit.

The next cartoon began. My mind was frantic for a new idea, like a crazed little man yanking stuff out of drawers and closets. Commercials for kid's food and paper towels return and it's my time once again. Were the instructions for the tape player clear? Did it work ok on batteries? Melissa made little grunts, replies somewhere between ok and don't talk to me.

Aw, shit. Once again, the wall. The moat filled with the spirit-puncturing monster. Mt. Melissa, degree of difficulty: Impossible.

I exhaled. I pushed back on the vinyl couch and smiled grimly at Wile E. Coyote going over the cliff. All I had to show for my effort was right here, hanging out, watching cartoons with my daughter. If only I could have felt peace or even gratitude. I wondered if Melissa was aware of our physical closeness and unhappy as I that we were a universe apart.

Gloria returned from the kitchen and announced that it was time for Melissa's afternoon treatment. Melissa went to her room. Gloria and I talked some more before I gathered up the gifts she'd wrapped. I went down the hall and knocked on Melissa's door to say good-bye. I leaned towards the door and heard the whooshing nebulizer as Melissa inhaled her medicine. I waited a moment, then left.

I trudged to the park at the center of town. Around the yellow and turquoise gazebo, there looked to be the same old people from 1990 glued to benches and low walls. I stood at the spot where Melissa and I first met. I told myself it had been worse, much worse. I crossed the street to a bench under trees towering as high as the cross atop the old cathedral. To comfort myself, I made a mental list of the week's developments:

1. Melissa received a new supply of medical products.
2. We made eye contact several times.
3. We watched TV together.
4. Merilyn revealed family secrets.
5. Melissa introduced me to her dog.

I thought, *Ok. Not great, but ok.*

Then, *Oh, Jesus. "Introduced to her dog." Who am I kidding?*

I felt real bad.

The sky in the west turned the blackest blue. I couldn't return to the hotel in such a pathetic state. I walked back to the house. I went through the gate and knocked on the door. Ruby barked, then Melissa opened the door. Before I saw her outline through the screen I heard her cough. She sounded like a 5-pack-a-day smoker.

"Is your mom here?"

Melissa, looking down at Ruby, turned her head from side to side. "No."

No invitation to come in. I paused. "Well. I'm glad I saw you today. I'll come by again tomorrow morning before I go home."

Her eyes looked past me into an imaginary distance.

I moved towards the gate, then turned. I didn't know what to say, so I said what came to mind.

"Are my letters to you private?"

She shook her head no.

My Spanish wouldn't allow me to express any of the things in my heart. I hadn't a clue what was in hers.

"Ok, see you tomorrow."

* * * * *

I arrived at Ascension's house, my shirt drenched in sweat. Sitting on the narrow porch were Marvin, Melissa's English-speaking cousin, and, surprise, Gloria. I greeted them, but was in no mood for small talk. I pulled a lawn chair forward so I could see the two of them.

"Marvin, please translate for me. Tell your aunt that I'm doing everything I can, but I'm going crazy. This summer was the hardest time of my life. I need her support."

Gloria looked almost startled, as if she had never heard me speak like this.

"Everyone is acting like they are afraid of me! What can I do? What power do I have? I live in a vacuum! I can't even find out why Melissa ignores me, why she always acts angry and cold. Come on, Gloria, this is a two way street."

I went on like this for a while. It was a monologue sparked with passion. I felt powerful and a bit self-impressed, but big fucking deal. It ended with the same question of most soul-bearing, indulgent monologues. Did it get us to a new place? Of course not.

A loud noise interrupted the moment. A truck with a round tank in back rumbled around the corner blowing fucking Agent Orange or some pesticide in acrid clouds over the house and the entire street. There was nothing to do but press my bicep over my mouth and curse into my shirt sleeve. *My kid's lungs are battling deadly infections every fucking day and the government is spraying tons of shit into the air she breathes.*

* * * * *

As the poisonous cloud began to drift away, Bita brought me a watermelon *liquado.* She looked down at my sandals and gave me a sly grin. "You and Melissa have the same feet." I had to laugh.

She turned to Gloria and gave her earful about the importance of Melissa going to the USA. I hid a smile. Gloria sat looking down the street. When Bita finished her lecture, she disappeared into the back of the house. Gloria stood up to leave and I kissed her on the cheek, told her I'd see her tomorrow. Marvin came out onto the porch and watched her walk away. "My aunt, she's very difficult."

They invited me to stay for a dinner of grilled beef, potatoes and salad. I dined with the men. Merilyn and her mom, I presumed, ate later. After dinner, one of Ascension's little grandsons appeared from the rear of the house so granddad could read Bible stories to him. The scene, coupled with the smells of dinner, comforted me. I wondered what Melissa was doing at her house.

Merilyn joined me at the table and, with Marvin translating, told me how much her family loved me. I told her I could never thank her and her family enough. She asked me what had taken me so long to return to Esparza.

"I've been working for them to come visit me for most of the year. But really, I wasn't sure it would do any good to visit Melissa. She hasn't shown any interest in seeing or talking to me."

Merilyn smiled, as if she were the keeper of some special knowledge. "It's the same with Melissa's Father in Heaven. He loves to hear His children talk to Him. Her father on earth loves to hear from her, too."

"Needs to," I added.

When it was time for me to leave, Bita, half my size, gave me a monster hug and told me to come back, "*pronto.*" Ascension took my outstretched hand, put his other hand on my shoulder and looked me in the eye. He choked back a feeling. "I am very grateful...for all that you are doing for Melissa. Very grateful." He patted his heart. Tears filled my eyes.

They thanked me for the camera and everyone repeated, "God bless you," more times than I could count. I stepped down the porch steps, and headed into the dark street. I was touched and saddened by the blessings of the Reyes family. They reminded me of how lonely and shut out I felt around Melissa and Gloria.

* * * * *

The next morning I returned to say a final good-bye to Melissa and Gloria, not knowing when I would see them again. Gloria and I spoke for a few minutes about Melissa's school and medical expenses and about staying in touch and all that. Gloria went to get Melissa. Her door was locked. Gloria knocked and called, and then made warnings. Melissa emerged, her hair in all directions, her face its usual unexpressive mystery. She shuffled towards me in fuzzy slippers and I bent over in my chair. She offered her cheek for a kiss.

My eyes were level to hers. "I love you very much. Write to me and tell me about your life and how you are doing in school."

She glanced at me, then lowered her head.

I drove back to San Jose, gazing at the Costa Rican hillsides without seeing them. I sat in the airport terminal, my mind a blank. I took a seat on the airplane home not knowing who I was or where I was going.

If only I could have arrived at their house with the cache of some charismatic Latin hero, like Che or maybe Zorro, a childhood television favorite of mine. Irresistible, suave, and fluent in Spanish. Oh, yes, I would have swept into Ramon's house, bravado oozing, teeth sparkling under the cool black mask tied at the back of my head.

> *From beneath my cape, I pull out airline tickets to San Francisco and, with a flourish, drop them onto the table. Melissa and her mom look at each other, big smiles. Melissa walks over to me, hands outstretched. I kneel and her arms encircle my neck. I peel off the mask, close my eyes and we hug. She kisses me on the cheek and calls me "Papá." I look in her eyes and tell her not to ever be afraid of me. She nods and cradles her head on my shoulder. I tell her I will always be there to protect and guide her and get her the best medical care in the world.*

But I was not Zorro, I was Olin, and the road to Esparza was littered with my failures.

34. Initiation—December, 1993-January, 1994

On the flight to San Francisco I recalled my last night in Esparza. Sleepless, I pulled on my clothes and wandered through town under yellow lamplight. The houses and shops were empty, like me. A feathering breeze changed gears and began to wail, forcing trees to roll and bounce like bottomed-out bungee jumpers. The air grew thick with an aromatic moistness just before the rain exploded. Within minutes, the street was a racing river. I leapt a gutter spilling over with smelly sewage water onto a sidewalk and huddled under a tin overhang fronting a little shop. Droplets of spray wet my face. Paper cups, candy wrappers and plastic bottles flowed past and disappeared into the night. The deluge pounded roofs and palm fronds with a deafening roar.

As the rain began to wind down, I detected a jerky movement in the shadows at the periphery of my vision. I turned and saw an enormous tarantula picking its way across the wet street. It was the size of a football. Its hairy, hinged legs moved up and forward in slow motion. Although the spider walked at an angle away from me, my heart raced and I stood paralyzed, lest it sense my anxious presence, turn and run up my leg.

At 30,000 feet, I mused about the storm and the tarantula. The experience embodied every dimension of my visit with Melissa. Unsettling, alien, and darkly absurd. At the same time, my midnight stroll was like my relationship with Melissa, leaving me fully alert and alive. The past three years had mostly sucked, but for the entire time I'd been totally engaged in life.

It was depressing to sit on a plane headed far away from Costa Rica and my daughter, like I was leaving my heart and my life. A song floated into my head, Leon Russell's "Stranger in a Strange Land." And one line in particular: *Oh, such a sad, sad state we're in.*

I pressed my head to the window to glimpse the sapphire Caribbean beneath a stream of clouds. I dreamed up a fierce letter to the entire Reyes family, calling out Gloria and requesting Ascension and Bita to convene something like an intervention for an alcoholic, to move their stubborn relatives into gear. But, once home, I doubted that Gloria could be convinced to give up her belief that God would work a miracle in Esparza. Nor did I believe in her ability to make Melissa board a plane. Melissa, by herself, possessed a resistance that approached rabid, possibly for fear of being stuck in San Francisco for an extended hospitalization. And then there was Gloria's new hubby, Ramon. I'd heard stories from Laura of Costa Rican men who wouldn't flush their own toilets, a task left exclusively to their wives. I suspected that Ramon was a non-flusher who probably gave Gloria a no-fly order. The Reyes family and I were powerless against that trio. In the end I chose to send a short letter to Melissa, expressing my happiness at seeing her and adding that I would write again before Christmas.

As much as I needed get on with my life, it didn't happen immediately. I arrived home to learn that searchers had discovered Polly Klaas' body in Cloverdale, a rural community several hours north of Petaluma. A memorial was scheduled in town at St. Vincent's Church. I considered attending, but my feelings about the kidnapping and abuse were still too raw to absorb the grief of the huge crowd which I knew would pack the church.

The day after my return, my landlord cut down a flowering tree, my favorite, from the lawn in front of the duplex. I was sickened beyond words and averted my eyes every time I left the house. Then came the flu, a five day body slam, the kind that makes you wonder if death wouldn't be better. While bed-ridden, I received a phone call from a prospective client who revealed that he was a convicted child molester. The thought of sitting in a room with a man who'd willingly abused a child made me cringe and I referred him to a colleague.

The month of December was a time of emptiness, rooted in the fear that CF would take Melissa away before I could see her again. As near as I could tell, our relationship had gained no ground. Even though she had referred to me as father at her birthday party and written a thank-you for my concern, there were no signs we might ever be close.

I had never known a 15-year-old so hidden and passive. Did all Costa Rican daughters act like this with their fathers or was she was merely shy, sensitive, and too pissed to try to relate. Perhaps she was happy that I came to see her, satisfied just to watch cartoons on the couch with her dad. The distance felt like the non-stop cut of a knife which I couldn't live with. But what choice did I have?

I did the wondering/maybe/what if thing until my head hurt. I was in the dark as much as ever about who she was and how I could communicate my love. I knew I would not abandon her. I would always provide financial support and correspond. But my visits were expensive ventures with little to show. All my efforts with the hospitals in San Jose and San Francisco and the cystic fibrosis community, buying and smuggling prescription meds, studying Spanish, hiring translators… *Pfwat.* My Bridge Project was a lame attempt to bring Melissa to the States. I remembered my earlier decision to let go and accept her right to live and die any way she chose. My thoughts of pulling back when her very life was under assault seemed like time wasted and a complicity in bad choices by her and her mom.

For weeks, I drifted from tired to detached, from lonely to melancholy. One day, I sat in my office with a client, a woman happily married whose marriage had grown stronger by our work together. But the life she'd made was threatened by her immense creative and spiritual dissatisfaction. At some point in the hour a thought crossed my mind. *I must find someone to love.* The next day, I began to run and answer personal ads in San Francisco and Marin newspapers.

* * * * *

As the holidays approached, I composed a two-part letter.

Dear Gloria,

I am happy that I was able to visit you, Melissa, and your family last month. I am glad to know that everything is going well. I am sending you all photos of my family and if you would send me photos of you and Melissa, I would appreciate it very much.

Dear Melissa,

I am happy that I visited you and talked to you, your mother and your family. I saw how much you have changed. I saw the young woman emerging in you: proud, independent and pretty. You wrote your grandparents that this is the age which is most difficult and beautiful for a woman. I sincerely hope that this age has more beauty than difficulties for you.

I hope that you are enjoying the tape player, the earrings and other gifts. It would please me if you would write and tell me about your plans for Christmas and your vacation activities. Also tell me if Ruby decided to have any more puppies.

Merry Christmas!

PS Do you enjoy Gloria Estefan or no? Who are your favorite musicians?

I devoted many hours to building my practice, something I'd neglected for the latter part of the year. I resumed lessons in Spanish, hoping I might use it someday, somewhere. I zipped through Francisco Goldman's novel of Guatemala, "The Long Night of White Chickens," fueling fantasies of returning to that troubled country or possibly, Nicaragua. Maybe I'd swing by Costa Rica while I was in the neighborhood. My hunger for more closeness with Melissa was replaced by a fumble of plans, poor replacements for my deepest wishes.

Several days before Christmas, my greatest professional inspiration, family therapist Carl Whitaker, appeared in a dream. Dr. Whitaker was an idiosyncratic genius in a field short on brilliance. He often amused and provoked family members and students with sly, koan-style remarks. I memorized several of them, such as: "If there is no confusion, there can be no change, no progress. Life goes on as living dies." He spoke frequently of craziness and hate, the demands of psychotherapy, and the dangers inherent in trying to help others. I never missed his annual workshops in Santa Barbara.

I'm sitting at a table with my father, my sister, Jan, an unknown grandmother figure, and Carl Whitaker. We are participating in a family therapy session with Dr. Whitaker. He points out that no one in our family was raised to "have dreams of family." Dad admits to the truth of this, as if he were responsible. After our meeting, the family goes out to breakfast. I look around for someone I never see. Crowds pile into the restaurant and we wait endlessly for our food to arrive. Dad gets up to lead us out, and the food arrives.

I lay in bed, alert, thanks to Dr. Whitaker's appearance. I weighed the differences between my father's emotional removal from family life and my current, chosen distance from Melissa. The dream left me uneasy. In the restaurant, Dad (a symbol of me?) wants to leave just as the meal is ready to begin.

* * * * *

Mr. Dodson,

My heart and prayers go out to you. I truly believe that God is using you as his instrument to help your daughter. I hope that they can understand soon. Please, let me know if I can do anything to help. It would be my pleasure.

May the Lord bless you.

Xiomara Cubillo

(Merry Christmas!)

To Xiomara, God's purpose was simple: help Melissa. At one time I would have agreed. I knew Melissa and I had come together for a reason. But after three years, Melissa had received little help. So much for God and His or Her purpose. I searched elsewhere for meaning.

Frances, a spiritual-type friend, suggested that I was receiving one of life's lessons in letting go. I thought I had let go before my trip, when I decided Melissa could live and die in the way she chose. That spiritual achievement ended the day I returned to Esparza. One look at Melissa and "letting go" got up and went. What I'd called letting go was like a false summit on a mountain, the one you think is the top, until you arrive to see the real peak is a mile farther up. Frances' "lesson," as I understood it, was to emotionally back away from the table and cut my losses. I couldn't buy it.

I couldn't even buy the notion of a lesson. In spite of years of exposure to Northern California's occasionally off-beat values, it seemed that turning life experiences into "lessons" was reductionistic bull hockey. When did experiences stop merely being what they were? Suffering is suffering. And my entire relationship with Melissa was nothing if not a three year, non-degree education in smash mouth, emotional pain.

Sure, the suffering might one day lead me to a different "outlook" on life. Disillusionment was a distinct possibility, as well as despair. Now there's a "lesson" for you: Life can be bitter and unbelievably cruel. I bet you won't find a PBS seminar on coming to terms with a dying child. And those die-hard "lessons" people, how would they respond if I told them what I'd learned: life is a heartless road trip. Would they say, "Oh, honey, you just learned the wrong lesson"? Lessons, I figured, were for people with a need to turn hell into something positive.

Some days I was simply insanely fucking angry. There was no answer. No solution. If letting go was the big lesson, then good for all those lucky students who learned it. If I ever learned it, it would be in another lifetime.

* * * * *

I received a little Christmas card from the Reyes Family and, the following day, a separate note from Bita on lined tablet paper.

> *Monday, December 20, 1993*
>
> *I greet you, affectionately, together with the family, and as you receive these lines we hope you are well. These are our wishes. Many thanks for the card and all that you give. I can tell you that your daughter is doing well. This year she is going for the 4th year of high school. Melissa's health is very good. Sunday the 19th we went to the beach with her and she enjoyed it very much. All of my family is doing well, thanks to God, and I hope your family is also. Greetings from Merilyn and from the rest of the family. I say goodbye to you now, wishing you a Happy Christmas and a prosperous New Year. May the God of peace protect you now and always. These are, above all, the wishes from our hearts.*
>
> *Respectfully,*
>
> *Lesbia of the Reyes*

Bita, Xiomara, Gloria, Merilyn, Frances. Each thought about God's will and prayed daily for His assistance. There was some comfort being around people who searched for the deity's presence in their lives. As for me, hunting for God was identical to my quest to be a father to Melissa — and equally elusive.

I did not lack for angels. On New Year's Day, 1994, I walked into a San Rafael coffee shop and saw Isabel Allende and her husband, Willie. We greeted warmly. Isabel would look smashing doing laundry, but there were lines on her face I'd never noticed before. She told me a story as if she had been waiting for me to re-appear in her life. She had read a newspaper article about the introduction of Pulmozyme (the new medicine which had been so helpful to Ana and Isa Stenzel), and it left her and Willie wondering what happened with Melissa and me. I gave them a sanitized version of the year's events. I described Melissa's first letter to me in three years, and my happiness that she had a joyous *quinceañera*, and, most importantly, how she remained out of the hospital for most of 1993. As I talked, Isabel's eyes teared. Whether out of happiness for me or because she suddenly was reminded of her daughter, I couldn't say. I thanked her again for being such a great support.

In early January, Melissa appeared in a dream.

> *We're together alone in an open landscape. The sky is cloudy. We sit at the edge of a huge body of water, a lake, in which the water level is rising very quickly. The water moves so powerfully that it creates waves. I glance around and see that the land, which is four feet above the water, will soon be covered.*
>
> *Melissa and I stand up and move to higher ground. She sits at my left, just like she did on the couch at her house, but at an angle, so she faces me. In Spanish, I ask, "Do you swim?" With a pained look on her face, she says that she doesn't. She begins pouring words out and, though I listen carefully and nod my head, I cannot understand what she is trying to say to me. She surprises me by moving into my arms, crying. I hold her, like "The Pieta."*

When I wake up, I am the one sobbing. Melissa's dream presence, as always, was deeply stirring but we were no longer giggling or playing patty cake. The symbolism had moved up a notch and become spiritual. I couldn't grasp the meaning of The Pieta, I saw only the reflection of my crushing suffering intermingled with a love like I'd never known.

Mid-January came and went. Still no Christmas card from Gloria and Melissa. Loss drained me each day. Then, another dream.

> *I'm working as a laborer on the 3rd floor of a factory or mill. I leave and go to a nature park. I see an island in a lake where a bear and a visitor are embracing. The bear stops and glares menacingly at me and I feel a sense of doom as it lumbers over and embraces me. The bear is transformed and becomes a woman. The scene shifts and we are in a tent with beads and trinkets, and she "takes me into another realm." Her breast hangs into my mouth and throat, then she withdraws it. No milk, no satisfaction. I am aware in the dream that somehow, this is the first stage in an "initiation."*

The dream signaled the turn of a kaleidoscope. Maybe it wasn't permanent, maybe I would have to return to this place again and again, but I let go. For the moment the Bear-Woman and the Pieta offered clarity, a reminder of another dimension and the grand scheme of Life and Death in which my efforts and urgencies were of little significance. The message was evident. *It was not for me to decide.*

On the heels of that little epiphany came an awareness that my approach to Gloria and Melissa had taken a wrong turn. The curtain of my emotional confusion parted enough for me to see that our relationship had devolved into Me Push-They Resist. In part, this resulted from my not making a space for them. I decided to step back and hope they would enter that space. In truth it felt like the only available path, born of desperation and failure. I would no longer pepper them with requests. If they wrote, I would not reply immediately. I wouldn't indulge my sadness, wouldn't feed my regret. I would find a way to restrain my reaching out and see what happened.

35. A New Year—February-May, 1994

To the Reyes Araya Family-

I hope this letter finds your family in good health. I know you have a new president. I hope he will be a good leader for your country. Thank you for the beautiful Christmas card and the inspirational letter from Bita. I hope you received my Christmas card.

I am happy to tell you that the $2000 Rotary Club grant will soon be ready. The money is going to Dr. Castro and the cystic fibrosis program at the Hospital de Niños for equipment and medicine. The Rotary Club here has worked for more than a year on this project.

Once again, thank you for everything you do for Melissa and for being so welcoming to me. Spending time with you was one of the best parts of my visit last November. Please pass along my love and best wishes to Melissa and Gloria. I have not heard from them since my visit, but I hope everything is good in their lives. I told Gloria that I will not continue to ask them to come to San Francisco because all of the rejection makes my heart hurt. But I said when they are ready they should tell me and I will make all the necessary arrangements and welcome them with great happiness.

Please stay in touch.

With affection,

Olin

As winter deepened my mood lightened. Business picked up and I received twenty-eight letters in response to a personal ad I ran in the Marin Sun. Laura Lee called to announce an upcoming vacation to Costa Rica and offered to take gifts to Melissa. I sent her a box of water-soluble Vitamin K, still hard to find in Costa Rica. I attended a journaling workshop designed by Dr. Ira Progoff, who had inspired my journal-keeping in the early 70's.

Two days of contemplative writing helped me to gain clarity about my work and my plans for the year.

February passed without a word from Melissa. There were underlying feelings of frustration and anger, my companions for as long as I could remember. But something had changed. I understood that I had never wanted to be anywhere other than with Melissa and all that meant: three years of anger, fear, helplessness and failure. I wouldn't have passed up a single moment of those years where the shit/happiness ratio was about 1000/1. There was no relationship without pain, no miracle of being found without crushing rejection. There was not even Melissa without cystic fibrosis. The whole of her and the experience was all there was and it outweighed every individual piece of it. No trade-offs, no bargaining. Nothing else, nothing different.

For surely the first time in my adult life, I wasn't calculating pleasure versus pain, profit and loss, credit and blame. I wasn't hanging back or figuring the odds. Melissa led me to a greater acceptance of life on its own terms.

It must have been the suffering which changed me. Melissa's perpetual rejection forced me to face my perpetual selfishness. My hopes. My dreams. My agenda. I couldn't have all I wanted. At times it seemed that all I had were questions. What is most important? How am I going to handle the pain? How do I conduct myself?

I wrote Melissa, enclosing a check inside a letter reminding her that I thought about her all the time. I requested photos from her birthday party and asked her to describe her visit with Laura. The PS told her that her *abuelos and tías* always asked about her.

Then came the Night of Jeff's Gumbo. I drove down to Topanga Canyon for one of my regular visits with Jeff Jacobson, his wife, Marnie, and their son, Henry. Jeff often traveled in his work as a freelance photographer, but had committed to being at home the last weekend in February and throwing a party featuring his infamous Iowa Gumbo. He had frequently raved about their former next door neighbor, Claire, a movie producer who had worked with Carl Jung's friend, Laurens Van der Post. The recent earthquake had caused her to flee Southern California and move back to Santa Fe. She was in town on movie business and Jeff assured me that meeting Claire and friends and feasting on his gumbo would make for a memorable evening.

Claire showed up late with a male friend just as the group of ten was sitting down to the table. She commanded my attention with green cowboy boots, a short skirt and a black blazer, somehow making it all work. She started the table talk rather peculiarly, I thought, by asking the assembled if it was anyone's birthday. I alone answered. "My father's." Which started the two of us on an animated cross-table conversation about our shared family roots in east Tennessee. Claire's dark eyes gleamed brightly with a fierce intelligence, and her cynicism was funneled through a biting wit.

The next day Jeff and I couldn't agree on a movie matinee so I suggested we visit Claire. He phoned and arranged for us to go out for lattes. Jeff remembers that when Claire answered the door, he heard a *sotto voce*, "Whoa," leap from my mouth. She wore the same boots and skirt as the night before, but something about her jewelry or jet black hair, maybe even her framed glasses, set me back a step. We walked to a sidewalk café in the Pacific Palisades and continued our exclusive conversation, leaving Jeff and Claire's friend, Jill, pretty much on their own. Later I said goodbye to her with a kiss on the cheek and told her I was sure we'd see each other soon. Heading home on the Pacific Coast Highway, I asked Jeff, who was driving, if he thought Claire heard my "whoa." I had barely finished the question before Jeff began to laugh so hard I thought the van would go into a ditch.

Claire and I raced into high gear with a stream of high-velocity phone calls once, twice, then multiple times a day. Flying to meet her in LA or Santa Fe became an unstoppable practice. Sitting atop Atalaya Mountain under an icy blue New Mexico sky we shared life stories. We hiked in Will Rogers Park in Los Angeles and ate lunch at Mort's in the Palisades. I met her dogs and some of the less important beings in her life. Every moment we shared was enthralling.

On March 3, I dreamed of Melissa.

A friend brings me a letter from Melissa scrawled on the back of an envelope. It's written phonetically in English, translated as "I liked the presents, thanks for coming to see me."

The dream was a premonition.

It was a winter of other dreams to remember, with repeats of the dog and lake motifs.

> *In one dream two snarling dogs confront me. One of them bites me on the hand. I bite back tearing a piece from its rump. Then a scrawny mutt with a multi-colored, brown-ish coat brings me an old sweater and sits beside me, sort of adopting me.*

Ferocious dogs replaced by a compassionate mutt complemented the earlier dream where the bear embraces me and turns into a woman. Like suffering and letting go were more than I had ever imagined.

Bodies of water returned in two dreams. In the first, I once again drove my car into a lagoon. In the second

> *I'm a woman and I step into a boat on a lake. It feels like a scene from a Native American past. I sit down in the boat. There is a long pink rope beside me. I prepare to "cast the line" out onto the water. I pull my arm back and my visual field goes dark. I feel the rope wrapping around my neck and I awaken laughing.*

These dreams seemed directly connected to Melissa. First sinking into water, the symbol of grief and sustenance. In the second dream, the rope was cast out then returned to strangle me in a pleasing way. Strangled in love, but not to death.

* * * * *

Melissa had spurred me to re-examine my attitudes about relationships. From puberty onward I never thought much beyond a girl's or a woman's beauty, intelligence and love of good times. When our relationship became more serious, those factors were not enough. My freedom and self-confidence felt jeopardized, and I froze. With Melissa came a different experience of love and commitment. Both were imposing, but I wanted their rewards.

Claire had had as many disastrous relationships as I, the big difference being that several of hers had led to the altar. She was disillusioned about marriage but I took comfort from her repeated remarks that she'd never known a man like me. She had no children but didn't seem to be hung up about it. In fact, "Get Over It" was Claire's motto for herself and others and there were few times I ever heard her express a regret. She was quiet on the subject of Melissa, something I attributed to her never having children. She did enjoy the story and the photo album but rarely asked questions about Melissa unless I initiated the conversation or received a letter from Costa Rica. Like the one from Gloria in April.

March 23

Hola. Como esta.

Melissa had an appointment with Dr. Gonzalez on 2/21/94 and another time on 3/7/94 and was admitted for treatment on 3/18/94. Dr. Gonzalez talked with me for a long time and she told me many things and among them she said she didn't understand how you didn't find her when you were here. I explained to her but she did not seem very happy.

Olin she wants you to help her with a conference. She explained to me that it is very important. I showed her the vitamins that you sent Melissa and she said that this is what she wants for the children here. She recognized these vitamins are the best for them and many thanks for obtaining them for Melissa.

Write Melissa now that she is in the hospital. I am sending you photos of Melissa's cumpleaños. Later I'll send you more. I have problems obtaining them.

Olin, the doctor always talks to me about the hospital politics. Well, you already know this.

This Sunday something happened that had never happened before. I was robbed in San Jose. My bag and all the documents. And it took a lot for me to get over it. I had a nervous crisis and a very bad stomach.

Ok, hasta luego. I tell Melissa always to write you.

I held the three photos to the window and peered closely to catch every detail of the party I had missed. In the first, teenagers in clean, modest clothes stand at a long table covered by a plastic cover. Most have their hands clasped behind them, their heads bent in prayer. Melissa's eyes are closed, her face partially hidden by long thick curls falling over her left cheek and shoulder.

In the second photo, Melissa stands alone at the table, in front of a pink cake topped with a gaudy gazebo structure which doubles as a girl's pink hoop skirt. She wears a satiny pink dress. It is unclear what is taking place at the moment the shutter clicks. Girls sit casually on either side of her. Her eyes appear to be closed and her face has a slightly puffy look, as if she might have been crying.

The last photo is posed. She sits in a chair, holding a pink basket covered with gauzy pink ruffles and plastic flowers. Wrapped in enough dress for her and a friend, Melissa stares open-eyed at the camera. It's that Mona Lisa smile again. Her long fingers curl below the basket, their clubbed tips faintly visible. I kissed the photo.

I re-read Gloria's letter with cynicism. She was pulling the strings of my paternal love, as if they needed pulling. Maybe she'd thought long and hard about my visit and my obvious frustration. She was aware that I had pulled back and possibly fearful that I'd move further away. Even so, how could she think a letter from me would reach Melissa in the hospital, unless she was going to be there for a month. The letter provided Gloria's usual grating nothingness of details about Melissa's condition. We had agreed that she would call me in the event of a crisis so I could only hope and assume that by the time I received the letter Melissa was back home and going to classes. My assumption was confirmed by a second letter from Gloria just a few weeks later.

April 2

Olin,

How is everything there. Here we are good.

Melissa is very good. We received the check dated 2/11.

Melissa had a lot of vacation time. We went to Panama beach.

Greetings to your family and to the parents of Laura. For Meli, this year is her fourth year.

Ok, hasta luego.

I breathed a sigh of relief about Melissa's health followed by a shock when another letter arrived, this one from Melissa.

Hola. Como esta.

I am well. I have not written because I don't have time. At home I have to study a lot if I want to pass. Thanks for visiting me and bringing the things that you gave me. Thanks for giving me the tape player.

Perhaps you think that I'm writing you in order to ask you for something, but I'm only writing to say hello to you and express appreciation for everything.

I bid you good bye because I have to study. I have an exam tomorrow in chemistry.

Until soon, write.

Melissa Reyes

Astonished, I read her words again and again, returning to the single line, "I am only writing to say hello and express appreciation for everything." I danced in delight as a gratitude for life arose within me.

In a quiet, distinct, young adult voice, Melissa had turned towards me.

Something inside said to respond gently. I would take time, then write.

*****

I sent Isabel Stenzel a copy of Melissa's medical records, the same ones Dr. Hardy had reviewed. I wanted to know how Melissa's tests and lung functions compared with hers. I knew Isa well enough by now to know that she would provide the brutal honesty I wanted and dreaded. The first time she told me by phone she was ready to share her observations, I declined. "Let's talk about it when I have more time."

I called her a few days later, unable to think of a good reason to delay any further. Isa was chronically apologetic before applying the hammer. "I'm sure you know, of course, her lungs are really crappy. I probably shouldn't use that expression."

"No, that's okay. I want to know what you think."

"Well, she has *Pseudomonas Aeruginosa* like so many of us..."

"Right. Dr. Gonzalez told me that when I first met her."

"It's the bacteria that becomes resistant to antibiotics and starts the vicious cycle of damage to the lungs. She's had it since she was 9. That's what, 5, 6 years. Damn, she's got to be really tough. Because if you look at the FEV1 and the RV..."

"Wait, slow down."

"Sorry! See the sections called "Spirometry" and "Lung Volumes"? Look at the lines pre and post and you can see that the "post" numbers don't improve that much. And that's after 17 days in the hospital."

I looked at the numbers as she spoke. I'd never seen, or I'd forgotten, that Melissa's lone hospital visit in 1993, the one I'd boasted to Isabel and Willie about, had lasted for a staggering 17 days. It didn't register, I'd been in denial.

I suddenly felt stupid and at the same time, as if I were sinking into darkness. *Melissa has more to deal with than I've ever known. More than I've ever faced. How can she push through school when she's so sick. No wonder she always looked punky and unkempt.*

When I heard Isa's voice again, she was in mid-sentence.

"...that explains why she is on oxygen every day. But her normal days, her *normal* days! are like Ana's and mine when we are really sick. Man, she's got to be a fighter. I've known many people like your daughter who live in this gray area of sickness and perceived wellness."

"What do you mean?" I pictured Isa shaking her head back and forth. I sat like a statue.

"Simply that she's in a tricky stage where she might think she could subsist this way forever despite the reality of limited capacity and functioning. Let's face it, she's hanging on with 30 percent lung capacity. And she weighs 66 pounds! I'm sorry, is this depressing you?"

I lied. "No, please go on."

"Just that I've known people who live like that for years, while others fell apart very quickly. She's really tough, that's the good news."

Thank God for that.

I said goodbye to Isa and walked around my house screaming at God until I ran out of screams and the tears began again.

36. Pen Pals—June-November, 1994

Eight days after receiving Melissa's letter I mailed my reply.

Dear Melissa,

I hope you and your mom and all of your family are doing well.

I enjoyed your letter and I want to thank you very much for what you said. I hope you did well on your exams and are enjoying school.

Things here are up and down. The economy in California is in a slump and things are a little hard for almost everyone I know. Still, I was fortunate to be able to visit New Mexico recently. Northern New Mexico, in particular, is very beautiful with spectacular vistas and colorful mountains.

Right now I am busy preparing a lecture on dreams for a psychology class of 70 students at the local university. Well, it is not exactly a lecture. The professor, who is a friend, said I could do anything I want for 90 minutes. Since a long lecture would be torture for most people, part of the time I will lead a discussion which I hope will be challenging to the students.

The subject of dreams is very interesting. The night before I received your recent letter, I dreamt about you. This happened two other times the night before I received letters from you or your mother. Very interesting, don't you think?

I want to mention especially the beautiful photographs which I received from your mother a few weeks ago. Tell her thank you very much. I made color Xerox copies to send to your grandparents.

Melissa, I am happy you are well. Please give my love to your mom and your family, and write again soon.

I love you,

Dad

PS I am planning to move to another house in Petaluma in a few months. For now you all can continue to write me at my present address or my office.

My letter must have crossed in the mail with Gloria's.

Olin,

How are you.

Melissa is well and taking vitamins.

I want to know if you received some photos of Melissa a few months ago because there have been problems with the mail. If you can write me when you receive this.... I want to wish you happiness on your birthday and I hope that you are in good health and that this day is passed in happiness. I sent you three letters. Olin I hope that Melissa will have a friendship with you but she is in a difficult time of adolescence.

Greetings to everyone.

Gloria

Gloria's letter was peculiar. It contained more lapses in spelling than usual and there was one line I couldn't make sense of. The request for me to be patient with Melissa left me doubting that she knew Melissa had written me. I had already thanked Melissa for the photos so there wasn't much to respond to in Gloria's letter and I didn't.

* * * * *

Between March and May, Claire and I had run up huge expenses from phone conversations and airline tickets. We agreed that it was ridiculous to give Southwest and Pac Bell so much money when we could spend the same amount or less talking in person and living together.

Santa Fe seemed like the best option for a number of reasons, but I couldn't up and leave my clients. Claire volunteered to move to Petaluma for a year or two after which we would re-locate to Santa Fe. We began looking for a rental and lucked out with a beautiful old Victorian near downtown. I flew to New Mexico in July and with helpful muscle from a friend, we packed a U-haul with Claire's furniture and belongings and drove west. Before we left we shopped for a piece of art to honor and symbolize our relationship. We were drawn to an original, unusually shaped pottery bowl in a shop near Santa Fe's plaza. It was a clay and straw composition, glazed with an earthen orange patina.

We glided into a sweet summer groove, waking up together and enjoying the natural beauty and great food of the Sonoma wine country. It wasn't a fairy tale. We had conflicts and moods that only primates would find endearing, but we never stopped wanting to be together. I loved Claire's keen mind as well as her vulnerability and generosity. My feelings were a never-ending meteor shower, everything from fascination to fearful of losing, from sweetly to fiercely affectionate. I felt secure in myself that Claire could never overwhelm me and that I wouldn't lose myself in her. My ability to love was rooted in what Melissa had taught me.

In late August, I took Claire to Sea Ranch where I had rented a spacious house with a million windows facing the ocean. We cooked and walked through the sand dunes and I proposed marriage. We had begun discussing the idea a month earlier but my question and her acceptance, in a grove of trees on a sunny Saturday morning, made it official. Walking out of the grove immediately afterwards, I ran headlong into a low tree branch and fell on my ass. It was almost head over heels, a fitting punctuation to my finding a woman who was just right for me.

> *I have an extraordinary dream of a sky, its color an incredible, glowing burnished brown. The moon is full and luminescent and all the stars are ablaze. The scene overwhelms me so that I'm forced to stop what I'm doing and I wake up.*

We soon settled into a new routine. Claire traveled to LA every week, a separation which was easy compared to the one with Melissa. Knowing I might be moving soon, I confined my out-of-the-office work activities to teaching classes and doing short term projects. She and I inevitably bumped into parts of each other which were challenging, to say the least. Her insecurity had a saw-toothy persona which one of her friends called Attila the Hun. But in those honeymoon months, we rarely ventured too far into conflict without pulling back. Except for one occasion.

We were dining at a French restaurant, talking movies, when I mentioned my enjoyment of the work of a particular director. Claire almost choked on her asparagus. She called him a sexist, despicable animal, known throughout Hollywood for his crude manner. I hastily clarified what I liked about his movies, drawing a distinction between the man and his work. The distinction meant nothing to Claire. I thought the whole matter boiled down to something minor, but she kept on the attack, and with each question and answer the disagreement became stickier and more emotional. I suggested we change the subject. Claire refused and accused me of sleeping with the enemy. The night was one to forget. The director's name was never spoken again, not even in jest.

Summer turned into autumn. When I thought about Melissa it was with a sense of resignation, practicing letting go by writing her only when she wrote. I imagined that she seldom thought about me in spite of her uncommonly friendly letter in April. Gloria was surely aware that I had not responded to her July letter. Perhaps I had muddied the waters by not sending them money in September. Money had been tight since Claire moved to Petaluma and my bank account was legitimately low at the usual time for sending a check. But the deeper truth was I was spending money on Claire and me and my omission was a petty and passive-aggressive way of communicating my disgruntlement.

On October 18, I awoke from a dream in which I asked Claire what we were going to do about children. Melissa was there with us. I lay in bed thinking, *To hell with holding back.* I got out of bed and wrote a letter.

Dear Melissa,

I send love and best wishes to you and your mother.

It is hard to believe that almost one year has passed since I visited you. I hope it has been a good year for you and all your family. My parents and my sisters also send you greetings and wish you a happy birthday.

1994 has been filled with many activities and events. My family has been fortunate this year. My sisters have passed through difficult times. My parents are happy and in good health.

Shirley and my father visited Petaluma last month and next month my fiancé, Claire, and I will visit them in Arizona. Yes, Claire and I became engaged and next year we will get married, possibly in Los Angeles. I hope you and your mother will come to the wedding.

Melissa, as you turn 16, I send to you my best wishes and prayers for you to have all the best things in life: love, health, happiness and opportunity. I am always here to help in any way I can. I think of you every day and I hope we can get together next year.

Write soon.

With love,

Olin

PS Please give my love and greetings to everyone in the family of your uncle, especially Ascension, Bita, Merilyn and Marvin.

I completed the letter and did household chores. When I went to pick up the mail I found a letter from Melissa resting in the box. Her words were inscribed in blue ink on lined tablet paper. I cradled it in my hands, gaping at its length, half the page!

Hola!

How are you? It's been some time since I received a card or letter from you.

This trimester my exams have gone well. If God wihes, I am going to Irazu Volcano the 8th of October. A class trip. And the 23rd of October I am going to Monteverde Reserve with the church.

I received a scholarship for English for school vacation in December, January and February, but I don't know if I will go because it is in Puntarenas and I don't have enough money. If I decide to go I'll tell you.

You may be surprised that I'm writing you, but I'm crazy.

I say hi to everyone around you.

Respectfully,

Wendy Melissa Reyes Reyes

I let out a big breath and my body shook with delighted energy. This was the fourth time a letter followed a dream of Melissa. How did that happen?

My eyes roamed happily down each line of the letter, trying to take in all the information and mostly, the surprises. School and church trips. "I am crazy!" *Delightful!* The opportunity to study English. Her gentle reminder of my silence. My daughter was making herself vulnerable.

But what was *not* said was the best of all: not a single word of sickness or hospitals.

I placed the letter softly against my nose, hoping to catch a scent of my daughter. We were almost pen-pals. Living so far apart, maybe this was as good as it could get. Separately dreaming and wondering, fearing and hoping, intertwined in a relationship of letters to feed our hearts and help us grow into our own version of daughter and father.

As I ruminated, dark suspicions gurgled up. Melissa's birthday was just around the corner. Her letter could be a manipulation, but truthfully I was manipulating her and Gloria as much if not more. If you won't write, I won't. If Melissa was manipulating me because of her impending 16th birthday, that was ok. Better that she "use" me directly and not by silence. Looking back I saw that my missed check, after months of regularity, might have had an unsettling effect that I'd not intended. It wasn't fair to be indirect and leave them guessing. I resolved never to miss a check again.

I was crazy with curiosity about Melissa. I added an addendum to my letter.

Melissa,

I finished writing this birthday letter to you and planned to mail it tomorrow, then only one hour ago I received your letter. I was very happy to read it and I want to congratulate you on your accomplishments in school. If you want to study English during vacation, please let me know how much school and your expenses will be and I will send you the money.

No, I do not think it is strange to receive a letter from you. It is rare but in fact you have written two letters in the past several months and maybe it will be common for us to exchange letter more frequently in the future. In the meantime, I hope you will be very happy and again I send my hope that you have a very happy birthday. With the money I am enclosing, please buy yourself something you like.

With love,

Dad

I invited my translator to the house for a phone call to Melissa. My letting go had lasted for almost a year. It was time to revise the strategy.

Elizabeth, a bespectacled young woman from Mexico City, joined Claire and me at the house one week after I'd received Melissa's letter. I was still high from Melissa's mention of studying English and hoped she would open up even more on the phone.

We dialed the number at Ramon's house and got a recorded message that the number was not a working number. Figuring I'd dialed incorrectly, I tried again slowly and got the same recording. My excitement turned into confusion, alarm and then confusion again. We called Ascension's house. Another recording. I stood up and paced the room. We called international information and got a new number for Ascension. Bita picked up and told us that all of Costa Rica's phone numbers had changed. She gave us Gloria's new number. I thanked her and we tried the new number. My mouth tasted bitter. I shook my head. "Gloria," was all I could say.

She answered the phone. I composed myself, asked how she was. "I'm fine, but I'm taking Melissa to the hospital." I looked at Claire and mimed a heated "Fuck!" before my mind short-circuited. Gloria didn't elaborate beyond saying that Melissa felt sick and they were going to the hospital. Melissa was too sick to talk. I told Gloria to tell Melissa I loved her and to call me if there were any complications.

I set the phone in the cradle. Melissa could be taking a turn for the worse. I paid Elizabeth, thanking her as cordially as I could. After she left the house, I collapsed into a chair, surrounded by my own darkness. Claire squeezed next to me, her arm around my shoulder. Fucking cystic fibrosis. Just when Melissa reaches out, she goes down. Just when my hopes grow, they go down, too.

Claire took me to lunch and drove us to a spa in Calistoga. We sat in the hot pools until sundown. "This is how the last four years have been. Like crap. I'm so tired of the bullshit." I sputtered the words. "And Gloria, she's been useless. How could her phone number be changed and her not tell me?" We both knew I was scared shitless for Melissa. Frances once said the mind is a bad neighborhood. The spa waters barely eased my despairing thoughts. Love and hope were betrayers, always turning into grief.

I was emotionally busted. Writing letters to Costa Rica was the only productive thing I did for the next week. I heard no more from Gloria and assumed the best.

Dear Gloria,

I hope all is well for you, Melissa and your family.

I was surprised and very upset to hear the news about Melissa's hospitalization in November. And I was unhappy to find out that your phone number had changed and you did not tell me.

Gloria, it is extremely important for you to keep me informed by letter or fax about major events like this in Melissa's life. Would you please spend a few colones of the money I send to you and write me in times like this?

Many thanks.

Respectfully,

Olin

My words might have been a waste of time, but they had to be said.

Dear Family,

Love and best wishes to everyone. I send apologies to Bita for not talking longer with her on the phone. I was frantic because no one had told me your phone numbers had changed and it took many frustrating minutes to obtain the new numbers. This experience upset me, then it was worse when I received the news that Melissa is going into the hospital.

After four months with no letters I had concluded that Melissa's and Gloria's interest in a relationship had ended. That is why I stopped writing and sent only money. When I received Melissa's letter recently, I was very surprised, but happy. I do not receive important information about what is happening in Melissa's life. Can you provide information about what happens to me?

Great thanks and affection to all,

Olin

Four days after the phone call, Claire confronted me over my emotional distance. It led to a fight, and then another argument, this one about her anger. We eventually regained an affectionate equilibrium, but only after a painful, sobering weekend in which we both distanced ourselves. Even a week after the call, I still wasn't quite back on track. The roadblocks seemed insurmountable.

*****

It was November 9, Melissa's birthday. Driving home from the video store, a radio DJ announced a special request for someone's 16-year old daughter. It was the Beatles' "Yer Birthday." I sang at the top of my lungs all the way home.

37. Interruptions—November, 1994-April, 1995

I sent Melissa and Gloria a Christmas card and inserted a letter to Melissa.

Dear Melissa,

I hope that you had a happy birthday. Did you receive my card and the money from Claire? Please give my greetings to your mother and to each one in your family. I hope that things are going very well for you.

Claire and I are going to take a trip at Christmas. I gained a free ticket to fly anywhere in the US. So we are going to visit her family in Tennessee and afterwards my sister, my nieces and friends in Georgia.

I have been very busy with work, which is good, but the elections here in California and the US were horrible. The results were in general, terrible, and I ask myself if we are going to go through a dark period of time in the US. Time will tell.

For now I want to wish you and your mom a very Happy Christmas. I hope that you are enjoying your school vacation. Spend the money I am sending you on something you can enjoy.

Write soon and tell me what you are doing.

I love you,

Olin

On December 1, I received a letter from the Reyes Araya Family. In English, it must have been transcribed by Marvin. He was gaining proficiency in English but wasn't quite there.

Dear Olin,

We hope you and your family are all well and that you are enjoying these last days of the year.

We had a great time with your letter, though we are concerned because of Gloria's incomprehension for you. For us her behavior is difficult to understand. We haven't written to you about Melissa's health because, in our humble opinion, the proper people to do it is Gloria, isn't it? However thanks to your letter, we have discovered Gloria isn't interested in communicating to you Melissa's news so we are willing to help you and we'll try to establish closer contact.

Now the Reyes are in, Gloria is out. Maybe she was offended by my last letter. How could she not want to communicate what was happening with Melissa? The more I thought about it, the less I cared. Gloria's communication (or lack of it) and her support (or lack of it) had never seemed to make that much difference. I preferred having the other Reyes on board.

With Melissa, what concerned us most is they are very reserved and avoid giving us any explanation about them and no doubt you know very well this situation. About Melissa we can tell you she is fine in her studies, except in three courses, they are Spanish, English, and mathematics. Two months ago, she was at Irazu Volcano and the cold affected her too much. Short before, she visited Monteverde Cloud Forest Preserve and the cold and height affected her again, first-aid being necessary. In both times, she had vomits, sickness and severe sinusitis, but fortunately she recovered quickly. Regarding Melissa's hospitalization this month, we don't know nothing, for sure it's a false alarm because Melissa is taking her final examinations.

Finally, Melissa told us she wouldn't go to your wedding because she wouldn't like to produce a riot in your honeymoon. Furthermore she wouldn't have anyone to go for a walk and talk.

Oh, how I would love for Melissa to produce a "riot" at the wedding! If only, if only she would come to California for the nuptials. We'd walk and talk until one of us collapsed.

These are all the news about Melissa we know. We hope to give you better news in the next letters so be patience and keep the faith. You are an honest and kind man and sooner or later you'll have your reward with the love of your daughter.

We are terribly sorry with you about our phone number, we forgot to tell you since March 31, all the phones across the country have one more digit.

At home we are fine, however we have passed hard times with my mother. When a hernia grew too much, they decided to operate her. At present almost have passed three months and her health has gotten better. We are concerned because she must not get fat so she is beginning a special treatment ten days from now to lose weight, that's the best way to avoid a new hernia.

Merilyn was working in a National Bank branch in San Jose for three months, but she didn't like it so she was back to Esparza on November 17.

My father is probably working his last days in the Costa Rica Electricity Institute, because he will retire very soon.

We owe you an apology for forgetting to write you and we are sorry we took so long to do it.

It was a pleasure to receive your letter and know you are worried, as always, about Melissa's health. We hope you are enjoying reading these lines. Please say "hi" to your family for us.

With our best regards,

Reyes Araya Family

As I held the letter, sadness mixed with gratitude. My heart was touched by these people who had not given up hope for Melissa and me. Their letter confirmed Isa Stenzel's impression that Melissa was terribly fragile and amazingly strong. I admired the girl who took big risks with her health to visit volcanoes and rain forests with her friends.

I wondered if Melissa felt any pain about our distance and, for that reason, held back. Or did she prefer to hold me at arm's length until she had a better reason to bring me nearer. The 12-year-old who was so excited to meet her dad, what happened to her?

I remembered the day in 1991 when Jeff and I drove down to the beach south of Malibu. It was a damp, grey morning and we walked with hands dug firmly in coat pockets. Gulls caught the wind and shot past us like rockets. I was going on about Melissa's emotional remove and how I couldn't make any sense of her.

Jeff stopped and I turned around to look at him. "Boy, she sounds really smart," drawing out the word, 'rea-lly.'

"This girl has no idea if she will ever see you again. She doesn't know you, doesn't know if you are a man of your word. Why should she just give herself over to you?" Jeff's voice grew louder with self-assured intensity. I loved that side of him. "She is rea-lly smart."

By her silence Melissa always forced me to examine myself, my assumptions and my actions. Now, four years on, instead of merely dismissing her as closed and controlling, I was beginning to appreciate that she was fighting me for a relationship she could handle. My 16-year-old Latina child had instincts for love, security and self-preservation. Her concerns were essentially no different than mine.

* * * * *

In January, a giant, sparkling Christmas card arrived from the Reyes Araya family. The envelope was marked "*Expres/Entrega Especial.*" The card jinglebelled when I opened it and inside were little notes from Marvin and Merilyn.

Marvin:

> *Unfortunately, we must give you bad news about Melissa. She was hospitalized on December 2 and we don't know how long she is gonna be in the hospital so you can call up to the Children's Hospital and ask information about Melissa's health.*

Merilyn:

> *Hi Olin,*
>
> *Melissa told me about your wedding next year. I hope that God blesses your love and you can be happy, they are my wishes. I went to see Melissa in the hospital yesterday, 12-6-94 and she is doing well. They have her on oxygen all day. She has Chemistry left and she has to take an exam in February to know if she can pass to the fifth year.*
>
> *Hasta pronto.*

Feliz Navidad,
Merilyn

I was blessed by Merilyn and Marvin.

*****

Claire was in LA when I drove to Berkeley to return a few Christmas gifts. It was Martin Luther King's birthday and on my way home, a public radio station began playing one of his sermons. I settled in for the long drive across the Bay grateful for the company. The sermon was titled "Interruptions."

After reading a single line from the Luke's gospel, King described how our lives had been interrupted, not just by loss and difficulties, but by a series of wars from WWII to Vietnam. He moved into a deep groove of pauses and rhythms which were both musical and mesmerizing.

> *The major problem of life is learning how to handle the costly interruptions, the door that slams shut, the plan that got sidetracked, the marriage that failed or that lovely poem that didn't get written because someone knocked on the door.*

"The door that slams shut." His message had become personal. I moved into the slow lane on the Richmond-San Rafael Bridge and forgot the traffic.

> *We may take our interruptions resentfully…The person who pursues this path is likely to develop a callous attitude, a kind of cold heart and a bitter hatred toward God, toward those with whom he lives and toward himself. In short they become mean. You've seen people like that, they have a great disappointment in life. Some great dream that they dreamed, some great hope that stood at the center of their being…And then it didn't come through and their response to life was bitterness and resentment.*

King's words reminded me of my recent resignation to bitterness. I wanted to stop the car and give the radio my complete attention, but the bridge had no shoulder. I took the Sir Francis Drake Blvd. exit towards San Quentin and found a turnout.

> *People…fail to see that interruptions are part of the scenery of life. Storms are part of the normal climate, like the ever-flowing waters of the river, life has its moments of flood and its moments of drought, like the ever-changing cycle of the seasons, life has the soothing warmth of its summers and the piercing chill of its winters.*
>
> *…The way to deal with the interruptions of life is to face them as realities but then develop something on the inside of you that gives you the power to endure them and thereby transcend them.*

King's voice broke, then rose to a shout.

> *When the darkness of life hits you! When things seem not to be working all right! When it seems that you are burdened down with the greatest*

trials and you wake up crying sometime! The question is whether you're gonna stretch your wings forth and then go on above the storm, that's the question! It's life's question.

Goose bumps covered my neck and arms. I leaned on the steering wheel as if it were the back of a pew. King told the story of a man standing on a bridge in Knoxville, Tennessee, contemplating suicide because of a lost love. But, "in that moment of heartache, he started thinking and he wrote a little song called, 'Goodnight Irene.' And he ended up making $75,000 on that song!" The congregation erupted in laughter. I joined them.

Oh, when life's problems hit you, don't jump! Somehow think up a song! Produce a song!

The sermon wound down and ended and I hit the off button, exhausted from holding my breath. *Endure and transcend.* After a time, I started the engine and drove home.

* * * * *

The wedding became a major topic of conversation. We researched churches, created a list of invitees. Claire flew to Santa Fe on business and looked for a house. My application for a counseling license in New Mexico was approved by the state board.

Melissa returned to her cave. It was three, then four months without hearing from her, longer for Gloria. No thank you's after her birthday, nothing at Christmas.

In what seemed like the proverbial blink of an eye, sixteen months had passed since my last visit to Esparza. Mine was a strange, schizy life: longing miserably for Melissa, happily embarking on marriage and a new home in New Mexico.

In March a dream of Melissa and Gloria preceded another surprise letter.

Hola!

How are you, I am very well. It's been 15 days since I left the hospital. I received the present from Claire and your card. Congratulations on your wedding with Claire.

I would like to tell you I passed my exams and I am going into my 5th level, this is the last year and I am going to need more money because I have to buy many books. Since my mother doesn't work, but thanks to God we found you. The new president has raised everything, taxes have gone up, and also school books and pencils and things that I need. You said that when I need something I could ask you.

The telephone number has not changed it is the same.

If you talk with your mother or father by phone, tell them hello for me.

Bueno, hasta pronto,

Melissa Reyes Reyes

I folded the letter and kissed it. It's tone was conversational and grown-up. I noted how Melissa offered no details about her health and referred to her hospitalization only in passing. Her main concern was school, as in previous letters, though I'd never noticed it quite so much. I began to more fully grasp that my role was to give Melissa what she wanted and needed, whatever it was. In this case it was school supplies.

Whether she called me Father was not the point. Nor did it seem so critical that she receive medical care in the States. Once more, I kissed goodbye the dream of being God's gift to a fatherless, sickly school girl. I did so without regret. The old fantasy had become irrelevant.

Melissa's letter woke me, as if she'd slapped a playing card down on the table, revealing that my hand was not what I thought. I was the father of a Costa Rican teen-ager. Pushing my outdated dream on a girl I didn't know or even perceive very well had caused us to battle each other. Now, what was being asked of me? My answer had three parts: Dump my agenda. Remain constant. And, finally, pay attention and trust that Melissa will tell me what she needs.

* * * * *

Soon afterwards yet another letter arrived from the family, in Bita's handwriting.

Dear Olin,

First of all, greetings for you, your family and Claire. We hope all of you are very well.

It's a pity to learn that your translator Elizabeth came back to Mexico City because Marvin is starting to work next month so we'll have some problems to reply to your letters in English but Merilyn is able of understanding written English and we hope Marvin may help to us. If not I guess there will always be a good way to keep in touch. Merilyn says it's easy to understand your clear handwriting.

About our family, thanks to God, we are all very well, especially mom and dad. Merilyn is receiving a conversational English course paid for by Costa Rica National Bank. Marvin is gonna work as a French teacher at Esparza High School and he'll continue his studies to get his Bachelor's at the Central Costa Rican University.

With regards to Melissa, she had a great success with her exams so on March 1, she'll be starting her 5th and final year in high school.

On the other hand, Melissa had some health troubles three months ago and she was hospitalized. Now she's having trouble again. Her feet became inflamed, respiratory problems and sinusitis has appeared again. Fortunately she is receiving good medical care. We suppose Melissa doesn't take the treatment as doctor recommended her and that would be the reason why she is suffering continuous relapses.

Furthermore, doctors want to do a lung transplant and they already talked with Gloria and Melissa to know their minds. Doctors told them there are various steps to follow but the first one is Melissa must get fat and psychological work with the aim that she understands all about the transplant and this one would be held at Children's Hospital.

Please give our regards to all.

Take care,

Reyes Araya Family

The hospitalization of three months ago which they referred to had occurred before Christmas. I was confused why Bita didn't mention the later one Melissa referred to in her letter, unless she wasn't aware of it. It was exciting to know that Children's Hospital could perform a transplant, but with Melissa's ongoing health struggles, transplant seemed a distant possibility. Perhaps the "Nova" program on transplants was an early sign of what was in store for her—and me, if she could accept an adult lung.

I wrote to Melissa in early April, to assure her that she would be able to buy the books and school supplies she needed.

Dear Melissa,

Thank you for your letter. I am sorry that I was slow to write this letter but my life is so crazy and busy, in large part because of the wedding.

Please give my greetings to your mother, your tía and tío and your primos.

As you can see it is necessary to write in English, but I hope Merilyn or Marvin can help with the translation.

Everyone here is fine. I know you are very excited to be in your final year of school. I hope it is your best year, filled with lots of wonderful experiences. You have worked harder than I can ever know. When I think of your determination to graduate I am filled with appreciation and respect for you. I hope you will express some of your thoughts about continuing in school in your next letter to me. I will begin sending you more money each month soon.

Claire and I will have our wedding ceremony on April 21 in San Francisco. We are very happy and excited. We selected our rings and next week we will meet with the minister of the church. We plan to invite only 20 people. There will be a dinner afterwards. I am sorry that you, your mother and your family will not be attending. But I will send you photos as soon as possible.

Claire and I are planning to move to New Mexico in July. I will tell you more when the final decision is made.

The newspaper article is from the New York Times. It describes positive benefits from a medicine similar to aspirin. Please share it with your mom and doctor.

Melissa, I hope you are feeling good and happy. Everyone here sends their love and interest.

I think of you and your mother every day.

Write! I wish I could see you soon!

Love, Dad

PART FIVE
1995-1997

38. Santa Fe—May, 1995-March, 1996

In early July, Claire and I moved our belongings to Santa Fe. Our final weeks in Petaluma were a fast-forward of boxing possessions, cleaning the house, the all-day yard sale, cancelling/starting utilities and cable television, sending out our new address, and saying goodbyes to friends in the Bay Area. I had many endings with clients as well, some of whom had worked with me for ten years.

Our new life was headquartered southeast of Santa Fe in a community known as El Dorado. We had made a financial plan with care. I would get a job and/or build a new counseling practice. She would fly to LA every other week and, with her business partner, develop scripts and try to land film production jobs. We decided to postpone a honeymoon until a time when we were more settled. Our neat scheme went up in smoke when Claire and her partner were hired to work on a blockbuster movie scheduled to be shot in New York City. She left in mid-July. Our moving-in period had lasted little more than a week.

The move and the chaos of unpacking, briefly hosting her brother and nephew, then packing her luggage for a change of seasons in New York, made the wedding seem like a distant memory. We had selected the historical Swedenborgian Church in San Francisco as our wedding site. We were joined there by twenty of our best friends, including Jeff, Marnie, Britt and Sally. The brief ceremony concluded with our guests encircling us and, in response to a request we authored for the occasion, pledging to support us through whatever difficulties marriage might bring.

Somehow I had ceased thinking about Melissa's possible passing, forgotten Elizabeth Glaser's experience, never had an inkling that marital difficulties could ever occur. But Jeff received a foretaste directly from Claire. She had predicted to him that Melissa's passing would be "very difficult." As Jeff described it years later, he knew that Claire was not referring to the repercussions for me, but for her—and us.

The wedding capped a week of exhausting excitement touched by the discord of events elsewhere. The Federal Building in Oklahoma City had been bombed several days before the wedding and the aftermath seemed to shroud us in conversations and via television and newspaper vending machines on the streets of San Francisco. I later learned that Dr. Carl Whittaker died the day of our wedding. A professional father figure to me, Dr. Whittaker believed in marriage as a critical rite in an individual's development. The synchronicity of his death had an unavoidable symbolic meaning to me, like a child being given away by his parent at a wedding. I was on my own, literally.

*****

El Dorado sits on a mesa at the north edge of the Galisteo Basin, a stunning expanse of land. The views of the blue heavens and silhouetted horizons intoxicate. That first summer, the landscape seemed like a moonscape of relentless light, low humidity and eerie dust devils, sometimes towering to the heavens. Juniper, chamisa, and needle-nubbed cholla dotted the parched land. The sunset apologized for the day with a glowing rose and persimmon which made my eyes tingle. The night skies were another marvel. I held my breath on summer evenings when dry storms flared up in all directions. I would step away from the house, slowly turning in circles to catch revolving, distant explosions of silver lightning, like silent Independence Day fireworks.

I would picture Melissa beside me, eyes aglow at the lightning storms. Wonder-struck at the road runner which flitted through the neighborhood. Eating a honey-covered sopapilla at Indian Market. Peering into the darkness of the kiva at the Pecos Mission Monument. My day dreams always dead-ended in reality since, at 7,000 feet in Santa Fe, Melissa's lungs would labor in misery. I dreamed anyway.

My search for a job was conducted with little enthusiasm, since a 9-5 would preclude me from having time to visit Claire. I accepted an offer to coordinate legislative lobbying activities for two New Mexico counseling associations. When not painting the house or nurturing our new trees and shrubs, I hiked the Sangre de Cristo Mountains and the Pecos Wilderness. It was a great life as such, offset by the lack of local friends, regular withdrawals of savings, and a wife 2000 miles away. She and I talked on the phone every night. Her movie was a nightmare and, as line producers, she and her partner were in the center of the craziness. On any given night she could sound desperate, almost like a stranger.

In mid-August it was time for the first of four trips to New York that I would take that fall. I pulled out overflowing folders of my correspondence with Costa Rica, the Lees, the Cystic Fibrosis Foundation, Reina and Mirta. I thumbed through each of them and felt a familiar sad bewilderment. So much work, for what? For the past year or so I'd been nothing more than a paycheck to Melissa and Gloria. If Melissa were to die suddenly, I would never know what, if any, effect I'd had on her life.

I wondered about my recent epiphany to simply pay attention to Melissa. From a distance, there was nothing to pay attention to but the silence. My so-called insights could seem pretty nonsensical.

When I returned from my first New York trip, Britt Dean, my childhood friend, came to visit for a couple of weeks. We did some work on the house and took a few day trips around Santa Fe before setting off on an overnight to Chaco Canyon. We took Highway 84 north to Georgia O'Keeffe country near Lake Abiquiu and then headed west. Watching the afternoon sky turn to pastel, I thought about Melissa and absent-mindedly put Bonnie Raitt on the tape player. "I Can't Make You Love Me" came on, and when it ended, I rewound and played it again. And again. Finally Britt interrupted my trance. "It's about time we put that to rest, don't you think?"

* * * * *

By late October, it had been seven months since I'd heard from Melissa and I was more resigned than ever to the distance and her silence. I was puzzled by the flurry of correspondence, abruptly ended, and my desire to fuel the communication had waned. I continued to send monthly checks and wouldn't deny her if she wanted something, but…

I sent her a bubbly birthday card and three weeks later a Christmas card with a letter tucked inside.

November 15, 1995

Dear Gloria and Melissa,

Greetings from New Mexico! I am sending happiness and love to you both and to your family in Esparza. I have hope that everything is well in your lives, with much happiness, good health and friendships.

My life in New Mexico is exciting but difficult. New Mexico is a place of so much beauty, with spectacular views, mountains, blue skies and magical light. The people here are friendly. I am learning much about the Hispanic and Native American cultures which make New Mexico different than the other states in the US.

The thing most difficult now is that Claire had to go to New York with her job for six months. She and her business partner work in the field of production for a big movie. It is very hard to be apart now. We talk on the telephone each morning and night. We are going to meet at the house of my mother-in-law in Tennessee for ten days over the Christmas holidays.

Everyone in my family is fine. Recently I went to Arizona where my father and his wife Shirley live. It is no more than one hour by airplane to get together with them and my sister, Jan, from Oregon. It has been a long time since you have written. I have hope that you have not had a difficult time in your life. Did Melissa have a happy graduation from high school?

I am going to stop for now. I want you to have a Merry Christmas and Happy New Year. I have a hope that we will get together soon. You can visit Claire and me and her dogs anytime. I send you and everyone love. Write soon.

Love,
Olin

I spent Christmas with Claire's clan, coupled with a side visit to Atlanta to see Britt and his wife Sally and my sister Kay's family. New Year's blues kicked in on my flight home. Claire had flown directly to New York and the movie still had no wrap date. New Mexico was buried in a blizzard and around mid-night, as I crept north on Interstate 25 near Algodones, Interstate 25 disappeared in a white-out. I turned back for a bleak sleep in an Albuquerque motel.

A day later, picking up my accumulated mail in Santa Fe, I ignored everything but the beautiful red and blue international envelope snuggled in the middle of the stack.

Hola!

I hope that you are well. I am very well since the day before yesterday. I don't know if I passed my exams or what the results will be.

I will tell you that if I pass the exams, all of them, Merilyn will reward me with a trip to Turtle Island.

For now I am on vacation and we are in summer. Mommy hasn't told me if she is going to reward me, surely it is a surprise.

My dog has just had a puppy. The puppy is very small and black. It is very pretty. It is a Christmas present. Speaking of Christmas, Merry Christmas, and if this letter arrives later, then Happy New Year.

When are you going to visit me? It has been two years since your last visit, nor have you written me a letter. Perhaps you don't have time......

Ok, I say goodbye now. If you talk with your family, say hi from me.
Respectfully,
Melissa Reyes

"Merry Christmas"? When will I visit? It seemed almost too good to be true. I was cheered briefly but anxiety and misery infected every good mood. Claire's movie shoot had been extended and there was no end in sight. My credit card debt had grown as my bank account shrunk. The knowledge that I couldn't take advantage of Melissa's invitation dragged me down. Her comment about not receiving a letter bothered me. Was my Christmas letter lost, delayed, or was Melissa asking for something addressed solely to her?

Several glorious feet of snow covered northern New Mexico but to me the winter wonderland sucked. Santa Fe life had been hard and disorienting. Each day I made a list of chores and activities to provide me with order and structure. Each day the list was the same. Look for work. Study Spanish. Exercise. Study psychology. I volunteered time with the Santa Fe Rape Crisis Center. There was no more house to paint.

When I was feeling better, I studied Melissa's letter. Nothing had passed between us, there was no sign of a change in health or her feelings about coming to the U.S., but there it was: an interest in me coming to see her. I was wary of becoming overly excited; I could picture myself going there and finding the same withdrawn girl. Still the Melissa I knew would not say something she did not mean.

A woman I met at the legislature referred me to a work associate from Spain, a potential translator. I met Maria for coffee at the Old Santa Fe Trail Book Store near the State Capitol. She was tall, thin and moved like a dancer, with long brown hair reaching to her waist in a pony tail. I gave her a summary of the last five years. As she read it her large eyes widened and grew wet. Maria "got it."

I took out the letter I'd received and asked her if she would translate it aloud. She read down the page to where Melissa asked when I would be visiting again. "It has been two years since your last visit....Perhaps you don't have time." I grasped the line for the first time through Maria's lips. Never had Melissa written a word of acknowledging, wishing, liking, wanting, missing a letter. And here she was speculating, suggesting, worrying that I was too busy for her.

It was a tiny giant step towards a full-blown relationship years down the road. Would she live long enough to see it or would she retreat for another six months? Maria gave me an excited smile and I forced one in return, fearful of the future.

* * * * *

I sent off a letter in late January.

Dear Melissa,

What a happy surprise when I returned home from Christmas vacation and found your letter! I'm delighted to know that you are well and I hope the same is true for your mother and all your family.

Things here are going well, although a little, well, in fact a lot more difficult that I am used to. At Christmas I spent time with Claire at the house of her mother. But afterwards she had to return to New York to continue her job on the movie. Unfortunately the progress with the movie is very slow. Soon it will be six months since Claire left and there remains about two more months for the movie to end. She is miserable and me too, but we intend to endure the situation the best we can. The end is near, but New York is a freezer these days and here in New Mexico the house seems empty.

All the family here is doing well except for Shirley. She is going to have an operation on 2/22 to replace her hip with a plastic one! We are concerned for her because she is a good person and she cares about everyone in the family.

I am busy finding a job as a counselor and talking on the phone with Claire every day. In addition for one month during the convocation of meetings by the lawmakers of the state, I move around the building of the government of the state of New Mexico which is here in Santa Fe. The professional association of counselors, of which I am a member, is fighting for better laws and economic support for the benefit of children and families. Because the association selected me as intermediary with the legislature, every day I put on my suit, meet with legislators and talk with them about the subjects for which we need their votes. At the moment it is something hard but enjoyable and the results we're obtaining are good.

I want you to forgive me because I haven't been very good about writing letters. I feel a little embarrassment because I can only write you in English since we moved. Also I want to say that you have not written me as frequently as I would like. But now I have had the luck to find a woman from Spain, Maria, who will help me with the translation of my letters. Do you notice the Spanish influence in this letter??

OK, Melissa, I hope that one way or the other, 1996 will be the year that we can get together again. I hope with all my heart that the results of your exams were as you hoped. As soon as you can, send me the results.

Please pass along my affection to your mother and the rest of your family. I hope to receive your news soon.

With affection,

Olin

Unexpectedly, after I opened my bank statement, I needed Maria for another translation.

February 26, 1996

Dear Melissa,

How are you?

Today I learned that the checks that I sent you for your birthday and Christmas have not been processed by the bank. I worry that perhaps you did not receive them.

Could you write me as soon as possible to tell me if you received them or not? Thanks.

Pardon me for ending so quickly but today has become a very busy day. I will write you again soon.

With affection,

Olin

PS Greetings to your mom and everyone.

Spring brought more than one thaw in my life. In March I received interest from several potential employers. I even interviewed for a job in both Spanish and English. Soon I was making counter offers and turning down jobs, waiting to hear from the counseling agency which most interested me. Then came word that Claire's movie had set a "wrap" date. She would be home in six weeks.

But the news that my heart had longed for more than a job, more than Claire to come home, or winter to end, arrived in a long air mail envelope with those beautiful red and blue stripes on the borders and a red, black and tan Costa Rica stamp in the upper right corner and Melissa's name opposite. The letter was folded so I could see immediately that there was writing on the front and back. I opened up the page and saw the two beautiful words,

Hola, Papá.

I grew still and sat down quietly, like I'd walked into church late. Barely breathing, I continued to read.

> *How are you? I am very well since I came out of the hospital. I left February 16. I was three weeks there. It was a little boring.*
>
> *Bueno, here my family is very well. I passed all the exams and graduated December 22. They gave me the title of high school diploma. This year I would have entered the university but since I was in the hospital I was not able to return to the "U." There are several drawbacks. The second is that I don't know what to study, although the first year student doesn't enter a course without having to do a year which is called general. There are only 4 subjects the following year if you already know what you are going to study, then you can enter what is the course. The third drawback is the cost of each course. They are from 10.000 mil to 15.000 mil colones per semester. When they come back I will send you the photos that I have of my graduation.*
>
> *When are you going to come to visit me. I have been thinking of going in January of next year when I have already reached 18 years of age, an adult, I communicated this to my mom. My cousin Merilyn wants to go with me but I need for you to tell me that you will send me the cost of the ticket to go. I hope that you won't have to work in order that you can take us around and show us some places. And also how is the climate? One question is about the altitude of that place because I can not be in a high place. I turn purple. It's called sinusitis. OK these are details that we can talk about soon if you can.*
>
> *I would like for you to come this year.*
>
> *Respectfully,*
>
> *Melissa Reyes*

The University! Another milestone and another goal, another chance for Melissa's spirit to exercise its sinews. I rubbed my wet eyes and leaned back in my chair, rolling my head back and forth. My daughter, a 17 year-old pre-college student interested in traveling to see me, had replaced the sullen 15 year-old.

"Dad....I would like for you to come this year." There had been many dreams of Melissa visiting but I'd never imagined her claiming me, never. The words came from the place in Melissa I always wanted to touch. Claire was unavailable on a movie set so I sank into the lush, moist air which signaled the end of a devastating drought.

That night I drafted a letter to Melissa. How odd and wonderful to correspond about travel plans.

Dear Melissa,

I was very happy to receive your letter last week. I am proud to learn of your success with your exams and your graduation! I'm sure you are also pleased and proud of your accomplishments. After so much hard work, not to mention the obstacles such as the hospitalizations which were placed in your way. Speaking of which, I am sorry to hear about your recent stay in the hospital. You said you were bored and I can understand that perfectly after visiting you in the hospital in 1991.

Please give my best wishes to everyone especially your mother. Everyone here is fine. Claire's movie in New York ends soon. This is very good news! She and the dogs will be home by April 15. At last! Most of my work at the legislature is complete now and I have decided to find a job working in a clinic for the time being. There are three places which say they want me but I must wait until next week for a formal offer from the place I most want to work.

Your travel plans are very interesting. I'm sure Claire and I can help you and Merilyn to have a vacation to remember! Because Santa Fe is at an altitude higher than San Jose, Claire and I will arrange to meet you somewhere near sea level like Los Angeles, Florida, Arizona or San Francisco. We can probably arrange for you to visit two cities. What would you like to do and see? Do you need some help in deciding? When you tell me what you want to do, how long you can stay, etc, I will buy your plane tickets and you can obtain your visas. I will take time off work when you are here. This will be fun! New York is also an option as a great tourist destination. The weather is typically miserable in January but there is much to do. We may have to buy you both polar bear coats!

Claire and I also hope to visit you too. I'll let you know more just as soon as we know more details.

Your decision to attend the university is more good news. I think it's great that you want to continue your education and I'll do whatever I can to help, without a doubt. I'm eager to know more about your plans. Would you live in San Jose, or commute? Do you plan on taking a full schedule of classes or only attend part time? And when is the deadline for enrollment? This question is especially important so that I can know how much time you and I have to work out the details. Also how does your mom feel about your decision? (By the way, when I first attended the University here, I had no idea what I wanted to major in until my second year. Here at least that is very typical).

I guess that's about all for now. Except I almost forgot to tell you. Once again, just before your letter arrived I had a dream about you. I wish I knew how to explain this!!

Bueno, I look forward to hearing from you soon. Give my affection to everyone.

Dad

There was one problem. Claire expressed no interest in travelling to Central America so soon after returning to Santa Fe. I told myself she was tired, looking forward to being home. I overnighted her several Costa Rica travel brochures, convinced I could persuade her to accompany me for this incredible opportunity.

I told the Clinical Director of one of the organizations interested in me that I would prefer to begin work in July or August. It would give Claire and me time to visit Melissa and simply hang out together in our house for the first time. The director was amenable to the idea while reminding me that I hadn't yet been offered the job.

My imagination churned gaily, freed from its two-year lockdown. I thought it would be ideal if Melissa and Merilyn could visit us in June or July. After all I'd been through, it was about time for a little bit of "ideal."

Claire and the dogs returned on April 15. In the weeks preceding her return, she'd been prickly on the phone. She'd remarked that, at the end of a movie, everyone in the production suffered from anxiety over returning home again and never knowing if they would work again. I tried to express understanding of her anxiety but my attempts mysteriously stirred up her feelings of distrust. She rebutted my comments until I gave up trying to express any empathy.

Still I was happy to have her around for the foreseeable future, happy to cook, walk the dogs and make love in our own bed. The counseling agency I liked offered me a job as I hoped with the stipulation that I begin work in late May. It meant that Claire and I could head to Costa Rica almost immediately, a fact that was confirmed with the arrival of another letter from Melissa, her second in four weeks. This one was four long, dense pages so, without even attempting to translate it myself, I phoned Maria. She met Claire and me in an open air café near the plaza in downtown Santa Fe. It was a perfect spring afternoon and I moved my chair close to the corner of the table craning my neck to see the words as Maria translated the astonishing letter.

39. Melissa's Story—April, 1996

The four pages were divided into two sections. There was a brief opening letter.

Hello! I received your letter today. The situation with the check is that yes I got it, the one for my birthday. I cashed it and bought a bag I needed for school, the other one was very old and stained. The check for Christmas and the one for January I cashed and bought a dress that I saw at the store. But my cousin who works at the bank says that you have to change the date. So you have to send them again.

Tell me if you already got my previous letter. It is already 22 days since I sent it. Write me.

Sincerely,

Melissa Reyes

**Pass along my greetings to your parents*

Maria turned to the next page.

I was recently reading the story that you wrote me about your life, how you and mommy met. At the end you said that you wanted me to tell you mine.

I will try to write about what I feel like and what I remember.

We were living there, with my uncle, in that house, but we had to move to Mojon, to another place. When I was really little, my mom told me that I had a dad who was a North American named Olin Dodson. I sometimes thought about you, that I would get to meet you one day, or that you could have died. I had so many questions, but nobody had any answers, not even my mother because she had tried to find you but she never got news back from you.

I want to say that my mom never was a bad example to me about messing around with older men. Men never put a foot in my house. Until 1989, my mom worked ironing clothes and then she met Ramon. Around 1990 we moved to that house, in the school area, a friend told me that a gringa was going to teach English classes. She was Laura. I thought maybe she could look for you. My mom talked to her and that was the case. I want to tell you that my mom did all that for me because Ramon was opposed to us looking for you. I think it was jealousy. The day that Laura told us that she had spoken with you on the phone I don't know if I was emotional or what, but I got more emotional when I knew you had replied and that you were acknowledging that I was your daughter. You know that not every man accepts that responsibility. I congratulate you. That day I was surprised that you had not gotten married nor had children. That was good fortune.

The day that I met you in the park I did not know what to do. I never had a dad. My feelings were messy when I met you; and that was the year my mom got married and with a man that I don't like. He is a drunk. Don't talk to anyone about that because my mom is capable of beating me if she finds out I've talked about it.

During that time, I was a little girl and my mom made me treat Ramon well and also you. Do you understand? I was angry. I did not want her to get married. I had so many questions to ask you but I was angry perhaps, and you did not know Spanish too well. You could not communicate with me. Now that I am older I regret not wanting or being able to take advantage of that time.

[Melissa switched from Spanish to English for three words]

I am sorry.

I will like it if you could come here by yourself. I don't mean to leave your wife out. You have a right to be happy. I want to go there in January or February. I want to meet you but you have not answered to me about the airfare. Only Merilyn will go with me.

About my health, I am well but I can't go to cold or high altitude places. Last year they did a lung transplant on a 13 year old boy. He is fine but had complications. They also did one on a 12 year old girl and she died six months later. They want to do one on me. Papa, I do not have faith. I fear making the decision.

I had to change doctors. Doctor Castro is who sees me now; I feel better with him. The doctor said that if I don't want to do it, that it is my decision. This is a procedure that they did not used to do until just recently. I could have a better life, breathing better, but after the transplant, it is like two months in the hospital and after that I have to go to the hospital every eight days for a series of tests. It's too much of a sacrifice if I don't know how long I am going to live.

They showed a documentary on TV of a young woman in the United States who had a transplant but with lungs from one of her parents whose lungs were compatible with hers. I wouldn't really like to have a transplant.

End of story.

That was it: "End of story." Maria looked up from the page and with Claire turned to me. They didn't have to guess my reaction.

"We've got to go see her."

Then I sat almost mute in thought. Melissa's apology and invitation erased the pain of the last five years. Melissa had considered my invitation for a story, and, exactly three years later, responded. The story, what a story! It gave me personal history and a window into her that our correspondence about doctor's appointments and money and school had never equaled.

Three years, it was nothing. One minute you are stranded at the South Pole, starved, desperate and frozen—and the next, you are invited into a shelter with a fire, warm food and companionship. It was wonderful and oddly disorienting to have my life turned upside down again.

We said goodbye to Maria after making arrangements for her to come to our house to call Melissa. Driving home, Claire insisted that she was too drained from her job in New York to go to Costa Rica, leaving me in outraged disbelief. I bombarded her with reasons for her to accompany me, starting with Melissa's need to accept me as a married man, and meet the person she would have to share me with, for at least part of our visits whether in Costa Rica or the U.S. The bottom line was I wanted and needed Claire's support. Without saying why, she relented that evening.

We bought airline tickets the following day. Claire tended to business in her office while I took a walk on a trail near the house, along some railroad tracks. I came to an overlook where the tracks curved downwards towards the town of Lamy and looked south at the sun-splashed Galisteo Basin. I considered the transplant issue. When you go under the anesthesia, there is no guarantee that you will wake up or that your health will be any better off than before. The stories of two transplant recipients, one of whom died, must have terrified Melissa. She decided she couldn't take the chance and I couldn't disagree.

There were a few indistinct remarks in Melissa's letter such as the line about her getting emotional. It was just a matter of time before I would get to know her feelings and so much more. At last our dreams coincided. I lingered over a final look at the beautiful landscape before turning back.

Maria came to the house two days later. We used an extension phone so Melissa and I could speak directly to Maria to translate. It was the first time I felt free to listen to the music of her voice at length. Her voice was tiny but friendly with a nasal tone, a result of her perpetually clogged sinuses. I couldn't know if Melissa felt uncomfortable with yet another translator, but Maria's voice purred with warmth and every few seconds she encouraged Melissa with "Sí, sí," or "Claro." Melissa's answers were not unusual. I'm fine, Mommy's fine, my puppy's fine, etc., but on the subject of school she spoke in detail. She giggled frequently and even made little jokes. She coughed a few times, nothing scary.

She had apparently plunked down money for English classes and probably forfeited it because of her hospitalization. This didn't seem to concern her, saying she would study English later in the year. She expressed happiness that Claire and I were coming to visit in one week. When I said that Claire was looking forward to meeting her she echoed the sentiment. If she was disappointed that I would not be alone she did not say so. Will you be home next week? "Always," she answered, drily.

I asked if there was anything we could bring her and she said no, although a minute later she requested enzymes. I asked to speak to Gloria and told her of our travel plans. I didn't mention any of Melissa's letters, figuring Gloria probably had no knowledge of the latest one. The conversation was all very matter-of-fact, very easy. It confirmed the breakthrough and set the stage for our next meeting.

40. If Only—May, 1996

I woke up in El Dorado still tired after a night's sleep. I stared at the lime popsicle walls. The color reminded me of vomit.

It was two weeks since our return from Esparza and I'd been sick intermittently. I remembered a dream I'd had just before waking.

> *I was preparing to leave Central America, packing my summer clothes to take back to the States because I wouldn't need them any more. I went to a restaurant for my final dinner. Melissa sat across the table from me.*

I kicked the covers off and went into the kitchen to make coffee. Claire was in town getting a hair cut and picking up laundry before coming home to pack for another out-of-town job. I took my coffee to the kitchen table and eased down like an old man. I tried to recall details from the visit with Melissa.

I'd persuaded Claire to accompany me to Costa Rica by reserving a cabana at a beautiful resort at Playa Tamarindo, north of Esparza. First we checked into the Fiesta Hotel in Puntarenas and met up with our translator, a nice hotel clerk named Lorenzo. I'd hired him by phone before we left New Mexico. We'd set aside three days just to hang out in Esparza with Melissa and her family.

Claire, Lorenzo and I showed up at Ramon's house with a dozen presents, two for Gloria: clothes, jewelry, Christian music tapes (requested by Melissa), boxes of enzymes and water soluble vitamins. The house had a musty odor, a combination rest home and greenhouse. Gloria's physical appearance had not changed all that much, but her prim outfit and short hair reminded me of a nun. She and Claire greeted each other cordially and Ramon made a brief appearance to shake hands before departing out the front door. What Gloria felt in Claire's presence, after a couple of years of mostly silence between us, was impossible to know.

Gloria knocked on Melissa's bedroom door twice before it opened. Melissa came into the room, like an elderly woman, working to breathe as she neared the table. I greeted her with a cheerful hello, privately alarmed at her appearance. Colorless lips. Stringy hair. Pouches under her eyes like dead flower bulbs. She came to me and we kissed cheeks. She turned to Claire with a big smile and kissed her cheek. Then she sat, holding her posture upright. Her chest rose with each silent gulp for breath. She held her face in a stiff smile. I felt proud of her, also disturbed and afraid. Like her, I put on my best face.

I hunched over my coffee at the kitchen table, frozen by the memories running together. I talked with Melissa for hours about school, graduation, movies, and music. Had it really been hours? Remembering our conversation was difficult. Melissa answered every question in little fragments; revealing herself was foreign, maybe tiring. Even with my studied follow-up questions, the spaces were barely filled in. We reviewed sight-seeing possibilities in California or New York. She had such muted interest in every suggestion, I wondered if she harbored doubts the trip would ever happen.

I told her I wanted to give her a special gift for graduation. She couldn't think of anything in the moment, but nodded her head when I asked if she would think it over and write to me. To most questions she shrugged her shoulders, but if I only waited, she would answer. She shrugged when I asked her the name of her favorite movie star. "Jean Claude Van Damme."

Her awareness of the macho action star surprised me. "Really? Have you seen any of his movies?"

No, she had never seen his movies. There were no movie theaters in Esparza, and movies on tape were relatively new to Esparza. She'd seen his face on tv and perhaps in magazines.

"Do you think he is handsome?" She shrugged, and leaned her head towards her shoulder with a bit of a smile. "I think so."

We agreed that I would pick up Melissa on the following day and drive to the Puntarenas hotel for lunch. When Lorenzo and I arrived she was dressed nicely but said she felt too sick to come. We went into the living room and sat down. She let me look at her without turning away. Her eyes were the deepest I'd ever seen. We made idle chatter for a few minutes then I brought up the subject of transplant. I wanted her to look at my face and see that I understood her and accepted her decision. I guessed she might have more to say than the few lines she had written in her letter, and she did.

Her voice tightened and she began at the beginning. Doctor Castro had recommended a transplant. He told her that first she needed to put on weight and go into counseling. She said she didn't like counseling. She already ate as much as she could. Gloria obviously saw transplant as Melissa's greatest hope and told her she needed to do it. Melissa described the pressure her mother exerted on her with a steely glint in her eyes.

She related the stories of the only two children who'd received transplanted lungs at the Hospital de Niños. Melissa knew the boy with CF, Randall Herrera, from years of being hospitalized in the pulmonary ward at the same time. He was having complications from his double lung transplant a year earlier. I listened in silence. I forgot about her words, merely watched her face and listened. I somehow understood every word before Lorenzo offered his translation.

Other than her new doctor, I might have been the only person Melissa had shared her guts with. From time to time she pressed her lips together. Her eyes stayed glued to the distance. She related her fear of going under an anesthetic and never waking up. When her eyes grew wet, mine did too.

I watched her face until I was certain she had finished. I spoke slowly to give Lorenzo ample time to translate my words and minimize the trembling in my voice. I said everything in my heart. It was unfair that, at 17 years of age, she was facing such a difficult decision. I regretted that she had to battle sickness and go to the hospital so often, but her toughness and her commitment to school made me proud of her. I recalled the television program on transplants and my dream of giving her one of my lungs. After listening to her story, I was convinced she was making the best decision and I was on her side completely.

I reached out and lifted her hand into mine. I looked at Melissa's delicate fingers with the round tips and touched her ring and commented on its beauty. When our eyes met I saw that she had been weeping and I had to force myself not to cry aloud.

We had talked for more than an hour and she had wearied. I told Lorenzo we should let her go and rest. I kissed her goodbye and said I'd return and check on her that evening.

*****

Later, Claire and I picked up Ascension, Bita, and Marvin and drove them to Puntarenas for dinner. Bita told us of Melissa's graduation, how she walked across the stage to get her diploma, how her classmates stood up and gave her a standing ovation. The three of them were sad about Melissa's condition but at the same time, resigned. They trusted in God, which meant she would live as long as He willed it. I listened and nodded my head sorrowfully.

We returned to Esparza and stopped by the house. As tired as she was, Melissa agreed to join us at Ascension and Bita's for dessert and photographs. I was so emotionally disjointed that, only two weeks later, the evening was a blur in my memory. The next morning, before Claire and I departed for Playa Tamarindo, we stopped in for a short good-bye. Gloria had not come to her brother's the night before and we had never managed to find time alone. Melissa looked horribly pale, her eyes drawn. Somehow I was able to

The last photo of Melissa and me together. With Ascension, 1996

make her laugh. I gave her money to cover her college enrollment. Claire put a rolled up $100 bill in her hand. We agreed to begin talking long-distance and figure out all the details for her trip in the winter. I pressed my lips to her cheek for as long as I dared, wild with fear that I would never see her again.

Every morning at the resort I pulled myself out of bed as if I'd never slept. I would trudge to the pool until one morning, floating on my back and staring into space, I had a sudden vision of a funeral. I bolted out of the water. Each afternoon, Claire and I drew the ebony linen curtains. As they stirred in the draft from the ceiling fans, we made love, then fell asleep. Except for the times I lay still and imagined Melissa listening to her Gloria Estefan tape or showing her new jewelry to a friend. I tried to think of something I'd missed, something which would make her feel better. But her joy and health were beyond my control. I could do little more than remain constant and help her realize her dreams as long as she was alive.

I fought the urge to drive back to Esparza to see Melissa one more time. I wanted magic, an eternal image of her to take with me. She was the incredible once-in-a-lifetime sunset. You promise you will never forget that moment, but afterwards your memory of the beauty is not the same and you are attempting to remember the feeling. I didn't want the feeling. I wanted to sit with her one more time, look in her eyes one more time. I wanted to pull her close and hold her so tight that the memory of her would fill me and be the same as her presence. For always. If only I could do that.

The cold coffee made a brown ring in the cup. I pressed my fist into my cheek, repeating the two-word refrain. If only. If only I could look in her eyes once again, I would never forget it. If only I could kiss her cheek, hold her hand in mine once more, I would feel better. I would gain some satisfaction. I could let go. But all the "if only's" were fool's wishes. The truth was this. If I could only see her one more time, I would feel the same as now. I would want more, never stop wanting more. I would never have her enough.

The trip had been unforgettable. Melissa and I sat together and talked. We looked at each other. We laughed together. She shared her transplant decision and we agreed to let go into the arms of an uncertain future. We cried. I held her hand. It wasn't enough. We couldn't remove our fears and sadness. We couldn't remove the emptiness of the years unlived together. We couldn't live together like so many daughters and fathers. We couldn't kill cystic fibrosis.

41. Life Apart—May-November, 1996

Dear Melissa,

Hi! How are you? I hope that you are feeling good and everything is going well.

You can't imagine how happy I was about visiting you in person. It would make me happy to be able to do that all the time. Claire and I are already talking about returning to see you again.

Melissa, I appreciated the friendly way that you welcomed Claire. I imagine that meeting her could have been a little uncomfortable but you did wonderfully. Our visit with you was very special and you are a person very special. Lorenzo, the translator, talked to me about this one day after we left your house. He said, "Olin, she is exactly as you said. She has so much depth. You can see it in her eyes."

I am sorry that we were unable to stay longer. The next time I hope that we can have more time together, here in the United States or in Costa Rica.

I will write you again in a couple of weeks. But, for now, more than anything I wanted to say hi and I am thinking about you.

I hope that you write soon.

Give my best wishes to everyone.

With love,

Papa

Dear Merilyn,

Claire and I want to thank you and your parents and Marvin for your wonderful hospitality. We feel happy to know all of you and to spend time with you. I am sorry we live so far apart.

Please give my love to Melissa. You can fax me anytime.

Everyone here is fine and working hard. Unfortunately Claire had to go to Los Angeles for several months.

We have some great photos of your family. We will send copies. We have your gift above our fireplace.

Claire and I met with Dr. Castro when we returned to San Jose. He said he is happy to give medicine to Melissa. He said it is not true that he is withholding medicine in order to motivate Melissa.

Claire and I send you our love. We think of you all the time. We hope to return to Costa Rica as soon as possible.

Write soon!!

Love,

Olin

Gloria sent her first letter in many months. The envelope contained two old newspaper articles about Randall, the boy with cystic fibrosis who'd received the first double lung transplant at the Hospital de Niños.

> *Hola, How are you,*
>
> *I want to thank you for the moral support that you gave to Melissa. For me it is very important. Thank you.*
>
> *In this letter I am sending you articles about the operation on one of the children that had a transplant. Melissa is in the hospital now. I would like you to write her, if you can give her words of encouragement. At times, she is sad thinking about her condition. We need moral support not money. Pardon me if before, I interpreted you wrongly. Thank you.*
>
> *I have had health problems. Melissa has been in the hospital alone for three days.*
>
> *I hope you all are well. Write.*

I unfolded the newspaper articles from 1994. One featured a photo of Randall, his mom, dad and younger sister. In the other, Randall, wearing a surgical mask, is waving at the camera like an astronaut ready to leave earth.

No longer calculating the timing of my letters, I wrote Melissa on Father's Day.

> *Dear Melissa,*
>
> *It is Sunday in the morning. I sit at the kitchen table in the pleasant morning sunlight. I listen to a quintet of Brahms on the stereo. Outside of that the house is still.*
>
> *It is the 16th of June, Father's Day in the United States. I hope you are well. I received a letter from your mom a week ago saying you had gone in the hospital. More unhappy news. I hope you did not need to stay there for a long time and are now feeling better.*
>
> *I arranged to have someone take an antibiotic for you to Dr. Castro from the United States. I have not been able to track her down since she returned, but I hope the medicine was delivered without a problem (and more importantly I hope it helped you to feel better). If so, I will try to find someone else to bring you more soon. Claire and I cannot visit you again until November. Unless of course you need me to come sooner for any reason.*
>
> *Claire and I began new jobs two weeks after we returned from Costa Rica. I knew I would, of course, but Claire's new movie was unexpected. She had to leave again, destination: Los Angeles. It appears that she will be there until October. The good news, however, is that LA is only a 90-minute flight from here and tickets are cheap. So we pledged to visit each other two weekends each month.*
>
> *Claire enjoyed meeting you and is already starting her Spanish lessons. When we returned to New Mexico I came down with a peculiar respiratory illness. I was sick and unhappy for a week. In part I think*

it was a reaction to leaving you again. I continually had the miserable thought of so many miles between Esparza and Santa Fe.

Seeing how you had changed into a young woman filled me with so much happiness. You have become not only beautiful and dignified but intelligent with a witty sense of humor. Once again I commend you on your courage in seeking contact with me. You wrote and acknowledged me for responding to you six years ago, now it is my turn to applaud you.

This day means very much to me this year. I have more to say....next time.

Con cariño,

Papá

PS I sent Merilyn a fax at her bank a week ago. I hope she received it. Write soon! How do you like the music tapes? Do you wear the clothes and jewelry we brought you? Tell me please. Also tell me what you think about going to the University and visiting the US.

I am planning to call you by phone in the middle of July. Unfortunately I do not know exactly when because Maria and I have to find agreement; the hours and days of her job change every week. But Maria will call you ahead of time in order to decide on a good day and time for you and us.

I wrote an imaginary letter in my journal.

Dear Melissa,

There is so much...... There are so many conversations we never had. Words never said. Experiences never shared. Trips never made. Touch, laughter, confidences....Never.

I won't live a life of regret but this had to be said.

I want to see you and I can't.

Live life. Follow your dreams.

I had lived a good life filled with great friends and wonderful experiences and opportunities, and now I had a relationship with my daughter. Mostly via mail, but I embraced that. I had come to share Melissa's happiness that I had no other children. How could I not be grateful for all that did and did not happen, that every event in my life and many others took place exactly the way they had? Every turn, every stop and start joined a conspiracy of moments which led to Melissa's arrival in my life. My acceptance of the job at the voc rehab center in 1975. My Outward Bound trip. My decision to quit my job and travel to Latin America. The exact days I chose to leave Guatemala and El Salvador and Nicaragua. Not having a ticket out of Panama so I'd be kicked off the bus, waking up when I did in San Jose, going to the café where I met Gloria, and rooming with the snorer who told me I'd be an idiot to leave Costa Rica. I could look into the past through cosmic binoculars and there's Shirley and me, crossing paths at the State Fair. There is Laura deciding to volunteer in Costa Rica, and Bob and Anne Lee making that one final phone call to my former co-worker, and Gloria enrolling in English class, and so forth, on and on forever, all of it. The strands of time and events and decisions intertwine and fade into the past until they disappear. Each one is an essential piece of the tapestry and to remove a single thread would mean No Melissa.

In July, we began a series of phone conversations. I drove to Maria's house near the capitol building in Santa Fe. I plugged a portable phone into a jack in the bedroom while Maria sat in her kitchen.

Melissa answered the phone. Her voice was upbeat. Although I took my usual active role with questions and topics, she held up her side of the conversation. Melissa thanked me for the Tobramycin I sent her; it worked well, similar to the antibiotics she was used to.

She told me she'd written me a week earlier. In a coy tone she warned me the letter contained something which might give me a heart attack. In spite of my attempts to persuade her, she would say no more, other than it was related to my wallet.

She was non-committal about any further plans for visiting me. Her focus was on her upcoming university enrollment, just a few weeks away. I followed her lead and asked her questions about her possible classes and reaffirmed my pride in her.

We decided to end for the moment. "Claire sends you her love."

"*Igualmente.*" (Equally)

"If I have a heart attack from your letter, I will call you from the hospital." Melissa giggled. It was one of the best phone calls of my life.

The last six years had been a repeated exercise in imagining a world I did not know. I returned to that world after our conversation ended. Melissa is walking unhurriedly to her room after putting down the phone. She has a contained, secure feeling. She is pleased by her father's love, warmed by his attention and curiosity, strengthened by his wish to see her, delighted by his responsiveness. She has begun to believe that he is a safe man and she can ask for his assistance. She can step forward into the world.

I imagined us sitting next to each other, me cradling her hand like I did the first time we met. My heart was full.

Soon, another jewel.

> *Hola!*
>
> *I am well. Last week I went to an appointment at the hospital and I am very good.*
>
> *I am happy that you enjoyed your visit, also that you are thinking of your next trip. In your letter you said if it was difficult for me to meet Claire and just look, no, I enjoyed having met who you had decided to live your life with.*

One week after your visit, I had a stay in the hospital for 15 days while I was there a new treatment arrived that you had talked about with Dr. Castro. Regarding your trip the doctor asked nothing.

If I can go it would make me happy, in part to go to someplace beautiful, perhaps to Sea World. Further on we'll see.

With respect to the letter that you sent to the family, saying that you had spoken to Dr. Castro, that it was a lie that he did not have medicines for me, but they left me without medicine for one and a half months. This is true because I went to my last appointment and they ordered me nothing, but thanks to God, now I am fine.

I would be happy that whatever the doctors say to you, you tell to me or my mother and no one else, not my family because I want them to know nothing, don't mention nothing about this please. Thanks.

I think that when this card arrives, it's already passed, but I hope that you had a Happy Birthday.

I want to ask you something. According to what you told me there you have a celebratory custom, something big. It's going to sound crazy, but some day I want to ask you, I want you to buy me a car, it would be easier to transport myself to the university or trips that I have, but you could help me pay the taxes, my girlfriend there said they are cheaper there than here. Please answer me soon, don't mention this to anyone, thanks.

Write soon, thanks.

Sincerely,

Melissa Reyes

The request for the car made me laugh. I couldn't wait to tell her it gave me a heart attack. The entire letter delighted me, especially the fact that she was dreaming of Sea World. I'd become a confidant, we had a secret.

I was not happy that she had spent two weeks in the hospital, but the letter was spirited and positive. The wording was wonderfully direct with an unmistakably mature feel. Planning a trip to the United States, she must have guessed that a visit to a CF specialist was inevitable. No longer the sullen, depressed girl. No more "*No Voy!*"

I phoned her several days later, serious about her request. I held a list of things I'd prepared to say to her. First, how much I appreciated her thoughtful idea. Second, a car would cost more money than I had, my own car was eight years old. Third, her request was appealing since it would help her to travel to school and back. Always I spoke in a matter of fact tone, hoping to minimize the chances of her feeling embarrassed or rejected. I asked her to think of an alternative, something a bit less expensive. I emphasized how much it meant for her to tell me what she wanted, even if I couldn't say yes.

I couldn't convey the joy I experienced from our conversation, one which was, I imagined, just like fathers and daughters sometimes have in real life. This was my dream for Melissa and me: real life.

Late July brought an unsettling dream about Claire.

> *We are in a department store Christmas shopping. She's walking several steps ahead of me, oblivious to my whereabouts. She walks onto an escalator with several people between us and, to get her attention, I stop. But when I go downstairs there is no sign of her. I look around everywhere. Rather than question her leaving me, I second-guess myself. I wander out into the parking lot, thinking I should have paged her.*

On August 21, Melissa and I spoke again, our fourth phone conversation. She said she felt ok but her tone was unconvincing. I asked what was wrong. She said one of Ruby's puppies had wandered off a couple of days earlier. She had placed an ad on the radio, one of those local programs where people sell things and pass along messages of love. "You were very smart to do that."

We talked a bit more and I said, "Maybe if she doesn't come back, she's found a home where she is well taken care of."

Her response was brief. "I don't believe that."

We left it there. I told her of my recent illness, misery and medicine, highlighting the part of the story about having a doctor I didn't like. "I thought you could relate to that." When she responded with a big laugh, I was a happy man.

I asked if she needed money for school. She wanted to ask something but said it was a bit embarrassing. "Why have you not sent money, it makes me think perhaps you are not serious about helping me."

I chose my words carefully, hoping Maria would translate them with clarity. "Yes, I am serious. That is why I brought up the subject. Thank you for being so honest. I want us to always be honest with each other. Like the day we talked about transplant." I paused. "How much money do you need?"

Approximately $150 for tuition, books and bus fare. I promised to send it the following day.

We spoke again several weeks later. It was September, classes had begun and Melissa had purchased her books and paid her tuition. We had a simple conversation. I described my plans to visit again before Christmas. Had she come up with an alternative graduation present? "Yes, a VCR." I said I would be happy to give her a VCR. We agreed to shop for one when I returned to Esparza. Had she ever watched a DVD she especially liked? "Yes, "My Life."" I knew of the movie. Michael Keaton played a man dying of cancer. "I haven't seen it, but I'll rent it."

As a rule our phone chats were quite matter of fact. Periods of silence were common, so I always prepared topics for us to talk about. I looked forward to discussing "My Life."

No letter had come from her in a while, but I sent her one anyway.

Dear Melissa,

I hope that you are feeling well and happy.

Everything is going well here although Claire, sadly, finds herself in Los Angeles for work and I continue making visits to the doctor, this time for high blood pressure. The doctor practices Chinese medicine and acupuncture. Have you ever tried it? It's very relaxing to me and doesn't hurt. Also I drink Chinese herbal medicine 3 times a day. It tastes bad.

Give my greetings to everyone. I hope you enjoy the photos I am enclosing. Could you give some to your aunt and uncle please?

It would make me happy if you would write and tell me about your clas

If you want some music tapes and anti-biotics when Claire and I come in December, tell us soon!

Take care,

Dad

In late October, we spoke for the sixth time. She was attending class and feeling good, and once again very upbeat on the phone. Her voice was easy going and she responded readily to everything I said or asked. She had not made any progress in getting a passport. She was happy to hear of my firm plans to visit again in early December. In response to my question she asked for cassette tapes of two gospel groups I was unfamiliar with.

I noticed a pattern in our communication. As we neared the conclusions of our conversations, Melissa would bring up new things to talk about. I was usually anxious about the length of our chats and her becoming bored, but she didn't seem to want the phone calls to end. Maria later offered the same observation.

Soon the postman brought another letter from my favorite pen pal. I'd had a strong foreshadowing that her letter would arrive that day.

Hi!

How are you? Good, I hope.

I received your letter. It's been 4 weeks since I've written you because I had to study for two exams. It went well for me in both.

I am sending you a document, perhaps when Maria returns from Spain she can translate it for you, because you are not going to understand it. In the future the amount that you had to pay for tuition I am going to need each month for transportation and to eat something there when I have to stay all day.

If you could send me the money at the beginning of each month, it would be the easiest. With respect to the music cassettes, don't bring me anything for now, thank you. For medicine, I would be happy if you could bring me ADEK AND Ultrase vitamins. It would make me happy also if you could bring me a VCR although perhaps it would cost you too much. You don't have anyone else who asks you, only me. This week I have to go to an appointment with the doctor. Hasta Luego.

Sincerely,

Melissa Reyes

**Write me*

Melissa was accepting me as a part of her life and renewed energy propelled me through the days. I'd be with her soon. Her health seemed stable. Her doctor's appointment was probably nothing more than a regular check-up. I'd almost blocked out my worries about cystic fibrosis.

Dear Melissa,

As you turn 18, I would like to wish you the most happy of birthdays! I sincerely hope that the year which will soon begin will be the most happy of your life. I enclose for you two checks. The little one is for school stuff. I hope you spend the big one on a party or on things for yourself that you would not ordinarily buy. Whatever you do with it, enjoy it!

With affection,

Dad

PS I enjoyed talking to you on Wednesday. Soon I will send you a long letter with details of our visit in December.

I watched "My Life," scarcely moving. Early on a doctor bludgeons the Michael Keaton character with the news that he has an incurable health condition with only months to live. Keaton leaves the office then rushes back and bursts in on the doctor, going completely wonderfully ape-shit. Melissa was surely enthralled by the scene. Later the Keaton character is laying on a healer's table when he flows into a spectacular shower of light and beauty, a transcendent vision of life after death. God, what I would have given to see the movie at her side.

Maria wasn't available for calling Melissa on her birthday but I thought about her all day. To my knowledge no one with CF in Costa Rica had reached the age of 18. When Merilyn had told me that it would be age 18 before Melissa opened up, I wondered if that time would ever come. But she had arrived ahead of schedule. I found myself dreaming about her future with a sweet boy, discovering a different kind of love.

Several days later when we did speak, our conversation soared with an amazing revelation. Melissa said she would like to bring a friend to Tamarindo with Claire and me! I responded affirmatively, holding in shouts of joy. Melissa also reported that her new doctor, Jose Pablo Gutierrez, would like to meet me. It would mean lots of driving back and forth from Tamarindo to Esparza and San Jose, but I'd make it work out. There were no developments in her travel plans. It looked like there would be no trip to the US over the winter. We never did talk about "My Life."

November 13, 1996

Dear Melissa,

I hope this letter finds you happy and feeling good. Please give my best wishes to everyone especially your mom.

I began this letter a few months ago, on Fiesta Day in Santa Fe, a half day holiday for many New Mexicans. Fiesta celebrates the return of the Spanish to this area after the Native Americans threw them out in 1680. Today there are processions and special masses.

Unfortunately this weekend Claire and I can't be together. So I will spend the weekend alone–and outside as much as possible. Also I have to sit by the telephone for six hours as a volunteer on the crisis line, a free phone service that victims of domestic violence can call for assistance. I believe that men should act to stop domestic violence. This is one of the activities I do in my free time.

While I sit by the phone I will write you. I also have to find something in a book, or write something that can be read at the wedding of a friend, Britt. I have known him since I was 12 years old. Unfortunately, we can't attend his wedding in Atlanta, but he has asked me to send him something for a friend to read during the ceremony.

Then I remembered something. I found one of the poems which was read at my wedding with Claire. I am sending it to you, because it is beautiful and because it was written by a Spanish poet, Antonio Machado. Are you familiar with him? Let me know if you like the poem, "Last Night As I Slept."

Everything here is fine. My intensive classes in Spanish were cancelled, not enough students to fill the class. And so I returned to my workbooks. Now I study fervently and in fact I know more than ever. Claire is also using tapes in the little free time she has. I admire her for doing it.

You know, I don't think I told you much about my new job. It is very interesting. I enjoy very much the majority of kids I work with. There are a couple of boys with emotional problems, another one that saw his mother die, another that was sexually abused, and two teen-age mothers. The majority of the kids have parents that do not live together.

Just now as I wrote this fact, I thought about you growing up with only your mother. The fact that you have grown up and come to be a motivated student and a young woman so honest and thoughtful is a true achievement on your part.

The past spring you wrote me and apologized for the way you had treated me. Your words touched me deeply. Naturally I was hurt. But I hope you understand, as I did, that you were only a child. I knew that you had much to work through for yourself, more than I could understand.

Merilyn and your tios helped me a lot. They always believed in me and you. As your father I chose to try and remain strong and maintain the faith that one day your heart would open. I continue wanting to understand how you changed. Could you put it into words?

We made plans to fly down on December 7. We will visit Esparza for three days and afterwards go to Tamarindo for three days. Perhaps you can join us in Tamarindo for 1, 2, or 3 days. I know your health is a consideration. We will have a car to take you rapidly to Esparza or San Jose in case of an emergency. And if you only want to stay one night I can take you home the following day. You can bring a friend if you wish. The hotel in Tamarindo is extremely beautiful. Claire and I would enjoy it if you joined us, so I hope you will consider it seriously.

After Tamarindo we will return to Esparza for a few hours before returning to San Jose and our flight home. This is a short vacation, very short, but I want to see you and it offers Claire a rest she desperately needs.

Often I think about our visit last spring. Often I think about our close conversation in your living room. I felt so touched by your openness. I don't know if I ever mentioned your bravery in the face of imposing circumstances. I don't know if I ever told you how much I respect and solidly support you in your decision. In light of all you told me I can imagine myself making the same decision that you made. For someone who is so important to me, it saddens me greatly to see you suffering. If only my love was powerful enough to ease your suffering.

Something more that struck me about our last visit was sitting and laughing with you and Claire. I hope we can do more of the same in December.

Until then.
Love,
Dad

Last Night When I Was Sleeping
By Antonio Machado

Last night when I was sleeping
I dreamt—blessed illusion—
That a fountain was flowing
Inside my heart.
Tell me, hidden aqueduct
Water, why do you come to me
Spring of new life
From which I never drank?

Last night when I was sleeping
I dreamt—blessed illusion!—
That I had a beehive inside my heart;
golden bees making
white wax and sweet honey
from my old sorrows.

Last night when I was sleeping
I dreamt—blessed illusion!—
That a fiery sun shone inside my heart.
It was fiery because it gave off colors of a red home
and sun because it gave light
and made me weep.

Last night when I was sleeping
I dreamt—blessed illusion!—
That it was God I had
Inside my heart.

42. A Single Flower—December, 1996

It was no dream, we were on our first road trip, a half-hour drive to Puntarenas to buy Melissa a VCR. She sat beside me, not really close, in the front seat with Claire and the translator behind us. I watched her from the corner of my eye, looking for a sign, some kind of message. It was like those days of going to the mail box and finding nothing. She stared forward and spoke when spoken to, sparingly and without feeling. I tried to tell myself this was a great experience, shopping with my daughter. I had hoped the fresh air and change of scenery would pull Melissa out of her shell. If she wasn't intending to push me away, she was doing a good job.

We walked around town and found a VCR she liked in the second store we visited. It was more expensive than one I could buy in the States, but I had wanted us to shop together and consult on the selection, no matter the cost. When we drove back to Esparza, the big box sat on her lap. She never cracked a smile, as if expressing happiness would threaten her world. By the time we arrived at the house, the remnants of my good mood had soured completely. We'd come here for what?

The excitement of the departure date for Costa Rica had built like a tidal wave, then crashed. Once again Claire threatened to stay home. The pattern had grown more common. One night I hawked tickets in front of the Lensic Theater because she'd suddenly reversed her mind about the book reading I was eager to attend. On the morning of our raft trip down the Rio Grande, she decided to spend the day shopping in Taos. We never honed our skills in marital negotiating. If I pushed too far, she switched into a "Take No Prisoners" mode. The raft trip disagreement went something like this.

But I paid for your spot.

I'll pay you back.

I've waited to do this with you.

I've rafted the river before.

That was it. Case closed.

She didn't want to go to Costa Rica because of the possibility we'd have Melissa and her friend sleeping on a roll-away in our cabana.

Look at it as something new and different. Melissa wants to join us and what if she gets sick in the night? Do you want her friend having to run get us?

That's my point. This won't be a vacation for me.

Come on, we will have time to ourselves. This is only one night!

I don't want to share our room.

This is about seeing Melissa at a really important time in her life, in our life. I can't believe you don't want to share in it.

Well you are not the one who spends most of your time away from home.

Claire didn't give an inch.

Two days before our flight, Gloria faxed me to say that Melissa had contracted the flu. She was being watched closely in case she developed pneumonia. In my office, I quietly closed the door when I broke into tears. I had never felt terror but I knew it when it hit. The Executive Director of my organization told me he would put Melissa on his prayer list. I was touched and scared. His words crystallized the fear that this would be the last time I'd see Melissa.

I told Claire I'd rent another cabana for Melissa and her friend and she agreed to go. I had a feeling that Claire's cabana issue was a smoke screen for something else which I never understood. But I didn't think much about it; I was merely glad I wasn't going alone.

Melissa's flu had turned out to be not as serious as Gloria's fax had indicated. But Melissa's clean white t-shirt and shorts couldn't disguise the fact that her heavy eyes were about the same as before, maybe worse. Something else had changed. I studied her interesting features and the upright way she carried herself. She was now a young woman.

She sat with us but gave nothing away. She claimed to feel fine. If true, there was no explanation for her dishwater pallor or her flat reaction to our arrival and attempts to engage her. She was non-committal about joining us in Tamarindo.

Later at the hotel Claire patiently listened to me vent my frustration. She said we couldn't know what was going on in Melissa. My reply was that Melissa was being self-indulgent and not showing the least bit of appreciation. In truth my criticism was a classic case of projection, accusing her of an attitude scarcely different than mine.

The next morning Claire and I drove back to San Jose to see Dr. Gutierrez in his private office. He was a handsome guy, about 35, friendly with no hint of ego. He was low-key, not the type to rattle easily. I could see why Melissa liked him. He apologized for having only thirty minutes to see us; he had appointments with many children. I could sense he was, like most Central American docs, hyper-dedicated to his work, foregoing big money in Miami or Houston.

Dr. Gutierrez knew Melissa had been sick and was currently being treated in a clinic in Puntarenas. He stated his belief that Melissa's best chance for survival was a lung transplant. Unfortunately she was too underweight to have such a major surgery and, besides, she was fearful of the operation. But her faith in God was strong. She kept her appointments and took her meds as directed. He said if she could maintain her health, perhaps she would change her mind. I didn't tell him about my conversation with her about transplant. Nor did we go into great detail about Melissa's health. Perhaps Dr. Gutierrez realized that there was nothing to be gained by alarming me.

When I asked how Melissa related to him, he said they had a good relationship and he believed that she trusted him. He gave her books to read and discuss with him. The one she liked best was Antonio Skarmeta's *El Cartero de Neruda*, the basis of the movie, *Il Postino*. It was a romantic movie and I wondered if the book fed love fantasies for my 18 year old.

Dr. Gutierrez said Melissa spoke with admiration for me and had discussed with him her wishes to visit me in the future. We discussed how that could be arranged. He said she would need to travel with oxygen and only when her health was stable. Special medical arrangements could be arranged with the airlines after Melissa got her visa and I bought her plane tickets. We exchanged phone and fax numbers, agreeing to talk again when Melissa's travel plans were firm.

We returned to Esparza to visit with Melissa. She said she felt ok but she looked fatigued and her cough made me cringe. I told her about our chat with Dr. Gutierrez. She didn't react when I told her about our discussion of her plans to visit the States. She declined another invitation to join Claire and me in Tamarindo and my heart sank. I asked why and she just shrugged. I waited but there was no explanation. I reminded her that there was still time to change her mind.

We drove to see Ascension and Bita. They hugged us warmly and enjoyed my stories of the phone calls between Melissa and me since I had last visited. They knew of her feelings about transplant. Ascension listened without comment but Bita was not so shy. She said the university was very important to Melissa and Doctor Gutierrez had been very good for her. As for Gloria's silence, Bita dismissed it with a little grunt and a swing of her hand towel. Ascension rolled his eyes.

The next day, we stopped by to see if Melissa would join us, knowing she would not. She was waiting for an acquaintance to come by and set up her VCR. Claire and I handed her a video of the movie "Babe" (the smart pig) dubbed in Spanish. We said we'd return in a few days and make sure the VCR was working properly. I asked if we could pose together for photos. She refused.

Claire and I spent three nights at Tamarindo. The beach and the sunsets and ping-pong under the palm trees were enjoyable but it all felt like marking time. I was boxed in. If I insisted on returning to Esparza, Claire would never forgive me. And there was no hint that Melissa would welcome it. I couldn't help but wonder what had happened to her. It was one thing to be faithful correspondents and pen pals, but in-person pals we were not.

On our way back to San Jose, we stopped in Esparza for a few hours. A group of people, mostly Merilyn's friends, were gathered in the living room of Ramon's house to watch a soccer game between the US and Costa Rica. I pulled for Costa Rica but they couldn't mount any offense and lost the match. Melissa's hack was edgy but everyone ignored it until it got so bad she went into the bathroom. Merilyn and I shared pensive looks.

As Claire and I prepared to leave, I knelt beside Melissa and said take care, I love you, I look forward to seeing you in the US. I hugged her lightly and kissed her cheek. She looked at me with wide eyes, saying nothing. It was an anti-climactic end to a disappointing visit.

Three days before Christmas, I drove over to Maria's and we phoned Melissa. Maria had called ahead to ensure she would be home. It took a retreat of a couple of thousand miles just to have the pleasure of hearing Melissa's voice and get over myself. No matter the miraculous gains Melissa and I had made, she was still a teenager and one with a serious chronic illness. It was unreasonable to think that she would be able to set all this aside and suddenly be the girl I wanted her to be. Idealistic parental fantasies were of no help.

I gave Melissa a synopsis of all that had happened since we returned and we briefly discussed Christmas. For many Costa Ricans, Christmas was not a materialistic show day. The only Christmas activity Melissa mentioned was going to Church. I talked about our families visiting and sitting down to large meals. Melissa apologized for not letting me take her picture. I accepted her apology, saying it was nothing. I remembered what it was like to be a teenager, self-conscious and picky about your photo being taken. But to see yourself in the mirror, your face lacking life, your body beanstalk thin, fighting for your breath, coughing up mucous, feeling your spirit worn out, honest to God, I had no idea.

43. June, 1997

Dear Melissa,

How are you? I send you my best wishes for a Happy New Year. I hope you are doing well. Please give my regards to your mother and all your family. Claire and I had a busy Christmas with all of her family visiting. It was nice to be with them for two weeks and run around with them. Now our life is returning to normal, with a bonus: lots of snow.

I hope you had a beautiful Christmas and are receiving enjoyment from your VCR.

I have not heard any news from your doctor. Have you made any progress in obtaining your passport?

How is school going?

I hope to hear from you soon.

With affection,

Dad

The weeks passed slowly, with no word from Melissa or Dr. Gutierrez. I had hesitated phoning her, thinking any day I would receive a letter. Through January and February we didn't speak.

February 27

Hola. How are you both? Well, I hope. I am very well because I am finished going to the hospital to receive a treatment. Here everything is the same, everyone is in good health.

I already began the university. Soon, in one month I will have the first exams and in May I will have the others and finish the course.

I have a doubt always that we have discussed about when I travel there. You told me that you would pay everything for a passport but you have not said when you would send me the money for obtaining a passport. You didn't say anything when you came, also in your letters.

Another thing I am going to travel alone. Merilyn will accompany me on the second trip another time.

I hope that you send me your answer quickly so that I can begin to make the trip [to obtain] the passport. Hello to Claire.

Sincerely,

Melissa

I fell back in my chair and growled. Almost three months since my visit and no action on the passport. I could forget about seeing her anytime soon. On top of this, she was blaming me for not mentioning money for the passport. Had I really overlooked this? Wasn't she to blame for letting this go?

I dropped off a copy of the letter at the store where Maria worked. She phoned me that night. She told me that, in Spanish, Melissa's words didn't have the accusatory tone I invested them with. Maria said it was pretty factual, nothing I should take offense to. I said, "I thought we had an agreement that I would send her money when she knew the cost. Why did she take so long to mention this?" Maria, of course, did not have an answer.

I decided to write Melissa my own factual letter. Still not knowing how much money to give her for a passport, I enclosed a check for $25.

Dear Melissa,

I was happy to receive the news that you are feeling good and that you making constant progress in your studies.

Things here are good, not great. It seems as if almost everyone in Santa Fe has been sick lately, including Claire and me. Work had been difficult because for two weeks I have had to do my job and my supervisor's, too while she is visiting her father.

Regarding your question, I am happy to send you money for your passport. Please tell me how much it will cost and I will send you a check.

Please give my best wishes and affection to everyone there.

I hope to hear from you soon.

With affection,

Dad

I was happy that she was feeling good and anxious to get her passport, not so happy that I had to gear down, forever waiting for her to make a move. I'd once heard all cystics described as control freaks, a description which definitely fit Melissa. Loving her was a lot of preparing to jump through hoops when she raised her starter's pistol, then jumping when the gun was fired and then being called back for a false start. Just when it seemed we were taking a big step in our relationship, like the Tamarindo trip, we took no step.

When I tired of whining, I would always remember how difficult her life had been, and feel selfish for feeling such impatience and judgment.

I put in some calls to the Consulate to learn about the visa application process, and then to American Airlines to see what they required in order for Melissa to fly with oxygen.

Melissa's next letter arrived in early May, almost two months after her previous one.

Hola.

How are you both? I hope that you are well. I haven't had time to write you I've been studying. In a week I have final exams for this cuatromester. With respect to the University I need you to send me money for matriculation in the first week of May and to buy materials, the same that you gave me in December when you came.

Here everyone is fine, without anything new.

With respect to the trip, the cost of the passport is around $50, without a visa, that is separate, I don't know when I will know.

Doctor Gutierrez told me that he would write you when I could do it.

OK, that's all.

Sincerely,

Wendy Melissa Reyes Reyes

It was Melissa's shortest letter in a long while and its appearance was peculiar. The left side margin angled down and to the right, making the body of the letter a rectangle with four uneven sides. I was perplexed that Melissa's communication had reverted to such brevity.

"I don't know when I will know." The visa and the trip had been moved into the future somewhere. Disappointed that the trip had gained no traction, I could do nothing but wait for Dr. Gutierrez' approval.

Dear Melissa,

I was happy to receive your letter and to learn that everything is going well. Please give my greetings to everyone. I would like to express my best wishes for you to have great success on your exams.

I think I gave you $150 last time (for tuition) so I am sending you a check for the same amount for next semester and $50 for the passport. Once you obtain the passport, we can discuss your visa and what would be the best dates for you to travel.

This has been an extremely busy and chaotic time. I will be changing jobs in a few weeks. I will work in a town called Espanola, which is 25 miles north of Santa Fe. I will work as a counselor in remote areas of northern New Mexico, in a unique project, completely innovative and new, where I will counsel families in their homes. Normally Hispanics are hired to work in these areas of the state, so it is a big honor that I have been selected for this position.

Recent months have been difficult for a few people in my life, like my father's wife, Shirley, and Claire's mother, both of whom have had health problems. Two friends at work have lost parents.

Love helps us to persevere. Ok, that's all for now.

Stay in touch. Tell me about school, video movies you recommend, stories about your dogs, etc.

I hope to receive news from Dr. Gutierrez. In the meantime, enjoy life!

With love,

Dad

Claire went off to Europe with her business partner, a nice decompression from the rigors of another movie. She wrote impassioned emails from the south of France wishing I was there, urging us to travel there together as soon as I could get time off. In three weeks we would re-unite and fly to Raleigh for her nephew's wedding.

She left the same day I began my new job in Espanola. I was excited about my responsibilities, counseling individuals and families in Rio Arriba County, an area devastated by heroin.

Sleep one night in mid-June was interrupted with a disturbing, violent dream. I was at a convention of some sort. I and some companions began shooting people with rifles.

Later that week, on a Friday night, I tripped down the anxiety highway. I'd had the occasional catastrophic fantasy where my secure life suddenly turned inside out, but this one was ridiculous. This particular evening turned ugly over my New Mexico counseling license. I began to obsess about lacking a sufficient number of continuing education units to renew my license. The panic engulfed me to the point that I couldn't think rationally. I went so far as to plan how I could make a living when I lost my license and couldn't keep my job. I spent the weekend, sleepless, before calling the Board on Monday and learning I was ok, my license was secure. For nights afterwards, in spite of assurances from the Board, my anxiety didn't diminish, it merely changed the subject. I woke up well before dawn each morning worrying about clients I barely knew.

Those June nights were peculiar. And dreamless.

Part Six
1997-2004

44. Faxes—June, 1997

My new job as family therapist in Espanola, north of Santa Fe, began in early June. I joined a culturally diverse staff of highly dedicated people, mostly Hispanics from the surrounding valley. Ray, the executive director, was a former Episcopal priest, while Nurit, the clinical director, had immigrated from Argentina. Both worked out of the Santa Fe office where I had spent the past two years.

The third week of my job began on the second day of summer. Cresting the lip of Opera Hill outside Santa Fe was like stepping into another world. The salmon cliffs of the Espanola Valley shone in the sunlight. I took the turnoff through the old Spanish community of Santa Cruz, past Holy Cross church, down a narrow street crowded by stucco walls. I said to myself, How happy I am to be alive.

There was just the single car in the lot when I pulled in. The office manager, Linda Garcia, always arrived early and opened the office, a converted house near the high school. She walked up to me with a quizzical look. "Do you know anyone by the name of Marvin?"

"Not offhand. Why?"

"There is a phone message this morning—in broken English—and your name is mentioned."

We walked over to the phone machine and Linda hit the play button. It was a garbled voice on a bad connection but the voice of Melissa's cousin, Marvin, was unmistakable. Like Linda, I couldn't make out his message and was puzzled as to what he wanted and why he called me at work.

I went about opening the garage door of the house, part of the daily morning ritual. I heard a noise and looked up to see Nurit's car coming up the driveway. She and Ray stepped out of the car. Their faces looked tight and unhappy. They walked directly towards me and I froze.

Nurit carried two pieces of fax paper. She handed them to me. "I'm afraid we have some bad news. These came to the office over the weekend."

Both faxes were signed by Dr. Gutierrez. I understood everything as soon I read the first line.

> *June 21, 1997*
>
> *Dear Olin,*
>
> *I am sorry to notify that Melissa's health has started to deteriorate over the last days. My concern is that she is going to leave us on the following days and she asked me to inform you about her. Please feel free to use the fax number below or my e-mail if you want to send her a fax or note.*

June 22, 1997
Dear Olin
I am sorry to inform you that Melissa pass the way this afternoon. Her mother is expecting you to call home today or tomorrow, so the arrangements for the funeral can be made.

Tears exploded from my eyes. I collapsed onto a couch and heard repeated long wails, as if from a distance. I shook as I sobbed.

Someone phoned Claire. Ray took my car keys and drove me home. I lay my head back and stared vacantly at the landscape all the way home. My attention was on a far away place.

* * * * *

We had plans to attend the wedding in Raleigh later in the week. Claire changed the itinerary sometime that day. Someone, maybe me, called friends and family. In the evening we flew to Dallas or perhaps it was Miami. I looked and didn't see, like the time I went into shock after an auto accident. Everything was stripped down and almost peaceful, except for the hole in my gut which seemed to be mainlining pain into my chest.

Which shirts and slacks in my luggage? Chicken for dinner? Want to go to the room? Ready for bed? I did not care. Somehow we got to San Jose, rented a car and drove to a resort hotel in Puntarenas. Someone, Claire undoubtedly, had called Gloria to delay the funeral an extra day. I remember eating breakfast under a fake thatched roof and looking down to see the food blur beneath my tears.

I lay on the bed, paralyzed, and stared at the hotel room windows. Condensation blocked the view. Little rivulets ran down the windows night and day.

That evening we walked into the church. I'd been there before, the time Melissa had moved away so Gloria would be between us. Someone told us that the service would last through the night. People were scattered throughout the rows of benches and chairs. Everyone seemed to be whispering. A guitarist and an electric pianist played music I didn't recognize. A man spoke, but I couldn't focus on his words. I looked around but didn't see anyone I knew. Later Gloria told us that the parents of Randall Herrera were there. He was the boy who had died after his lungs rejected.

The scene was a dream in a fog. A huge casket sat at the front where the pews ended. Claire and I walked forward to sit in the front row. A few people stood in line waiting to look down into the casket through a clouded Plexiglas cover. From time to time, people walked up after looking at Melissa and shook my hand. They said they were sorry. They kept their heads down while they spoke.

When I finally walked to the casket I glanced in then quickly looked away. Melissa's dress was frilly and colorless. Her face was bloated with chemicals. She looked strange, ugly. I feared the memory would haunt me. It wasn't the

Melissa I wanted to remember.

The next morning, I awoke and stared at the running windows. I tried to think of something to say at the cemetery. We drove to the church with a translator from the hotel. We sat in one of the back rows near Gloria and Merilyn and the rest of the family. We stood for songs and sat for eulogies. The service ended and I found Gloria. We hugged like ghosts.

Some men picked up the casket and I joined a listless herd in blinding sunlight. We crossed the highway and trailed through neighborhoods. The heat from the pavement burned through my shoes. A large cemetery with decrepit tombstones and grave markers awaited us. Tall trees drooped and scattered shadows over the grounds. Utter stillness made the scene feel like more dreamscape.

At the opening in the ground, the men had difficulty getting the casket into position. I stepped into the hole and helped them push it into place. The minister spoke and people threw flowers onto the casket. I hesitated until the end, then threw mine in.

People of every age stood among the tombstones and burial plots, wherever there was room. I fought to keep my balance; my limbs were numb like they'd been shot up with novacaine. I thanked everyone for loving Melissa and coming to the funeral. I forgot the words before the translator finished.

Everyone wandered off in small groups, except for Merilyn. Some family members returned for her an hour later and pulled her away from the graveside.

Clare and I drove back to Gloria and Ramon's house. Gloria moved and spoke as if drained of all life. She escorted us into Melissa's bedroom. Her bed was now just a frame and a naked mattress. The walls and closets were gray and barren. A room never looked more empty.

Gloria gave me the silk sash that Melissa wore over her high school graduation robe. It was navy blue and gilded in gold fringe and letters which read simply, "Esparza, Graduation, 1995." I thanked her, too enfeebled to ask if there was any special meaning to her gift.

We sat at a table and drank something cold. Someone handed me a clipping from a newspaper announcing Melissa's passing. I looked at it later in the hotel room. The last line surprised me, but as with everything, my reaction was swallowed up in grief.

WENDY MELISSA REYES REYES

Passed away in her 18th year. Aunts and uncles, cousins and other relatives express their sorrow. The funeral will take place today at 10 a.m. Her body will be buried in the Cemetery of Esparza.

Her mother: Gloria Maria Reyes Reyes

Her adopted father: Ramon Campos Campos

45. Night—1997–2000

We took a one-stop out of San Jose to Raleigh. Touching down at Miami International my imagination envisions horror. The plane hits the tarmac and one wheel snaps off, causing the fuselage to cartwheel. The catastrophe unfolds in my mind's eye in slow motion, allowing me to linger over the carnage and death.

Claire and I had spoken little on the flight out of San Jose. While we waited for our connecting flight, she called friends on her cell phone. I sat unmoving, a lost spirit. A stream of travelers tugged at luggage and children. They went about their business ignorant of my grief. I felt distantly resentful.

In Raleigh I spent hours lying in bed at our B&B while my wife and her family socialized. The heavy drapes were pulled tightly. The room was dark, but not as dark my thoughts. I had spent so much time focusing on our new relationship and Melissa's education and her upcoming trip to the States, her passing stunned me as if I'd forgotten it could ever happen. I felt a great shame that I'd been caught off guard.

Claire was with her family one afternoon when I lurched around Raleigh. It was all I could do to decide where to walk, then find my way back. There was a dinner and a wedding and a reception. I watched myself go through the motions, pretending to be there when I wasn't. I didn't remember any of it a week later.

A letter from Gloria awaited us when we returned home. Written two weeks before Melissa died, the letter, after a casual intro, said that Melissa had been released from the hospital with a "heart problem." Gloria added, "the doctor told her she had to be on oxygen night and day. Last week he told me he was going to write you… I was very sad to see her this way. She is studying and wants very much to go there (to the US)… At times I feel sad and tired."

I lay on our love seat for hours at a time, like a ball of flab. I felt flimsy and unprotected from anything unexpected which might come and hurt me.

One day Claire and I took a slow walk through the old South Capitol neighborhood of Santa Fe. It was a still, sunlit afternoon. I said, "This has just the right amount of stress."

Claire looked puzzled. "This has no stress." I nodded.

I returned to my job ten days after the funeral. Jim, my boss, came up to me. "You look like shit. What are you doing here?" I didn't honestly know. I went home.

There was a section of highway near our house where the road was cut out of rock face. Driving past, I wondered what it would be like to crash my car into the cliff wall. This thought became a daily habit.

I wished I could have traded my life for Melissa's. I had experienced so many things: love, travel, sex, independence—which she never had. It's staggering to know that you would give your life in an instant for your dead child, and immensely sad to know you can't.

The impulse wasn't so noble. Deep inside, my life felt worthless and utterly disposable. These were the facts: a beautiful, innocent teenager, having been sick for most of her life, came to a three-week period when the disease suddenly intensified and sucked the life out of her. I'd spent maybe one night in a hospital in my entire life. I'd never lost a friend or close family member. The unfairness of it all sickened me. It told me that life is random and extraordinarily ruthless. Some part of me soured on life and wanted to quit it in disgust.

Jeff Jacobson was one of my few friends who'd experienced an unexpected major loss. His dear friend, Ethan, had died accidentally at a young age. Jeff kept in close touch with me in those early months. I told him that the life had been speared out of me and the world was a place I didn't care for. Being a professional photographer, Jeff often had a different lens on life, and one rarely lacking in compassion. He was silent for a moment then acknowledged my loss of Melissa and my being crushed by it. "On top of that, you and Melissa were a part of something larger. And it was something many people would have turned away from...and you dove right in."

I broke into tears. When I could talk, all I could say was, "I don't want to dive in anymore."

I received cards and letters of condolence. Melissa's death elicited poetry from some, fluff from others.

"God calls those He loves the most to be with Him."

"Be happy. Melissa would want you to be happy."

"Life can only be measured by quality not time."

Such trite remarks, however kindly motivated, only fed my rage, and the rage bled into despair.

One day Frances, a friend from graduate school, phoned. Frances had lost her husband, John, when she was a young mother. Alone she'd raised her daughter, Heidi, and two sons. She'd earned her guts, was never afraid of hearing the details of my grief. She asked how I was.

"Well, I've gone through an entire day without crying. So I guess I'm doing better, at least today."

"I'm so glad to hear that. I phoned Heidi today and we were talking about you and how difficult it must be to lose your beloved Melissa. Olin, we both broke into tears right there on the phone." I choked when Frances said that.

I re-entered the world of the living through work, but not because I cared. I merely came to the realization that I could probably get through a day without my emotional scabs being ripped off. Numbness had become trustworthy armor, along with selective dishonesty. When people asked how I was doing, I said ok. I didn't see the gain in being brutally honest about my despair and wish to die.

After a couple of weeks, the acute pain seemed to subside and shifted into lethargy. More than once I walked into my office, said "I can't do this," and drove home. At those times, I knew if the entire world imploded I'd probably just stare at it. However sad or sick I felt, nothing could make me weep or vomit. Sleep was the most welcome activity of the day.

I visited a hospice counselor. Claire joined me two or three times before business took her out of town. The counseling sessions were unpleasant. Regurgitating painful stories seemed meaningless. My thought of creating some sort of memorial to speed my healing led nowhere. My counselor seemed excessively interested in talking about Claire after she left. I couldn't confront him, I couldn't confront anything. I stopped making appointments.

I put in long hours of work. I forgot each day once it was over. In the words of my mentor, Carl Whittaker, life went on as living died.

A month after Melissa's passing, nothing much had changed. Some anger and irritability had come to the surface, but little else. Defeat hung over me and didn't lessen. The world seemed overwhelming and crazy. There didn't seem to be much to live for other than people's kindness.

My unhappiness was compounded when on the same day two new clients asked if I had children. Each time the question rattled me, and each time I wanted to run away. I couldn't be real and say, "I had a child, but she passed away." I couldn't say yes and have to face the next question: "How old is she?" So, I lied and said no. I ended up feeling like I'd betrayed Melissa twice. After the second exchange, I packed up and left the office. I couldn't lie again but I didn't know how to be honest and talk about Melissa's death.

On another day, soon afterwards, I struggled just to get to work by 9:15. Opening my office, I thought, "I shouldn't be here." But I didn't know where I should be. In a counselor's office? In church? With Melissa's family? Alone? Claire was having work anxiety and was emotionally frazzled. She had been there for me all along but for now, I was on my own. She was, too.

I sleepwalked through the days, looking at the world dully, with burning eyes. After making love, staring at yet another dark ceiling, I could feel my face frozen and hear deadness in my voice.

The Crime Victims Reparations Commission referred two young siblings to me for counseling. They had been sexually abused by their estranged father. I decided to meet with them together at first. We spent those meetings playing games and making light conversation. I felt their trust building and it gave me a good feeling to be in their circle of spontaneity and delight. I looked forward to our times together. One morning the DA's office called to say that the children's mother had phoned and demanded that the counseling sessions end. She gave no explanation and, in spite of the case worker's plea, refused to re-consider her decision. The news tore at my heart. I sent the children a goodbye card, even though I could not be sure they would ever see it. The loss of contact with those children ripped off my scab. I knew I couldn't endure those kinds of feelings ever again. My days of counseling children were numbered.

September 15, 1997

Dear Melissa,

Every day something reminds me of you. I still become very sad that there is so much we never did together. I become sad over the daily suffering of your life and the fact that your light was extinguished so early. I wish I knew why you had to suffer like you did. It is so very unfair. You did not deserve all the illness and difficulty you endured.

We missed out on so much. I played with friends' children more than you and I ever played in 7 years. But we weren't about play were we? No we were about something weightier, dad and daughter learning to be together, working through pain and anger and staying connected.

And we did. Thank God you never, never turned your back on me for good.

I always loved you. I love you still. That is something all those other kids never had: all of my heart.

That was me three months later, still professing my love, still thanking Melissa for hanging in with me and still bitter about the injustice of her living in a chronically fucked-up body. Her illness and short life left me distraught and confused, without answers to explain or justify hers or any child's incurable physical and emotional suffering.

I looked back to 1990 and all that had occurred. Never had I been more alive. In meeting my fate, as Jeff described it, I had lived life on another plane. The force of life which sustained me, even in times of great pain, disappeared with Melissa's death.

Life had played its cruel joke, asserted its true nature. Work, marriage and most of all, love, seemed arbitrary and pointless. Nothing brought light to the darkness in and around me. My eyelids and facial muscles felt as if they had weights attached.

Gloria and I exchanged letters, each of us groping with emotional devastation. In the third letter, Gloria described her emptiness and physical ailments. She asked if she could correspond with me about Melissa. I answered back affirmatively, but Gloria never wrote again.

I received outpourings from Merilyn, the first one written over the course of several days in July. She was obviously in great pain, having been unaware of Melissa's dire condition in the days before she passed. Merilyn was hanging onto her faith in God, but she sounded no better nine months after the funeral than I was. We invited her to come be with us at my expense. She agreed, but said she didn't want us to think of her as a replacement for Melissa. I reassured her that we didn't feel that way. Later on, I wasn't so sure. Our correspondence petered out after April, 1998. My last letter had these words:

> *Even now, ten months later I cannot completely believe she is gone. When she was alive, I talked to my family and friends about her all the time. Now there is nothing to say. I cannot talk about her life, her letters, her school, her travel plans...nothing. Each day her life is one more day in the past. They say, "Do not look back." But looking back is all I have of her–and I never want that to vanish. You know, my memories are all I have.*

I rented "My Life," thinking that the movie which meant something to Melissa might lead me to feel better. Twenty minutes into the movie a mountain of grief mushroomed inside me, like nausea, and I punched the off button.

What had I said about accepting everything about Melissa, including her diseased condition? It was a romantic, self-centered, stupid idea. Being born with cystic fibrosis in Costa Rica was a virtual death sentence.

A year after Melissa's death, I joined Claire for a long holiday weekend at a lakeside resort outside Toronto, where she was working on a TV movie. We had an argument, possibly over my disinterest in having fun, enjoying conversation or making love. She yelled at me to get over it. I argued feebly that it wasn't as simple as that, but, honestly, it is impossible to advocate for the grief process when you are struggling to stand upright. She won the argument or at least made her point. One year is a long time to be deep in grief, although "get over it" is advice of extreme idiocy to a person drowning in sorrow.

I tried hard to make an attitude adjustment but grief doesn't go away easily.

Another year and half passed before Frances' husband, Lee, and I signed up for a Sierra Club hike in southern Colorado. Looking at the schedule and photos of the year's trips in the Sierra Club catalog, something stirred within me. Sleeping beneath the stars, surrounded by expanses of natural beauty seemed the perfect remedy. I began to work myself into shape by hiking near my house with a backpack filled with books. Claire was not thrilled about my being out of phone contact in the Rockies for a week, hours from emergency medical care. Her concern felt good.

The trip in the late summer of 2000 was a tremendous physical hardship. We hiked and camped in the rain for several days. My training hikes had not prepared me for the 70 pounds of gear I carried on my back. The group returned to the trail head after six days, weary, but rejuvenated. Then we hit a steep incline of about a quarter of a mile leading to the parking area. Even in the pleasant light of an August morning no one was happy to discover this final challenge.

Melissa came to mind as I panted and slowed down alongside my companions. I considered how she never could take breathing for granted and didn't have the luxury of merely slowing down in order to catch her breath and feel better. So I decided not to, either. I committed to myself and perhaps to her that I would reach the parking lot without stopping.

I passed several companions and moved steadily up the trail as my lungs began to feel white hot. I circled two others and picked up speed at a steady marching pace. Leaning forward, I pushed my pack upwards to distribute its weight on my back and counter the incline. The ground beneath me filled my vision. I wondered how many steps remained to the parking lot and began to groan aloud with each exhale. I opened my throat wide to take in air; phlegm and spit poured from my mouth onto my chin and shirt. My lungs cried until tears streamed down my face. I stepped up onto the pavement of the parking lot and bent over, heaving, for several minutes. My throat made a gagging sound as air rushed to fill my chest. Melissa was right there.

Claire was a continent away from Colorado on a movie set. When I called her from the motel in Alamosa, she was too busy to talk. She didn't call me back that night as she had promised. The next time we spoke she was at her mother's house in Tennessee. She said she had been unhappy for a long time and wanted a divorce.

I pulled the drapes tight once again.

46. Cocooned—2001-2002

I guess I took the "death til we part" business more seriously than Claire did. She wouldn't even discuss it. We had four, maybe five conversations, mostly about dividing our stuff, before I saw her one final time. We agreed to meet at a café in south Santa Fe so she could unload a few things I'd left at the house when I moved out. I asked her to bring our "love bowl," for a ritual kiss off. A numbing fog had engulfed me since Claire's phone call but clarity arrived like the cavalry for this one event. After a worthless cup of coffee we took our positions on a sidewalk near our cars.

The bowl rested beneath us, a pricey work of pottery on life support.

"Ready?"

"You do it."

"Uh-uh, that's not what we agreed to. On three," I said, and counted. Together we stomped, me more than once, until the bowl was tiny shards.

*****

I dived headfirst into a new job as Director of Clinical Affairs for a large medical and behavioral health organization headquartered in Santa Fe. As if the work would be some sort of antidote to my grief. This idea, totally plausible at the time, shows how misguided a typically sound intelligence can become. Distraction is not grieving.

I functioned passably and passively. I bought a house and managed my work duties. A trip with Frances and Lee to their mountain cabin near Truckee, California, brought me the healing of the Sierra and the warmth of caring friends.

We hiked and kayaked and spent every chilly, radiant sunset next to a crackling fire. But I felt the long weekend's joy as if it was a blanket stuffed in a box of blankets. Claire's departure had set me back to square one, if I had ever truly moved beyond it.

I unpacked my interest in mountain hiking. The torture of straining upwards to reach spectacular views of the landscape was somehow therapeutic. In the summer of 2001, on a cloudless morning, I scaled Mt. Princeton, one of the 20 highest peaks in Colorado.

At the four-hour mark my map indicated that I was above 13,000 feet. Looking up I guessed that I had only to circle the knob in front of me, cross a field of talus and a short saddle before toughing out a final steep climb of several hundred feet. My deficiency in map reading soon manifested itself. A young couple hastening down the trail delivered the news. I was two hours from the summit, still hidden from view. They warned me about the shaky scramble to the saddle and showed me a gash on the woman's shin. I faked a cheery thank-you.

The trail disappeared into a broad swath of rocks and boulders which forced me to climb on hands and feet for several hundred yards. Then came the talus which, with its sliding footholds, was like climbing straight up a giant truck bed of gravel.

I began to pant, stopping every few feet to milk the thin air. I exhaled forcefully to rid my lungs of as much carbon dioxide as possible. Ninety minutes later I overtook a church group with Iowa t-shirts, all of whom heaved like me. I passed them and began to count steps. One to twenty, then stop and breathe. I pictured Melissa, straining and coughing mucous. My fight for oxygen at 14,000 feet resembled the struggle she often endured at sea level.

I reached a high saddle with a view of endless mountain ranges. The sky had turned hard blue and the flap of the wind was the only sound. Just ahead, four teen-agers doubled over in misery. I offered water to a girl who couldn't move. Her face was pewter.

I was ten, maybe fifteen minutes from the summit. In between stood a man bent over a blonde-haired girl leaning on a boulder. He yelled at her in apparent fury but drawing near, I sensed it was a father exhorting his daughter. "You can do it! Hang in there!" She shook her head, weary and beaten down. Tears blurred my vision. The man was shouting the wish I held for Melissa all those years.

At the highest point of the mountain I stopped and looked back. The girl and her father slowly climbed towards my perch. I thought of Melissa's harsh walk, the one I tried to take with her. I turned and gazed at rows of peaks, baked brown. There were no more walks for us.

*****

Experiences like the hike on Mt. Princeton and the Sierra Club trip were powerful, but they didn't assuage my grief or my nights of anguish. Nothing helped me to sleep. Exercise. Diet. Nothing. It had been five years since Melissa passed away. Happiness, hope, anticipation and their relatives were behind me. I tried a prescription sleeping pill for thirty days but stopped for fear of developing a habit. Alcohol, after a childhood with alcoholic parents, was never an option.

I hatched an idea for a memorial to Melissa. I would present a Central American kid with a school scholarship, perhaps a child in Esparza. I talked to friends and even emailed the idea to Melissa's uncle, Marvin. I visited a local foundation to learn if I could set up the scholarship as a tax write-off. I was told they would need a healthy sum of money to draw down, an amount I couldn't afford. The idea went on hold.

Certain dates and anniversaries knocked me flat regardless of how well I prepared for them. November had two of those dates back to back: Melissa's birthday and the day we met. In June, it was Father's Day, followed by June 22, the day she passed away. At those times, whether the pain hit early or late, whether it stayed three days or two weeks, it crushed me like a medieval torture device, a paralyzing cocoon of despair.

My grief, I believed, was boring, a burden to others and a family gathering served as proof. My father and his wife Shirley brought their relatives together in Sherman, Texas, to celebrate their wedding anniversary. It took place two months after my divorce was finalized. Not a soul from my immediate family asked how I was holding up nor did I bring up the subject. How true we were to our hardtack, east Tennessee heritage.

Sometimes I gazed at people quietly going about their jobs: office mates, bus boys and girls, gas station clerks, hotel maids. I wondered if their insides, oblivious to others, were twisted in loss and sadness.

Certain books, music and movies let me dip into my loneliness. "Crouching Tiger, Hidden Dragon" was one of those. Each of the major characters embodied a combination of longing and lost love. Zhang Ziyi's character, in her pride and stubbornness, resembled Melissa and represented the ferocious young woman my daughter would have become. She even looked at the master, Chow Yun Fat, with the same spite Melissa had shown me in the hospital. One's death led to the other's. All of it made my insides spill over in the darkness of the theater. I returned to watch the movie, start to finish, five times.

Friends did what they could. Sharon sent a Father's Day card each year, a practice continuing to this day. Frances framed an original watercolor entitled "Melissa is the New Star in Heaven." It was a comfort to look at the starry blue universe above my desk and feel Frances' belief in Melissa's eternity.

Everyone grieves in their own way, in their own time. Or not. There was such a long time when my pain was never-ending, you might say it was unfortunate that it took several years for my real grieving to get jump started But the way events unfolded leaves me little cause to second-guess what I did or did not do. The entire tapestry has to be considered. And life was to lead me to unimaginable places.

47. Britt—May, 2003

Several years of not seeing my two oldest friends, Jeff and Britt, surely made my road longer and more difficult. Then Britt came to visit in May, 2003.

I first met Britt Dean in Miss MacDonald's 6th grade elementary class at R. L. Hope Elementary School after my family moved to Atlanta, Georgia. We both remember reading MAD Magazine in my back yard as the initiation of our friendship. In fact, it was the entire span from grades 6-12 which set us in motion for fifty years.

Throughout our adult lives, Britt lived in the greater Atlanta area while I resided in Northern California and Santa Fe. As a result, seminal events in our lives, like his second marriage, to Sally, took place with each of us far away from the other. I suppose it was shared values, a mutual willingness to be engaged by music and creativity, and a perfectly matched offbeat sense of humor which provided the bonding material. We have always loved to make the other laugh, and I would take the sum of those laughs—totaling hours or likely, days of our lives—over most life experiences.

We never knew each other's parents or siblings very well. We have lived in some sort of timeless, encapsulated world in which Britt seems virtually unchanging: gregarious, creative, forgetful, reflective and wickedly funny.

Since he had planned to fly out for a short visit in September of 1990, I decided to hold off and break the news of my parenthood until he arrived. We met at the Downtown Berkeley BART station. He emerged from the train, skinny as ever, with his curly hair tinted some crazy orange. We lugged his bags to my car while falling into our comfortable patterns of laughing and clowning then grabbed a fast dinner. No time to tell my story in the rush to make a Sonny Rollins/Branford Marsalis concert on the UC Berkeley campus. We both tired during the concert and left early for the long drive to Petaluma. Still not a good time.

The next morning we agreed to take advantage of the gentle morning and breakfast in a downtown diner. As we ambled through a city park halfway to town, I broke the news. Britt stopped and staggered to a nearby bench. He exhaled an elongated "Ah-h-h-h-h-Yi!" like some indigenous cry as he crossed one leg over the other. I could see his wet eyes blazing towards some distant horizon as he drank in the entire event and its meaning for me.

Then he erupted in a resounding, "YES!" His head nodded up and down to some ethereal music. "Yes!...Yes!!" He nearly shouted as I looked on in delight. Then he rose and hugged me until it hurt.

By his mid-fifties, Britt had suffered hard losses in marriage and business, but I knew he was uncomfortable talking to me about Melissa's death. Nor did he much care for my sad condition, 6 years later. We took a drive north of Santa Fe to Georgia O'Keefe country, the area around Ghost Ranch and the Perdenal. We drove a stretch of road along Abiquiu Lake where the canyon rock reflected the sun into a million jewels of red, black and brown. Emblazoned in my memory is one thing Britt said on that drive.

"Sally asked me what it would be like to lose you, Olin." He paused. "I couldn't talk about it." We arrived at the animal shelter as a sudden cloudburst pounded the car with such ferocity that we had no choice but to sit without speaking.

The next day, we hiked up Aspen Vista trail in the Santa Fe National

Forest. The area was experiencing some late spring gloom. Low clouds darkened the landscape. The trail was empty of other hikers. Thirty minutes up the mountain, Britt began to relate a story of a friend back home who had recently died of reccurring breast cancer. She was in her 50s and part of a close association of friends and colleagues Sally and Britt ran with.

In spite of the exertion required to move up the trail, my attention sharpened upon hearing Britt's story. Over our three days together there had been no mention of Melissa's death nor of my continued slippage into despair. It made me edgy that he had not brought it up. Perhaps his story was the opening to talk about my grief. Britt went on to describe how people had visited their friend in her final days and on the day she died, gathered on her front porch for a memorial service. He said it was a beautiful event.

I bit off my words. "I can tell you, they're not all like that."

Britt grunted. "Losing a child is the hardest thing anyone can go through." His head turned towards a grove of aspen.

The aphorism, coming from my friend's mouth, chilled me. I glared at him, now several yards ahead of me. I had presented an opening, a cue for Britt to give empathy, inquire about my pain, be my mommy for a moment and…nothing. A sow's ear.

We made it to a rocky outcrop two hours up the trail. The Espanola valley was shrouded in clouds and mist. I was too cowardly to mention the slight I'd felt. I retreated into my grief hole. Britt left town the following day. Melissa's name never came up.

*****

I, too, left town, for Cedar Mesa in southeastern Utah. A previous weekend exposed to the extraordinary beauty of the area had whetted my appetite for an extended visit. I had never backpacked solo, carrying water, stove and gas canisters, but a stint in the wilds would surely soothe my spirit still rattling from Britt's visit.

I drove to Bluff, Utah, for a night at the Recapture Lodge. In the parking lot I assembled my new camp stove and practiced starting a fire. I inventoried food and studied a map, dreaming about ancient petroglyphs in the canyon. The hike would last six nights, just like my Outward Bound trip thirty years earlier. No big deal.

My adventure began with a quick stop. I picked up my permit and quizzed the ranger about the weather and parking options at the trail head. His instructions were clear, but thirty minutes down a dirt road brought me to an unanticipated fork. The clearing to the right looked promising but for a series of low flat rocks. Easily passable for a high-carriage SUV but not my rented sedan. I carefully negotiated the rocks and came to several half-buried boulders. Further ahead, the road appeared to worsen, even disappear. I turned the car around to the road not taken. It too dead-ended so I shifted into reverse and drove backwards to the fork, a quarter mile away.

The shade of a tree looked like an excellent place to study the map. Perhaps I'd missed a turn back up the road. If so, it wasn't on the map. The low boulders on the first fork were a risk. Returning to the ranger station might be a bigger humiliation than I was in the mood for. I looked around me blankly, like a cow chewing on my options, then placed the map on the seat and drove out.

I came to the highway and pulled the hand brake. Nearby Blanding was an option, as was Moab. A return to the trailhead tomorrow for a day-hike was a possibility, maybe even a re-start up the canyon. Or I could drive home, go back to work and make up an excuse for my early return. I hurt myself. I got sick. My pack broke. My car broke.

I sighed. I was hundreds of miles from a friend to walk me through this. I popped the brake and turned west away from civilization in the direction of Bridges National Monument. There, from a pay phone at the main office I called Frances in Sonoma and unloaded everything. My inability to make a decision and enjoy the wilderness. My total dissatisfaction with my job and my social life. My inability to feel good. The absence of hope. Frances made grunts of understanding during my frantic rant and, when it ran down, pointed out that my instability could only be treated with a vacation of the low-stress variety. She invited me to join her and Lee at their summer cabin in the Sierra in a few weeks.

Utah was sunny and a dark womb was unavailable. I returned to the Recapture Lodge and grabbed the key from the desk clerk. After a nap and dinner, the world looked different. A return to the park for a day, maybe an overnight, seemed like a fine idea. Forty-eight hours under an open sky would be easy. But over breakfast the following morning, my anxiety sheared and I was home in my own bed by nightfall.

Ignoring my lonely stomach the next morning I did laundry and emptied the car, storing the stove and gas canisters in the garage. I looked over the list of therapists covered by my insurance plan. Britt and I exchanged innocuous emails, reminding me of our friendship and the opportunity to connect with him I'd missed three weeks earlier.

It took a few days for my vacation stress to subside. One night, buried in Dennis Lehane's "Shutter Island," I came across a disturbing line, re-read it, then closed the book and went to my laptop. I pounded out the truth I'd kept from Britt on the mountain. I hit the save button and flopped on the couch in front of the TV. Bill Moyers was talking to Biblical scholar Elaine Pagels about the deaths of her child and husband, and her faith. She quoted from the Gnostic Gospel of Thomas, something I'd heard before. "If you bring forth what is within you, what you bring forth will save you." The next line was something like, if you don't bring forth what is within, it will destroy you.

I woke up wide-eyed in the middle of the night and stumbled to my desk. I finished the email and sent it off.

The time of denying the deep wound had ended.

48. The E-mail—May 17, 2003

Hey Britt,

Tonight you got chosen. I remember you said losing a child is the worst...But I suppose until you have the excruciating inner pain that brings you to your knees and, in one form or another, hangs around for years, you have no idea. If you can't hear me on this, simply push the delete button or save. There are the two letters from Melissa's doc which I hang on to, but can't read. There are the 8 letters from Melissa which I can't read. These are your most valuable possession, except for the photos, but you can't bear to read them. I have to write this and you got chosen. I told Helen, who lost one kid to CF, some of this and she understood. But there was a point she said, "You can't let yourself think that." But I do.

Did you ever read "Mystic River" and "Shutter Island"? Both books have this real beautiful gripping sadness. In "Shutter Island," I just read these words: "And if I knew for certain that all it would take to hold her again would be to die, then I couldn't raise the gun to my head fast enough."

That gives you some idea. Helen has two other girls, she has a grandchild. God help the person who loses all. It twists everything to WISH you had the choice and to know you would hand over all you have in an eye-blink. It makes you angry that you were not given the option.

My stomach wrenches to think about it. But something weird happens when you hear yourself say that you wish it could have been you. That you would trade all you have, your life, if it would somehow mean that she could have had a life: a boyfriend, a husband. Children. How easily I would give it all up even just to see her a little longer, just to spend another hour with her! If you call that unresolved grief, then I don't care about resolution. When someone in my profession begins to prattle on about resolving grief, I feel disgust.

I haven't come close to solving the problem which hammered me when a beautiful child-my child-leads a sick life, struggling to just take thousands of fucking breaths most days and finally wearing out when all around her are healthy and mobile and can laugh without coughing. I can't even now accept the whole thing and the whole thing is this life. I can't see a God in this. If this world is in the dominion of the devil then that's the only theology which makes any sense. At its heart it's deeply, deeply reprehensible and ugly. It's what obscene means, forget all the other definitions.

Your beliefs don't really help out on any of this, but you struggle like a fish on a beach to make sense of what doesn't. I didn't get it when Isabel Allende said to me, after her Paula died, "I'm just so confused." But that was before Melissa died.

I wrote the above around 10:00 and it is now almost 2 am and I can't sleep. There is the darkness underlying your daily reality and probably no one knows that this is your most basic truth and if they have heard about Melissa they definitely don't want to know any more about the whole thing. And you feel cut off and sort of leper-ish around this, and sometimes just feel sick, like it is this thing which may come forth at any moment and pull you in. You say, "I have to go home now, it's the anniversary of my daughter's death and I can't be here," and they look at you like you said I want to fuck your dog. Or they say stupid things like, "How did she die…suicide?" That, from a doctor who managed to momentarily forget that children die prematurely from chronic and terminal illnesses.

Life, a very different life, goes on. Time goes on and it's no solace at all. You look up and it is 6 years since she died and you're unhappy the further away her life becomes, because you sense the memories shrinking and fading. And the reality of her skin and her deep eyes and her laugh go further away. And you want that process to stop. You don't want her life to be 10 then 11 then 12 then 20 years away.

Sometimes when I get a notion that she is there looking at me, even if I can't all the way believe it, I can believe it just enough that I fantasize it would be better there in her company than it is here. Maybe because we never had enough time. My goal was always to have her know that her dad loved her. Her next to the last letter told me that she got it. Then before we could settle in and enjoy the relationship she was gone. Six and a half years, 7 (mostly tortured) visits. We never had enough time together.

If some day you hear that I've died unexpectedly, willfully, it will be because I believed in a reunion just enough, at a time when life was being real hard, to take the gamble. I don't see signs that the suffering has made me stronger, I think it's made me weaker, like a boxer who's been knocked around and just can't take a punch anymore.

Probably wasn't that resilient to begin with……

Olin

49. Cedar—June, 2003

Even before Britt responded to me, I returned and stared at my words on the computer screen.

I couldn't see what his saying, "it's the hardest thing" had to do with anything. So he failed to bring up the subject of my loss. I'm raging at my oldest friend because he didn't read my mind?

Then there was my desperate warning that, in a moment of weakness, I could destroy myself. Seeing the words on my computer screen gave them a different impact than spitting them out. Hope had died when Melissa passed away. I got the message. Life could not go on this way.

Maybe I had more anger than I knew. Maybe it was anger not just about Melissa, but over the fact that I'd existed for six years in darkness, unconvinced that I would ever live again, furiously wanting the pain to stop but not knowing how to make that happen.

In the course of two long treks in the mountains around Santa Fe, my mind cleared and the self-recrimination over the Utah debacle eased. I made a few decisions and followed through. First I dumped my SUV, Claire's former vehicle and a remnant from the marriage. Habitat for Humanity accepted it as a charitable donation. It would be a dependable ride for someone, well maintained with good tires and, for good luck, a gold wedding ring wedged underneath a seat frame where it could never be found. A pillow Claire and I had shared went into the garbage can. My load lightened briefly.

The window of days preceding Father's Day and the sixth anniversary of Melissa's death approached, bringing sleepless nights meditating on her death and mine. I re-discovered the desolation of pre-dawn hours. Memorial Day weekend found me in the emergency room for strange chest pains. No matter what I did I hurt.

I'd attended a professional luncheon in Albuquerque several years prior. The PowerPoint futzed out, leaving the speaker, a therapist, to give one of the smartest off-the cuff presentations I'd ever heard. It was filled with common-sense, humor and humanity. I saved her name, Cedar Koons, just in case. I phoned her. She was leaving town and kindly asked if I could wait a month for an appointment. I said yes.

How to summarize the work and impact of our therapeutic relationship? I will say this: there were a few things I needed to do in order to re-embrace the world.

Cedar spurred me and watched as I started, faltered, resumed, hesitated, and pushed on down the road. Early on we addressed my isolation. Then my confused conclusion that life had ended. Later my lack of creative expression. And finally, or I should say throughout, there was my uncompleted bereavement.

A major roadblock was feelings. I'd long had a collegial relationship with many types of feelings. But my grief terrified me, threatened my sense of control, and I could only feel it to a highly constrained point, whether in or outside of a movie theater.

Anger got me into therapy; grieving got me back into life. Cedar never preached. Ok, let's just say she kept it to a minimum. There was no point to her dancing around the obvious. When I told her I couldn't bear to re-read the faxes from Melissa's doctor about Melissa's final hours, I may as well have raised a giant balloon and pointed: Either I do this, or I continue not living.

Cedar never nagged me about the faxes, just quietly asked about them from time to time. She recommended I buy a book of poetry by a long-ago Sufi master named Hafiz. His poems teased and prodded and sang about the gift of life, as if it were a party happening right in front of me, in my house and I was oblivious.

50. Losing—October, 2003

I attended several meetings of "Compassionate Friends," a support group for parents who have lost children. The people sitting around the table seemed nearly inconsolable. Excruciating stories about beloved children, overdosed or run down by drunk drivers, had little I could identify with. But every parent who nursed a child through a long goodbye made me think of Gloria. My heart went out to her.

One night, Melissa appeared in a dream.

> *She shows up from out of nowhere, happy and energetic and gives me a bunch of little kisses on the lips. The scene changes and I'm on my back bouncing her on my chest like a baby. In the next scene we're playing gleefully.*

For the first time in six years, I felt grateful to be alive and for the wonder of having Melissa.

I saw an ad in a weekly Santa Fe paper and phoned the instructor. She said all the right things and signed me up for the personal monologue class. In person, she invited each class member to select "something personal and close to the heart" to be the topic of a seven-minute monologue we would write and read to a live audience. There was only one story to tell.

I faced the room packed with mostly strangers. When I came to the part which covered the last six years, cotton mouth set in. I pursed my cheeks and tried to make enough spit to carry me through.

The grief slammed me down hard. For weeks I did little but lie on the couch or walk slowly to the corner and back. When I began driving again, I would obsess about jerking the car off the road or into oncoming traffic. Three and a half years later, a therapist would tell me, "You climbed into the grave with your daughter." It was one of those nothing statements I seemed to hear frequently. Statements like, "That is just the hardest thing a person can go through." Having no idea. One annoying woman lowered her voice knowingly to say, "You know, God calls those he loves the most to be with Him." I wrote an old friend to ask for guidance. She, too, had lost a daughter, age 12, to CF. I knew I was in trouble when I read her response. "Olin, I don't have an answer for you."

My wife's version of advice came after a year, when she clenched her teeth and told me I needed to "get over it." Two years later she phoned from the East Coast to say that the marriage was finished. Then a friend in Atlanta was diagnosed with prostate cancer and another friend in Sonoma got a nasty mass in her lungs and went off to an attorney to set her affairs in order.

I was beaten to my knees. The thing was, I couldn't tell if I had ever gotten up off them. I literally did not know how bad I was doing, if I was coping well, if I was only reacting the way anyone would, if I was healing at my own pace — or what.

I spent about a year-working full-time, but otherwise holed up, listening to "high-lonesome" bluegrass music, taking long hikes in the Sangres and Rockies, and reading novels about life in neighborhoods and small towns. Next came a year of deliberate 50+ hour work weeks, in a corporate setting where "success" is a good word, and "defeat" not good. I kept my defeats to myself and hoped that time would work its magic. But time alone could not heal my heart because I had cleared out a barren space around it, to keep it safe and impregnable.

I have taken a long road to acknowledge something that, as a man, I don't do easily or well. I've grown up in a sub-culture where winning is not just everything, it's the only thing. I like winning. I like my team to win. At my age, winning now means things like getting good deals! If I can get 30% off a nice shirt or a pair of slacks, I almost feel as if I've won Wimbledon.

And losing — losing at cards, losing hair, losing an erection, losing a friend, a marriage, a daughter — these are practically shameful. As if they say something about who I am as a man. Otherwise, why couldn't all us guys talk about stuff like this??

But the biggest loss was taking that cleared out space around my heart

and building a castle around it, the kind with a moat and drawbridge.
Rilke, in his poem, "The Man Watching" writes about loss like no one else.
He describes a man struggling in vain with an Angel, and says,
"This is how he grows: by being defeated, decisively,
By constantly greater beings."
Well, I've been defeated, decisively.
I have not been a winner with death or grief.
I have not put either behind me, nor will I avoid either in the future.
I will find a way to live with them.
And the castle will come down.

The monologue ended there. The night before, as I polished the ending, those final lines came out of nowhere. Not the Rilke stuff about being defeated, but the part about the castle coming down. It surprised me, it really did.

51. The Gift—November, 2003

November's ninth day brought Melissa's birthday anniversary. I looked at the photo album in tears. I missed her, all of her, and the magnificence of life she brought. I missed my heart no longer full. I wanted to live. I wanted to bring Melissa back into my life.

I can't describe what led me to bring those faxes to Cedar's office the next day. I do know it was not a simple A-B-C process. And what difference would it make if I could define how it came about? You've already been there, or it's irrelevant blah-blah, or if you need to do something big in your own therapy it will look different anyway. As I said earlier, everyone's path and time table are different.

It must have been critical to read those faxes in the presence of someone I trusted, someone who could understand my pain. I read, and when I felt myself breaking apart, I stopped and took deep trembling breaths. Cedar sat quietly, attentive, with a slightly furrowed brow. When I finally gave in and broke down, I looked up to see tears running down her cheeks.

I had read the faxes on only two occasions, once in 1997 when they first arrived and again on the 3-year anniversary of Melissa's death in June, 2000. Each time I found them unbearable and pushed them deep into my desk drawer.

On July 2, 1997, I wrote Dr. Gutierrez and thanked him for taking care of Melissa. I asked him to pass along my deepest appreciation to Dr. Castro, Dr. Gonzalez, and a nurse who I knew only as Inez. I asked that he provide some information about Melissa's final days. Ten days later I received his reply.

Dear Mr. Dodson,

I received your fax this week as I returned from my holidays last Monday. Here are the answers to your questions.

The cause of death was "cor pulmone" which is a condition related to the pulmonary hypertension that most of the CF patients develop as their pulmonary disease gets worse. Melissa wasn't awake when she died. We put her on an infusion of morphine the day she passed away. It was her decision to be awake the day before and on the morning of that Sunday, she decided that she got enough and decided that the time was right to be sedated. She slept for awhile and at the time she died she was not in any pain or suffer. I talked to Melissa (and Gloria) about death on her final days. Since last year, (when I met her) we talk from time to time about death on her final days. She was well aware that her day to go was close.

She was concern about you. She wanted you to be informed of her condition although she didn't expected that you will organize things fast enough to trip to Costa Rica before her death. She was concerned about leaving you as she was concerned about leaving Gloria. You know that who dies is concern about causing pain to people they love. Things such as they don't want to see people crying or being concerned of their situation bother them. I guess she wanted to make sure you know that she thought of you and tried to say good-bye.

Unfortunately we didn't have your home number (Gloria didn't have it with her and Melissa didn't know it for sure) to organize a phone call.

Well, Olin, please feel free to ask any other question you may have. For all the CF team, Melissa's departure was very hard. It was very easy to love her. She gain our hearts and she was very brave on her final days.

Best personal regards,

Jose P. Gutierrez

I sent more questions several months later. Dr. Gutierrez' reply arrived on November 10, 1997.

Dear Mr. Dodson,

I'm sorry to this late reply at your email dated November 4, 1997.

Melissa was a religious person and I think it helped her a lot on her final days. As a doctor I never discussed her religious beliefs. I always try to avoid it anyway with any of my patients as these discussions can produce an imposition of my beliefs and values. I let the family and patients to sort out their beliefs in the way they want to.

Yes I did tell Melissa that her death was sort of close about 8–12 weeks before she died. I was really surprised that she accepted it very "easy" and honestly. I think she knew it before I told her. I did not see

Melissa depressed or sad and she always tried to keep her soul at the highest possible level. I think I sometimes felt more sad for her than she was for herself.

Melissa let behind her plans to fly (to the States) around March or April. I think she felt scared to get really sick in the plane or to get sick over there. Who knows, she probably was right.

I explain to her what the morphine was for. I explain that the morphine will help her with her dyspnea and sensation of panic or pain, but also I did explain that we would not put her to sleep until she really wants to. She felt very tired at the end. She wanted to sleep and have a break but she also knew that with the morphine she may not wake up again. We waited until she asked for it. This really give her the time to say good-bye to me, and to her mother.

She said good-bye to me approximately 24 hours before she died. I went to visit her the day before just when she started to get really sick. After I explain to her about the final hours she interrupted me. She ask me why I looked serious and sad? She told me that I always make her laugh and she thanked me for that. I gave her a big hug. I knew she was saying good bye. I thanked her also for making me happy.

Well, Mr. Dodson, please feel free to write again. I hope these lines make good on you. I can just imagine your feelings but again, let me assure you the love she had for you and that she never expressed to me any regret.

Jose P. Gutierrez

The faxes helped me to understand the depth of Melissa's bravery and compassion. She accepted her death and lived life with great heart. She wanted her mother and me to be spared the agony of experiencing her departure. It might have been her final wish.

From the moment Laura Lee told me I was a father, I had wanted to be Melissa's gift. Dr. Gutierrez' words told me unequivocally that she was the gift, to her final breath. I was blessed to have nearly seven years with her.

52. The Stream—February, 2004

The hole in my life was tied to the years which were moving further and further away as each day passed. I had visited Melissa six times. We spoke on the phone seven, maybe eight times. She'd sent me eight letters and one fax. The number of stories I could replay in my head was meager at best.

Esparza was all I could think of, after its absence from my mind for six years. I pictured myself at the dining room table at Ascension and Bita's, encircled by the entire family. Our tears and laughter would leave my soul replenished. Fifty family meetings would not fill the vacuum in me, but I knew that table was the place to start.

It was 2004 and not 1997, so I was able to send emails to Costa Rica to prepare everyone for my visit. I resumed Spanish classes and began a packing list. Old dreams to explore other parts of Central America returned, especially after I read Giaconda Belli's Nicaragua memoir, "The Country Under My Skin." I tacked on an extra week to visit Nicaragua. In 1978, it was a grim country on the verge of revolution. I was curious to see how the country had recovered from the devastation of Reagan's War in the 80s.

One month before I left the country, I emailed Britt and described my ongoing sadness. He wrote back quickly.

> *Olin,*
>
> *...My latest take on these emotional upheavals is that we float on a multi-layered stream, a deep river of emotions, and that it doesn't really take all that much to tap into one of the currents... The river is the way I explain to myself how I can be happy with Sally and so sad about being divorced. Even though it feels like the only part of that stream is the heartbreak of losing Melissa, it is not the only one.*
>
> *While we were in Maryland last weekend to attend a wedding, I had an interesting reaction to the ritual. The ceremony was held out on a little point on a small inlet off the bay behind a lovely old rambling inn. When I heard the Episcopal priest, decked out in a cassock and stole, crank up with the traditional wedding, I moaned internally. Then to my complete surprise, as a young woman began to read from the Song of Solomon, Chapters 2 and 8, I was riveted by this age old description of love as stronger than death and all I could think about was you and Melissa.*
>
> *"Many waters cannot quench love. Neither can the floods drown it."*
>
> *These are not words for a wedding. They are not for dearly beloved but for dearly departed.*
>
> *I love you, Olin, and I cherish your sharing your life with me. It is a gift I honor. Be well, and be sweet to yourself as you think about Melissa and as you take on your new life.*
>
> *Britt*

Hope, missing in action for nearly seven years, had re-emerged with Britt's affectionate words. He and others had said "I love you," in the dark time following Melissa's passing, but it had been a long while since that expression, or even the simple word, "future," had carried any real meaning for me.

The Stream. His words conjured up an image of a universe of primal emotions roiling beneath waking consciousness, like that massive, awe-inspiring subterranean river near Oaxaca, Mexico. It occurred to me that love, too, is a stream, more a mad gusher, really. Impossible to quench or drown. In the years since Melissa found me, love and the search for love met in a confluence with hope and grief: the unending, everlasting waters of life.

53. Longing—April, 2004

I landed in Managua on Good Friday when the April evening air was hot and humid. A short bus ride took me to Granada which was virtually closed for Holy Week, *Semana Santa*. Granada's springtime heat can stand toe-to-toe with Atlanta's in the pit of summertime. After two days watching people wade in Lake Cocibolca for baptism or simply to cool off, and sitting in my hotel pool from 9 in the morning, I needed to move on. A young hotel clerk named Idania had suggested a popular tourist destination. I would take a bus south to San Jorge and connect to a ferry for Ometepe, a remote island in Lake Cocibolca. It wasn't until my bus neared the area that I glimpsed the island's double volcanoes and remembered my passage on the same highway in 1978.

The waters of gigantic Lake Cocibolca, the largest freshwater lake in the hemisphere, break in little waves on the westernmost shore of the island. Ometepe had everything I wanted: limited access, cabanas near the pounding surf, excellent food, trees painted with floral blooms, sweetly dispositioned people, and always in view, one or the other of the volcanoes. My spirits lifted in the island's soft breezes. I rode horseback to view ancient petroglyphs and walked along the lakeshore at sunset. In a beach chair, I worked in my journal and reflected on my dream to set up a student scholarship in Melissa's name. And I worried, for the first time, that the family might have sad stories which could re-awaken my depression.

One morning I took a bus trip to one of the island's tiny towns. Altagracia is a sleepy farming community with a few small hotels and cafes and fewer paved streets. No airport. No Internet. Bulls pull small produce carts with wooden wheels. Outdoor schoolrooms in the town plaza. I wondered how much the island was even touched by the Revolution or the Contra War. People of all ages stared at me and if I smiled back, they often registered surprise and broke into delighted smiles. The broad grins disarmed me with their vulnerability and openness.

I wandered into the local museum, a couple of rooms overseen by a young girl who swept floors for twenty minutes as I wandered among the dusty exhibits and stellae. I strolled the sidewalks encircling the town square, killing time until my bus returned. It was Thursday, and a decision faced me as to whether to cross the border before the weekend crowds, or climb the volcano known as Concepción. Lost in thought, turning the final corner of the town square, I was stopped short by three third-graders in blue and white school uniforms. The girl in the trio held up a ceramic piggy bank on which was taped a piece of paper. There was a barely legible inscription, something about school supplies.

Looking left I saw some thirty sets of eyes glued in my direction. I looked down at three smiles and eyes wide with hope. I was helpless. From my wallet I extracted a Nicaraguan bill worth about $7 US. The class erupted and leapt out of their chairs, screaming and laughing. Quickly surrounded by chattering children, I held out the bill to the teacher, who now stood in front of thirty empty chairs. She smiled and shook her head, and pointed to the pig. Like a magician, I held up the bill for all to see. I folded the bill three times then pretended that the bill would not fit into the opening. Silently I looked to the girl for help. The class laughed gleefully and when she pushed the money through the slot, they erupted once again. Standing in the center of a group of applauding, laughing children immediately joined the list of my life's great joys. The class agreed for me to take a group photo as I thought to myself, I should do this again tomorrow, and every day.

But Costa Rica beckoned. Early the next morning I began the multi-stage trip to the border. An hour-long jeep ride took me to the dock, where I boarded a ferry to San Jorge. Most of the "commuters" from Ometepe sat in a large room below deck in front of a huge television, hypnotized by a soap opera which was featuring a wedding. I sat serenely looking at the water as Bach's "Jesu, Joy of Man's Desiring" played and replayed for almost thirty minutes. From the dock, noisy at 10:00 a.m., it was a brief taxi ride to Rivas.

Unknown to many tourists, Rivas is a bustling town with a considerable place in the country's history. Like Esparza, several hours south in Costa Rica, it is mentioned in the travel diaries of American archeologist John Phillips Stevens, and by Che Guevara. It is the birthplace of Nicaragu's first woman President, Violetta Chamorro. The peace treaty ending the Contra War was signed not far from town. I was there only to catch a bus to the Costa Rica border. How could I know that I would see Rivas more than once?

By mid-morning, the temperature was making me groan. The marketplace, which doubles as a bus terminal, was surrounded in blinding sunlight, noise and dust. After a quick survey to determine that there were no buses preparing to go south, I found a shard of shade beneath a tin overhang and stood motionless, hoping a border-bound bus would arrive before I shriveled up. Shriveled up, like the elderly woman in a grey cotton dress walking directly towards me. She had wrinkles whereever her skin showed, and toted a small basket of vegetables on her shoulder. She locked her eyes onto mine. The sweetness of her expression made me smile. She spoke. "*Vas a ir a la frontera?*" Are you going to the border?

"Yes, I am."

She said something I couldn't translate.

"*Lo siento, no entiendo,*" I replied. Sorry, I do not understand.

She repeated herself and I was forced to wistfully shake my head.

She paused, looked away briefly then asked "*Está bien usted?*" Are you okay?

I was caught off guard. "Yes, I am fine," was my gentle reply. "Thank you."

She smiled and walked away. I shook my head in delight and amazement. My bus pulled up almost immediately. I took a seat behind the driver and looked up. On the space above the windshield were big gold letters forming the words "Santa Fe." The gods were smiling. We were soon barreling southward, a reggae version of Cat Steven's "Wild World" blasting from the sound system, and Ometepe's volcanoes rising in the east.

At the border, people congregated below the bus's open door, shouting and waving food and sodas for sale. I paused on the bus steps, uncertain of my next move, until a uniformed man called out to me. He studied my passport as a flood of people pushed me past him through a gate. I followed the flow to a distant building and a long glass cage of clerks with dead faces. There was a form to fill out and sign and a fee to be paid. I fell back into the porch space, fumbling money, passport, wallet and shoulder bags, then kneeling to reorganize my things. Almost immediately a little girl called out to me. I looked up, but didn't see her, only the notebook she carried.

I was ready for her. A guidebook had prepared me for the scam with these official-looking—and completely meaningless—documents. "No, thanks," I grunted.

I collected myself for the toasty hike to the Costa Rican side of the border, remembering the wad of Nicaraguan *córdobas* in my pocket. The girl spoke once again. This time I looked at her. She was short and maybe 9 years of age. She asked if I needed to change money, said she could take me to someone who would do that.

This time I studied her. She had a serious eyebrow line and straight brown hair long overdue for a wash and trim. She wore nice jeans and a clean shirt with a little red purse over her shoulder. Her eyes were clear and direct.

I hesitated. "What's your name?"

"Guisell." "Okay. *Nos vamos.*"

Guisell struck out a few paces in advance of me. I felt a new calm, just to have a helper for the border crossing.

I tried to think of something to say, and the Spanish word for "guide" came to mind. I put it into a sentence: "*Guisell, usted es mi guia!*" You are my guide! I said it, pleased with my command of the Spanish language. But I was stopped short when a frowning Guisell turned and looked at me, clearly puzzled. "*Mi guia!*" I said it louder, the universal idiot response, where "louder" is supposed to equal "clearer." Her frown remained, spurring in me a quick inner dialogue:

"*Guia*" means "guide," I'm sure of that. Did I mispronounce the word...? No, impossible. It's a soft "*g*," right?? Like "guacamole." Or is it? Uh-oh, maybe, I did mispronounce it.

As I silently mumbled to myself, Guisell simply turned around and set off, south towards Costa Rica. I stumbled after her, quite unhappy and confused.

Abruptly, she halted and turned. "Oh, I get it! '*Guia*,' you meant '*guia*'!"

We smiled at each other. We walked on together.

As promised, Guisell took me to a money changer sitting in a car, then past the police standing at the door of the Costa Rican customs office. She waited patiently at each station, and moved among all the adults with ease. I had a glum hunch that she had been working here for a while. Before we parted, I gave her a generous tip and a ball point pen. It's good to have a helpful companion, however small.

I wandered over to the ticket office, looking for a bus to La Cruz, the first town south of the border. The woman behind the window couldn't understand me. I was flustered, wondering where my Spanish went, when, tap-tap, there was an elderly man at my arm.

"Are you having trouble?" he said in perfect English. He spoke to the ticket seller in Spanish for a minute, then turned to me.

"The bus doesn't come for quite a while. Why don't you take a taxi? They're fast and cheap."

I almost laughed. All I have to do is wait around for other people to come up and help me!

"Anything else you need??" I shook my head and thanked him profusely.

La Cruz, Costa Rica overlooks a wide, stunning bay on the Pacific Ocean. Amalia's Hotel takes advantage of the view and breeze, its hallways decorated with colorful original paintings. I checked in and, after a lunch of chicken and rice, found my room and flopped onto the bed by the table fan. The images of the day and my trinity of helpers instantly came to mind. I had an overwhelming, eerie feeling that they had been sent as personal escorts, blessing my return to Costa Rica. Tears filled my eyes and rolled down the sides of my face.

The words of my therapist, Cedar, came to mind: "Melissa brought you back to Central America in 1990, where your heart opened. Like in the Bible, a child led you… Now you are returning, to find your heart once more." Guisell came to mind, the child who had literally led me today. My insides burst and more tears poured out of me in waves of grief and gratitude.

My emotions exploded. I sobbed without control or the ability to understand what I was going through. Who were these three people? How could I think they "were sent?" Was I imagining this? "I don't get it. I don't get it…." I repeated the phrase again and again then slowly drifted off to sleep.

Night brought increased torment. I would sleep for maybe an hour at a time before waking up. At each waking, I thought about Guisell. Why isn't she in school? Who is watching over her? Can I help her in some way? Should I keep going or return to find her?

Towards morning, I was startled awake by a dream.

> *I'm playing in a soccer game, and we've lost two team-mates, including a girl who stepped out of bounds. The sun is sinking, so it is becoming difficult to see. Suddenly the ball rockets towards me, hits me in the head and ricochets into the net! GOAL!!!!!!!*
>
> *I fall back slowly onto snow-covered ground, arms extended, like when you make a snow angel. My team-mates jump on me, but I do not feel their weight. I see only their joyous faces.*

I opened my eyes listening to the table fan rotate back and forth. I knew immediately that the missing team-mate was Melissa and the girl who stepped out of bounds, Guisell.

* * * * *

Next morning I grab coffee and a pastry at the plaza and hail a taxi. We speed through the countryside while I try to devise a strategy. Will I wait at the border or go back through customs into Nicaragua? How long will I look for Guisell? What if she isn't working today? Will I look for her in Rivas? I have no answers.

We reach the border where I pay the driver and look over the long line of people waiting to enter the customs office. I walk around the building and wander into the relatively empty border zone. The questions have ended and my insides are quiet.

I scan the horizon north towards Nicaragua until a man in a black uniform approaches and asks what I'm doing. I give him the short version in Spanish. I'm looking for a girl who works around here. My daughter passed away in Costa Rica and I want to see if I can help this girl in honor of my child. He nods and walks off, and a minute later, up comes a dark, mustached man in a yellow shirt. I repeat my story and throw in something I've overlooked: I need a translator, too. Yellow-Shirt returns on the cross bar of a bicycle pedaled by a nice-looking fellow in a clean t-shirt. T-Shirt looks at me skeptically. I tell him about Melissa, my return to Costa Rica, and tie both stories to my hunt for Guisell. He nods, says he knows the girl. He signals the border guard, who waves at us and turns around, and the three of us walk towards Nicaragua. Soon we see Guisell walking towards us with a gringo in tow. When T-Shirt tells her I want to talk, without question or hesitation, she does an about-face. I buy sodas for all of us and we sit on the ground in the shade of a tree.

It's my first chance to study Guisell. She wears clean pants and a cotton shirt with broad blue and white stripes, and nice tennis shoes. Her face has a shadowy patina with a serious, almost tense expression, and why not? She's hustling pennies when most of her peers are at home playing with their friends. She has to be wondering what this meeting with the gringo is all about.

I begin by explaining the purpose of my trip to visit my daughter's grave, how I want to create a memorial to her. The guys have already heard the short version, but Guisell listens intently and unexpectedly asks a series of questions. What did she die of? How old was she? All three register horror and sympathy that Melissa died at 18. I'm off my agenda but I show them Melissa's photo from my wallet. I sense how Guisell, especially, needs some background on why I returned to find her.

I move on to my questions about Guisell. To my surprise, she's 12, not 9, and lives in Rivas with her mother and three brothers. She takes a 40-minute bus ride to the border every day after school and on weekends. She doesn't know her public school teacher's last name. Her class lets out every day around noon, but for some reason there was no school today. My good fortune.

Guisell says she plans to attend high school next year. "And after that, what would you like to do?" I ask. T-Shirt turns and glares at me. "*Oh, señor,* she has no idea....No idea!"

I pause as his comment sinks in. An embarrassing assumption had slipped from my mouth, one in which all the world's children dream wonderful dreams of their future. T-Shirt patiently awaits my next comment.

I say I'd like to write a letter to Guisell's mother. Guisell writes down her mother's name and address in my journal. I write down mine and, at T-Shirt's prompting, I add my phone number and email address. Guisell's mom, of course, has neither. It occurs that I haven't made it precisely clear why I came back to talk to Guisell. "So tell her how much I appreciate her being '*mi guia*' yesterday."

Guisell hears me mispronounce the word again. "*Guia*!!" she blurts out, and I laugh.

"To honor Melissa's memory, I want to write your mother. I want to ask her if she will agree for me to help you enroll in a good school."

T-Shirt begins the translation. I turn all my attention to Guisell, who responds before he finishes. Her head bows slightly downward and I see her hand go to her cheek below the right eye. Her finger slowly pushes the tears from that cheek and then the other.

My eyes fill then, and the men sit in silence as Guisell and I wipe our tears.

Soon afterwards, we begin the walk south towards Costa Rica. We take a few photos and I tell Guisell that her mom should receive a letter from me in a few weeks. We all say our thanks and goodbyes. Her tears and mine have sealed my commitment. Guisell is headed to private school.

54. Esparza—April, 2004

Coming south from La Cruz the bus stops short of Esparza at a taxi stand by the highway. My shoulder bag hits the back of a woman's head as I race down the aisle, apologizing over my shoulder. The cab drops me at a roadside restaurant/gas station where I down three cold sodas. I reposition my bags and set off towards the plaza trying to remember where Melissa's uncle and aunt live. Chickens scatter at the corner of the familiar street which leads to the old green clapboard house under an *almendro* tree.

Ascension and Bita come to the door with little shouts. Our loss makes us hold tight to each other. My Spanish skills are so suspect after the episode with Guisell I'm content to sit on their plastic front porch rocker and drink melon *batidos* until Marvin, the tri-lingual son, comes home. But Ascension has other plans. It's the day for his visit to the cemetery. He goes to house-keep the graves of Melissa and his mother, Victoria. I accompany him with a façade of willingness but, as we walk, I'm distracted by wondering how I'll react at the graveside.

The cemetery is a flat space, overgrown and broken-hearted. Melissa's coffin has been moved to a family plot near a long white wall at the edge of the cemetery. Black, iguana-type lizards with bulging legs stroll around with raised heads. Unkempt grave-markers and headstones are carved with names like Lisimacho, Eustoquio and Belarmina, with birth dates going as far back as the early 1800s.

Ascension, in a white baseball cap, sets down his wash pail beside a block of white tile, maybe 4 by 8 feet. At one end is a raised tile header with Melissa's name on a metal plate. Ascension balances himself on one hand and reaches out to pick little shoots of grass from the spaces between the tiles. Then he rolls water from the bucket and wipes the tile with his hand. I watch, oddly numb, as if the hot afternoon air has turned my feelings to sludge.

Later, I join Merilyn on the front porch of a little house she recently purchased. She is a successful climber of the corporate ladder in banking, a tough world for a Costa Rican woman. She wears a rose-colored, sleeveless pants suit decorated with flowers. Effusive but elusive, Merilyn speaks about Melissa in a tone which manages to be both matter of fact and personal.

She begins with the most difficult subject. She admits to rarely visiting Melissa's grave; it overwhelms her. I think that even after all these years one little push could send her into a cascade of grief. I listen and say little.

She tells me that in the later years Melissa had given Merilyn several letters to mail to me. The letters were their secret, Melissa's way of protecting herself and Gloria from any conflict or anxiety which might arise from Melissa showing too much interest in me.

I understood that it was Gloria's fear as much as Melissa's that kept her from coming to San Francisco in 1993 for a medical work-up. Melissa suffered from the emotional complexities which had filled the spaces between her mom and me. It left me with a bitter taste.

By age 17, Melissa openly risked her mother's displeasure by reaching out and planning a trip to visit me. Merilyn emphasized how much Melissa had wanted to go with me to Sea World. Melissa's courage and stubborn integrity were undeniable, similar to what I'd witnessed in other people with cystic fibrosis, like Isa and Ana Stenzel.

Merilyn made it clear that Melissa had more to overcome than CF. Gloria had lied to her, telling Melissa that I knew Gloria was pregnant when I left Costa Rica in 1978. It explained in part Melissa's ambivalence, remove and anger. But her own experience of me perhaps kindled her passion and fostered a final miracle: Melissa's embrace of me. I was happy that Melissa felt loved by me and maybe loved me in return.

Then Merilyn launched into a story which swept me up in waves of emotion.

Do you know Rio San Jeronimo? Well, I went there camping with Melissa, and she didn't want to go to sleep at all, she stayed up all night long looking at the stars, listening to the sound of the waves with the light of the moon reflected on the water; and there I was, telling her off to go to bed. She said: "How can I sleep having this landscape in front of me? You don't come to the beach to sleep."

It is a place of difficult access, the first time that we went there, she scared us, she turned very purple trying to grasp for air. Two ladies and I stayed along her side to help her but she didn't want us to help her, and she got there the best way she could. I was so worried, that I started praying to God that everything would go well. How would I get her out of this place if she gets sicker? Melissa got there and sat down on the sand, she said: "At last!" She seemed so strong that the other young people of the Church would laugh to see her so happy. The second time we went to the ocean it was very rough and the waves burst against our voices, but she was not afraid and she entered into the water to have a good time. There were so many things we didn't do, places we didn't go and never will go. There are so many memories that I will like to freeze some in time and stop remembering and stay with the ones I liked the most.

I believe that in my family secrets are traditions. Later I knew that the Doctor told my mom that Melissa knew about her own condition some time ago, I don't know if I can believe it or not. Clearly, she is not here now to blame it on her; that torments me; how much solitude she felt upon knowing the bad news and kept it for so long. I cannot accept that she hid that from me. She always trusted me.

We had so many dreams: our professional careers, our weddings, ironically, she wanted to have children but I didn't so much, family, trips that we never made, and new experiences like to navigate the Sarapiqui's rapids, to take rides in an aquatic park called Acua-mania, to fly in an airship in Greece, to go to a Torre Fuerte musical concert—"Strong Tower" is the name of the band—and to attend a baseball national selection game and shout during the whole game and take pictures only of the most good-looking players, etc. There were things that we never did together and to be honest I don't know if I want to do them all by myself. If I try, I think that I will cry all the way through. Well, I don't know, but, through prayers, I think that she is a different woman. The one that lives in me.

I could have listened to Merilyn talk all night.

*****

Marvin, age 34, came to his parents' house after dinner for the second table talk. His parents would wander in and listen, then leave, then come back. In the faint light we spoke in English and he occasionally translated for his parents. They in turn offered brief comments. A public school French teacher, Marvin's English had a peculiarly beautiful accent. He shared memories of Melissa referring to her "papá," which told him that she accepted me many years before I had any inkling. Once he teased her. "You love your father, don't you?" She pursed her lips tight like she was afraid the word "yes" might burst out. Marvin said they both knew the truth, adding that Melissa was captured by her mother's worry that I would come between them.

Melissa's death had shaken Marvin's faith and he told me of his great anger with God. He drank alcohol excessively until God spoke to him and he stopped. Grief had crushed every member of the family differently. At evening's end, Marvin stood and hugged me hard.

* * * * *

Following Merilyn's directions I drove my rented Suzuki down a steep hill, across a narrow bridge then turned right onto a hundred yards of an old river bottom. I braked often to prevent the rocks from ripping off the muffler. On one side was a row of living spaces connected duplex-style, on the other a steep slope covered with trees. I stopped at the last blue house on the right and got out. Jessica pulled up behind me in a faded sedan which sat high off the ground. Her kinky curly hair was highlighted with blond streaks. She approached me with a look of great happiness. I wondered aloud, "Haven't we met?" She smiled mysteriously.

Jessica introduced me to her three beautiful daughters and handsome husband. She and I sat in her back yard on kitchen chairs, knees almost touching, and I got a chance to look closely at her. She was small and muscularly built. An intricate tattoo extended from her left clavicle to somewhere underneath her top. Ordinarily I might have stared at it, but I didn't really look at anything but Jessica's magnetic blue eyes. Her energy was like that of a stallion at a starting gate but before she could complete her first sentence I interrupted to say why I was there. Then she was off, speaking almost nonstop, while I tried to hang on with my pen and journal.

> *Melissa is my best friend. I carry her with me always. Always. She make me laugh whenever we were together. Even when she was sick she made me laugh. My father...well, he spanked me. I had two brothers and he treated them differently, you know how it is. Anyway no matter how I felt, Melissa would make me laugh. And I could tell her anything and she would tell me it would be all right.*
>
> *We were both skinny and smaller than everyone else and you know how kids are, they would pick on us. But we never let on how we felt. Melissa never complained or talked about her problems, even when she was really sick. We weren't interested in boys, we were too shy. If we saw a cute boy and we had to walk past him, we would go the other way-around the building. Our main interest in life was to help others.*
>
> *When she missed school, I would take her books and homework to her house and explain the assignments to her. She was so smart sometimes she would end up helping me, and understand the homework better than me even though she missed the classes. She was a serious student. No matter how much time she was in the hospital, she would work hard to complete her assignments. Her penmanship was really good. Sometimes*

she would make homework cover sheets for me. They looked good.

Wendy, I was the only one who could call her Wendy, always look and smell real nice. Here smell my hand. She love this perfume. It was all she would ever wear. She always put lots of powder on herself, and this perfume. She always smell good like a new baby.

I remembered Melissa's fax, the one she sent after my first visit, was signed, "Love, Wendy." It was her special name.

We always were laughing. Sometimes when she would cough and make that terrible sound it would make us laugh even more. I remember her lying in bed with that mask and the oxygen and the machine that you bought her. I thought she had asthma. She never talked about it. She kept a lot of things to herself. She hated to have to take her medicine at school.

I don't want to hurt your feelings, but Melissa had, I don't know the English word, "resentimiento."

Resentment.

Yes, resentment.

I understand.

Because you weren't with her mother.

Wendy was my only friend. I tell my daughter, you can have many amistades, people you can have fun with, but they are not your amigos. An amigo is someone you can trust and love. Wendy was my amiga. She is with me everywhere I go. I have a few photos, but I'm not a picture person. I keep everything here and here. [Two fingers touched her head, then her chest.]

She took care of everything you gave to her, kept it in a box. I think you sent her a box of gifts for Christmas. I can't remember all the things you sent, but it was really nice. She gave me some of the gifts: post-its, stamps, things like that. I think she wanted to be with you. She looked forward to visiting you. I was in the States then, but she wrote letters to me. I think she never wanted your money or anything, she just wanted you.

She had me. I never loved anyone more.

I feel the same way. I was in the States when my mother called and told me she died. When I returned to Esparza, I sat at her grave for two hours. I never saw her body or had a funeral to go to. She was gone. There was just a blank there. I couldn't remember her face. Then I had a dream.

It began with this big beautiful light. And there was beautiful music. Beautiful music and all this light. She was coming down from the light and she had long white braids down to her butt. She had on a white dress, it was blowing like an angel's, and her cheeks were pink. Her blonde hair was in these little braids and I thought, Jesus, how long did it take to do those braids?

After that dream I was calm. I knew she was fine and I felt calm.

With the recounting of her dream, Jessica stopped and we sat in smiling silence. Her stories of Melissa's thoughtfulness reminded me of Dr.Gutierrez' faxes. How had he phrased it? *She always tried to keep her soul at the highest possible level.*

I was thrilled that their childhood relationship was used to teach Jessica's daughters, Skylin and Angeline, about true friendship. I loved the image of Melissa with braided hair coming down from the light.

I thanked Jessica for loving Melissa so much. She handed me several photos of the two of them, to make copies. One, from their grade school graduation, shows a giddy Melissa, holding her friend with all the obvious affection Jessica had just described.

Jessica hugged me twice when I got up to leave and her two girls did the same. It would have scared Jessica to know how much I wanted to hold her. I felt the same feelings for her that I had for Laura, Anne and Bob Lee: appreciation, affection and a crazy wish to give her a gift as precious she had given me.

* * * * *

The following morning Bita and I spent time alone. Gloria had moved to a nearby town. We spoke briefly on the phone, but she did not come to Esparza. Bita in flip flops, holding a worn kitchen towel, had always been a great supporter of me. She brought out the family photo albums. One standout photo showed Melissa getting her hair done for high school graduation. In person I had never seen my daughter so happy, full of glowing young womanliness. Another page held a photo of Melissa as an upright toddler, pre-cystic fibrosis. It reminded me of the early years of Melissa's life, the holding and kissing and touching that I missed. Tears trickled down my cheeks until Bita walked over to me and held my head to her bosom. She reached across my shoulder and removed the photo and placed it in my hands.

Soon, it was time for Ascension to take me on another walk. Our destination was the bank on the plaza where his daughter worked. Merilyn, we learned, was out for the day, but we toured the building. Everyone smiled and greeted Ascension as if he were the mayor. We walked outside and I looked straight ahead, startled to suddenly recognize something important, something I hadn't thought about in years. I took Ascension's arm and pulled him across the street as I pointed. "There! There is where Melissa and I first met!!!"

I pulled him to the low wall extending out from the park rotunda where

Melissa and I looked in each other's eyes for the first time. I'd memorized the location from photos for fourteen years. Ascension and I sat on the wall and asked a school girl to take our photo. We held each other and smiled like loons.

It was as if I'd discovered the fount of love, the center of the all life, with "sacred" being the only proper description for it. For the next two days, after each visit to the cemetery, each conversation I had there with Melissa, I returned to the place of immeasurable joy. Each time, I sat on the wall for an hour or more, looking around me, remembering, and feeling.

On the final day of my visit, I repeatedly kissed my fingers and touched them on Melissa's grave. I did the same at the wall in the park and buried a small gift in the dirt. I had been foolish to fear what I would find on my return to Costa Rica. In looking for stories, I found much more: caring relationships with Melissa's family, Melissa's dear friend, Jessica, and two precious places on this earth: the plaza in Esparza and the border zone between Costa Rica and Nicaragua.

55. The Return—October, 2004

Santa Fe's color and charm were dim compared to the incandescence of Costa Rica and Nicaragua. Thanks to a rehabilitated imagination, my work days were richer than they deserved to be. Something inside had changed, as the prospect of mentoring Guisell took on a reality. I had drafted a letter to Guisell's mother, Neyvi, on my return flight, and after quickly getting it translated, sent it off. I kept it short, describing my life, my work, and my reason for being in Nicaragua and meeting Guisell. I directly asked for permission—as a memorial to my daughter, Melissa—to assist her own in obtaining a good education.

Six weeks passed before the acceptances came to my mailbox. Neyvi had composed a response of clarity and grace, handwritten in perfectly even lines. She offered a portrait of her life with four children: Guisell, 13, and three boys: 16, 14 and 2. Neyvi worked out of her home, selling cosmetics and giving manicures in other people's houses. She made no mention of a man in their lives. She concluded with the following:

> *If you are willing and have the wish to help, whatever amount however small would help us a great deal. I want to tell you that your friendliness is very pleasing, it is the first time a person has been concerned about us and even more a total stranger... I am very sorry for what*

happened with your daughter. If you do this, I promise that Guisell will honor her and keep her uppermost in her memory…

With much affection,

Neyvi

Guisell's brief letter bounced with adolescent energy. Her script was like decorative art, filled with exclamation points and circular dots, resembling hearts, above the "i"s.

Dear Godfather… I am very happy because I received your letter! I had thought that what you said was a joke but now I see that you are serious. I hope that you will come back to see us! It would make me happy if you would be my godfather, because you are a good person.

Take great care and may God bless you.

I love you lots,

Guisell

Greatly touched, I pulled out plans previously sketched out, plans which I could now commit to. The next step was to help Guisell identify a private school and arrange the transfer. I desperately needed a contact in Nicaragua to serve as an intermediary. With no friends there, I turned to the young woman, Idania, who had worked the front desk at my hotel in Managua. The morning I checked out we had discussed life in Nicaragua for a solid twenty minutes. I told her that "The Country Under My Skin" had strongly influenced me to come to Nicaragua. Idania knew of the book's author, Giaconda Belli, but had never read her sensuous memoir, so I sent her a copy. Now I emailed her to see if she would lend a hand by passing communication to Neyvi and Guisell through a family friend who had a cell phone. I told her I would pay for her time. Idania quickly emailed me an enthusiastic yes, but expressed no interest in being reimbursed, saying only that "an education is the best gift you can give a child."

Her response meant that I could now dream with more certainty. I envisioned a door beginning to open for a virtual street child. The dream and finding Guisell somehow left me feeling Melissa was involved in making all this happen. The claw-hold of despair on my heart began to loosen.

Several weeks later, I accepted a collect call, then a second. It had to be Neyvi but the woman's Spanish flew by me so rapidly I was unable to decipher any shred of meaning in her words, not even her name. Each call eventually dwindled into a long silence, followed by a faint background conversation, then a click and a dial tone. I was frustrated and puzzled.

Two emails followed and made sense of the phone calls. Neyvi began by offering an apology, explaining she did not want to abuse the relationship, then went on to say she had "economic problems." She asked if I could send her $150, "for things Guisell needs." Further details were scant, other than instructions on how to wire the money. I wondered what Guisell could need. Medical assistance? How mired in poverty was the family?

Friends cautioned me in terse voices, but I imagined myself in Neyvi's tattered shoes. In her position, I knew that, unless I were extremely passive, accepting everything as God's will, I would certainly try to get as much as I could from a charitable gringo. I thought it over and concluded that sending money would set an unwanted precedent. I had not signed on to be a financial helper to the family. I sent Neyvi a carefully worded letter. Politely, and honestly, I told her that I was not a man of great wealth and that my monthly income would only permit me to assist Guisell with her education. I added that I was nevertheless curious as to what Guisell needed and asked that she write me with more details. I never received a reply and the subject never came up again.

Meanwhile, Idania had contacted Neyvi through the friend with the phone. She was correct in her hunch that Guisell could not enroll in private school in mid-year. The soonest Guisell could begin a new school was January of 2005. I decided to return to Nicaragua in November to iron out the details and meet Neyvi. I signed up in a Spanish Immersion school in Granada, an hour from Rivas. For two weeks I lived with a family, studied Spanish every morning and finalized arrangements with Idania to travel to Rivas.

On Saturday morning at the end of my first week in school, Idania and I met up at Managua's noisy Huembes bus station and headed south for our pre-arranged meeting at Neyvi's house. Idania, at 22, looked impossibly cool in a clean white shirt and a blue skirt. Her outfit offset her smooth skin and generous, burnished brown eyes. This was only the second time we had met, but we chatted like old friends as our bus barreled south through the lush countryside. Almost yelling to be heard above the wind blasting through the bus windows, I asked Idania if she had heard of other foreigners sponsoring children as I was doing. "Yes, my cousins." She related the story of her four cousins whose parents had been killed, separately, fighting for the Sandinistas. After the revolution, one by one, the children had been adopted from their orphanage, two by a Finnish family and two by a Spanish family. The adopted parents had paid for each of them to attend the University, just as I considered I might eventually do for Guisell. To the east I glimpsed the two volcanoes on Ometepe.

Idania listened patiently as I played critic of my own plan. With the family living in such poverty how could Neyvi allow Guisell to give up her work and meager contributions to the family in order to attend private school? Wouldn't mom want my help in offsetting her financial sacrifice? Should I volunteer to give her money?

I studied Idania's expression, so serene and supremely sincere. Only when I inquired about her plans for the future did a cloud of worry crossed her brow. I sensed how burdened she must be by the choices she faced, not unlike Guisell, ten years her junior. Idania, industrious, principled and intelligent, knew that in Nicaragua only a perfect trifecta of smart choices, hard work and exceptional luck would maybe, only maybe, lift her out of poverty.

Rivas in November was like Rivas in April: hot, dusty and blindingly bright. We chose a honest-looking *taxista* and headed out. Idania firmly spelled out directions to the house and improvised suggestions when we became lost. South of the U.S.-Mexico border, house numbers are rare, if they exist at all, and the verbal map Neyvi had provided led us down empty dirt roads for 30 minutes. Wooden slat houses sat far apart and appeared abandoned. Finally we spotted a windowless concrete establishment and tentatively sidled in. A row of men and boys sat in the dark facing a wall lined with video game machines. We used the wall phone to call Neyvi's friend, but there was no answer. Idania's face, for the first time, showed a trace of worry. A man overheard us quizzing the manager and broke in, pointing through the wall and talking with assurance to Idania. Soon, in a different neighborhood, poking along in first gear, we were peering anxiously at another row of houses sitting under large trees.

I spotted Guisell's face peeking from a doorway in a little brick house. She turned and spoke to someone hidden from view. She skipped out on the porch and down the stairs. We hugged sideways, lightly touching, with the top of her head barely reaching my chest. Her hair was cut stylishly short. She looked like happy, delighted children look. Her eyes shone clear and vibrant.

I introduced Idania, then noticed Neyvi, dressed like her daughter in clean t-shirt and jeans, moving slowly off the porch carrying her two year old. She could have passed for 40 but was more likely in her early 30s. Her manner was quietly cordial, unquestionably distant. Where Guisell was bronze, Neyvi was mahogany.

Idania mentioned her need to return to Managua in three hours, then we moved the white plastic chairs into a circle on the porch and prepared for our business. I fumbled for words. Fortunately my chair had a crack in it which made it jerk as I shifted my weight. I flailed my arms, faking almost falling onto the floor. Neyvi and Guisell looked at each other and exploded in laughter.

I asked about the other boys. Neyvi said they were at the border, working. The police had swept the area a while back and kicked out Guisell and other young kids. Neyvi told us that Guisell had once attended a private school, but Neyvi could not keep up on the tuition payments. As Idania translated, while she spoke or listened to Neyvi, I observed everyone's body language. Neyvi's brow lowered as I spoke; then she looked Idania in the eye and responded sincerely and matter-of-factly. Guisell sat back smiling like a little buddha. Occasionally she would catch me glancing at her and her grin would grow even larger.

I directed a few questions at her. Are you still interested in attending private school?

Yes. Her face revealed the earnestness of her intent.

Do you have a favorite subject in school?

Science.

What advantages would you have in a private school?

Computers. Dancing. Physical education.

Would it be hard going to a new school and leaving your old classmates?

No, not really.

The conversation moved on to the logistics. Selecting a school. Determining if there were openings. The necessity of buying clothes, a uniform, a backpack, school supplies and books. Figuring out how to transfer funds for tuition and bus fare. Most of the work would fall on Neyvi and Guisell's shoulders. I asked for nothing in return other than some accountability by way of regular attendance and hard work. I wanted to see report cards. We did some rough calculations and figured that, including bus expenses, private school would cost $50 a month.

Ninety minutes into the conversation, the heat and the adrenaline had sapped me, but with agreement reached and everyone's duties carefully mapped out, I was pleased. Guisell was still smiling. I figured our work was complete. I asked, "Is there anything we haven't discussed?" There was a silence, then Guisell began talking. It was a rapid extended monologue delivered with animation in a serious, almost pleading tone. I liked her very much for speaking up.

Idania turned to me. "She says her elementary school graduation is taking place in four weeks. She would like to be in the ceremony but her mother can't afford to pay for the uniform and photographs and the other expenses. The kids who can't afford those things are not allowed to be in the ceremony. They are left to pick up their diploma backstage. It would mean a lot to Guisell to be in the ceremony. On top of everything it's on her birthday! She wants to know if you will help her."

I glanced at Neyvi. A sheepish look and a hint of a shrug told me that it wasn't her idea and I was on my own. I asked Guisell what she would need. Her answer: clothes, shoes, the photographs, the school's fee. I remembered my earlier decision not to be their financial helper, but I said, "Yes, yes, of course." Guisell smiled while I pondered the possible untended consequences of my decision.

Once again I looked around. "Anything else?" I knew departure was imminent. Guisell again had other ideas. She spoke only a sentence or two. I had to smile, eagerly anticipating Idania's translation. What she said gave me the jolt of my life. "Do you have the photograph of Melissa that you showed Guisell when you first met?"

My throat caught. Lowering my face, I fumbled for my wallet. Guisell walked over to me and took the outstretched photo by its edges. She presented the photo to her mother, proudly, as if Melissa were her own special friend.

Fighting back a surge of emotions, I began to recount the story of my first trip to Central America in 1978, the phone call and meeting Melissa in 1990, and the five hard years of her rejection. I related how she opened her heart for a miraculous year before her death. After her passing, it was three years before I began to feel alive again, and three more before I planned a trip to her graveside. I concluded by saying how my life had turned when, looking for an appropriate way to honor Melissa's life, I met Guisell.

Guisell was leaning against her mother as I finished my story and her expression was one of dreamy contentment. Neyvi's eyes were full and she gazed at me. Who can know what to say to one who's lost a child? "Do you still miss her?" "Oh, yes, of course," was all I could say.

I was overwhelmed by Guisell's surprises. Once again the tables had been turned on me in mystery and beauty. Once again the line between giver and recipient was blurred.

This little girl had, obviously, planned for our meeting with great care. After the private school discussion and decision came the request for me to help with her graduation. Next, the showing of the photo to her mother and the request that I retell Melissa's story. Guisell grasped her relationship to Melissa and embraced it with uncanny clarity. From that day forward, I began to see myself less as instigator and more as collaborator to a living connection between Melissa and me. I am not a person who sees an invisible hand all around me, but I knew Melissa had brought me to Guisell.

Finally we really did say our goodbyes. Idania and I set off down the road to find a taxi.

As we walked, we discussed Idania's side conversation with Neyvi. Idania had unknown family on her father's side in Rivas, including a cousin her age. Neyvi knew the cousin and agreed to help Idania find her. Idania vowed to return soon to meet her cousin. For her, as for the rest of us, a door had opened. I was very happy for her.

My thoughts returned to Neyvi. "Guisell's mom is really a good person and a good mother," I said, "but she looks very tired and stressed." Idania turned to me. "Yes, many women in Nicaragua have that look."

Several days later, I returned alone to Rivas. Neyvi, Guisell, and Nubia, the friend with a cell phone, led me on a shopping expedition around Rivas' busy shopping area. Neyvi seemed indecisive in every hot little store we visited, dithering over the price of every item. I figured she must be self conscious to have a stranger spending what was, for her, a fair amount of money on her daughter. Our shopping list consisted of a white shirt, socks, an undershirt, a pair of black shoes (extra sized for Guisell to grow into), and dark blue material for a skirt.

Guisell drifted in and out of the purchasing decisions. She was more interested in checking out the new styles of shoes and jeans. By the time we reached the photography studio, it was blisteringly hot. Nubia and I sat in the tiny lobby while Guisell and her mom disappeared behind a black curtain where a cap, gown and a camera awaited. Upon leaving the studio we were blasted by loud brassy music from down the block. We peeked through holes in a block-long plywood fence and saw a high-school marching band of 60 or 70 young people, half of them drummers. Each member was bedecked in a heavy uniform, black with gold buttons and epaulets. They were fronted by six majorettes in white jackets and red skirts flashing batons, and twenty or so cheerleaders waving yellow pom-poms.

I looked up from the fence hole to see Guisell at a distance, urging me to join her. She waved with her fingers down, the back of her hand towards me, as they do in Nicaragua. Nubia and Neyvi were disappearing through a gate into the practice area. I trotted towards Guisell and as I approached her, she took my hand and tugged me through the entrance towards a crowd of fifty people. Melissa had never reached out for my hand and, just for an instant, I hesitated. Guisell pulled me through the gate and touched the small of my back, escorting me into another world. We stood together for a moment before she left to find a vantage point with her mom and Nubia. I was surely the happiest, most thankful person in that crowd as the band filled the air with a celebratory song.

*****

Back in Santa Fe, only a few days after my meeting with Neyvi and Guisell, I found myself in another slow re-entry. A stomach bug kept me inside the house for several days. I lay around in a state of lethargic, unhappy separation. I slept fitfully and napped at odd times.

On my first Saturday at home, I flopped down on my bed just before lunchtime. I sank into a deep sleep and had the following dream.

I'm walking through a suite of beautiful offices trimmed in polished wood with heavy desks and book cases. Sun is entering the room through small windows high on the walls. Guisell is sitting at a desk, hunched over a map. "Where are you going?" I ask. She points to the map and says, "An aquarium." And she mentions a whale with a name like Shamu. She stands up and gently takes me by the hand. She leads me into a second room, and then a third, all dimly lit. We pass a small, thin girl sitting alone on a small couch or love seat. In the semi-darkness, with her head bent down slightly, I can't make out her face, but I know who it is.

I awoke, crying. Alone and anguished, I walked into the kitchen to boil water for coffee. I idly glanced at the wall calendar. The date was November 20, the anniversary of the day Melissa and I met.

Epilogue: Happy Birthday—November 9, 2007

The night before Melissa's 29th birthday, I scribbled 11/09/07! on a Post-it and placed it on the kitchen island. It would give me a happy jolt when I found it in the morning. For the first time in memory, I didn't worry about depression visiting me on this anniversary. In the writing of our story, Melissa had been next to me every day for three years.

Over the course of the preceding year, my spirits had been lifted by re-connections, via telephone and email, with people of significance in the story. Helen Dias helped me to locate Isa and Ana Stenzel, still living near Stanford University. I was delighted to learn that they were in fine health, thanks, in part, to double lung transplants. In Ana's case, two transplants, seven years apart: a "Double Double." The twins had competed in two National Transplant Games and lived amazing lives of service and physical feats, grateful for each day and every breath. They had published a book about their lives with cystic fibrosis and donor lungs entitled "The Power of Two." I was surprised they remembered our brief encounters fifteen years earlier. Both were excited to talk and to learn about both Melissa and Guisell. My relationships with Isa and Ana, in a short time, became profoundly affecting and overflowing with meaning.

One week before Melissa's birthday, from out of the blue, I received a phone call from Barbara Johnson, my first love who came to my Berkeley apartment in her hospital gown that autumn night in 1969. I learned that, in spite of suffering two more episodes in later years, she had made a good life for herself and become skilled at managing her mental symptoms. She finished college, worked steadily, got married, raised two girls and looked forward to becoming a grandmother.

Then came the news that Melissa's cousin, Merilyn, had given birth to a baby boy. It had been a while since I'd felt greater delight. New life springing forth in a woman and a family so devastated by the loss of a child gave me hope and happiness. I eagerly anticipated returning to Esparza to greet a cousin to both Melissa and me, Jose Joaquin. Melissa would have loved him, I know.

In Nicaragua, Guisell approached her 16th birthday. I had visited her four times in three years. She had not avoided many of the usual difficulties of adolescence but was still attending school and planning to graduate. Idania Mendez, my intermediary with Guisell, and I had remained in close touch as well. Idania had moved to Aachen, Germany to study at the university there. I became her sponsor of sorts, paying her tuition so she could focus on her studies without financial worries. During the summer of 2007, we had synchronized trips to Nicaragua, and we spent three enjoyable days with Guisell and her mom in Rivas.

Now, in the evening of Melissa's birthday, I roamed through the house looking at her photos, a common ritual on this date. My gaze lingered on the framed photo above my desk, the one of us sitting together at the river. Her smile told me that she truly was delighted that I had claimed her. Even if she, like me, felt that uninhibited joy for only a day, it was real and it resurfaced for good years later. I took out a CD Isabel Stenzel had burned for me titled "Melissa" and put it in the changer, along with a CD by Stevie Wonder. The first song on Isa's CD was Natalie Merchant's "Wonder." The opening lines struck me as if I'd never heard them before. They caused me to fall to my knees, there in front of the sound system.

Doctors have come
from distant cities
just to see me.
Stand over my bed
disbelieving
what they're seeing.
They say I must be one of the wonders
of God's own creation.
And as far as they see
they can offer
no explanation.

I bent over onto my elbows, in tears, like a broken Muslim in prayer. I thought about the one wonder of God's creation I had been blessed to know. I wanted to hug her more than I ever wanted anything.

A month before Melissa's birthday, I bought a double CD of Stevie Wonder's hit songs. He had occupied such a major position on my life's soundtrack through the 70s, 80s and 90s, and I owned most of his record albums. However, since moving to Santa Fe, I listened solely to CD's and never un-boxed my phonograph turntable. Stevie Wonder's CD sat in my collection, unplayed for some reason, until this night.

When "Wonder" ended, I hit a couple of buttons and played Stevie Wonder's "Happy Birthday." It was a song I had not heard in the ten years since Melissa's passing. The exhilarating tune honors Martin Luther King but, starting in the early 90s, I'd given it a new spin: celebrating Melissa's birthday. Most of the lyrics don't apply to her, but the ones which counted were just fine: "Happy Birthday to You! Ha-ppy Birth-day!" And the tune kicked ass.

At the river on the final day of my visit in 1990. Photo by Gloria.

The first verse began with me sitting like a rock. But the rhythms were irresistible: I stood up and began to dance. I grabbed my journal with both hands and moved it up and around as my body gyrated to the beat. I turned the volume up and sang at the top of my lungs. I danced as if possessed, remembering the dream I'd had in 1990 of Melissa and me singing this song, and more bittersweet tears streamed down my cheeks. The lyrics ended and a women's chorus began the fade out. Then came the tail end of the tune, which I'd forgotten: Stevie Wonder speaking, in a prayerful tone. His words about King's dream stirred me once more, capturing my longing for a world which looks after every one of its people. This part of the song always deeply moved me and tonight the words took on an added dimension.

We'll make the dream become reality,
I know we will,
because our hearts tell us so.

My mind locked on to my greatest dream: for Melissa to know I loved her. No less important were Melissa's dreams, including finding her father. I thanked God that those two dreams had been fulfilled, for both our sakes.

I remembered the dream Melissa shared with Merilyn: falling in love and getting married. Merilyn had told me how she loved to hear Melissa talk about that dream.

I believed other dreams filled Melissa's heart. As she lay in her bed gazing into the light of a morning, perhaps she dreamt of the day cystic fibrosis would be cured, dreamt for Gloria and me, for Merilyn, her *tíos* and the others in her family, for Jessica and Dr. Gutierrez, for Laura Lee and her parents. I am certain she loved each one of us and prayed for each of us to be happy.

I know too, that, far from her dreams, Melissa lives on in the thoughts and lives of many, including Idania and Guisell. Should they ever have families, Melissa's life and story will be passed along to their children and, perhaps, their children's children. Jose Joaquin, too, will hear many stories about his cousin, the wonder of God's creation whom he never met.

Melissa is talked about by my friends and acquaintances, and she lives wherever I tell her story. And I am aware of her when I find myself in a place of great natural beauty, or hear music which stirs me, or witness an extraordinary kindness. The ripples of a mighty love, tested by defeat, never end.

When Melissa passed away, I feared that I would never stop crying. I fear no more. The door to grief will never close, nor do I want it to. One day I saw a father ruffle the hair of his young daughter and I bent over in a terrible weariness. But I receive the grief, experience it, even invite it in. When I feel out of sorts and know my grief is bottled up, I seek it out. It is no longer attached to despair or a desire to leave life. It simply is. The tears, I understand, will never end nor will my profound gratitude for Melissa and the life she gave to me.

Acknowledgments

While writing the concluding chapter, "The Return," two additional dreams came in the night. I put them into my journal and only found them as the manuscript of *Melissa's Gift* was near completion two years later.

In the first dream, I was taking a long hike to a mountain peak. It was my second hike there and I came upon a "final section" I'd never seen. It was "the true zenith," although nothing more than a short walk. The daylight was fading and I worried about going further and having to find my way back down the long trail, when I found a flashlight in my pocket. With it, I proceeded to the top.

Three weeks later, I dreamed I was in a foreign country, somewhere in Central America. It was dark. Guisell brought me a gift, wrapped incompletely in paper featuring "designs which told a story across three sides."The gift sat in a big shoe box. I asked Guisell if I should open it now or later. She paused then said, "Later." Our dream exchange duplicated a conversation which Melissa and I had on my first trip to Esparza.

These dreams, like the aquarium dream in 2004, depicted powerful connections between Melissa and Guisell. Re-visiting these and other dreams in my journals has enriched my sense of fundamental mystery at the heart of this story.

Many people, including virtual strangers, dreamed with me for Melissa's heart to open. They taught me that love, grows within a community, even when the love relationship may never be directly witnessed by the community. I have been blessed by many friends who gave selflessly of themselves in personal conversations and other ways they can never fully appreciate. They include Britt Dean and Sally Wylde, Jeff Jacobson and Marnie Andrews, Frances Freewater and Lee Doan, and Sharon Felton. Other givers of precious gifts include Isabel Allende, Celia Graterol, Helen and Ed Dias, Heidi and Philippe Rerat, Joan Schweighardt, Cedar Koons, Karen and Jim Spehar, Maria Jose Rodriguez Cadiz, Mirta Rios, Della Vigil, Susan Hyde Holmes, Leticiá Marquez Rutledge, Miriam Hill, Deyonne Sandoval, Judy Richardson, Anita Eliot, Debbie Brooks (for her bears), and Tanya Taylor. A special appreciation to David Cole of Bay Tree Publishing for his truly collaborative approach to publishing. For their continuing support and interest,

I thank my sisters, Janice and Kay, and my father, Olin, and his wife, Shirley, both deceased.

As I wrote *Melissa's Gift*, I took great inspiration from two extraordinary women, Ana Stenzel and Isabel Stenzel Byrnes. Battle-scarred from life-long struggles with cystic fibrosis, they now embrace life with transplanted lungs.

I wish to thank Rotary International, the Cystic Fibrosis Foundation in Bethesda, Maryland, and Dr. Karen Hardy for their generous contributions made in the course of this story. I thank Dr. George Whitelaw for his support and for his non-profit, Children Without Borders, which provides essential medical services for underserved children in Costa Rica.

My deepest appreciation goes to Carroll Jenkins, Executive Director of the Cystic Fibrosis Research Institute in Palo Alto, California, who, along with her board, donors and researchers, and thousands of untold others in the greater, amazing CF community, support each other and work for a cure for cystic fibrosis.

Laura, Anne and Bob Lee set this story in motion. Since handing me over to Melissa and Gloria, they've gone on about their lives with family and humanitarian work. My heart holds them eternally.

I have been fortunate to meet many lovely people in Central America. They include, in Costa Rica, the Reyes Araya family, Ascension, Bita, Merilyn and Marvin. Each, in her or his way, gave me endurance and light in the darkest hours of the journey. Jessica Benavides will long rest in my heart for her stories and love for Melissa. Dr. Jose P. Gutierrez offered himself to Melissa as a friend and person in the way of all true healers. The best treatment available in Costa Rica was provided to Melissa by Dr. Reina González, Nurse Inez Gutierrez, Dr. Oscar Castro Armas, Dr. Arturo Solis-Moya and the entire staff of the Cystic Fibrosis Clinic at the Hospital de Niños in San Jose. May God bless each of them.

Parental love in its highest form can often be witnessed in those who care for children with chronic health conditions such as cystic fibrosis. Gloria Reyes is one of those. Because so much takes place in relative privacy, few, except for God and other parents, can ever know what CF parents do and endure. I honor Gloria for her years of selfless acts of love and devotion to Melissa and for never giving up the hope of finding me. More recently it has been my happiness to become acquainted with the members of the *Asociacíon Costarricense de Fibrósis Quística* and its president, Jorge González. They are tireless fighters for children and families touched by CF.

The people of Nicaragua welcome me into their hearts wherever I travel in their beautiful country. The open arms of Idania Mendez Aguilar, Nubia

Aguilar, Neyvi Jimenez Sevilla, and, of course, Linda Guisell Pasos Jimenez, changed my life forever. Without them, this story would have had a much different ending.

Melissa led my heart to open and break and be touched by life. May every parent be similarly blessed by their children.

Made in the USA
Lexington, KY
04 March 2012